The
Clinton
Presidency

Recent Titles in the Praeger Series in Political Communication
Robert E. Denton, Jr., *General Editor*

Campaigns and Conscience: The Ethics of Political Journalism
Philip Seib

The White House Speaks: Presidential Leadership as Persuasion
Craig Allen Smith and Kathy B. Smith

Public Diplomacy and International Politics: The Symbolic Constructs of Summits and International Radio News
Robert S. Fortner

The 1992 Presidential Campaign: A Communication Perspective
Edited by Robert E. Denton, Jr.

The 1992 Presidential Debates in Focus
Edited by Diana B. Carlin and Mitchell S. McKinney

Public Relations Inquiry as Rhetorical Criticism: Case Studies of Corporate Discourse and Social Influence
Edited by William N. Elwood

Bits, Bytes, and Big Brother: Federal Information Control in the Technological Age
Shannon E. Martin

Warriors' Words: A Consideration of Language and Leadership
Keith Spencer Felton

Electronic Magazines: Soft News Programs on Network Television
William C. Spragens

Political Campaign Communication: Principles and Practices, Third Edition
Judith S. Trent and Robert V. Friedenberg

Candidate Images in Presidential Elections
Edited by Kenneth L. Hacker

Earthtalk: Communication Empowerment for Environmental Action
Edited by Star A. Muir and Thomas L. Veenendall

The Clinton Presidency

Images, Issues, and Communication Strategies

Edited by Robert E. Denton, Jr., and Rachel L. Holloway

Praeger Series in Political Communication

Westport, Connecticut
London

Library of Congress Cataloging-in-Publication Data

The Clinton presidency : images, issues, and communication strategies
/ edited by Robert E. Denton, Jr., and Rachel L. Holloway
  p.   cm.—(Praeger series in political communication, ISSN
1062–5623)
 · Includes bibliographical references and index.
  ISBN 0–275–95109–X (hc : alk. paper).—ISBN 0–275–95110–3 (pb. :
alk. paper)
  1. United States—Politics and government—1993–   2. Clinton,
Bill, 1946–   . I. Denton, Robert E., Jr.   II. Holloway, Rachel L.
III. Series.
E885.C553   1996
973.929'092—dc20   95–37650

British Library Cataloguing in Publication Data is available.

Library of Congress Catalog Card Number: 95–37650
ISBN: 0–275–95109–X
     0–275–95110–3 (pbk.)
ISSN: 1062–5623

First published in 1996

Praeger Publishers, 88 Post Road West, Westport, CT 06881
An imprint of Greenwood Publishing Group, Inc.

Printed in the United States of America

The paper used in this book complies with the
Permanent Paper Standard issued by the National
Information Standards Organization (Z39.48–1984).

10 9 8 7 6 5 4 3 2 1

To those who enter the arena, who choose to serve in a time of great risk and great promise, who are called to account, and who answer the call. This book is dedicated to the men and women who serve their fellow citizens in national, state, and local government.

Contents

Series Foreword

Those of us from the discipline of communication studies have long believed that communication is prior to all other fields of inquiry. In several other forums I have argued that the essence of politics is "talk" or human interaction.[1] Such interaction may be formal or informal, verbal or nonverbal, public or private but it is always persuasive, forcing us consciously or subconsciously to interpret, to evaluate, and to act. Communication is the vehicle for human action.

From this perspective, it is not surprising that Aristotle recognized the natural kinship of politics and communication in his writings *Politics and Rhetoric*. In the former, he establishes that humans are "political beings [who] alone of the animals [are] furnished with the faculty of language."[2] And in the latter, he begins his systematic analysis of discourse by proclaiming that "rhetorical study, in its strict sense, is concerned with the modes of persuasion."[3] Thus, it was recognized over 2,300 years ago that politics and communication go hand in hand because they are essential parts of human nature.

Back in 1981, Dan Nimmo and Keith Sanders proclaimed that political communication was an emerging field.[4] Although its origin, as noted, dates back centuries, a "self-consciously cross-disciplinary" focus began in the late 1950s. Thousands of books and articles later, colleges and universities offer a variety of graduate and undergraduate coursework in the area in such diverse departments as communication, mass communication, journalism, political science, and sociology.[5] In Nimmo and Sanders' early assessment, the "key areas of inquiry" included rhetorical analysis, propaganda analysis, attitude change studies, voting studies, government and the news media, functional and systems analyses, technological changes, media technologies, campaign techniques, and research techniques.[6] In a survey of the state of the field in 1983, the same authors and Lynda Kaid found additional, more specific areas of concerns such as the presidency, political polls, public opinion, debates, and advertising to name a few.[7] Since the first study, they also noted a shift away from the rather strict behavioral approach.

A decade later, Dan Nimmo and David Swanson argued that "political communication has developed some identity as a more or less distinct domain of scholarly work."[8] The scope and concerns of the area have further expanded to include critical theories and cultural studies. While there is no precise definition, method, or disciplinary home of the area of inquiry, its primary domain is the role, processes, and effects of communication within the context of politics broadly defined.

In 1985, the editors of *Political Communication Yearbook: 1984* noted that "more things are happening in the study, teaching, and practice of political communication than can be captured within the space limitations of the relatively few publications available."[9] In addition, they argued that the backgrounds of "those involved in the field [are] so varied and pluralist in outlook and approach . . . it [is] a mistake to adhere slavishly to any set format in shaping the content."[10] And more recently, Nimmo and Swanson called for "ways of overcoming the unhappy consequences of fragmentation within a framework that respects, encourages, and benefits from diverse scholarly commitments, agendas, and approaches."[11]

In agreement with these assessments of the area and with gentle encouragement, Praeger established the Praeger Series in Political Communication. The series is open to all qualitative and quantitative methodologies as well as contemporary and historical studies. The key to characterizing the studies in the series is the focus on communication variables or activities within a political context or dimension. As of this writing, nearly forty volumes have been published, and there are numerous impressive works forthcoming. Scholars from the disciplines of communication, history, journalism, political science, and sociology have participated in the series.

I am, without shame or modesty, a fan of the series. The joy of serving as its editor is in participating in the dialogue of the field of political communication and in reading the contributors' works. I invite you to join me.

Robert E. Denton, Jr.

NOTES

1. See Robert E. Denton, Jr., *The Symbolic Dimensions of the American Presidency* (Prospect Heights, Ill.: Waveland Press, 1982); Robert E. Denton, Jr., and Gary Woodward, *Political Communication in America* (New York: Praeger, 1985; 2nd ed., 1990); Robert E. Denton, Jr., and Dan Han, *Presidential Communication* (New York: Praeger, 1986); and Robert E. Denton, Jr., *The Primetime Presidency of Ronald Reagan* (New York: Praeger, 1988).

2. Aristotle, *The Politics of Aristotle,* trans. Ernest Barker (New York: Oxford University Press, 1970), p. 5.

3. Aristotle, *Rhetoric,* trans. Rhys Roberts (New York: The Modern Library, 1954), p. 22.

4. Dan Nimmo and Keith Sanders, "Introduction: The Emergence of Political Communication as a Field," in *Handbook of Political Communication,* ed. Dan Nimmo and Keith Sanders (Beverly Hills, Calif.: Sage, 1981), pp. 11–36.

5. Ibid., p. 15.

6. Ibid., pp. 17–27.

7. Keith Sanders, Lynda Kaid, and Dan Nimmo, eds., *Political Communication Yearbook: 1984* (Carbondale: Southern Illinois University Press, 1985), pp. 283–308.

8. Dan Nimmo and David Swanson, "The Field of Political Communication: Beyond the Voter Persuasion Paradigm," in *New Directions in Political Communication,* ed. David Swanson and Dan Nimmo (Beverly Hills, Calif.: Sage, 1990), p. 8.

9. Sanders, Kaid, and Nimmo, *Political Communication Yearbook: 1984,* p. xiv.

10. Ibid.

11. Nimmo and Swanson, "The Field of Political Communication," p. 11.

Preface

The Constitution gives me relevance. The power of our ideas give me relevance. The record we have built up over the last two years and the things were trying to do to implement it give it relevance. The president is relevant here.

—Bill Clinton, April 18, 1995

In 1992, American voters elected William Jefferson Clinton president of the United States. The first baby boomer in the White House, Clinton offered what *Newsweek*'s Joe Klein called an "ambitious, expansive, romantic vision: with the end of cynicism comes a national rebirth, a revival of hope."[1] Clinton was "in touch" with the needs of the poor and the middle class and promised to make government work with them to solve a range of problems—economic insecurity, unemployment, health care, welfare, and crime. He was a "New Democrat" and one especially skilled in the "rhetorical presidency," a new communicator for a new time.

Then, almost immediately, Clinton entered a shaky marriage with Congress, the media, and the American people. With virtually no honeymoon, Clinton faced a travel office scandal, a tough budget battle, controversy over gays in the military, a last minute triumph on NAFTA, unrest in Somalia, Bosnia, and Haiti, Whitewater investigations, an inefficient and ineffective staff, a revolving-door Cabinet, a controversial wife, and a health care crisis. The president's first two years, despite legislative successes and a steadily growing economy, troubled an electorate, of which only 43 percent voted for Clinton in the first place.

By the 1994 midterm elections, Republican campaign ads across the country "morphized" Democrats into the president's image, potentially the most negative political image available at the time. Democrats actively distanced themselves from the president and then watched as Republicans swept into Congress with their first bicameral majority since 1946. The public sent a strong message. The president apparently was no longer "in touch," and so the people reacted with their own change. In the words of Elizabeth Drew, "his presidency was constantly on the edge. . . . Time after time, it appeared that his Presidency was in jeopardy, that its effectiveness and authority could come to an end. People have found it difficult to understand this complex and often perplexing man. His great strengths and his great flaws seemed constantly at war over his Presidency."[2]

The purpose of this volume is to offer some insight into the Clinton presidency, its promise and its failures, from primarily a communication perspective. The chapters individually and together create a picture of a presidency laboring under an inability to adapt its successful campaign strategies to effective governing, to maintain control of the media and issue agenda, to communicate its successes effectively, and to overcome an image of waffling, inefficiency, and lack of direction. Despite their critical observations, the authors paint a picture for potential reelection. The Comeback Kid may be down, but is far from out, if he has learned the lessons outlined in the chapters that follow.

We open the volume with Clinton's inaugural. David E. Procter and Kurt Ritter argue that Clinton's inaugural simultaneously reaffirmed the American national convenant and subverted the political community constructed by previous Republican administrations. Through his inaugural, Clinton created a bridge from the "jeremiad logic" of his campaign discourse into his new voice as president. He characterized the political past as a culture of "personal advantage," "deadlock," and "drift." He promised to renew the covenant of "civic citizenship," built on participation, service, and commitment to others. Procter and Ritter note that the media coverage failed to carry the subtle transformation of "change" into "renewal," treating the terms as equivalent and, in general, was not favorable to the new president's efforts.

The media's response to the inaugural set the tone for much of Clinton's early administration. The president's relationship with the media, his use of it, and the reaction of the news media is central to any analysis of a modern presidency. We focus on media issues in several chapters. In chapter 2, we take a look at Clinton's premiere campaign strategy, the town hall meeting, what it reveals about changing media demands and the presidency, Clinton's unique abilities in his use of the town hall, and its disadvantages as a governing strategy. We believe that Clinton faces a tough choice as he moves back into the campaign phase. Like George Bush, in the next campaign phase, Clinton will speak at town halls as a president with a record to defend, and he must adapt his style accordingly.

In chapter 3, Kenneth L. Hacker turns our attention to another communication innovation in the Clinton administration, the National Information Infrastructure

Initiative, particularly the White House e-mail system, and its potential contribution to citizen involvement and democracy. As revealed by discussions with Clinton administrators, the e-mail system, in principle, is an effort to support Clinton's principles of community and responsibility, but as presently designed falls far short of its objectives. Hacker argues that the system has not reached the ''interactivity'' necessary to enhance political communication and must be designed to accomplish involvement, if it is to serve democracy.

No matter how ''in touch'' a president attempts to be through his communication, one group, without exception, will reduce the president to a single panel and sound bite, focusing on the most trivial aspects of his work and image—editorial cartoonists. Edd Sewell provides a theoretical explanation of the unique nature of editorial cartoons as communication-play and their role in presidential image making. Sewell's content analysis found that on a range of domestic and foreign policy issues, Clinton appeared as a hostage, a battered soldier after basic training, or with his saxophone playing the blues. In his role of coach-as-president, Clinton was leading a bumbling team with no game plan. Interesting, Hillary Rodham Clinton appeared in 12 percent of the cartoons.

In a look at yet another mediated political forum, political advertising, Lynda Lee Kaid, John C. Tedesco, and Julia A. Spiker offer a content and interpretive analysis of political advertising in the NAFTA debate and health care reform efforts. Among other findings, the authors report some surprises—''for the issue'' ads (for Clinton's position) far outnumber ''against the issue ads'' on both issues; the Clintons did not appear in *any* ''against the issue'' or ''informational'' ads, quite the opposite from political campaigns. Equally contrary to predictions, the key players do not appear, even in the positive ads; Al Gore is not seen on NAFTA and Hillary Clinton does not appear on health care. The ads also literally did not give ''voice'' to women. Kaid, Tedesco, and Spiker remind us that what we do *not* see, in this case, may have greater significance than what we do see in policy advertising.

Rita K. Whillock looks to Clinton's broader image problems, starting from the inconsistency between Clinton's image as ''a failed and struggling president'' and his impressive legislative accomplishments at midterm in his administration. Whillock argues that Clinton contributed to the demise of his own image through his relationship with the media. His own campaign strategies eliminated a honeymoon period. Having alienated the national press corps and built up high expectations, Clinton's ''narrow-casting successes gave way to broadcast failures'' quickly upon taking office. Whillock argues that the many contradictions in Clinton's life and his political pragmatism made him especially vulnerable to the news media's emphasis on strategy that assumes and then reports an ''ulterior motive'' in every statement or position. While Clinton fulfilled many campaign promises, the media focused on promises broken or unfulfilled. The gay rights issue allowed Clinton's opponents to cast him as an extreme Liberal, not the New Democrat that he said he was. The health care debate left him with the image of a leader who promised more than he could deliver, alienating and uniting the white, middle-class male voter in the process. Despite Clinton's negative image, Whillock contends that reelection is not out of the question. If Clinton has learned the media relations lessons of the first two years and articulates and follows a clear agenda of reform in line with the public's interest, he may yet serve another term as president.

Hillary Rodham Clinton apparently has as many ''inherent contradictions'' as her husband and is one of the most controversial elements of the Clinton presidency thus far. Janette Kenner Muir and Lisa M. Benitez explore the rhetorical style of Hillary Rodham Clinton, identifying the many roles she creates in her discourse—the average person, the storyteller, the lawyer, the good Methodist, the ''first woman''—and the complicated reactions to her ethos. The diverse reactions to Hillary Clinton reflect, the authors argue, ''the larger issues of the tension between expectations and roles the First Lady must perform, and the expectations for Clinton specifically.'' She must continue to balance the rational/discursive aspects of her style with the spiritual, family-oriented identity she communicates. Both are central to her ethos.

Hillary Rodham Clinton's role was most obvious in the administration's effort to reform the American health care system. In chapter 8, Rachel L. Holloway analyzes the management of the health care issue and suggests that the Clintons' strategies were destined to fail almost before they began the intense fight for health care reform. The definition of the issue could not be sustained because it overreached what could be delivered and lost the support of the middle class. Clinton lost control of the debate through the delays caused by his own process, a shift in focus away from his early principled message, and eventually proposed a policy so complex that the status quo seemed preferable to the proposed overhaul of the system. Clinton opened the door to powerful and wealthy opponents and left his potential allies little room to maneuver without undermining the president's leadership on the issue. Holloway concludes that health care reform was possible, if defined more narrowly to realign political interests and to build bipartisan support, and if sequenced differently within the president's overarching reform agenda. Health care reform was both an opportunity lost and a promise unfulfilled.

In chapter 9, Denise M. Bostdorff draws similar conclusions in her analysis of Clinton's handling of the gay rights controversy as an exemplar of Clinton's issue management style. She argues that Clinton attempts to lead from the middle through a combination of transcendent moral appeals, attractive to all, and specific promises to specific groups. Due to his tendency to avoid conflict through conciliation to opposed groups, Clinton earned a reputation as a waffler, rewarded Democrats who thwarted him, played into his opposition's hands, and, at times, acted in ways that were less than courageous. In the end, all parties were dissatisfied with the outcome and the president's credibility suffered.

In the final chapter, Craig Allen Smith describes Clinton's ''centrist presidency'' as a blend of the strategies of bargaining, public approval, going public, and ideology of jeremiadic logic. Clinton's strategy is based on the formation of shifting legislative coalitions by bargaining with key elites and talking to functionally important issue-centered audiences, sacrificing approval ratings for a time in order to win specific legislative battles. This strategy prevented him from winning widespread acceptance of his ideology and teaching the public his jeremiadic logic. Smith argues that the strategy is especially problematic for Clinton because he failed to control the media's characterization of his actions and also did not change the way Americans think about political issues and solutions. As a result, he is not given credit for his successes, although they are many. Smith recommends that Clinton continue to focus his rhetoric on functionally related issue audiences, begin fireside "chats" to establish narrative authority, and teach Americans his way of thinking. If Clinton can successfully continue his strategy of "rough stretches and honest disagreements" while filling in its missing elements, Smith believes he will have developed a new strategy of presidential leadership.

It is rather dangerous to provide an academic analysis and discussion of a presidency in midterm without benefit of historical hindsight or perspective. The essays are too young to be considered "history," but are certainly more than journalistic first impressions. Collectively, the essays provide insight into the images, issues, and communication strategies of the Clinton presidency.

NOTES

1. Joe Klein, "And They're Off. . . ." *Newsweek,* January 25, 1995, 19.

2. Elizabeth Drew, *On the Edge: The Clinton Presidency* (New York: Simon & Schuster, 1994).

Acknowledgments

Editing a book is either an enjoyable process or nothing less than a nightmare. Luckily for us, the contributors made editing this project a most enjoyable and rewarding endeavor. Throughout the years, we have learned from their insights and analyses. It was a privilege to work with such noted scholars. Best of all, we are pleased to call them friends. We appreciate their willingness to participate in this volume and their insightful contributions.

We also wish to thank our colleagues in the Department of Communication Studies at Virginia Polytechnic Institute and State University. A faculty committed to scholarship provides encouragement as we juggle our many responsibilities within an ever-changing academic environment. To know that our efforts will be valued makes the long, sometimes frustrating, process worthwhile.

Finally, we wish to thank our family and friends who continue to ask about our ideas, read our work, and engage us in dialogue about this world of words in which we live. They bring us back to earth and hold us accountable for our work in ways that only family can.

Chapter One

Inaugurating the Clinton Presidency: Regenerative Rhetoric and the American Community

David E. Procter and Kurt Ritter

One of the functions of inaugural addresses is to unify the national audience by rhetorically reconstituting the concept of the American community. President Bill Clinton sought to carry out this function through an inaugural address that employed regenerative rhetoric. He employed the rhetorical form of the jeremiad to selectively reinterpret the core values of the national community, to decry the failure of the Reagan and Bush administrations to live up to those community values, and to call upon the people to join him in restoring America's true principles. The regenerative rhetoric that Clinton used to launch his administration attempted to subvert the public's allegiance to old political values based upon utilitarian individualism and attempted to reaffirm its allegiance to redefined and restored political values based upon community welfare.

In their book, *Deeds Done in Words,* Karlyn Kohrs Campbell and Kathleen Hall Jamieson (1990) detail four "interrelated elements that define the essential presidential inaugural address" (15). The inaugural, they contend, "unifies the audience by reconstituting its members as the people, who can witness and ratify the ceremony; rehearses communal values drawn from the past; sets forth the political principles that will govern the new administration; and demonstrates through the enactment of the inauguration that the president appreciates the requirements and limitations of executive functions" (15). While all of these elements work to characterize inaugural addresses, it is unlikely that all of these elements will receive equal emphasis in a particular inaugural address. Indeed, it is likely that one of the four elements will dominate the focus of the speech, depending on the circumstances of the particular election or times or the specific characteristics of the president.

In his inaugural address President John Kennedy emphasized the American principles that would guide our conduct in foreign affairs. President Lyndon

Johnson stressed continuity of the principles and policies begun by President Kennedy, while President Gerald Ford emphasized enactment of the presidency because of the crisis in the office after the Watergate scandal. The present analysis of President Clinton's 1993 inaugural address argues that the element that served to focus and organize his speech was Clinton's attempt to reconstitute the American people into a public who could witness and participate in the Clinton political agenda. Hence, this chapter explores the way in which Clinton's inaugural sought to rhetorically reconstitute the American political community.

REGENERATIVE RHETORIC AND CLINTON'S INAUGURAL JEREMIAD

The elements of inaugurals Campbell and Jamieson outline are cast into rhetorical forms utilizing specific strategies. These rhetorical forms subsequently guide political understanding and action that work to construct political community. As Walter Fisher (1992) has argued, "Communities are co-constituted through communication transactions in which participants coauthor a story that has coherence and fidelity for the life that one would lead" (214). Fisher has noted that "there are different forms of human communication with different relationships to community" including affirmative rhetoric, purification rhetoric, and subversion rhetoric (211). Fisher argues that the form found in most inaugural addresses is "reaffirmative rhetoric" or forms of communication that reassert "the validity of the community's creed or modes of ceremonial, communal transactions" (211).

Campbell and Jamieson have outlined rhetorical forms specific to inaugurals, noting that "the language of conservation, preservation, maintenance, and renewal pervades these speeches" (20). Likewise, Ernest G. Bormann (1982) wrote that Reagan "used the fantasy type of 'Restoration' " in his first inaugural address. According to the restoration theme,

the original founders of the new nation set standards of the United States. Subsequent failures of the government and the society to meet these standards were not evidence that American institutions and American society were outmoded, structurally flawed, or inherently at fault. Rather, the problems stemmed from a falling away from the authentic and true basis of society as established by the founders. Reagan's restoration fantasy directed the nation to return to its original basis and rightness (136).

Likewise, Bill Clinton's inaugural address in 1993 was cast into a rhetorical form, one that can broadly be labeled "regeneration." Regeneration is similar to the renewal and restoration forms previously noted, except that regeneration includes not only the "reaffirmative rhetoric," but also a "subversion rhetoric" (Fisher, 1992, 211), not found in those other forms. It is our argument that Bill Clinton worked to regenerate the American community by specifically: (1) reaffirming an American national covenant based on a heritage claimed by the

"New Democrats"; (2) subverting the political community constructed by the previous Republican administrations by decrying America's failure to live up to that version of the national covenant; and (3) envisioning a regenerated political community based on America's "true principles" of community welfare.

The notion of regeneration comes originally from the religious and natural orders. Fundamentally, "regeneration is a system of change, of generating, of producing anew" (Procter, 1992, 173). Glenn Hewitt (1991) explains that "regeneration implies some change in the human subject. There is a new birth, bringing new life, a new nature, a new personality" (163). In regeneration, however, this new life comes from a concomitant process of degeneration. Regeneration suggests that through death, life is renewed. From a religious perspective, Hewitt contends that "the person who experiences regeneration is said to die to sin or self and be reborn into life in Christ" (4). Similarly, in the natural order, biologists speak of plants regenerating each spring through the decay and death of the previous winter. David E. Procter has noted elsewhere that "regeneration, then, is a dual process of the new emerging from the destruction or death of the old" (173).

This framework of regeneration is relevant to the study of inaugural addresses in general and Clinton's 1993 inaugural address in particular. Inaugurals are considered "an essential element in a ritual of transition in which the covenant between the citizenry and their leaders is renewed" (Campbell and Jamieson, 1990, 14). Inaugurals outline a relationship between the American people and the American government, celebrate the peaceful transition of government, and reaffirm faith in that government. The inaugural address, then, represents a moment of change and transition in America and therefore is an address that reorients or "reconstitutes" the American audience into a political community. Political regeneration is one way presidents work to reconstitute the American political community, and this process occurs when significant social, economic, and/or political changes atrophy elements of existing political narratives (Procter, 1992). Changes in political administrations, recessions or depressions, and world events causing changes in the national mission are all examples of contextual events that could precipitate a weakening of the narratives constituting political communities. Political rhetors then utilize significant rhetorical moments such as inaugurals to rhetorically destroy old political communities by further "undermining the coherence and fidelity of the opposing [political] story" (Fisher, 1992, 211).

Importantly, regeneration does not imply total destruction and death. Instead, regeneration suggests that, like a seed of a plant, the core values of the community survive and reconstitute themselves according to new relationships among the political rhetors, auditors, and context. Robert N. Bellah (1985) connects this idea to political rhetoric, explaining that the fundamental American "themes of success, freedom, and justice . . . are found in all three of the central strands of our culture—biblical, republican, and modern individualist—but they take on different meanings in each context" (28). In political regeneration, rhetors articulate their interpretation of the nation's core values. They then attack opposing political narratives undermining unwanted political attitudes, actions, and policies, stripping the political community to its core values and fundamental persona. Rhetors highlight these essential values as the internal resources necessary to withstand political change and to chart the new and true political course. These political speakers then reconstruct political community by explaining how the community's essential values translate into "appropriate" attitudes, actions, and policies. This rhetorical form, then, allows the political culture to change and regenerate itself through times of sociopolitical transition (Procter, 1992, 171).

As Bill Clinton prepared to deliver his inaugural address, he faced a rhetorical situation in which existing political narratives were losing their force. A vacuum existed that allowed Clinton to begin to regenerate American political community. During the first days of the Clinton administration, John Judis (1993) observed in the *New Republic* that Clinton's challenge as president was not merely to revive the nation's sagging economy: "He confronts an equally difficult task of restoring America's faith in her future. . . . The nation's spiritual doldrums have a certain life of their own. They stem from expectations about America's future that no administration may be able to meet—expectations that have deep roots in our religious past" (41). Judis perceptively argued that with the end of the cold war, Americans' sense of their national mission must be redefined. Having vanquished the Evil Empire, Americans were no longer clear on their millennial mission. Judis warned that "Clinton's challenge as president will be not merely pragmatic but evangelical—to articulate a new understanding of America's millennial hopes" (44).

President Clinton used a specific form of regenerative rhetoric—the political jeremiad—to organize his inaugural address. Many scholars have argued specifically that the jeremiad has served as the organizing principle in several inaugural addresses, including those of Franklin D. Roosevelt, Lyndon Johnson, and Ronald Reagan (Ritter 1993a, 1993b; Smith and Smith, 1994, 138–48). Clinton (like most modern presidents—and their speechwriters—facing the daunting prospect of presenting an inaugural address) first reviewed the inaugural addresses of past presidents. Significantly, Clinton devoted special attention to Lincoln's second inaugural address, which is a classic use of the jeremiad form in American political rhetoric (Ifill, 1993, A13; Von Drehel, 1993, F11; Bormann, 1985).

The jeremiad is the old Puritan sermon form that has become fundamental to American political rhetoric. Indeed, the jeremiad has been called "the most American of all rhetorical modes" (Popcock, 1975, 513). The jeremiad has evolved into a secular form in modern American rhetoric, but it retains a critical connection with its religious origins in America: the notion that America has a special covenant—a national mission—that it must strive to fulfill. In its modern form, the jeremiad has three themes: (1) the *promise,* which reminds the American audience of its covenant; (2) the *declension,* which scolds the audience for not yet having fulfilled its covenant; and (3) the *prophecy,* which assures the audience that if they will reform their ways the nation can yet fulfill its national covenant (Howard-Pitney, 1990, 8; Ritter and Henry, 1992, 37–53).

The jeremiad as regenerative rhetoric functions to (1) remind the American audience of its covenant based on the nation's fundamental values; (2) point out that America has not fulfilled its covenant because citizens have followed the flawed policies of the previous political administration; and (3) envision a nation fulfilling its national covenant when adopting actions consistent with the values articulated by the new administration.

ESTABLISHING THE CORE VALUES

In order for the political community to regenerate, the audience must first understand and rely on their core values—as interpreted by the new president. Likewise, the key move in any jeremiad is to establish the first principles of the community that constitute the audience. "The promise," as it is known in the jeremiad, is the covenant between the people and a higher force. For Puritans, the covenant was directly with God. In its secularized form, the political jeremiad speaks of a covenant with our past, with our heritage, with our land, with those who have died to maintain America's freedom. The interpretation of the covenant is crucial, for it allows political speakers to link the adoption of their policies with the historic purpose of the nation (Ritter, 1980, 158–71).

Reagan-Bush rhetoric used the core American values of freedom, success, and justice to articulate a conception of political community focusing on what Bellah would label utilitarian individualism. This conception of community argues that the most important thing about America was "the chance for an individual to get ahead on his/[her] own initiative" and that "in a society where each vigorously pursued his/[her] own interest, the social good would automatically emerge" (Bellah et al., 1985, 33). For Reagan, "the primary aim of government [was] to safeguard the peace and security necessary to allow self-reliant individuals to pursue their largely economic aims in freedom" and "although there is some need for the government to provide a 'safety net' for individuals who fail in their quest for self-sufficiency, such government assistance must be reduced to the minimum necessary to protect the 'truly needy,' and if possible, restore them to self-reliance" (Bellah et al., 1985, 263).

For Clinton, the covenant is with "America's ideals—life, liberty, the pursuit of happiness. Though we march to the music of our time, our mission is timeless. Each generation must define what it means to be an American" (Clinton, 1993, 1).[1] Of course, Clinton's notion of the American covenant differs sharply with the covenant proclaimed by recent Republican presidents. Clinton follows the Democratic Party's tradition of defining the covenant as an obligation to create a community where all share equally in the fruits of happiness. The new president urged all Americans to "take more responsibility, not only for ourselves and our families but for our communities and our country" (2).

It is worth noting that Clinton repeatedly tied his interpretation of the covenant to the nation's founders: "When our founders boldly declared America's independence . . . they knew America, to endure, would have to change. Not change for change's sake, but change to preserve America's ideals" and later he contended that "Thomas Jefferson believed that to preserve the very foundations of our nation, we would need dramatic change from time to time" (1). Hence, the ideal of a cooperating and mutually supporting community was the goal; "change" was the means for creating such a community.

It is no surprise that Clinton employed a jeremiad as the vehicle for this regenerative rhetoric in his inaugural address. As Craig Allen Smith has noted, Clinton's entire 1992 campaign employed a "jeremiadic logic," which attacked the policies of the Reagan and Bush administrations as being unfaithful to America's true values (Smith, 1994). Clinton's inaugural address served as a rhetorical bridge between his campaign discourse and his presidential speeches. As with other presidents, his inaugural address was not only the first speech of his presidential administration, but also the last speech of his presidential campaign (Ryan, 1993, xvi). From the first speech of his campaign, Clinton had declared: "We need a new covenant to rebuild America" (Clinton, October 3, 1991). Throughout his campaign, Clinton had been honing the theme of regeneration that would become the organizing principle of his 1993 inaugural address. At Georgetown University he spoke on "a new covenant: responsibility and rebuilding the American community" (October 23, 1991). The next month he spoke of "a new covenant for economic change" (November 20, 1991), and yet another month later he called for "a new covenant for American security" (December 12, 1991). More than eight months later when he accepted the presidential nomination of the Democratic Party, he titled his address, "A Vision for America: A New Covenant" (July 16, 1992). Indeed, as Craig A. Smith (1994) has observed, "Bill Clinton began his jeremiad in his announcement speech and continued it into his inaugural address" (96).

Yet, Clinton's inaugural address was not merely a restatement of his campaign rhetoric. It was an attempt to translate his campaign themes into a statement of core values that would not only guide his administration, but, he hoped, would guide the nation back to what Clinton saw as its historic roots of community and cooperative action through government.

UNDERMINING THE PREVIOUS POLITICAL COMMUNITY

Clinton's short inaugural address had barely begun when he began to undermine the community constructed by the former Republican administrations. Through a jeremiad theme of declension, Clinton argued that America had not yet lived up to its promise; it had not yet fulfilled its covenant. Such a posture, of course, has been typical for first-term presidents displacing an administration from an opposing political party. Woodrow Wilson (1995) had done so in 1913 when he warned the nation: "There has been something crude and heartless and unfeeling in our haste to succeed and be great [as an industrial power]'' (684). So had Franklin D. Roosevelt (1995) in 1933 when he remarked that ''only a foolish optimist can deny the dark realities of the moment'' (720). Similarly, Ronald Reagan's first inaugural address in 1981 declared: ''These United States are confronted with an economic affliction of great proportions. . . . It threatens to shatter the lives of millions of our people'' (155–56). Each of these presidents then identified the national sins that they claimed had led America into calamity.

Clinton's inaugural followed the same pattern of subversion and degeneration. As a political community, he argued, America had failed to live up to its national covenant. Clinton's inaugural worked to subvert the old political community, which he portrayed as having created the sins of greed, government ''deadlock,'' leaderless ''drift,'' and a culture based on ''personal advantage'' (1–2). The former administrations' policies created a public debt that had ''enriched'' the privileged elite, ''who are able to compete and win.'' In contrast, Clinton continued: ''Most people are working harder for less; . . . others cannot work at all; . . . the cost of health care devastates millions and threatens to bankrupt many of our enterprises'' (1).

In particular, Clinton found Washington, D.C., to be suffering from a selfishness, which he portrayed as inherent to the Republican Party's ideology of individualism. Speaking on the West Front of the Capitol, Clinton contrasted the beauty of the scene with the corruption beneath its surface: ''This beautiful Capital, like every capital since the dawn of civilization, is often a place of intrigue and calculation.'' It was only as he spoke that he added the word ''often'' to soften the unqualified condemnation in the advance copy of the address. He continued: ''Powerful people maneuver for position and worry endlessly about who is in and who is out, who is up and who is down, forgetting those people whose toil and sweat sends us here and pays our way. Americans deserve better'' (2).

Instead of facing up to its failure to create a sharing community, Clinton charged, America had ''drifted and that drifting has eroded our resources, fractured our economy, and shaken our confidence'' (1). This sorry state of affairs had resulted, in part, from ''the bad habit of expecting something for nothing, from our government or from each other'' (1).

This regenerative strategy sought to destroy the legitimacy of the previous political community, which was based on Republican interpretations of America's national covenant. Clinton's speech reduced that political community to the core values highlighted by the new president. His inaugural then completed the regenerative form by projecting a regenerated American political community.

PROJECTING THE REGENERATED COMMUNITY

Clinton asked his audience to look forward with him to the prophecy—to the ultimate fulfillment of America's covenant. Indeed, he devoted the largest portion of his inaugural address to his vision of a regenerated America—a vision of political community that might be called civic citizenship. This form of community is a participatory process, one characterized by citizens and groups taking responsibility for discovering answers to public policy issues (Bellah et al., 1985, 28–31; Kemmis, 1990, 111–15). Clinton called for increased responsibility: "Let us all take more responsibility, not only for ourselves and our families but for our communities and our country" (2). He called for service to those in need: "I challenge a new generation of young Americans to a season of service—to act on your idealism by helping troubled children, keeping company with those in need, reconnecting our torn communities" (2). And he called on Americans to recognize their interdependence: "In serving, we recognize a simple truth: We need each other. And we must care for one another" (2). Such a commitment, he acknowledged, required dedication: "It will not be easy; it will require sacrifice. But it can be done. . . . We must provide for our nation the way a family provides for its children" (1–2).

To repent its sins and reform, Clinton asserted, Americans would have to "revitalize our democracy." The voice of the people had to replace "power and privilege" in Washington; Americans had to "put aside personal advantage" so that they could "feel the pain" of the less fortunate members of the community. This renewal, ultimately, would require Americans to "meet challenges abroad as well as at home." In short, the welfare of the American community required a concern for the world community: "The world economy, the world environment, the world AIDS crisis, the world arms race . . ." (2).

Halford Ryan (1993) has noted that Clinton's inaugural address echoed the "hortatory subjective" style of John F. Kennedy's inaugural (302). This parallel was particularly clear when Clinton assumed a prophetic voice: "Let us resolve to reform. . . . Let us put aside personal advantage. . . . Let us give this Capital back to the people" (2). In closing, he called upon his audience to embrace the communitarian vision of America: "an idea born in revolution and renewed through two centuries of challenge; an idea tempered by the knowledge that, but for fate, we, the fortunate, and the unfortunate might have been each other; an idea . . . infused with the conviction that America's long heroic journey must go forever upward" (2).

The central point of the prophecy in the American jeremiad is that the nation can still recover from its errors and recommit itself to its covenant. In pursuing that theme, Clinton used a metaphor consistent with the process of regeneration—seasonal renewal. The first sentence of his inaugural declared: "Today, we celebrate the mystery of American renewal" (1). In the second sentence of his address Clinton observed: "This ceremony is held in the depth of winter, but by the words we speak and the faces we show the world, we force the spring" (1). Ronald Carpenter (1994) notes that in his major addresses, Clinton tended to "put all his figurative eggs in one basket" and that in his inaugural address "his significant metaphor is about spring" (126). Halford Ryan (1993) notes that Clinton's "spring" metaphor is introduced as part of an antithesis (an inauguration in the "winter" creates a "spring") and observes: "The audience knows that winter cannot be spring, but the antithesis entices listeners to conclude figuratively that winter—George Bush—has been shunted aside for spring—Bill Clinton" (Ryan, 1993, 303).

The jeremiad, however, demands that Americans make a choice to turn away from sin and return to the nation's first principles. Hence, a seasonal metaphor with its sense of inevitable change would not serve Clinton's purpose. Apparently Clinton and his speechwriters sensed this problem on some level, for instead of employing a straightforward metaphor of spring as a time of national rebirth, Clinton insisted that Americans would have to *choose* to reform. This took the form of "forcing the spring," as a horticulturalist might induce a plant to bloom before spring arrived by altering the temperature and light in a greenhouse. What might at first appear to be a conventional use of the spring metaphor as an ornament—as an attempt to dress his inaugural in a more elevated style—was actually a carefully chosen image to place the responsibility for American renewal not on the cycle of nature, but upon the will of the people.

As he neared his conclusion, Clinton once again made it explicit that America's renewal was an act of will, not of nature. After making the somewhat improbable interpretation that the vote in the 1992 presidential election represented a watershed in American history, Clinton declared: "Yes, you, my fellow Americans, have forced the spring. Now we must do the [community service] work the season demands" (2).

In calling for "a season of service," Clinton closed his address by restating his understanding of the American covenant. For Clinton, the American covenant was not a compact for individual liberty, but an obligation to put the community good ahead of individual aspirations. By recognizing that obligation, Clinton argued, Americans would grasp the fundamental values of the nation—the core from which an American regeneration could occur. Hence, he said: "Today, we do more than celebrate America; we rededicate ourselves to the very idea of America" (2).

THE MEDIATED INAUGURAL

In promulgating his regenerative rhetoric, Clinton had the mixed blessing of saturation media coverage. On the one hand, this gave him access to both an American and a world-wide audience for his address, while on the other hand, it placed the interpretation of his rhetoric in the hands of an army of broadcast and print journalists. The industry magazine, *Broadcasting,* reported that Clinton's inauguration "both drew unprecedented media coverage and media participation in the event itself" (Flint, 1993, 123).

The inaugural address was the centerpiece of inaugural coverage on January 20, 1993, that began at 8:00 A.M. (EST) with expanded versions of the morning "soft news" shows: ABC's "Good Morning America," NBC's "Today," and "CBS This Morning." At 10:00 A.M. PBS began a four-and-a-half hour version of the "McNeil/Lehrer Newshour." At the same time, CNN started its all-day news coverage. Half-an-hour later both FOX and C-SPAN joined the inauguration. Even cable entertainment channels MTV and "Comedy Central" covered Clinton's first day, with the former broadcasting from the "Rock N'Roll Inaugural Ball" (which MTV sponsored), and the latter presenting comedy highlights of the day's events in a program titled "America Gets the Bill."

In addition to their regular cameras, the television networks employed mobile cameras and robotic cameras, as they had for George Bush's inaugural in 1989. CBS, however, added a new feature: the "Bobcam," which derived its nickname from the circumstance that it was "a microminiature camera" mounted on the head of CBS correspondent Bob Schieffer as he covered Clinton's swearing-in and inaugural address (Sukow, 1993, 123).

For those unable to watch or uninterested in watching the inauguration live, the television network evening news programs presented distilled versions. A remarkably high proportion of news time was devoted to the inaugural address itself. Between January 18 and 22, 1993, ABC's evening news devoted over thirty-one minutes to the inauguration, with almost a third of that time (more than ten minutes) concerning the inaugural address. CBS and NBC had similar proportions, with CBS having over twenty-six minutes on the inauguration (over eight minutes on the address) and NBC having almost thirty-four minutes of inauguration stories (over nine minutes on the address).

The media interpretation of Clinton's 1993 inaugural address generally failed to grasp the communal values at the heart of his regenerative rhetoric, as well as their roots in American civil religion. The news media typically noted Clinton's theme of "renewal," which was treated as identical to "change" (especially generational change), and as merely a reworking of his campaign rhetoric. The *Washington Post* reported that the fourteen-minute speech was composed of "themes from a thousand stump speeches" recast into "an eloquent and simple statement of the values he [Clinton] will carry with him to the White House" (Balz, 1993, A1). Yet, what followed in the news accounts was often little more than a laundry list of topics. The organizing principle of "renewal" was treated as a slogan: "Ironically, Clinton blended his long-stated notion of reinventing America with the image of an 'American renewal,' which just happened to be part of the title of former president Bush's economic program, delivered too late in the campaign to save his presidency." For Clinton, perhaps the unkindest cut of all was the observation that "some of Clinton's rhetoric yesterday was suggestive of Bush's four years ago, when Bush attempted to step away from some of the unpopular aspects of Reagan's government" (Balz, 1993, A27).

Similar sentiments were presented by the press outside of Washington, D.C. The *New York Times* noted that "few will take exception to his message of hope and rebirth" but wondered if he could persuade the American public to make serious sacrifices for the community good (Apple, 1993, A1). The *Wall Street Journal* reported that Clinton's address "harked back to his campaign themes of change and renewal." Although finding the speech "at times moving," the *Journal* also suggested that Clinton had borrowed a line from the television series, "Star Trek" (Birnbaum, 1993, A16). The White House correspondent for *Newsweek* magazine found "renewal" an inadequate theme. Noting that "Clinton spoke of renewal last week rather than revolution or reform," the correspondent argued: "Renewal is a curiously neutral word; it has no enemies. It challenges exhaustion, not evil" (Klein, 1993). Overseas, *The Economist* complained that "through it all, Mr. Clinton behaved as if the campaign were on again" as he "revisited the economic and communitarian themes of his campaign" ("American Survey," 1993, 25). Of the major newspapers in the United States, the *Christian Science Monitor* was one of the few to take note of the religious basis of Clinton's regenerative rhetoric (Ingwerson, 1993a).

Why was the essence of Clinton's message lost in the news media coverage? Three factors seem to have contributed to this situation. First, the news media quickly transformed the concept of "renewal" into the notion of "change," particularly generational change. The news media searched for earlier presidents who had assumed office after a lengthy period of the opposing party being in the White House. Hence, "renewal" became equated with a shift in political power, and Clinton's inaugural address was presented as similar to Franklin D. Roosevelt's in 1933, John F. Kennedy's in 1961, and even Ronald Reagan's in 1981 (Leubsdorf, 1993, 1A; Safire, 1993, A25).

Almost every news account of Clinton's 1993 inaugural drew comparisons with Kennedy's inaugural address twenty-two years earlier. Clinton clearly encouraged the comparison. The day before his speech Kennedy family members had accompanied Clinton as he visited the graves of both John F. Kennedy and Robert F. Kennedy in Arlington National Cemetery. This was a media event and was shown on the evening news programs of both ABC and NBC on January 19, 1993. The news media found that Clinton's inaugural style echoed Kennedy's inaugural (Daley, 1993, A1). On January 20, 1993, Jeff Greenfield reported on the ABC evening news that the tone, substance, and themes of Clinton's address were modeled on Kennedy's speech—a point that was reinforced as the news program showed a series of comparative excerpts from both speeches. The impact of such coverage was to draw attention away from the substance of Clinton's regenerative rhetoric and instead to call attention to his relative youthfulness, to the circumstance that (like Kennedy) Clinton represented the rise of a new generation to political power, and to the transfer of power from the Republican Party to the Democratic Party.

The second factor contributing to the news media not focusing upon Clinton's regenerative rhetoric was that his own behavior as president-elect seemed inconsistent with the slightly self-righteous tone of his inaugural address. During the week prior to his inauguration, evening network news programs reported on a steady stream of negative news: interest-free loans were being solicited from large corporations to cover the $30 million cost of the Clinton inauguration (CBS, January 14, 1993); Clinton reversed his campaign position on Haitian refugees (NBC, January 14, 1993); other campaign promises on a middle-class tax cut, cutting the deficit in half, presenting economic legislation on his first day in office, and cutting the White House staff all seemed to be reversed (ABC, January 15, 1993); and Clinton's nominee for attorney general of the United States, Zoe Baird, had hired illegal aliens as domestic servants (NBC, January 16, 1993).

These difficulties made Clinton appear to be a typical politician, rather than the nation's moral leader. In its editorial on Clinton's inauguration, the *New York Times* observed that "his transition to governance has been filled with missteps, and his message obscured by awkward revelations about some of his cabinet appointments and by crablike retreats from some of his campaign promises" ("Mr. Clinton's Day," 1993, A22). Similar sentiments were woven into reports of the inauguration in the *Christian Science Monitor* (Ingwerson, 1993b, 1), the *Wall Street Journal* (Birnbaum, 1993, A16), *The Times* of London ("Inauguration Day," 1993, 17), and elsewhere. In particular, the press found Clinton's passionate denunciation of Washington politics a bit disingenuous: "Although stirring, . . . [such] comments contrasted sharply with Mr. Clinton's own transition to power over the past two months, which was highlighted by close relations with Congress and the appointment of many Washington insiders to high government posts" (Birnbaum, 1993, A16).

The third reason that Clinton's inaugural message resonated poorly in the press was that the speech itself failed to give sufficient attention to the principles that would govern his administration. The expectations of the media and the public encouraged Clinton to give a brief speech. Yet, a brief speech did not give him the time needed in order to develop both the communal and the deliberative functions of an inaugural address. Clinton chose to devote much of his inaugural to his most pressing problem: reconstituting the American audience. But this meant that he had less time to articulate the political principles from which his administration's major policy decisions would be derived. Quite possibly, Clinton chose to emphasize the function of reconstituting the American audience because his campaign rhetoric had equipped him with a well developed repertoire of communitarian themes but had not provided him with a clear ideology on which to base presidential policies. His decision to stress the reconstitutive function of the inaugural at the expense of the function of articulating political principles for his administration had consequences, however. It laid him open to charges (which plagued him later in his administration) that he did not have a set of principles to guide his policies.

Clinton had delighted in the massive television coverage of the inauguration, even mentioning in his inaugural address that "the sights and sounds of this ceremony are broadcast instantaneously to billions around the world" (1). But television comes with a price. It demands a concise speech with memorable "sound bites" for its news stories. Acting very much against his nature, Clinton limited his speech to only fourteen minutes—perhaps the third shortest inaugural address in American history (Fenney, 1993, 18A). His brevity won universal applause from the news media, especially in contrast to Clinton's nomination speech for Michael Dukakis at the 1988 Democratic National Convention and his own nomination acceptance speech at the 1992 Democratic National Convention—each of which had lasted almost an hour.

The brevity of his inaugural made it difficult for him to develop the principles of the Clinton White House. Too much was submerged beneath the surface of the speech. Instead of providing a clear bridge between his campaign rhetoric and his presidential rhetoric, the inaugural relied too heavily on Clinton's broad campaign themes. Perhaps he could have addressed the principles of his administration with pithy, memorable lines, such as Kennedy's "Ask not what your country can do for you . . . ," but the press noted that Clinton's address "lacked any such ringing phrase" (Birnbaum, 1993, A16). Indeed, the press concluded that Clinton "did not appear to reach for the single line, the memorable phrase that distinguishes inaugural addresses recalled down the years" (Daley, 1993, A1).

Shortly before Clinton's 1993 inaugural, Kathleen Hall Jamieson claimed that "one can say categorically the great presidents presented a great inaugural address. . . . If you don't come into office knowing how to use rhetoric to define yourself and the country, odds are you aren't going to find out sometime in your term" (Von Drehel, 1993, F11). After Clinton's inauguration, Jamieson criticized the address because "we didn't get a clear vision of the overaching principles that will guide his presidency. . . . It had the weaknesses that have characterized the Clinton campaign rhetoric. It had a little bit of everything" (Birnbaum, 1993, A16).

CONCLUSION

As John Judis (1993) has noted, the American mission needs to be redefined in the post–cold war world. Shortly after Clinton's inaugural address, Judis warned: "If Clinton is not able to articulate a new vision that buoys America's millennial hopes, many Americans could once again turn back toward a politics of reaction and apocalypse" (48). Indeed, for those sympathetic to the Democratic Party, the 1994 off-year election, which placed the Republican Party in control of both Houses of Congress for the first time in forty years, might have seemed to be a reaction to Clinton's inability to rally the American public around a clear vision of their national mission.

Yet, in fairness, it should be recognized that a single speech can accomplish only so much. Despite the need for a brief speech and the other difficulties occasioned by news media interpretations of his inaugural address, Clinton did capitalize upon his opportunity to address the American audience directly. His regenerative rhetoric did seek to respond to the nation's need for a reinterpretation of its mission.

Irrespective of Clinton's ultimate success or failure as a president, exploring the rhetorical form of his 1993 inaugural address helps provide insight into the community forms through which individuals live. The regenerative rhetorical form is coproduced by political rhetors and auditors to rhetorically strip an old political community down to its core values and to resurrect in its place a new political community. As Clinton's address reveals, the regenerative form is a variation of reaffirmative rhetoric especially applicable to inaugural rhetoric.

This rhetorical form eases the transition of government as rhetors and auditors symbolically destroy the old political community while retaining and celebrating the community's fundamental political values. A new president, such as Bill Clinton in 1993, then attempts to construct the foundations of a new political community using such rhetorical opportunities as the presidential inaugural. As Bellah (1985) argues, "American culture remains alive so long as the conversation continues" (28).

NOTES

The authors thank Carol Thomas (M.A., Texas A&M University, 1994), communications consultant, Ernst & Young, Inc., Cleveland, for her contributions as a research assistant.

1. Subsequent quotations from Clinton's 1993 inaugural address will be indicated by page numbers inserted parenthetically in the text of the chapter.

REFERENCES

"American Survey." 1993. *The Economist* (January 23, 1993): 25–26.

Apple, R. W. 1993. "A Change of Power, But Barely a Break in Stride." *New York Times,* January 21, A1.

Balz, Dan. 1993. "A Recasting of Themes: Campaign Ideas Echo Succinctly in Speech." *Washington Post,* January 21, A1.

Bellah, Robert N. et al. 1985. *Habits of the Heart: Individualism and Commitment in American Life.* Berkeley: University of California Press.

Birnbaum, Jeffrey H. and Michael Frisby. 1993. "Asking His Generation to Accept Responsibility for Governing, Clinton Becomes 42nd President." *Wall Street Journal,* January 21, A16.

Bormann, Ernest G. 1982. "A Fantasy Theme Analysis of the Television Coverage of the Hostage Release and the Reagan Inaugural." *Quarterly Journal of Speech* 68 (May): 133–45.

————. 1985. *The Force of Fantasy: Restoring the American Dream.* Carbondale: Southern Illinois University Press.

Campbell, Karlyn Kohrs and Kathleen Hall Jamieson. 1990. *Deeds Done in Words: Presidential Rhetoric and the Genres of Governance.* Chicago: University of Chicago Press.

Carpenter, Ronald H. 1994. "The Stylistic Persona of Bill Clinton: From Arkansas and Aristotelian Attica." In *Bill Clinton on Stump, State, and Stage: The Rhetorical Road to the White House,* ed. Stephen A. Smith. Fayetteville: University of Arkansas Press.

Clinton, William J. (October 3, 1991). "Announcement Address." Old State House, Little Rock, Arkansas. Text distributed by the Bill Clinton Presidential Campaign.

————. (October 23, 1991). "The New Covenant: Responsibility and Rebuilding the American Community." Georgetown University, Washington, D.C.

————. (November 20, 1991). "A New Covenant for Economic Change." Georgetown University, Washington, D.C.

————. (December 12, 1991). "A New Covenant for American Security." Georgetown University, Washington, D.C.

————. (July 16, 1992). "A Vision for America: A New Covenant." Democratic National Convention, New York City. Distributed by the Clinton-Gore Campaign. Also available in "1992 Democratic National Convention," ed. Joan Cameron. TapeWriter, Inc., P.O. Box 885, Lincolnshire, IL 60069 (transcribed from the address as televised on C-SPAN).

————. (January 20, 1993). "Inaugural Address." *Public Papers of the Presidents of the United States: William J. Clinton, 1993.* Washington, D.C.: Government Printing Office, 1994, Book I, 1–3.

Daley, Steve. 1993. "Echoes of JFK, But Less Electricity." *Chicago Tribune,* January 21, A1, A14.

Fenney, Susan. 1993. "Address Focuses on Renewal." *Dallas Morning News,* January 21, 1A, 18A.

Fisher, Walter R. 1992. "Narration, Reason, and Community." In *Writing the Social Text: Poetics and Politics in Social Science Discourse,* ed. Richard Harvey Brown. New York: Aldine De Gruyter.

Flint, Joe. 1993. "We Are the World Watching: Clinton Inaugural Was a Feast for all Eyes as Media Gave it Full-Court Press." *Broadcasting* (January 25): 123–24.

Hewitt, Glenn A. 1991. *Regeneration and Morality: A Study of Charles Finney, Charles Hodge, John W. Nevin, and Horace Bushnell.* Brooklyn, N.Y.: Carlson Publishing Inc.

Howard-Pitney, David. 1990. *The Afro-American Jeremiad: Appeals for Justice in America.* Philadelphia: Temple University Press.

Ifill, Gwen. 1993. "Clinton Hopes to Curb Tongue in Inaugural Address." *New York Times,* January 19, A13.

"Inauguration Day: President Clinton Ushers in an Age of Uncertainty." 1993. *The Times* (London), January 20, 17.

Ingwerson, Marshall. "Clinton Post Renewal as Theme for Presidency." 1993a. *Christian Science Monitor,* January 22, 1, 4.

————. 1993b. "His Agenda for Change in Hand, Clinton Steps into the Oval Office." *Christian Science Monitor,* January 22, 1, 4.

Judis, John B. 1993. "The Great Awakening." *New Republic* (February 1): 41–48.

Kemmis, Daniel. 1990. *Community and Politics of Place.* Norman: University of Oklahoma Press.

Klein, Joe. 1993. "Hoping for Passion." *Newsweek* (February 1): 30.

Leubsdorf, Carl P. 1993. "Democrat Sees Hope, Sacrifice." *Dallas Morning News,* January 21, 1A.

"Mr. Clinton's Day, and America's." 1993. *New York Times,* January 20, A22.

Popcock, J. G. A. 1975. *The Machiavellian Moment: Florentine Political Thought and the Atlantic Tradition.* Princeton: Princeton University Press.

Procter, David E. 1992. "Bridging Social Change through Mythic Regeneration." *Communication Studies* 43: 171–81.

Reagan, Ronald. 1992. "First Inaugural Address, January 20, 1981." In Kurt Ritter and

David Henry, *Ronald Reagan: The Great Communicator*. Westport, Conn.: Greenwood Press.

Ritter, Kurt. 1980. "American Political Rhetoric and the Jeremiad Tradition: Presidential Nomination Acceptance Speeches, 1960–1976." *Central States Speech Journal* (now *Communication Studies*) 31: 153–71.

———. 1993a. "President Lyndon Johnson's Inaugural Address, 1965." In *The Inaugural Addresses of Twentieth-Century American Presidents,* ed. Halford R. Ryan. Westport, Conn.: Praeger.

———. 1993b. "President Ronald Reagan's Second Inaugural Address, 1985." In *The Inaugural Addresses of Twentieth-Century American Presidents,* ed. Halford R. Ryan. Westport, Conn.: Praeger.

Ritter, Kurt and David Henry. 1992. *Ronald Reagan: The Great Communicator.* Westport, Conn.: Greenwood Press.

Roosevelt, Franklin D. 1995. "First Inaugural Address [March 4, 1933]." In *American Rhetorical Discourse,* 2nd ed., ed. Ronald F. Reid. Prospect Heights, Ill.: Waveland Press.

Ryan, Halford, ed. 1993. *The Inaugural Addresses of Twentieth-Century American Presidents.* Westport, Conn.: Praeger.

Ryan, Halford R., ed. 1993. "President Bill Clinton's Inaugural Address, 1993." In *The Inaugural Addresses of Twentieth-Century American Presidents,* ed. Halford R. Ryan. Westport, Conn.: Praeger.

Safire, William. 1993. "Clinton's 'Forced Spring.' " *New York Times,* January 21, A25.

Smith, Craig Allen. 1994. "The Jeremiadic Logic of Bill Clinton's Policy Speeches." In *Bill Clinton on Stump, State, and Stage: The Rhetorical Road to the White House,* ed. Stephen A. Smith. Fayetteville: University of Arkansas Press.

Smith, Craig Allen and Kathy B. Smith. 1994. *The White House Speaks: Presidential Leadership as Persuasion.* Westport, Conn.: Praeger.

Sukow, Randy. 1995. "Television Readies for President Clinton." *Broadcasting* (January 11): 123.

Von Drehel, David. 1993. "42 Men in Search of the Right Address." *Washington Post,* January 20, F11.

Wilson, Woodrow. 1995. "First Inaugural Address [March 4, 1913]." In *American Rhetorical Discourse,* 2nd ed., ed. Ronald F. Reid. Prospect Heights, Ill.: Waveland Press.

Chapter Two

Clinton and the Town Hall Meetings: Mediated Conversation and the Risk of Being ''In Touch''

Robert E. Denton, Jr., and Rachel L. Holloway

The 1992 presidential campaign was one of the most exciting and unique in recent history. The election signaled the end of the Reagan era, a revitalization of voter interest and participation, a generational shift of national leadership, the strongest third-party challenge since 1912, and the creative use of television and new communication technologies. Candidates were innovative in reaching the voters. Television and radio talk shows replaced the stump speech and sound bites on the evening news as the primary sources of political, issue, and candidate information. According to Dee Dee Myers (1993), Clinton's campaign communications director and later White House Press Secretary, ''The presidential campaign signaled a dramatic change in the strategy of political communication. The methods became part of the message'' (181).

It was presidential candidates Clinton and Perot that promised to institutionalize the electronic town hall meeting format. Perot's vision was most aligned to the notion of direct democracy. He advocated having major issues discussed on television and having citizens call a toll free number to express their vote or opinion on an issue.

Although Ross Perot is often credited with popularizing the concept of electronic town hall meetings, it was the Clinton campaign that recognized the potential role of new technologies to contact voters and provide more access to the candidate. For Clinton, the format was more strategic. It allowed more control over his message, greater access to specific audiences, and better opportunities for image management. More specifically, there were five strategic communication goals of the Clinton campaign (Myers, 1993, 182–83). First, the campaign wanted to provide the most rapid response around a ''get hit–hit back harder'' philosophy. One of the lessons of the Dukakis campaign was his lack of quick and timely response to attacks. Second, the campaign wanted to use various media and outlets to reach specific audiences. Cable channels and programs allowed Clinton to directly reach specific voter groups with targeted messages. Third, the campaign wanted to place Clinton in more than one place at a time. The use of satellite and interactive technologies expanded his contact with and exposure to voters. There is a greater likelihood of voter support if an individual has seen or heard a candidate in a more direct way. Fourth, the campaign wanted to use varied and longer format media opportunities. Campaign research showed that the more people saw and heard Bill Clinton, the more likely they were to support him. Finally, the campaign, in order to extend the reach of the candidate, used numerous surrogates who were associated with a particular issue, voter group, or region of the country.

Dan Nimmo (1994) argues that the electronic town hall meetings of 1992 served the candidates well, especially Clinton, and generally reduced the boredom of more traditional tactics of past campaigns. He concludes that the town hall meetings allowed the candidates to more easily target specific audiences, garner free air-time, confront more soft or polite questions, and play to the emotions of the audience and the melodrama of entertainment television (207–26). From a more theoretical perspective, the town hall meetings increased voter exposure to candidates, increased voter information and issue awareness, and energized the electorate, resulting in greater voter interest and participation.

Matthew Kerbel (1994) argues that the talk show appearances of the 1992 presidential campaign were a way not only to avoid the press but also to provide the appearance of "direct democracy and easy access to the candidates" (214). He notes that "the symbolism of accessibility can be as soothing as the real thing" (215).

For Clinton, the town hall meetings best represent the power and potential of successful mediated conversation as a strategy of public discourse and persuasion in the age of telepolitics. The purpose of this chapter is to investigate Clinton's use of the electronic town hall meetings as a means of communicating with the public. From a theoretical perspective, the electronic town hall meetings best epitomize the notion of mediated interpersonal communication. Such meetings, both in terms of form and content, best utilize the medium of television. Clinton is a master of the town hall technique of interaction. He possesses the skills and knowledge of effective interpersonal communication. But after two years, the Clinton administration stopped holding televised town hall meetings. From a political perspective, the electronic town hall meeting may be a great form of public communication for use in campaigns but is most problematic as a form of public communication while governing.

MEDIATED INTERPERSONAL COMMUNICATION

Today, it is only through the media that we come to know our leaders. And with the frequency of appearance we feel that we have come to know our presidents intimately. It is virtually impossible to distinguish between our political system and the media as separate entities. Television, as a medium, has changed the form and content of American politics. This change is not so much the result of *how* the medium is used as much as the requirements or *essential nature* of the medium.

Much of the twenty years of research on the nature and impact of mediated communication in the public policy arena focuses on media influence on the presentation, discussion, and evaluation of issues, leaders, and actions. Silvo Lenart (1994) argues that a medium as a conveyor of political information is only the starting point. One must also consider the importance of "interpersonal discussions" in shaping political attitudes (3–4).

There has been very little work on the interaction of media and interpersonal communication. Early studies found that, as sources of information, mediated information tends to reinforce preexisting opinions (Lazarsfeld, Berelson, and Gaudet, 1948; Katz and Lazarsfeld, 1955). Our concern is with the use of interpersonal communication on television or, as we call it, "mediated conversation."[1]

If viewers respond to television as if they were in an interpersonal conversation, then research about interpersonal communication generally and conversation specifically should inform our understanding of "mediated conversation" (Reardon and Rogers, 1988). Presidents now talk to us more than ever before (Hart, 1994, 1987). The way presidents talk and the medium through which they primarily talk has also changed. The days of impassioned, fiery oratory presented to packed auditoriums of live human beings are over (Jamieson, 1988). Today, presidents invite us, through the medium of television, into the privacy of their living rooms, offices, or studios for informal "presidential conversations."

Kathleen Jamieson (1988) argues that the interpersonal, intimate context created through television requires a "new eloquence"; one in which candidates and presidents adopt a personal and revealing style that engages the audience in conversation. Characteristics of "eloquent conversation" and research about nonverbal communication inform our understanding of the transformation of presidential communication strategies in the age of television. At the same time, television shapes the interaction in ways different from actual interpersonal communication contexts. The interaction of the television audience is "parasocial" and should be considered in that light (Cathcart and Gumpert, 1983; Pfau, 1990).

Conversation as Mediated Interpersonal Discourse

Thomas Frentz and Thomas Farrell (1976) define interpersonal communication as a communication episode consisting of a "rule-conforming sequence of symbolic acts generated by two or more actors who are collectively oriented toward emergent goals" (336). Through interpersonal communication, "people maintain and adjust their self-image, relate to others, cooperate in decision-making, accomplish tasks, and make order of their environment" (Cathcart and Gumpert, 1983, 27). Thus, conversation is a process of mutual interaction that establishes expectations, common goals, and a relationship that enables the mutual accomplishment of tasks.

From a structural perspective, interpersonal communication involves multiple channels (i.e., verbal and nonverbal) and interchangeable sender-receiver roles. Successful conversation requires openness, reciprocity, empathy, commitment to the interaction and continual awareness of one's role as speaker and listener as well as to the rules of social interaction (DeVito, 1988, 186–94). From a content perspective, conversation is most often personal, intimate, and revealing. In conversation, individuals attempt to communicate and to perceive personal characteristics and attitudes, from warmth and honesty to control and poise as well as conventional meanings and understandings.

Like interpersonal communication, the electronic media affect social behavior as well as relationships formed between sender and receiver, having consequences for both the television audience and the televised speaker. Marshall McLuhan argues that "societies have always been shaped more by the nature of the media by which men communicate than by the content of the communication" (McLuhan and Fiore, 1967, 8). There is a sensory involvement in any given medium. Televised conversation, while drastically increasing the potential size of the audience and the number of participants, still provides a personal, direct interaction. Television brings a president into the living room. The walls that once separated the public from its leaders have disappeared. We see them jog, eat, and even fall asleep in meetings. For the viewing audience, the experience is "real." In fact, Tony Schwartz (1973) argues that "experience with TV and radio stimuli are often more real than first-hand, face to face experiences" (44). In fact, the "captured reality" of media is preferred to personal experience. Television engages the viewer and demands attention.

Television is essentially expressive, presentational, and analogic (Meyrowitz, 1985, 93–103). Television conveys nonverbal behaviors that create impressions by their mere presence—gestures, vocalizations, facial expressions, movements, and so forth. These expressions, which cannot be stopped, are directly tied to the expressor. People gather social information about someone from television in much the same way they do in face-to-face interaction. The public looks a president in the eye, watches the subtle shifts of expression, and listens for emotional vocal cues. The visual information creates a personalized context for the president's words.

The information gleaned from television also is much more direct than meanings conveyed primarily through words. Unlike words, no arbitrary social meaning is attached to visual impressions. Citizens simply "know" what they see. As Meyrowitz (1985) notes, "There are no isolated units with independent meaning in a smile; there are not discrete degrees of sincerity in a handshake" (97). Therefore, nonverbal communication adds context and meaning to the candidate's verbal communication and may be as strategic and conscious as the words a president or political candidate chooses.

As a medium, television is intimate, ordinary, familiar, and immediate. Television requires a "spontaneous casualness" rather than a projected voice, character, or gesture as in film, on stage, or before a large audience. The key, according to Schwartz (1973), is that the role of the audience is altered. Instead of being targets for communication, audiences become participants. But it is a different kind of participation than that found in "true" conversation. Television provides viewers with the illusion of participation. Television allows the audience to observe presidents in much the same way as they do those in their everyday lives (Cathcart and Gumpert, 1983). Unlike true face-to-face interactions, however, television offers viewers the additional safety of anonymity and the potential for scrutiny that comes with it (Meyrowitz, 1985, 122). The availability of nonverbal cues, the proximity of close-ups, and the luxury to react and judge in the privacy of their own homes invites citizens to stare openly and judge without fear of, or opportunity for, response. Thus, their participation is passive, and because televised images do not respond to audience participation, it lacks authenticity.

According to John Langer (1981), good television also personalizes, "rarely using a concept or idea without attaching it to or transforming it through the 'category of the individual' " (352). Television presents, therefore, a world of personalities who organize our reality and articulate our social agendas. But, of course, not all personalities are right for television. A successful television performer must achieve a low-pressure style of presentation. Thus, not only must the message conform to the medium, but the focus is on the person delivering the message who must also conform to the medium.

As a technology, the modern media carry a connotation of rationality. Because of this, according to Altheide and Snow (1979), both communicator and audience are oriented toward a "rational means-end" type of communication. Audiences view the information shared as accurate, objective, and current. As a society, we have come to depend upon the media. Pictures and visions make the world understandable and shape the environment. What is projected affects what is seen and what is not seen. Individuals, of course, see things differently. From a political perspective, Doris Graber (1993) argues that audiovisual communication is simply more appealing to the public for several reasons. It makes information more accessible. Audiovisual communication does not require unique skills or training in order to receive and comprehend the communication. Second, the experience is closer to that of a personal experience than printed communication. It provides more emotion and receiver involvement. Third, audiovisual communication carries more information, verbal and nonverbal, than other forms. Finally, it provides more context and memory associations (329–30).

Given this theoretical context, we can now address how media impacts presidential communication or transforms it into mediated conversation. First, television is best at "one-to-one" interaction—mediated communicator to viewer. Because of television's dominance, the impassioned orator has been replaced with a warm, sincere, conversational speaker. Jamieson (1988) argues that "in intensity, style, tone, and even length, the new eloquence is more constrained than the old'' (56).

Second, television is best at reflecting or mirroring the everyday and the routine. It provides a sense of simple optimism and a sharing of who we are and what is on our minds. As an intimate medium, television requires a "comfortable" projection of self, "a sense of private self, unself-consciously self-disclose, and engage the audience in completing messages" (Jamieson, 1988, 81). Conversation is simple and utilizes short sentences and recognizable images. To engage an audience is to appear to talk with them, not at them. And, above all, the message must be personal, not institutional.

Third, television is best at presenting reactions, immediate responses rather than thoughtful reflections or ambiguity. Television, as a medium, is best suited for answers, not questions; solutions, not problems; and good old-fashioned "horse sense," not wisdom. Television is not suited for the presentation or discussion of complex issues and policies, at least not in dissertation or extended formats. Complexity confuses, simplicity aids understanding and identification. Drama on television draws the public's attention better than small group or ordinary discussion, celebrity discussion more so than private, unknown individuals, and so on. The media deals in dichotomies—win or lose, right or wrong, good or bad. Television is very good at conveying experience, not facts (Schram, 1987, 52). Television, at its best, is a sales medium presenting a dynamic message in the simplest form possible.

Finally, television does not just convey, but construct. "The mass media do not mediate. They restrict themselves to telling about themselves. They are the origin of the sense of unreality and the process of de-realization" (Ferrarotti, 1988, 13). As a result, everything for Franko Ferrarotti (1988) is spectacle. "The making of reality into spectacle seems thus to appear as an essential characteristic of the mass media. . . . Thus television ends up paradoxically transforming reality into a seemingly realistic spectacle. Reality lessens, but in its place there does not arise even the true spectacle of pure representation" (14–15). Thus, public address by a speaker to a crowd has been replaced by "private, interpersonal conversations" between a leader and the public. While television is best at presenting conversation, it is important to note that "mediated conversations" are different from nonmediated face-to-face interactions.

Presidential Conversation as Mediated Discourse

Scholarly attention is increasingly becoming focused on the nature of the "plebiscitary presidency" (Lowi, 1985) and the various strategies involved in "going public" (Kernell, 1985; Denton and Hahn, 1986). Presidents who increasingly rely on the medium of television are forced into playing the communication game by television's rules. This not only means shorter speeches, it also means speeches that are crafted specifically for television. Presidential speech is increasingly familiar, personalized, and self-revealing. Reagan's use of contractions, simple, often incomplete sentences, informal transitions, colloquial language, and frequent stories transformed his "formal" Oval Office addresses to conversations with the American people (Jamieson, 1988, 166). His skillful adaptation to the camera simulated direct eye contact with individuals in his audience. It had all the appearance of conversation. This conversational style "invite[s] us to conclude that we know and like" presidents who use it (Jamieson, 1988). Ronald Reagan first excelled at this style, which stands in marked contrast even to the conversational style of Franklin D. Roosevelt, for example. For where the strength of Reagan's rhetoric is that we feel we know and understand him, the strength of FDR was that he knew and understood us. Bill Clinton through his mediated conversational style accomplishes both, especially in the town hall meeting format.

Certainly with Clinton, presidential conversation was to be the primary means of conveying policy orientations and image projection. These "one-on-one" sessions, sometimes with viewer call-in or a live audience, moved the president one step closer to the public. Participation and interaction were encouraged. Settings are becoming more informal, giving the appearance of a casual interaction where the audience simply "eavesdrops" on the conversation.

It is important to note, however, that mediated conversation does not parallel the process of human communication. We know, for example, in the media interview format, questions to be asked are often known ahead of time and presidents rehearse desired responses prior to a mediated event. In some cases, topics and areas of discussion are issues of negotiation. In addition to lacking spontaneity of interaction, there can obviously be no "turn taking" with the televised audience. Naturally, the interviewer gives a great deal of deference to the president. Thus the partners in the interaction, whether it is the audience or the interviewer and president, are not equal in terms of control, power, or reciprocity in any phase of the conversation. There is not a mutual exchange of asking questions, voicing opinions, or stating facts.

Presidents may make themselves "physically" available but not accessible in terms of openness and a willingness to share and disclose feelings, beliefs, and attitudes. Likewise, there is little commitment to the interaction or relationship and, from a presidential perspective, the "conversation" is more often a means to a political end. In short, there is no intrinsic value to the conversation. In mediated presidential conversation, competition over control and message rather than cooperation is the norm. Although interaction takes place, it is, quite simply, a different kind of interaction.

Not only is the structure of mediated presidential conversation different from nonmediated conversation, but the content of the interactions differ as well. Interviews on television differ greatly from those in print. On television, how one responds is as important as the content of the response. Was there a hesitation, a shift of the brow, an expression of emotion? Remember the shot of Bush, in the 1992 Richmond presidential candidate debate with Clinton and

Perot, taking a quick glance of his watch? This simple action communicated a rather callous, cavalier attitude toward the audience and the event.

Perceptions of personal characteristics conveyed primarily in nonverbal communication influence viewer perception of specific presidential performances. Measures of cooperative attitude, equality, absence of superiority, warmth, interest, similarity, friendliness, sincerity, and honesty account for substantial variance in likelihood of viewers voting for a candidate, as well as perceptions of credibility and judgments about competence, sociability, and character (Pfau and Kang, 1991, 124). The secret, therefore, is a controlled response best suited for the medium of television. "More than print," Meyrowitz (1985) says, "electronic media tend to unite sender and receiver in an intimate web of personal experience and feeling" (96). The public's reactions are personal and "real," shaped by feelings and intuitions as much as by rational analysis and interpretation. In the end, the public believes they "know" the president.

Presidents should adapt to the medium of television through higher levels of intimacy and expressiveness. The "presumption of intimacy" attempts to make the audience feel as if they know the president as a dear friend and to force the audience to render positive, personal judgments. Frequent "conversations" lead to friendship, trust, and intimacy with the nation. Issue disagreements are less important and tolerated because of the appearance of friendship (Cathcart and Gumpert, 1983).

From this perspective, mediated presidential conversation is best characterized as performance rather than interaction. According to Erving Goffman (1973), interaction is defined as "the reciprocal influence of individuals upon one another's actions when in one another's immediate physical presence," whereas performance may be defined "as all the activity of a given participant on a given occasion which serves to influence in any way any of the other participants" (15). Political consequences of actions, sentiments, and opinions can never be ignored or forgotten.

Goffman (1973) further distinguishes between "front region" and "back region" behavior (106–33). Front region is the area of behavior and interaction that is for public view and inspection. It reinforces the desired images and arguments. These very public performances must keep up the desired appearances and manners. In contrast, the back region of behavior and interaction are those not seen or constructed for public view. It is the place where the performer can expect that no member of the audience will intrude. It is what goes on behind closed doors. We only allow those we trust to see the back regions of our life. In the back region we are more honest, open, and genuine. The concepts can be illustrated by contrasting the cleanliness and order of our homes on a regular week to our homes when entertaining company. Much as we create a more pleasing "back region" for guests in our homes, presidents reveal a strategically constructed back region through their conversations with the public. Through revealing the "real" person behind the office, presidents hope to engender the public's trust. Candidates even invite us on casual and relaxed tours of their home. We literally see the private side of the White House as the president and First Lady chat with our media stand-in.

But these conversations are no more real than any televised performance. The "conversation" is at least loosely scripted and practiced for timing, camera angle, and content. Some subjects and areas are off-limits. The media tourist cannot spontaneously change the spaces to be included in the tour or surprise the First Couple with a tough policy question. Finally, the product is edited to meet the constraints of the medium and the expectations of the audience. The audience receives its "televised invitation," a promotional advertisement, to the open house. It is both performance and production.

Because they are so revealing, politicians must at all costs protect their "true" back regions. Many Americans were surprised at the language of Richard Nixon revealed in the Watergate tapes. Americans were shocked at Carter's revelation that he too had "lusted in his heart" for women. Reagan's playful comments of blowing up Russia when testing a microphone before one of his weekly radio broadcasts, perhaps revealing his true intentions toward the Soviets, frightened many Americans. Presidents must be on guard without appearing guarded.

While Reagan proved that television's intimacy could heighten audience identification, the 1992 presidential campaign moved a step further with an interpersonal mediated context—the televised town meeting. As already noted, it is Clinton's mastery of the town hall meeting format that epitomizes "presidential mediated interpersonal conversation." While the format is effective, it can be misleading. It may also be great for campaigning, but what about for governing?

ELECTRONIC TOWN HALL MEETING

In 1641 the town hall meeting was established as an element of governing with the adoption of the "Body of Liberties" by the Great and General Court of Massachusetts (Nimmo, 1994, 213). The "Bodies of Liberties" specified that every man was free to attend town meetings and "either by speech or writing to move any lawful, reasonable, and material question." As the ability of citizens to provide directions or opinions on issues of daily governing became impractical, periodic town meetings became public forums of sharing opinions and views with elected officials. According to Nimmo (1994), the town hall meetings as a deliberative body was short lived. They became primarily an instrument of consensus-building rather than conflict airing or legislative development (214). As noted, the televised town hall meeting today best epitomizes the notion of mediated interpersonal communication.

The fundamental shift in the town hall meeting is its transformation of the relationship between audience and candidate. A televised town hall meeting expands and elevates the audience's role beyond what it is in speeches, press conferences, or interviews. First, it heightens the television audience's ability to observe immediate interaction. People watching the televised discussion observe the president's demeanor and attitude toward a "public surrogate," sometimes identifying with the president and at other moments taking the role of the audience member, as it happens. When a subjective camera angle is used, the television audience may be placed in the immediate situation and look the president in the eye, as if they were seated next to the citizen questioner. At other moments, the camera takes the president's point of view and the audience may see the situation from the president's perspective. When the camera pulls back to an "objective" position, the audience watches the relationship created between president and surrogates in interaction. The audience's vantage points are multiple.

The interactive format moves the audience literally and figuratively closer to the president. The journalist/panelist no longer sits between the audience and the candidate. Rather than prearranged questions and areas of discussion, the people dictate the topics. In this sense, the relationship is direct.

Perhaps more important, the town hall meeting allows the television audience to move beyond its observer role to become a participant. Surrogates ask questions, offer nonverbal feedback, and even interrupt the president. Peers in the immediate audience interact with the president. The audience helps to shape the communication. The format clearly allows the audience to set the agenda based upon the questions asked and empowers the audience as part of the democratic governing process. As a result, the town hall meetings are much more "real" to the public and elevate the status of both the immediate audience and the television audience. It is the ideal setting for what Horton and Wohl (1956) call "parasocial interaction." The audience participates in a relationship vicariously and comes to "know" the president's persona "through direct observation and interpretation of his appearance, his gestures, and voice, his conversation and conduct in a variety of situations," much as individuals develop a relationship with other television personalities (216). More than other televised formats, the town hall meeting creates an intimate, interactive mediated forum similar to a television talk show. The president talks face-to-face with "real" people. Rather than inviting us into his world, the president moves into ours. And identifications, and the demands on the president's communication abilities, shift accordingly.

One of the major functions of a campaign is to "breed familiarity" between the candidates and the public. As noted, media coverage provides the bases for candidate selection. In addition, candidate preferences are shaped by group discussion (Lenart, 1994, 105). What better way to get to "know" a candidate or president than to be incorporated as part of the "group" as a participant in a town hall meeting.

Horton and Wohl's (1956) research on the relationships created between television audiences and talk show hosts provides insight into the "Oprahization" of presidential politics. They argue that viewers build up a sense of who the "host" is and use that as a basis for further interpretation. A successful television host develops a "character" and a "pattern of action" that reveals self to the audience. The "character" is strategically constructed and coached. Although it may appear that we see the same person "backstage" and "on-stage," the separation is false. The "host" that the public views is an overall "persona" that occupies a "middle region"; a space somewhere between formal former front region behavior and informal back region behavior. Meyrowitz (1985) recommends that politicians make the most of the middle region by exposing only "selected, positive aspects of their back regions in order to integrate themselves with the public" (217). The middle region requires a consistency previously unobserved by the public. To be successful, politicians must maintain a unified image across contexts. While voters will accept a multifaceted individual as president, they will reject anyone whose fundamental "character" changes dramatically according to context. The politician must move flawlessly across situations, adapting accordingly and yet always fundamentally the same.

Nonverbal Strategies

To maximize the potential of the electronic town hall meeting, politicians must adopt verbal and nonverbal communication strategies that simultaneously reinforce positive persona as well as communicate political positions. Verbal strategies take on greater significance when placed into their visual, nonverbal context. Television not only captures nonverbal communication but also frames it strategically. The camera captures some physical behaviors and eliminates others. The director selects shots, angles, and distances that all contribute to audience perception. Freed from a podium, open floor space provides opportunities for movement and more relaxed and physically immediate interaction. Standing up and moving toward an audience member creates a physical relationship with that person, as the president literally captures "center stage." In addition to the development of a relationship with audience members, the movement also constrains camera shots.

Holding the floor, or talkativeness in conversation, is related to perceptions of leadership, friendliness, and attractiveness. Cappella (1985) reported that talkative persons are perceived as more productive, task-oriented, more leader-like, more influential, more socially adept, and better liked than less verbal people (78). However, people may exceed positive levels of talkativeness. When respondents evaluated a hypothetical person according to percentage of floor holding time, perceptions of power, influence, and competence increased up to about 60 percent and then began a decline. If someone seems to move toward monopolizing conversation, perceptions become negative (Cappella, 1985).

Eye contact reinforces relationships created in space and time. Length of gaze indicates warmth, interest, and involvement in an interaction. A negative facial expression may assert dominance or threaten the other person (see Duck, 1991, 13–15). Dovidio and his colleagues (1988) report that looking at a listener while talking communicates high power whereas less powerful or less expert people tend to look only while listening.

While these factors are known to influence interpersonal communication, several analyses of televised presidential debates also attribute perceptions of a candidate's image to nonverbal factors (see Hellweg, Pfau, and Brydon, 1992, 89–93). Eye contact patterns (Berry, 1987; Katz and Feldman, 1977; Patterson et al., 1992; Wingerson, 1982), physical tactics such as entering the stage and handshakes (Martel, 1983), and facial expression (Rosenberg and McCafferty, 1987; Henry, 1985) all are identified as contributing to televised images.

Beyond audience judgments, movement, eye contact, and other nonverbal expressions make for good television. In attempts to produce a well-paced television show, directors will choose shots that promote attention and interest, shots that promote a sense of clash, drama, action, personalization, and interaction (Drucker, 1989, 1990; Morello, 1988a, 1988b, 1992). Reaction shots have always been controversial in political debate negotiations. Morello (1992) asserts that reaction shots misrepresented the degree of clash in the 1988 presidential debates. The shots were often cued by ad hominem attacks and offered an opportunity for nonverbal refutation overriding the "equal time" conventions of verbal responses. Thus, the television director, through reaction to the president's and the audience's nonverbal behaviors, creates a mediated reality different from the experiences of the immediate audience.

Verbal Strategies

Verbal strategies of mediated conversation parallel those of interpersonal communication. In everyday conversation one fundamental perspective that leads to eloquence is "other directedness" (Daly, 1990). Persons perceived to be eloquent elevate the importance of the person to whom they are speaking, legitimizing the other's participation in the conversation and the importance of their ideas and feelings. Eloquent conversationalists turn the focus of the talk to the other party and diminish attention to self. Research indicates that individuals who adopt "other directed" messages are perceived more positively in a range of situations and on several affective variables (see Burleson, 1987).

Verbal strategies that express "other directedness" include open-ended questions (i.e., "How does the government most influence your life?") or explicit invitations to others to expand on their views in an unthreatening way (i.e., "That's interesting. I'd like you to tell me more about that."). Eloquent conversationalists validate the other through seeking information about their interests and concerns. Duck (1991, working from Daly, 1990) reports that successful conversationalists generally "avoid a competitive or argumentative style, steering away from disagreement or dogmatic statements and towards an attentive and accepting, if gently interpretative, manner" (43–44). They listen carefully and create an equal relationship with their conversational counterpart.

Involvement and commitment to the conversation are communicated by summarizing the others' statements and referencing past points in the conversation (i.e., "A moment ago you said that . . ."). Successful conversationalists are able to phrase the same idea in many ways, allowing them to adapt easily to different audiences (Daly, Vangelisti, and Daughton, 1987; Duck, 1991).

The sense of relationship created through conversation is also influenced by references to others and self. Something as simple as pronoun choice influences perceptions of relationship. Inclusive pronouns presume or create a relationship between speaker and audience. For example, if a president uses "we" as opposed to "I," the dynamic shifts. Presidents may align themselves with the public or with others.

"Other directedness" is not just a matter of style but also of substance. Walster and his colleagues (1966) reported that a person is more credible when he or she argues against his or her best interests, perhaps because it is perceived as an indication of trustworthiness and respect for others. Eagly and her colleagues (1978) found that a communicator who takes a predictable line of argument is less persuasive than one who speaks in contrast to the direction one would expect.

The televised town hall meeting offers a president a unique opportunity to use a personal, intimate conversational style in the traditional front region. Such performances give the appearance of unselfconscious responses and interactions but are, in fact, contrived, purposeful presentations. "Because the media are fixated on differences between the private and public self of public figures," according to Jamieson (1988), "a comfort with expressing rather than camouflaging self or at the minimum an ability to feign disclosure, is useful for a politician" (83). So, in a town hall meeting, are we seeing the "real" Bill Clinton in conversation with citizens or is it a public performance before the nation? For Meyrowitz (1985), it is both, which makes it neither. "To the extent that actions are shaped to fit particular social settings, this new setting leads to new actions and new social meanings. . . . We have not only a different situation, but also a different president, and—in the long run—a different presidency" (43).

CLINTON AND THE ELECTRONIC TOWN HALL MEETING FORMAT

The Richmond debate during the 1992 presidential campaign demonstrated the power of the town hall meeting format and Clinton's interpersonal communication skills. John Meyer and Diana Carlin (1994) evaluated citizen reaction to the town hall debate format. They found that the town hall format was the most favored, seemed the most open and honest, heightened voter interest, and made people "feel good" about the experience. Citizens very much liked the notion of "average people" being able to participate and ask questions reflecting their concerns, not those of reporters (78–79). Clinton was so successful with the format that he intended to incorporate the "technique" of mediated conversation into governance. He committed to at least two live appearances a year on the "Larry King Live" show (Kerbel, 1994, 215) and to conduct weekly town hall events across the nation (Drew, 1994, 164).

Clinton wanted to avoid the Washington press corps and traditional news outlets, not because they were "unfair" but rather because of their "commercial imperatives." Traditional news stories did not provide enough time to adequately answer questions. In addition, because of network competition, there is a great deal of pressure for reporters and correspondents to find a unique and often contrary angle or twist in coverage. In fact, members of the White House were convinced that the press today has gone back to the mean-spirited, picky, bull-dog approach of the Carter days and nearly as bad as during the Nixon presidency.

Initially, Clinton's media strategy was twofold: to rely upon longer, more informal program formats and to generally avoid the Washington press corps (Gersh, 1993, 12). According to media advisor Mandy Grunwald, this approach solved two problems. First, specific talk shows reached very targeted audiences, audiences who may not read newspapers or watch the evening news. The programs also allow a more personal and in-depth look at the president. Second, talk programs allow the president to go directly to the people and address their concerns. Grunwald contends that the White House press corps tends to ask questions largely irrelevant to the general public. Audiences ask more reasonable and relevant questions in contrast to a more "yes-no," argumentative style of reporters. For Grunwald, the strategy is about connecting and relating to the audience. "We need repetition, you need news" (12). This perspective provides more control over message, audience, and context of interaction.

Thus beginning with the Richmond debate during the 1992 presidential campaign and subsequent town hall meetings as president, Clinton's nonverbal and verbal behaviors maximized strategies of interpersonal communication. He regularly moved away from his seat to answer almost every question and moved toward the questioner. In fact, even when people asked questions from a remote site, Clinton moved toward the television monitor or screen. By maintaining eye contact usually with only the questioner throughout his answers, Clinton reinforced the sense of a one-to-one interaction with audience members. Movement allows for camera shot changes, increased pacing (stationary "talking heads" are considered boring television), and visual variety. Usually, there is a close-up shot of Clinton directly answering the question. Because Clinton does not look into the camera but maintains sustained eye contact with the questioner, the camera places the television audience in a seat near the questioner; the television audience is able to observe Clinton very closely.

Clinton adopts an equally "other centered" discourse by the frequent use of the inclusive first person plural pronoun, "we." Such usage creates a relationship between the president and the audience, uniting them in common purpose. Together, Clinton and the public will find solutions to problems or at least discuss solutions to problems. Elizabeth Drew (1994) observed that Clinton "would express his sympathy with their plight—and then spell out some program he had proposed that would deal with it. Clinton's empathy, actual or feigned, became one of his trademarks'' (95). Clinton's discourse establishes an ongoing public influence.

Simple acts of courtesy and direct statements of acknowledgment reinforce Clinton's eloquence. He refers to questioners as "sir" and "ma'am," and thanks individuals for their questions. He also asks questions of audience members and engages them with nondefensive statements and interactions.

In reviewing town hall meetings during the campaign as well as in the presidency, one is struck by Clinton's openness. Even receiving hostile questions, he is careful to show respect for the questioner, acknowledge the perspective of the hostile question, often asks follow-up questions to explore the questioner's position, and will even take a minority or "unpolitical" position in answers. Clinton disagrees but never argues with questioners. Such tactics enhance the perceptions of openness, equality, and genuineness.

The town hall meetings are Clinton's most preferred form of public communication. The format maximizes his style as well as control. The town hall meetings are carefully orchestrated events. The authors were present for the televised town hall meeting in Charlotte, North Carolina, on April 5, 1994, from preplanning and rehearsals through its broadcast and follow-up. The NBC news channel that sponsored the meeting retained the services of freelance producer Jean Bowman, who previously worked in the Advance Office of the White House. She knows the Clintons well, has carefully studied the president's style, and produces nearly all the town hall meetings acting as a paid consultant. A station executive stated that Bowman was recommended by the White House to assist with the scheduled town hall meeting. Implicit was the notion that retaining Bowman would improve the likelihood of the president's accepting the invitation. Perhaps more pragmatic is the simple fact that Bowman's knowledge and experience would prove invaluable in staging such a national event with less than seventy-two hours notice.

Bowman briefs the stations on audience selection, camera positions and stage construction, and personal likes and dislikes of Clinton, and moments prior to the meeting briefs the audience. Most interestingly, Bowman provided a one and a half hour "dress rehearsal" working as a stand-in for President Clinton. She copied his movements, mannerisms, and even answered questions according to his issue positions. Bowman even copied such details as sipping water, pauses with the microphone at chest level, hand gestures, and so forth. The rehearsal allows directors and camera operators to anticipate and plan for the best coverage of the president. The rehearsal was surprisingly similar to the actual town hall meeting, even to how and where Clinton would begin to shake hands with audience members at the end of the meeting. Details from the briefing were likewise very accurate. For example, Bowman told the director to anticipate twenty-five questions for the hour and half program. Twenty-three were asked.

The Washington press corps was not allowed in the studio for the town hall meeting. However, a large television monitor was provided for them, and every few minutes during the broadcast, the Office of the Press Secretary for the White House would distribute a transcript of the town meeting in progress. As a result of casual conversation with members of the national media, their frustration with the lack of access to Clinton at such events was most noticeable. It is important to note that the impression and basis of the press corps reports were the televised program, not first-hand experience of the event. The Washington Press Corps was forced to watch the meeting literally from the public's perspective, a role they refuse to accept. At the same time, because they are forced to remain outside the event, their ability to "lift the veil" on what they define as a public relations "illusion" is limited.

Clinton's "mastery" is a combination of factors, verbal and nonverbal interpersonal skills in an interactive, mediated setting. Beyond specific issues or political philosophy, Clinton knows how to engage an audience and to create a sense of identification.

Of course, Clinton's communication style is not altogether without precedence. In fact, it extends trends in presidential communication started by Ronald Reagan (Denton, 1988). Reagan was conversational in televised speeches; Clinton engages in televised conversation. Reagan's self-disclosive style allowed the public to get to understand, know, and trust him. Clinton's interactive style invites the public to disclose, so that he knows and understands them.

The shift in direction of communication and understanding mirrors a shift in public expectations. Jamieson (1988) argued that Reagan's success as the "Great Communicator" was a serendipitous mesh between his "natural style and the appetites of both television and the citizenry. . . . By disposition and practice, he was a storyteller at a time when storytelling met a powerfully felt social need" (243). Clinton's natural style as a facilitator and conversationalist met the public's special need for involvement and participation in 1992. Holloway (1994) argues that a shift in the public's political orientation from a private interest to a public interest ethic shaped the issues in the 1992 presidential election. That same dynamic, in which the public demands a voice and active participation in politics after a long period of disinterest, favored Clinton's communication style as well as his policy positions. The intimacy of television generally and the vicarious interaction of a televised town hall meeting provide a "place" for the public and a candidate to interact. In 1980, no one element alone created the unique phenomenon of Reagan's popularity. In 1992, a shift in public sentiment, a new television format, and a candidate's natural style came together almost magically in a victory.

A 1991 Kettering Foundation study reported that Americans "want an ongoing relationship, especially in between elections, in which there is 'straight talk' and give-and-take between public officials and citizens" (Germond and Witcover, 1993, 517). Of the three candidates in 1992, Clinton was the only one whose communication created a positive, ongoing relationship with the voters. Bush's style asked for deference; Perot's called for direction; Clinton's favored discussion and mutual decision. In the end, only Clinton engaged in a conversation with the American people, a conversation he seeks to continue as president. But winning the office and governing require different skills and strategies. The town hall meeting is a strategic tool of governing of the Clinton administration. However, its effectiveness was short-lived.

Within days of Clinton's first town hall meeting in Michigan, some Democratic observers in Washington were concerned that "Clinton was running the risk of being too informal and too accessible," jeopardizing the very "dignity and majesty of the office" (Drew, 1994, 54). Indeed, over time the nature of the questions asked by citizens changed. They became more directional and more challenging or argumentative. Below are several examples from the April 5, 1994, Charlotte, North Carolina, town hall meeting.

Q: Mr. President, with recent news reports about the First Lady's cattle futures earnings, and with all these Whitewater allegations, many of us Americans are having a hard time with your credibility. How can you earn back our trust?

Q: Mr. President, are you one of us middle-class people or are you in with the villainous money-grabbing Republicans?

Q: Mr. President, in 1993 when interest rates were declining, your administration took credit for that. But now both long-and short-term rates are higher than when you took office. Will your administration now take responsibility for higher rates?

Q: Mr. President, I don't mean any disrespect, because I'm an avid sports fan. But I'm also concerned about frivolous spending in government. I would really like to ask what did it cost taxpayers for you to attend the games?

According to Drew (1994), the town meetings created several problems for Clinton. They provided a temptation to mention an idea before having thought it through. For example, at an "Ask Bill" event in Chillicothe, Ohio, the president mentioned a "value-added tax" as something we may need in the future. This statement not only caught the White House staff by surprise, but also grabbed the headlines. Clinton often failed to fully appreciate the impact of what he said (85). Because of the range of topics and questions asked in town hall events, it is difficult for the White House to control the headlines and focus of legislative initiatives. On the day of the House of Representatives vote on the deficit reduction bill, President Clinton held a televised town meeting on "CBS This Morning." Drew reports that a key democrat later said, "I don't believe the town meeting was a useful device. When you have those town meetings, a hundred subjects come up and there is no message" (169). Finally, Drew questions whether or not such exposure and interactions "display the commandingness people want in a President. Did the American people want a Phil Donahue in the Presidency? Clinton slipped into the culture, became part of it" (95).

After nearly two years of town hall meetings and disastrous midterm election results for the Democrats, Clinton's new chief of staff, Leon Panetta, drastically altered the president's public access. Panetta thought the president was overexposed. The dignity and stature of the office had been eroded by presidential appearances on too many talk shows and town hall meetings. Panetta increased the ratio of press conferences to other appearances (Drew, 1994, 424). Clinton looks more presidential behind a podium than sitting on a stool.

IMPLICATIONS OF MEDIATED PRESIDENTIAL CONVERSATIONS

The new presidential "public address" as mediated conversation has several implications in terms of campaigning, governing, and the quality of citizen democracy. Mediated presidential conversation fails to properly inform and educate the public on political matters. Mediated presidential conversation encourages citizens' continued emphasis on character rather than substance of policy (Schram, 1991). As the public becomes even more reliant upon television as a source of political information, the medium increasingly simplifies the information and, consequently, the ability to recognize, perform, and appreciate complex social issues also declines. Ferrarotti (1988) observes that "as we are informed, we know everything about everything, but we no longer understand anything. It is purely cerebral information that does not manage to touch the deeper levels of human beings" (13). For Roderick Hart (1994), "television miseducates the citizenry but, worse, it makes that miseducation attractive" (12). In reality, the public does not know what they think they know and the public does not care about what they do not know. Politicians no longer try to change minds through argumentation; rather, they attempt to say something we in the audience can identify with, to project an image by what they say, to communicate something about their personalities by the audiences they choose to address.

Members of the press, of course, think they can do a better job questioning and presenting the president than members of the general public can. According to Tom Wicker, former reporter and columnist for the *New York Times,* members of the press are better at focusing on issues, identifying specific aspects, dimensions, or complexity of issues. Equally important, he thinks the press is better prepared to ask questions resulting from topic research and study (Conn, 1993, 18). For Howard Fineman of *Newsweek,* "talk-show democracy is a driverless vehicle which anyone with money can commandeer" (18).

The staged mediated presidential conversations offer a mode of discourse that Neil Postman (1985) characterizes as "accessible, simplistic, concrete, and above all, entertaining" (18). He argues that "the problem is not that TV presents the masses with entertaining subject matter, but that television presents all subject matter as entertaining. What is dangerous about television is not its junk. Every culture can absorb a fair amount of junk, and, in any case we do not judge a culture by its junk but by how it conducts its serious public business. What is happening in America is that television is transforming all serious public business into junk" (15). Not only does mediated presidential conversation trivialize public issues and thought but its overall effect is one of confusion.

Through mediated presidential conversations, our presidents become media celebrities or personalities. A celebrity is a "human pseudo-event" where people are "known for their well-knowness" (Nimmo and Combs, 1983). President Clinton is a "national Oprah." The mediated conversations provide a false intimacy because they do not reveal the true back regions of presidents' thoughts or ideas. They are backstage interactions performed on frontstage. The illusion is one of spontaneity and accessibility. In Clinton's case, Joe Klein (1992) noted that "there is a facile opacity to this style of leadership: even though we get to hear about his 12-step program, his stepfather's alcoholism, his mother's cancer, his brother's drug addiction, the host himself remains elusive, a kaleidoscope of comforting images" (35). We participate vicariously in his life through "artificial interactions." At best, according to Roderick Hart (1984), "television gives us a one-dimensional presidency. It presents our presidents to us in their Sunday best but without their souls or feelings" (54).

This illusion functions to hide the power relation inherent in any presidential relationship, allowing presidents to use (or misuse) the appearance of intimate conversational relations as a mechanism to delegitimize criticism and secure his power base.

Further, this illusory conversation allows for a divorce between reality and public presidential speech. Such interaction often generates unreal expectations. The exchanges, for the benefit of the audience, are always fun, revealing, and predictable. The intimate knowledge the electorate feels they have of the president is not intimate at all. Information so widely shared is neither reciprocal nor privileged. Politics and political relations based on such an illusion can be neither healthy nor authentic.

Perhaps the most damaging aspect of all mediated conversations is the public's open acknowledgment that all political talk is performance. During the Charlotte town hall meeting, one author watched the event at a remote site. Unlike the Charlotte participants, who saw the president in person, or the media audience, who saw him in close-up and interacted vicariously, the once excited remote audience quickly fell into silence as the town meeting progressed. Much as Dorothy and friends were angered, disillusioned, and wiser when the wizard's curtain was drawn back, participants outside of Charlotte were overwhelmed by the artifice and production. They heard the reports of satellite problems, the director's updates and cues, the anchor's interaction with the control room. When "their turn" came, the questioner stared awkwardly at the camera, while on a monitor nearby the president appeared to be looking directly back at him. Ironically, because of the placement of the monitor in the studio, the questioner never saw the president. Worse yet, because of audio problems, the president was speaking to an image of a citizen who never even heard his answer.

Martin Schram (1991) argues that the public's recognition that all presidents are ultimately "acting" merely leads to acceptance of the ability to perform as the essential qualification for office: "The quest for personal leadership becomes a self-destructive quest in which all pretenders are found to be just that. In the end, the grammar of electronic electioneering teaches people to be content with their inability to find a 'real leader' and to be comfortable with elected officials who are comfortable faking it'' (215).

The mediated conversations also create a short-term political environment. The focus is on the person, not the issue; the momentary emotion, not the long-term commitment; the immediate image, not the long-term solution. Through the conversations, presidents engender trust and identification rather than the process of rational decision making. There is, as Jamieson (1988) notes, a continual divorce between speech and thought, character and ideas (215).

Perhaps above all, mediated presidential conversations invite the potential for abuse. They emphasize style over substance, fantasy over reality, and demand a skill of "conversation." To use a medium effectively implies control, planning, and proper execution.

CONCLUSION

Presidential communication increasingly resembles "conversation," but it is not conversation. The public is not being exposed to "back room" communication. While Goffman and Meyrowitz argue that the glass walls are being constructed between the front and the back room, thus exposing the audience to "privileged" communication, we argue that the "back room" is being purposely and intentionally constructed for us in the front room. The "real" back room is now the place where these purposes and intentions are discussed, and the construction is planned. As in a theater, the appearance of reality is part of a constructed set designed to portray a specific and narrowly focused view of the world. In the case of the president, the set is designed to engender trust in the person of the president apart from the specific policies espoused.

The facade of "conversation" is just that—a facade. Presidential "conversations" are, in terms of the degree of management, scripting, and staging involved, as formal a mode of discourse as a presidential inaugural or campaign address. The difference is that the public does not perceive these "conversations" as formal communication because "conversations" lack, at least for now, the rituals that attend most forms of formal communication.

Despite the limitations, the public's desire for such interaction, however limited its eventual form, should not be dismissed lightly. After President Clinton answered questions for several hours about his proposed health care plan on a special "town hall meeting" addition of "Nightline," host Ted Koppel said, "There is something wonderful about being able to bring an American president and an audience of 1,000 of his constituents together for this kind of exchange" (September 23, 1993). What is wonderful is a distant approximation of true democracy, an exchange of ideas among a leader and the citizenry.

However, as presidents reduce the level of formality between the mass public and themselves, as they spend more time in "the back room," as they increasingly engage in "conversation" with the public, the public will, in turn, come to expect the continuance of such behavior, and will come to treat presidents as they treat other members of conversational dyads.

The founders designed the presidency to be insulated from the pressure of public opinion. The distance of formality was intended to protect the president and provide for a certain degree of freedom of action within the constraints of democratic accountability. Ironically, the staged "conversations" have replaced, to a large degree, the formality of status and access, reducing both the protection and the accountability. Town hall meetings destroy the distance between the office and the people. They can not provide perspective of the issues discussed. Television makes the *process* the story, not the action or result. From the president, they demand "instant wisdom," "infinite knowledge or solutions."

We live in the age of candidate-centered politics and the personal president. Ironically, there appears to be a continual decline in presidential popularity. Martin Wattenberg (1991) argues that "the focus on personal attributes has been a major component of the decline in candidate popularity" (81). Town hall meetings continue the process of familiarity which further breeds contempt. The politics of personality makes the president personally accountable. Unlike earlier presidents with equally notorious personal reputations, President Clinton's personal past has produced civil suits and tabloid headlines. His guilt or innocence is not of interest here. What is relevant is the willingness of the public and the media to participate in the preoccupation with his personal actions at the expense of political analysis. Had he been on less friendly terms with the public, if he had created a more distant and superior presidential persona, would he face such scrutiny? If a president meets the public on its own terms as an equal, he must accept a changed relationship, with both its good and bad consequences.

One of the great paradoxes of American politics is that we want one of us, an average citizen who knows us and understands us, to run for president. But once elected, we demand greater strength, greater insight, greater knowledge than the average person. We expect the president to provide uncommon leadership. Thus, "mediated conversation" is the best form of communication for campaigning, but not for governing. We agree, of course, that the interpersonal conversational style is best for television. But should the medium of television dictate who runs and who is elected president? Lance Bennett (1985), in discussing communication and social responsibility, notes the dangers of communication forms or constructs developed for social control rather than participatory interaction. "The communication of simple, self-fulfilling representations may be indispensable for mobilizing both opinion and unreflective action, but impoverished representations are not useful for enriching the human experience, developing a critical consciousness of the relationships among symbols and things, or increasing the chances for ordinary people to participate in the discovery and transformation of their own condition" (259). Such is the ultimate danger of mediated presidential conversations. The obvious requirement is a politically active citizenry who receives information from a multitude of sources and interactional contexts.

NOTE

1. The notion of "mediated conversation" was first developed and discussed in "Presidential Communication as Mediated Conversation," by Robert E. Denton, Jr., and Mary E. Stuckey in a paper presented at the annual meeting of the Speech Communication Association, November 1990. See Philo Washburn, ed., *Research in Political Sociology,* Vol. 7 (Greenwich, Conn.: JAI Press, 1995), 91–115.

REFERENCES

Portions of this chapter appear in Philo Washburn, ed., *Research in Political Sociology,* Vol. 7 (Greenwich, Conn.: JAI Press, 1995).

Altheide, David L. and Robert P. Snow. 1979. *Media Logic.* Beverly Hills: Sage.

Bennett, Lance. 1985. "Communication and Social Responsibility." *Quarterly Journal of Speech* 71: 259–88.

Berry, Joseph P., Jr. 1987. *John F. Kennedy and the Media: The First Television President.* Lanham, Md.: University Press of America Inc.

Burleson, Brant R. 1987. "Cognitive Complexity and Person-Centered Communication: A Review of Methods, Findings, and Explanations." In *Personality and Interpersonal Communication,* ed. Jame C. McCroskey and John A. Daly (pp. 305–41). Newbury Park, Calif.: Sage.

Cappella, Joseph N. 1985. "Controlling the Floor in Conversation." In *Multichannel Integrations of Nonverbal Behavior,* ed. Aron W. Siegman and Stanley Felstein (pp. 69–103). Hillsdale, N.J.: Lawrence Erlbaum.

Cathcart, Robert and Gary Gumpert. 1983. "Mediated Interpersonal Communication: Toward a New Typology." *Quarterly Journal of Speech* 69: 267–77.

Conn, Earl. 1993. "The Press and the Omnipresent President." *Editor & Publisher,* August 14, 18, and 33.

Daly, John A. 1990. "Competent Conversation." Paper presented at the Iowa Ideas Forum, University of Iowa, February.

Daly, John A., Anita Vangelisti, and Suzanne M. Daughton. 1987. "The Nature and Correlates of Conversational Sensitivity." *Human Communication Research* 14: 167–202.

Denton, Robert E., Jr. 1988. *The Primetime Presidency of Ronald Reagan.* New York: Praeger.

Denton, Robert E., Jr., and Dan F. Hahn, 1986. *Presidential Communication: Description and Analysis.* New York: Praeger.

DeVito, Joseph. 1988. *Human Communication: The Basic Course,* 4th ed. New York: Harper and Row.

Dovidio, John R., Steven L. Ellyson, Caroline F. Keting, Karen Heltman, and Clifford E. Brown. 1988. "The Relationship of Social Power to Visual Displays of Dominance between Men and Women." *Journal of Personality and Social Psychology* 54: 232–42.

Drew, Elizabeth. 1994. *On the Edge.* New York: Simon & Schuster.

Drucker, Susan J. 1989. "Televised Presidential Debates: A New Tradition." Paper presented at the annual meeting of the Speech Communication Association, San Francisco.

————. 1990. "The Impact of Mediation on Argumentation in Presidential Debates." Paper presented at the annual meeting of the Speech Communication Association, Chicago.

Duck, Steve. 1991. *Friends, for Life: The Psychology of Personal Relationships,* 2d ed. London: Harvester Wheatsheaf.

Eagly, Alice H., Wendy Wood, and Shelly Chaiken. 1978. "Causal Inferences about Communications and Their Effect on Opinion Change." *Journal of Personality and Social Psychology* 36: 424–35.

Ferrarotti, Franko. 1988. *The End of Conversation.* Westport, Conn.: Greenwood Press.

Frentz, Thomas and Thomas Farrell. 1976. "Language-Action: A Paradigm for Communication." *Quarterly Journal of Speech* 62: 333–49.

Germond, Jack and Jules Witcover. 1993. *Mad as Hell.* New York: Warner Books.

Gersh, Debra. 1993. "Mixed Messages." *Editor & Publisher,* April 10, 12–13.

Goffman, Erving. 1973. *The Presentation of Self in Everyday Life.* New York: The Overlook Press.

Graber, Doris. 1993. "Making Campaign News User Friendly." *American Behavioral Scientist* 37: 328–36.

Hart, Roderick P. 1984. *Verbal Style and the Presidency.* Orlando, Fla.: Academic Press.

————. 1987. *The Sound of Leadership.* Chicago: The University of Chicago Press.

————. 1994. *Seducing America.* New York: Oxford University Press.

Hellweg, Susan A., Michael Pfau, and Steven R. Brydon. 1992. *Televised Presidential Debates: Advocacy in Contemporary America.* New York: Praeger.

Henry, William A. III. 1985. *Visions of America: How We Saw the 1984 Election.* Boston: Atlantic Monthly Press.

Holloway, Rachel L. 1994. "A Time for Change: The Issue in the 1992 Presidential Election." In *The 1992 Presidential Election: A Communication Perspective,* ed. Robert E. Denton, Jr. (pp. 129–67). New York: Praeger.

Horton, Donald and Richard R. Wohl. 1956. "Mass Communication and Para-Social Interaction: Observation on Intimacy at a Distance." *Psychiatry* 19: 215–29.

Jamieson, Kathleen H. 1988. *Eloquence in an Electronic Age.* New York: Oxford University Press.

Katz, Elihu and Joseph J. Feldman. 1977. "The Debates in Light of Research: A Survey of Surveys." In *The Great Debates: Kennedy Vs. Nixon, 1960,* ed. Sidney Kraus (pp. 173–223). Bloomington: Indiana University Press.

Katz, Elihu and Paul Lazarsfeld. 1955. *Personal Influence.* Glencoe, Ill.: Free Press.

Kerbel, Matthew. 1994. *Edited for Television.* Boulder, Colo.: Westview Press.

Kernell, Samuel. 1985. *Going Public: New Strategies of Presidential Leadership.* Washington, D.C.: Congressional Quarterly Press.

Klein, Joe. 1992. "The Bill Clinton Show." *Newsweek,* October 26: 35.

Langer, John. 1981. "Television's 'Personality System.' " *Media, Culture, and Society* 4: 351–65.

Lazarsfeld, Paul, Bernard Berelson, and Hazel Gaudet. 1968. *The People's Choice,* 3d ed. New York: Columbia University Press.

Lenart, Silvo. 1994. *Shaping Political Attitudes.* Thousand Oaks, Calif.: Sage, 1994.

Lowi, Theodore J. 1985. *The Personal President: Power Invested, Promise Unfulfilled.* Ithaca, N.Y.: Cornell University Press.

Martel, Myles. 1983. *Political Campaign Debates: Images, Strategies, and Tactics*. New York: Longman.

McLuhan, Marshall and Quentin Fiore. 1967. *The Medium is the Message*. New York: Bantam Books.

Meyer, John and Diana Carlin. 1994. "The Impact of Formats on Voter Reaction." *The 1992 Presidential Debates in Focus*, ed. Diana Carlin and Mitchell McKinney (pp. 69–83). Westport, Conn.: Praeger.

Meyrowitz, Joshua. 1985. *No Sense of Place*. New York: Oxford University Press.

Morello, John T. 1988a. "Argument and Visual Structuring in the 1984 Mondale-Reagan Debates: The Medium's Influence on the Perception of Clash." *Western Journal of Speech Communication* 52: 277–90.

———. 1988b. "Visual Structuring of the 1976 and 1984 National Televised Presidential Debates: Implication." *Central States Speech Journal* 39: 359–69.

———. 1992. "The 'Look' and Language of Clash: Visual Structuring of Argument in the 1988 Bush-Dukakis Debates." *Southern Communication Journal* 57: 205–18.

Myers, Dee Dee. 1993. "New Technology and the 1992 Clinton Presidential Campaign." *American Behavioral Scientist* 37: 181–84.

Nimmo, Dan. 1994. "The Electronic Town Hall in Campaign '92: Interactive Forum or Carnival of Buncombe?" *The 1992 Presidential Campaign: A Communication Perspective*, ed. Robert E. Denton, Jr. (pp. 207–26). Westport, Conn.: Praeger.

Nimmo, Dan and James E. Combs. 1983. *Mediated Political Realities*. New York: Longman.

Patterson, Miles L., Mary E. Churchill, Gary K. Burger, and Jack L. Powell. 1992. "Verbal and Nonverbal Modality Effects on Impressions of Political Candidates: Analysis from the 1984 Presidential Debates." *Communication Monographs* 59: 231–42.

Pfau, Michael. 1990. "A Channel Approach to Television Influence." *Journal of Broadcasting and Electronic Media* 34: 195–214.

Pfau, Michael and Jong Kang. 1991. "The Impact of Relational Messages on Candidate Influence in Televised Political Debates." *Communication Studies* 42/2: 114–28.

Postman, Neil. 1985. *Amusing Ourselves to Death: Public Discourse in the Age of Show Business*. New York: Penguin.

Reardon, Kathleen K. and Everett M. Rogers. 1988. "Interpersonal versus Mass Media Communication: A False Dichotomy." *Human Communication Research* 15: 284–303.

Rosenberg, Shawn W. and Patrick McCafferty. 1987. "The Image and the Vote: Manipulating Voter's Preferences." *Public Opinion Quarterly* 51: 31–47.

Schram, Martin. 1987. *The Great American Video Game: Presidential Politics in the Television Age*. New York: William Morrow and Co.

Schram, Sanford. 1991. "The Post-Modern Presidency and the Grammar of Electronic Engineering." *Critical Studies in Mass Communication* 8: 210–16.

Schwartz, Tony. 1973. *The Responsive Chord*. New York: Anchor Books.

Walster, Elaine H., Elliot Aronson, and Darcy Abrahams. 1966. "On Increasing Persuasiveness of a Low Prestige Communicator." *Journal of Experimental Social Psychology* 2: 325–42.

Washburn, Philo, ed. 1995. *Research in Political Sociology,* Vol. 7. Greenwich, Conn.: JAI Press.
Wattenberg, Martin. 1991. *The Rise of Candidate-Centered Politics.* Cambridge, Mass.: Harvard University Press.
Wingerson, Lois. 1982. ''Nice Guys Finish First: A Study of Facial Politics Concludes that a Candidate Should Not Lead with his Chin.'' *Discover* (December): 66–67.

Chapter Three

Virtual Democracy: A Critique of the Clinton Administration Citizen–White House Electronic Mail System

Kenneth L. Hacker

> Historians tell us that democracy is built on conversation—people talking to one another.
>
> —*Citizens and Politics,* 1991

In this chapter, I analyze the claims of Clinton administration planners for the new White House e-mail system, how the plans appear to be operating, and some theoretical bases for assessing the strengths and limitations of their efforts. Data for this analysis include numerous documents provided from the White House over Internet, interchanges with White House e-mail planners, and published criticisms by others who have looked over the efforts to use communication technologies to enhance democracy. Efforts to improve American democracy with e-mail are evaluated in light of efforts by scholars to articulate theories of democratic communication.

Developing objectives of improving democratic communication and empowering more citizens constitutes a noble task. However, such objectives must be placed within the political contexts in which they arose and are contested. This sort of analysis must therefore begin with both an understanding of the "Information Age" rhetoric of the day and the claims made by the Clinton campaign during the election of 1992. Eventually, we must also confront issues of who makes changes in democracies, whether or not it is possible to engineer democracy, and what role everyday citizens have in such redesigning processes.

According to early visions of the Information Age, today's society would be paperless, labor would be robotic in most factories, cash would be obsolete, and new communication technologies would have opened new vistas for education. Sadly, today's realities do not match what the visionaries presented in their tales of global villages, electronic cottages, and offices of the future. The Internet certainly offers new communication potential, but nothing close to the utopian scenes that were painted by those who saw answers to political problems in the emergence of new technologies. Recognizing this, we can work on realistic ways of helping the Internet develop into a tool of better human and political communication.

THE INFORMATION AGE MYTHOLOGY

Whenever new communication technologies are emerging, there are tales of both utopian and dystopian effects. The mythology that surrounds the Internet is the same kind of mythology of utopian effects that accompanies all new communication technologies. For example, Samuel Morse said that the trans-Atlantic cable was going to ensure a world of peace because it annihilated space and time and brought people together into a "common brotherhood" (Steffen, 1994, 13).

At least since 1971 when talk about a "wired nation" began, industry professionals and academics have predicted a "revolution" in communication that is always just over the horizon (Smith, 1972; Traber, 1986). These predictions declared that the revolutions in communication would bring about all new changes in economics, politics, and cultures. Cable television, for example, was supposed to bring about more education and services for the handicapped, aged, and minorities. Cable TV was also heralded as the beginning of home banking and instant access to emergency services such as police and medical attention (Traber, 1986).

Projections about communication "revolutions" occur with each new major communication technology. The microprocessor was invented at Bell Labs in 1971 by Ted Hoff, an employee of Intel (Rogers, 1986). In just a few years, there were visions about social transformation that would accompany microchip technology. A report by the Siemans Corporation predicted that 40 percent of office jobs would be lost, and a U.S. Senate committee report foresaw a twenty-two-hour work week by 1985 along with retirement at age 38 (Forester, 1992). Yet, despite the rhetoric about future shocks, global villages, third waves, megatrends, and the age of information, little actually changed. As Forester (1992, 134) observes, "Neither Utopia nor Dystopia has arrived on Earth as a result of computerization."

Politically, new kinds of democratization have been attributed to new communication technologies. Some of the predictions were about workplace democratization. More leisure time and flattened hierarchies would result from the new technologies. Evidence to support these hopes is nonexistent (Forester, 1992). Until recently, scholars believed claims in published studies of computer-mediated communication (CMC), which say that the nature of new technology is such that status and power factors of human interaction are lessened. Recently research has falsified or challenged some of those claims (Baym, 1995). Unfortunately, there is also no evidence that new communication technologies have expanded citizen involvement in democratic government. Political scientist W. Russell Neuman (1986) documents how the increase in media channels for political information in America actually parallels a decline in political sophistication. It is easier to stay at home and watch political events on television than to physically attend and participate in those events. And while more channels might seem to imply more information, the greater number of channels for messages also facilitates an absorption of disinformation (Traber, 1986). Michael Traber (1986) goes so far as to argue that the new technologies are not liberating anyone as much as they are consolidating the power of military and economic spheres. About 90 percent of all data flow via communication satellites is corporate data exchange (Traber, 1986). Despite visions of a global village, Traber (1986) points out that more than 80 percent of the world's international telephone traffic is conducted by the Western industrial nations. While on-line access to political information seems intuitively vital for citizen participation, we must remind ourselves that only about 1 percent of all U.S. households use videotext services and less than 7 percent are using computer networks in general (Forester, 1992).

It is common to hear that with the Information Highway, decision making is becoming more decentralized, that more people can communicate about political matters, and that our democratic republic is becoming more democratic due to increasing input from citizens. A sign of this political liberation, cited by Internet enthusiasts, is that people will be more able to choose from more options what they will consume and when. Hamelink (1986) cautions us to see that computerization or "informatization" is a follow-up to mechanization, a process motivated by goals of cost efficiency (9). As the change from serf to worker with the development of machines did not change power relationships of rulers and ruled, it is unlikely that real power changes accompany the change from industrial worker to information worker.

Instead of using more television outlets for more information, Americans are using the accelerating number of channels in cable TV for entertainment. This is not a function of the technology itself, however. The development of a communication infrastructure in France is instructive. In France, the Teletel/Minitel (Teletel = system, Minitel = terminals) videotext system has over 5 million users and offers more than 12,000 services (Arnal, 1990). Analysts attribute some of its success to the fact that the Minitel terminals were distributed free-of-charge by the French government. Also, the Teletel/Minitel system was designed to provide services that met known needs. One such service is the electronic directory, which serves as a replacement for paper phone books. This feature attracted whoever would later learn about other available services. At this time, about 85 percent of the users make use of the electronic directory. Other uses are home banking (18 percent of users), teleshopping (16 percent), and transportation (15 percent). Only about 4 percent of the users are using the system for messaging, and only 8 percent use it for games (Arnal, 1990). In the

United States, videotext systems have not met with such success. The videotext in Miami, Viewtron, for example, began in 1983. Charging $600 for its terminal and $12 basic monthly fee, it had only 3,100 subscribers by 1985. It takes time for new communication technologies to become known and accepted, especially when they have so many diverse functions. Still, mythologies about the technologies often create unrealistic expectations.

Mythologies help people to explain their experiences. However, an analytic view of mythology requires one to examine both its realism and its ideology (Hamelink, 1986). Today, we witness an ongoing myth of how we are shifting from an industrial society to an information society. This myth tells us that information is basic to everything important in human societies, including economic development.

Mythology is critical to the development of the Internet for many reasons. Americans view new communication technologies in a context of past technologies and values that are deeply embedded in their history. For example, Americans have trouble with having government planning of new technologies, in part because they see the nation as one of unlimited abundance and opportunities, where zero-sum scenarios simply don't make sense (Steffen, 1994).

The mythology of the Internet or Super Information Highway has many voices as well as a long history going back to fascination with the machines of the Industrial Age. A strong theme is that high technology can lead to a better life and world. Related to this is the belief now that high-technology communication will produce wider educational opportunities, less government centralization, and more economic inroads (Steffen, 1994). Science fiction writer Arthur Clarke is telling people that portable learning computers will make formal educational settings and teachers obsolete while creating a more enlightened and harmonious society (Steffen, 1994). Psychologist Carl Rogers sees high-tech communication as producing more cooperation and less destructive competition (Steffen, 1994). James Martin says that the technologies will deter encroaching federal bureaucracies (Steffen, 1994).

Historian Jerome Steffen (1994) argues that these kinds of projections have created "Edenic expectations of new technology" (14). In the Internet Eden, life is bucolic and citizens are content and can be seen occasionally glancing from their computer terminals out at the peaceful country landscape of rolling hills and idyllic villages.

Without being Ludditic, it is necessary to face the problems with present approaches to Internet. Nelkin (1994) describes three main problem areas with computer-mediated communication: privacy, "social control," and democratic values.

While not specified in the Constitution as an explicit right, most Americans believe they have a "right of privacy." However, they are also willing to let that right be infringed upon, when circumstances seem to demand that they do. For example, most people do not challenge the practices of stores videotaping them while they shop, exposure in the media of celebrities' personal activities, or drug testing for certain jobs. Computer data banks permit organizations to gain easy access to personal data on credit, school records, medical histories, and tax status (Nelkin, 1994).

Social "control" is enhanced when organizations and employers can gain access to personal data about employees through computer networks. Nelkin (1994) argues that new technologies are welcomed as creating a new kind of pluralism because of increased numbers of channels. In fact, she argues, increased channels will continue to provide the same kind of hegemonic messages that we have already. Some observers believe that the Internet is a great boost to democracy. Others see the opposite. Nelkin (1994) argues that inundation with information should not be confused with reasoned political dialogue.

Francis Bacon said that "knowledge is power." What he did not add is that most people do not have access to knowledge. This has not changed much with the development of the Internet. At this point, the primary beneficiaries are banks, stock brokerages, military facilities, and educational centers. As with foreign and even domestic policies, the guiding objectives for designing and implementing the Internet or Super Information Highway today are market objectives. Market objectives, present with the diffusion of all new communication technologies, involve control of labor forces, increasing work productivity in organizations, creating new markets for investments, and seeking of new capital. McDonald's planned to extend its golden arches into the Internet this year, by placing commercials on the American Online network (*Wall Street Journal* 7/21/94, B7). A brewing controversy now is how much advertising will be allowed on the Internet. The Clinton administration has not taken a position yet on such specific issues, but they have announced a strong orientation toward a corporate-driven national infrastructure.

COMMUNICATION BETWEEN PRESIDENTS AND CITIZENS

The issue of communication between centers of power and everyday citizens was dormant in American society for decades before the election of 1992. In the election of 1992, candidate Bill Clinton used the issue to strike responsive chords of voters. They wanted more connection to their president, and he promised that he would provide it. George Bush and his campaign staff appear to have missed the issue.

In 1991, the Kettering Foundation did a study of what Americans thought about their political participation and efficacy. The study was conducted by using six focus groups in various parts of the nation. Each group had about twelve people and talked for about two hours. The Kettering Foundation is a public interest organization dedicated to studying and promoting public participation in American politics. The findings of this study are important because they challenge conventional wisdom about American citizens and voters. They also provided information about Americans that provided key background information for the Clinton campaign strategies; no other candidate spoke more directly to the themes of the Kettering findings than did Bill Clinton.

Conventional wisdom often sees Americans as apathetic because of low voter turnout and skepticism in election campaigns. Journalists tend to assume that voters do not care about issues, and thereby conclude that it is appropriate to cover campaign strategies and personal lives more than issues. Conventional wisdom also assumes that citizens will only pay attention to quick, sound-bite driven newscasts. Additionally, it is assumed that Americans are too involved in their daily lives to participate in politics. The Kettering findings indicate that all of these assumptions are false.

The Kettering focus groups showed evidence that Americans were strongly dissatisfied with their political system. While history shows that it is common for Americans to be critical of politicians, big government, and corruption, this level of discontent went beyond what is considered usual. The participants reflected the typical pride that Americans have in their heritage, including strong appreciation for the struggles waged for suffrage, free speech, and rights. Yet, despite this loyalty, Americans were (and are) angry about the state of the republic in general and with their limited role in governing it. In 1991, Americans perceived Washington as a place run by a professional political class, comprised of politicians, lobbyists, and journalists. This class does not work for them as much as for interest groups with lots of money. The research also indicated that these people wanted to change all of this by adding more integrity to public discourse and more public input into discussions about policy issues.

The Kettering focus groups never indicated that people have a lack of information. Instead, Americans see problems with the quality of the information they receive. They believe that they are disconnected from power because they were forced out of political processes. Where they believe they can make a difference, they appear willing to engage in political processes. They were not looking for more accountability of leaders, but rather for a larger and more genuine role for ordinary citizens in defining issues and policy choices. They did not want to become better-informed spectators. An essential theme found in these focus groups was that voters spoke about disconnection from political debates. They believe that they cannot have any important impacts on government.

These focus groups provided indications of at least four necessary conditions for Americans to increase their political involvement. They are: (1) beliefs that they can affect or have input into debates, (2) seeing possibilities for creating and observing changes, (3) having an increased sense of belonging in their communities, and (4) seeing potential to act on their own interests (*Citizens and Politics,* 1991). They wanted more access to information about real issues, but also more open discussion about issues in which they participate. They wanted new ways for citizens and officials to interact in political discussions. Without such interactivity, citizens felt little connection with issues and little relationship with leaders. They were not likely to see letter writing as being effective. They wanted more access to the system, but did not know where to find it. They rejected the idea that public opinion polling helps democracy; they saw it as diminishing the voice of the people.

THE CLINTON CAMPAIGN COMMUNICATION TALK

The Clinton campaign of 1992 was one of the most focused presidential campaigns in terms of communication strategies. Advisers made decisions about all candidate communication actions including whom the candidate should talk to, whom to avoid, and how to hold a microphone (Golson and Range, 1992). Critical and effective decisions were made about what medium to use and when. For the debates, Clinton himself knew that he should demand the "town meeting" format to optimize his communication style. Clinton knew that he would do better to bypass journalists and interact directly with voters. In an interview done after the election, he said, "The media were more interested in the horse race. That's when we decided to go full steam ahead in a new way. . . . I think two-way communication on TV between the candidate and the people will be the story" (Golson and Range, 1992, 14). Clinton was aware of how journalists can turn rumors into news, such as the "story" about missing pages from his State Department file. Clinton acknowledged the important role of journalists in doing most of their campaign work and critiques, but also said that "anyone who lets himself be interpreted to the American people through these intermediaries alone is nuts" (Golson and Range, 1992, 15). Clinton promised that as president, he would continue to do "town meeting" discussions with citizens. He had done that, albeit less frequently.

While the Bush campaign tried to convince voters that the economy was not as bad as they thought it was, Clinton directly targeted their economic concerns. The Clinton campaign staff carefully studied the political zeitgeist and what voters were talking about. They learned that voters perceived government in constant gridlock and unable or unwilling to solve the most pressing problems (Denton, 1994). With this, Clinton talked about investing in people, providing opportunities with responsibilities, and reinventing government. More communication with citizens was promised by both Clinton and Gore. This culminated in discussion, plans, legislation, and task forces working on a National Information Infrastructure.

NATIONAL INFORMATION INFRASTRUCTURE (NII)

In September 1993, the Clinton administration announced a National Information Infrastructure initiative. This initiative stated that there is a "national consensus" that the construction of a NII will "help unleash an information revolution that will change forever the way people live, work, and interact with each other" (Background on the Administration's Telecommunications Policy Reform Initiative, 1994). Vice President Al Gore gave speeches announcing numerous legislative and administrative proposals for new information policies and government provision of information. Part of what Gore stressed was the need to encourage private investment in the NII, promotion of competition, open access to the NII, advancing universal access to the NII, and flexibility of the network. Some of what Gore and Clinton advocated was consistent with what some states were already initiating. In terms of investment, the Clinton administration pledged that there would be efforts to ensure more competition, but also enough government regulation of NII-related industries to protect consumers.

Universal service is a principle made common with the Communications Act of 1934. The Clinton administration argues that "the full potential of the NII will not be realized unless all Americans who desire it have easy, affordable access to advanced communications and information services, regardless of income, disability, or location" (Background on the Administration's Telecommunications Policy Reform Initiative, 1994). This commitment states that by the year 2000, all classrooms, libraries, and hospitals will be connected to the NII.

WHITE HOUSE PLANS FOR CITIZEN E-MAIL ACCESS

At the annual conference of the International Communication Association, in the Political Communication division preconference, held on May 27, 1993, in Washington, D.C., a key White House e-mail system planner discussed the theory underpinning the new plans for citizen access. The speaker was Jonathan ("Jock") P. Gill, Director of Electronic Publishing and Public Access e-mail to the White House. Gill talked about how the plans began during the Clinton campaign and how there are unanswered questions for the planners.

In the spring of 1992, people in the Clinton campaign looked for means to disseminate information directly to voters without the editorializing of journalists. Gill described this as a means of communicating with voters without "interpretation or filtration or manipulation." With the help of technical academics at MIT, from July on, every message uttered by Bill Clinton was sent to America OnLine and CompuServe. Then, with the help of the MIT specialists, all Clinton speeches and campaign talk points were distributed to discussion groups on the Internet. In September and October, the Clinton campaign received feedback from academics indicating that they were using the posted materials in their classes.

Gill says that he wrote about 7,000 messages in a hundred days to groups and voters. He was told by the campaign to answer the e-mail with the simple stipulation that he "make no policy; issue no opinions." Some answers had to be cleared with campaign policy experts. At the time that the campaign sensed a November victory, Gill was meeting with academics at MIT, businesspeople, and hardware/software companies to discuss political, philosophical, and technical implications of the computer networking they were doing.

Gill noted numerous issues that concern the White House planning of new electronic computer structures. One basic issue is how to effectively deal with message volume. No answer is yet apparent for that question. Gill argues that the communication structures used in the past are not adequate to meet the needs of America's large and complex culture. He argues for a new electronic "communications common." He suggests that we ponder if there is a relationship between citizen discontent and disconnectedness and the failure of present communication processes. He says that information drives change and reorganization. This means that more attention should be paid to issues of "haves" and "have nots" in the new designs. He raises important questions about who should build the new "communications commons" and if the government is responsible for creating an "information safety net."

Gill says that we must think about how redesigning communication between government and citizens affects the "robustness of our democratic traditions." In asking if the United States focuses too tightly on market approaches to communication structures, he says: "Is our country designed strictly for the market or is our country, in fact, designed to support democracy, and the market, and the arts, and education, health?" He argues that we need to ask questions about how our communication structures and architectures sustain our national diversity.

Gill uses two theoretical models from management theory to discuss changes in White House communication. The existing model was top-down and one-directional. People get their information from newspapers and short newscasts, for example. They have only the choices of paying attention or not; they cannot actively select the content that is sent to them. This "smokestack" model applies to messages about health, education, and management. The pattern is consistently downward. In this kind of communication structure, citizens do not talk with each other as much as gain information from above. An alternative model included two-way, upward-downward and lateral interaction.

According to Gill, the ideas for implementing the second model in the Clinton administration were a natural progression from how the Clinton campaign was organized. That organization was guided by three terms used by Bill Clinton: community, opportunity, and responsibility. Gill says that without community, there can be little opportunity or responsibility. Community depends on interactive relationships. He says that the top-down model works against community and interactivity. He says that the White House has an objective to reach out to people and "involve them as interactively as possible." Of course, that is not yet an objective which has yet been accomplished.

The work done by Gill at the White House is related to what is known as Americans Communicating Electronically. While this also involves electronic communication structures, there is a side goal of making sure that people who do not have computers can access drop-in centers where they can obtain needed government information and interact with appropriate government officials.

It is impossible to evaluate the work of Gill and others at this point in terms of total accomplishment, because the proposed projects are large in scope, technically abstract, and by nature, dependent on trial and error (testing and retesting) over several years. However, it is possible to evaluate the goals and preliminary steps taken by these planners. For example, the fundamental assumption they have regarding the centrality of communication structures to citizen access and empowerment is a sound one. Whether in organizations or in societies, power is always linked to information access, input, and participation in interactive discussions with those who make key decisions.

Empowerment of citizens is an issue that Gill and others in the White House address, but we must question what they mean by empowerment. At the 1994 annual meeting of the International Communication Association, Gill described empowerment in terms of government helping citizens to make personal decisions more intelligently and to become more responsible for their lives. An alternative approach to empowerment suggests that citizens need input into policy debates and policy formation. The second approach is less of an efficiency model than the first.

Gill works in the White House Office of Media Affairs. He began his work with Clinton e-mail during the 1992 campaign. He volunteered to work on the campaign and was given the job of answering the e-mail. When Clinton won, Gill went into the White House staff to continue his work. He told interviewers that the e-mail staff was working hard to correct the disconnection between parts of the federal government (Electronic Communication at the White House, 1994). He said that both President Clinton and Vice President Gore were committed to communicating directly with the public. Gill was one of the founders of Americans Communicating Electronically (ACE). ACE addresses the e-mail needs for those Americans who do not have computers and modems. Gill found that there are over 3,000 U.S. Department of Agriculture extension offices throughout the nation. People without computers can go to these offices now and use them for sending and receiving e-mail to the government. Gill claims that there are now thirty-seven government agencies now willing to accept e-mail from the public (Electronic Communication at the White House, 1994).

Gill recognizes the problem with assuming that simply providing new communication technology will change how people communicate. For four years, the city of Cerritos, California, for example, has had a full menu of interactive services such as movies on demand. Yet, hardly anyone is using the technology. Gill says this is not surprising since users will only take advantage of new technologies when they perceive useful purposes for it. In Gill's words, "Communication is much more context driven than technology driven" (Electronic Communication at the White House, 1994, 18). To be successful, in his view, the new technologies must help people solve their problems. Gill believes that education will change in America as part of the changes that the White House is encouraging. In other words, students will learn more about how to create new information from old information, and less about how to follow rules. According to Gill, President Clinton is working to create flatter structures from what are now hierarchical structures.

So far, the White House e-mail system consists of distributing documents that include speeches given by the president and vice president, press releases, and copies of bills and other important government documents. Citizens can access these documents through the Internet, Bitnet, CompuServe, America OnLine, The Well, MCI, Fidonet, Peacenet, Econet, and USENET/NETNEWS. Citizens can send messages to the president by addressing PRESIDENT @WHITEHOUSE.GOV or VICE.PRESIDENT@WHITEHOUSE.GOV to send their messages to the president or vice president.

Gill told interviewers for Educom Review that the White House receives more paper than electronic mail at this time. About 40,000 to 60,000 pieces of paper mail are received by the White House each day, while about 800 e-mail notes are received each day (Electronic Communication at the White House, 1994). He says this is not surprising since fewer people have computers than have pens and paper. Additionally, only about 7 percent of the people who do have computers use computer networks. Prior to the Clinton administration, there was no White House electronic mail department, staff, or budget. Gill's challenge was to build a White House e-mail infrastructure.

WHAT THEY SAY IN THE WHITE HOUSE

In April 1994, I traveled to Washington, D.C., to interview Gill. Speaking with him at the Old Executive Office Building next to the White House, I learned more about what the Clinton administration is attempting to accomplish with its e-mail system. I was surprised to hear Gill stress family and community as much as he did.

Gill sees family as antecedent to community. Dysfunctional families do not support functional communication. Still, Gill argues that community is a necessary, but not sufficient, condition for democracy. The White House e-mail plans assume that top-down communication was the style of previous administrations. In those systems, receivers had no control over the messages they received. According to Gill, passive, turned off people become hostile. He told me that he believes that there has been little discourse in recent years about what makes government legitimate. In the current system, governance appeared to be limited to certain strata of society. There was little discussion about common good.

The White House e-mail system, according to Gill, aimed to provide public documents electronically to any American requesting them. Mail notes are acknowledged electronically, and it is hoped that the system will be able to direct inquirers to related documents. Gill believes that if you can create bidirectional communication, broader levels of participation in government, and more unity of parents with their children, American society will dramatically improve. Where communication networks like Minitel have been adopted, the highest demand is for person-to-person communication.

People are learning more about computer networks, and the messages keep flowing into the White House via e-mail. Gill stated that there are in the neighborhood of 145,000 daily readers of White House electronic files or messages.

According to Gill, in the nineteenth century, public schools were mandated. He believes that textbooks of the future will be electronic. In his view, schools must be interconnected. Students need experience, access, and training. If they can get this, it is only a matter of time before new generations of students, in their K-12 experiences, become more fully and naturally integrated into society. This view, of course, is part of the overall vision presented in the White House descriptions of the National Information Infrastructure (NII).

Gill told me that President Clinton wants a "level playing field." The NII will provide more competition and let people sense that outsiders can participate and win. Generally, Gill said, people believe that they are uninvolved with the system. President Clinton seeks to get more people involved. Gill stressed that this is a long-term problem and it will take substantial time to change.

As part of these changes in community, Gill says that Bill Clinton wants to reintroduce work into community and common good into public discourse. The president believes in having a common good and a healthy private sector.

Communication infrastructure is the key to the Clinton e-mail plans. Gill points out how Franklin, Jefferson, Madison, and other colonials noted how necessary an informed electorate is for democracy. Gill argues that people need to understand the shift from top-down messages to a new kind of citizen access. One challenge now is how to integrate the bidirectional technologies into the political process.

The White House e-mail planners hope to get more people involved. Gill notes how important skills are to learning any new method of communication. For example, town meetings required that people know public speaking skills and how to be close enough to be heard by others. Agendas were distributed well in advance of the meetings to allow people time to think and plan their messages. Gill suggests that people start getting involved with the system, even with shallow issues. If they cannot use the resources that are emerging on the Information Highway, they will get left behind.

Gill believes that the top-down, mass marketing way of doing things is declining. People will use computer networks more and they will generally use those services that they experience positively. He believes that all of the Clinton e-mail and computer networking plans will take time. He argues that he himself is less interested in the technology per se than in what people do with their families and community. He mentioned systems theory and how the whole thing is not simple. He believes that the NII will allow people to learn how to find contacts and ideas.

As we sat on the steps of the Old Executive Office Building, facing a busy entrance of White House staffers and security personnel into the White House, I was impressed with how committed Gill appeared to be to the ideas that he was explaining. At one moment, he said, "Oh, there's Tony Lake." I had trouble looking since I was engrossed in this whole idea of a White House attempting to alter some basic communication patterns of politics and political communication.

WHITE HOUSE COMMUNICATION THEORY

The guiding theoretical ideas behind the White House e-mail plans appear to be derived from multiple sources such as management, political science, artificial intelligence, and physics. A document forwarded to me by Jock Gill was an abstract of a paper done by John C. Mallery and Roger Hurwitz, two scholars who are heavily involved at the theoretical end. The document indicates that there is a need for people in government, and for those who analyze it, to participate in the design and study of digital systems for political communication (Mallery and Hurwitz, 1994). The Artificial Intelligence Laboratory at MIT serves as the main distribution hub for electronic publications released by the White House. The easiest technical side of the system is distributing documents. The hard part is dealing with incoming mail. These scientists believe that they will be able to design technological solutions for the problem of citizen mail volume, however. One step is the development of conversation postings as distributed argument hypertexts. Citizens will be able to browse debates and then post their entries into those debates (Mallery and Hurwitz, 1994). Further technological innovations will include the design and employment of intelligent mail agents, data sharing in hypermedia environments, data mining steps with machine learning, and text modeling with natural language systems.

One article that the e-mail planners referred to me reports a physics approach to social dilemmas. The work of physicists Natalie Glance and Bernardo Huberman (1994) uses computer simulations to make predictions about how group cooperation arises and where it falls. While it is doubtful that the computational agents in their software programs sufficiently represent complex human decision making, there is some heuristic merit to their analysis. Their work begins with the challenge of explaining or learning more about how individuals can be induced to contribute more to collective efforts. They note that social phenomena like cooperation begin with decisions made by individuals. Social dilemmas involve choices that involve competition between collective and personal good. The connection to communication is that as groups communicate more about situations, they increase levels of cooperation (Glance and Huberman, 1994). As argued in game theory, these scientists argue that individuals choose actions that offer the most personal gain. Those who cooperate with a collective contribute to its common good and receive back some fraction of the added value. Free-riders who collect added value, but do not contribute, diminish the returns for everyone else. Members of collectives might choose to become free-riders when they see that the costs of cooperating exceed their shares of value. The smaller the size of the collective and the longer the perceived duration of the collective, the more likely cooperation can be sustained. People will continue cooperating if they see that a critical number of other group members are also continuing to cooperate. Using methodology from statistical thermodynamics, Glance and Huberman (1994) conclude that the two most stable states of groups are widespread cooperation and widespread defection (the opposite of cooperation).

From these opposite steady states, however, Glance and Huberman (1994) argue that members of collectives experience random perturbations caused by uncertainty regarding what others are doing with their behaviors. These scientists believe that this explains why there are abrupt appearances of social events, such as an upsurge in environmental activism. Recycling is an example of social dilemma. Uprisings against oppressive governments are another example. A key principle noted in this analysis is that changes toward cooperation are encouraged by members of the collective who have long-duration perspectives (called "horizons"). These people are the first to move from defection to cooperation. Other groups then follow. This spread of motivation to cooperate can be encouraged by methods of communication in which people share information. Of course, as these scholars note, there must be benefits for those who move toward cooperation.

While not a theory of communication, there is a perspective of communication and collective cooperation that emerges from the work of Glance and Huberman. That is, people in our society may be able to participate more in a reorganization of communication, wherein more people have access to the views of others and to certain key pockets of data and information. Of course, this may require what M. Lynne Markus (1990) calls a "critical mass" of communicators. According to Critical Mass Theory (Markus, 1990), a community depends upon density of communication. The key principle to the theory is that "only when all people in a community have access to an interactive medium does each member have the ability to realize full benefits from it" (Markus, 1990, 195). The theory also states that the surest way to create universal access is to provide the resources for access to everyone at the same time.

COMMUNICATION TECHNOLOGIES AND DEMOCRACY

It is commonly believed that new communication technologies such as computer mediated communication and computer networking will enhance participation of citizens in democracy. But there are numerous reasons to be skeptical about such a romantic vision. Foremost is the simple fact that technologies of communication can aid any number of political power structures. I would like to argue that a theory of political interactivity is a necessary condition for developing computerized communication systems in ways that enhance democratic communication.

The promises of new technologies of communication are reflected in the following claim made by Vice President Al Gore in his book, *Earth in the Balance* (1992, 359): "The best way for a nation to make political decisions about its future is to empower all of its citizens to process the political information relevant to their lives and express their conclusions in free speech designed to persuade others.'' Gore and many others, including many communication and information scientists, believe that adding channels to the political communication system will empower American citizens. They take for granted that these citizens are motivated and able to process political information. Like organizational theorists who make the error of assuming that more communication equals better communication, these experts may erroneously assume that the key reason that Americans do not have strong faith in government is simply that they do not have enough channels of input. Studies, such as those done by the Kettering Foundation, indicate the opposite. Americans do not want more channels as much as they want real solutions to real problems and real decisions made about what they have discussed with leaders. In other words, citizens want changes in the quality of political communication, not just in the quantity of it.

America faces what Neuman (1986) calls the "paradox of mass politics." While more people have access to information, more access has not increased political knowledge. Democracies rest on the assumption that citizens can govern themselves because they are informed. American citizens want to be involved with their political system, but existing means of information processing do not facilitate such involvement.

Many political communication and political science scholars have discovered that American citizens have low political awareness. Still, they wish to believe in their system and to make it work. Democratic communication in America can be improved with new communication technologies. However, such enhancement depends on far more than simple notions of channels, access, and state-of-the-art means of political messaging.

COMMUNICATION TECHNOLOGIES AND POWER

The use of new communication technologies cannot be equated with political empowerment. It is possible that these new media offer new channels for the kinds of content and relationships that already existed in older forms of communication. If this is the case, then new communication systems simply reinforce, even strengthen, existing power relations.

As the press is regarded as the "fourth estate," some observers may see a newer "fifth estate" in emerging networks of mediated communication. Neither the fourth, nor the fifth, however, is as independent from sources of political and economic power as certain technological visionaries would like us to believe. Looking back at the history of newspapers, Curran (1982, 212) notes that "the press barons merely amplified systems of representation furnished by others (politicians, civil servants, judges, the armed forces and so on) that legitimized a power structure of which they were only a constituent element."

There is little reason to doubt that the development of new communication technologies can offer new ways of disseminating ideas of political philosophy and protest. For example, the diffusion of the Bible in the fifteenth century decreased the power of Church monopolies over Scriptural interpretations. The printing press allowed wide distribution of political ideas. On the other hand, printing also converted thinking as a public process done orally, to a private process known as reading. Mass communication reinforced politics as private action. Computer networks have the power to go in either direction; users may be active or passive. Without interactivity, political perception may become detached from a public sphere.

The strongest centers of power in the United States insulate their political control by maintaining a system of political communication in which information moves downward through mass media channels and citizens rely on the media for information about governmental decisions. Expanding channels among people who have little input into national policy making may be meaningless in terms of political empowerment. History shows that communication is most related to power when those who have little input into decision making increase their input by using communication as a social, even revolutionary, force.

Political organization is closely related to means and methods of political communication. In the ancient Greek city-state, democracy was considered to be limited by the number of people who could discuss topics together effectively. Interaction among citizens was a necessary condition for participatory democracy (OTA, 1990). Today, cities, states, and nations are so large that only technologies of communication make large-scale democracy possible. Through radio talk shows, TV call-in shows, computer network conferences, and mass media news, citizens are able to share ideas about political topics.

In democracies, political policies and actions are justified in relation to citizen consensus or quiescence, participation in debate and persuasion, and competition for arguments and audiences. In ancient and colonial times, the right of free speech might be enough to provide access to audiences and public discussion about important issues. In the modern world, however, more is needed. It is necessary to have rights of obtaining information and distributing information. Some scholars also argue that we need the "right to communicate," meaning the privilege of gaining significant audiences for our arguments. This argument highlights the need for new thinking regarding democracy and new forms of communication.

Political communication creates political culture and communities. Without effective means of political communication, citizens in democracies cannot gather the information they need to make informed decisions about political issues. Nor can they organize others to take desired political actions. While input is always important, input should not be confused with participation. Participation entails more direct involvement by citizens in governing processes.

A constant issue in all of this concerns the tension between access and control. Citizens desire access while leaders desire control. Ironically, perhaps, both are accomplished through the same communication technologies. Today, leaders believe, as did Aristotle, James Madison, Joseph Schumpeter, and Bernard Berelson, that democracy is best preserved by having certain constraints on citizen participation (OTA, 1990).

Whether king, priest, or president, leaders have found means to control access to knowledge and abilities to interact with others about important issues. The invention of the printing press is hailed as a great liberation of human protest and growth. We should recognize, of course, that the printing of books, while invaluable for carrying written thoughts, also allowed the suppression and burning of those thoughts. A new form of access was born with magnificent potential. Still, a new form of control emerged concomitantly; with copyrighting rules, there would emerge classes of gatekeepers to determine where and how messages would be disseminated.

American political leaders, from the colonial days to the present, have recognized the correspondence between communication and power. Before the War of Independence, the British recognized the power of newspapers and pamphlets to become effective vehicles of protest. Networks of political communication existed long before computers. Paper communication and the telling of stories in printing shops and saloons contributed to the initiation of political movements. Later, the first American government administration would take steps to censor various forms of communication, such as theater, when messages were deemed potentially harmful to the new leaders. The colonials promoted the postal system as they recognized how much the dissemination and exchange of information was important to creating a nation. All of this illustrates how American leaders have learned how to expand communication access while also carefully managing communication control. A modern example of this is the recent Persian Gulf crisis. Reporters and the public had access to video coverage of military actions that brought the conflict straight into their living rooms. On the other hand, reporters would be kept, by force if necessary, from covering any aspect of the conflict in Kuwait or Iraq that was not cleared by U.S. military authorities.

Political communication is changed by technologies of political message exchange. For example, television had numerous impacts on politics. National issues took precedence over local issues. Producing news or news events became the major goal of political activists and campaign professionals (OTA, 1990). Because television is an entertainment medium and politics became increasingly dependent on TV, politics became more like entertainment than in the days preceding high television reliance. As political discussions occur more through computer networks, politics will again be transformed. The specific directions for such changes are unknown. While claims about better communication leading to better democracy are legion, it is necessary to question how democracy is being affected by new methods of message exchange.

Political communication scholar Dan Nimmo draws attention to the current glitter of town meeting status for new forms of campaigning. While championed by Bill Clinton as a way to get close to the people without journalists' interference, Nimmo notes the fallacies about town meetings in general. According to Nimmo (1994), town meetings, which go back to 1641 in the American colonies, were intended to assert the moral authority of the community. He says that the town meeting was "an instrument primarily of consensus-building rather than conflict airing" (214).

THE CRISIS OF DEMOCRACY AND COMMUNICATION

A crisis of democracy exists when the necessary conditions for a democracy are endangered. In America, there is a crisis of democracy for two reasons. First, citizens lack the kinds of political knowledge that are required for active participation. Second, American citizens feel disconnected from federal government in terms of meaningful communication. To have a voice in their government, citizens must have information and knowledge about issues, institutions, rights, and political processes. A minimal amount of information needed by citizens in a democracy is that which tells them about major events and the general nature of political problems (Graber, 1988).

Some political scientists blame voters themselves for not being more aware of political issues. Flanigan and Zingale (1991), for example, argue that voters have plenty of in-depth political information available through mass media. They state that only a relatively few Americans are motivated to inform themselves about political affairs. Neuman (1986) argues that political knowledge will not increase and has not increased in relation to an addition of news channels. Entman (1989) in fact, points out that political knowledge in America has declined as sources of political information have increased.

American participation in elections is lower than most people think it should be. Computer networks offer new means for participating in discussions about politics. Many conclude that this means that computer networks, therefore, offer ways of increasing political participation. However, political participation is not simply talking about politics. The effects of new channels of interaction cannot be predicted by assuming that more channels equal more public participation. In fact, television is blamed for contributing to the decline of voter activity, while it may have once been looked at as a means of stimulating greater citizen involvement in public affairs (OTA, 1990).

Contrary to the suggestions by some political scientists, low citizen involvement is not an indication of the health of the system. Instead, low involvement and participation indicates that citizens do not perceive the system to be useful in solving problems nor leaders as truly representing their most important concerns (Flanigan and Zingale, 1991). Moreover, studies show that education and affluence are strongly related to political activity (OTA, 1990).

The origins of the word and notion of democracy include the assumption that democracies depend on active citizen participation (Bertelsen, 1992). Concern for community above concern for individual privileges was part of ancient Greek democratic ideals. In light of the history of democracies, some communication scholars argue that new communication systems have enough interactive features to permit an informed citizenry and to allow them to express their political views. Others, however, note that these new means of political communication allow citizens to create political viewpoints while simultaneously removing them from actual participation in the governing. Bertelsen (1992), for example, notes that we may be confusing self-affirmation with political participation.

THE NEED FOR NEW MODELS OF POLITICS AND COMMUNICATION

In the presidential election of 1992, new formats for speeches, candidate-voter interaction, and debates were tested. Many of the changes appear to have contributed to increased voter interest. One interesting new form of communication among voters themselves is computer conferencing about candidates. Each campaign, for example, had representation on Bitnet with three conferences called Clinton, Bush, and Perot. The Clinton conference had input from Clinton/Gore volunteers in Little Rock. All three of the networks continue in operation, now with new purposes. The Bush computer conference is now renamed "Repub-L" and carries discussions that criticize the Clinton administration.

Westin (1993) notes that there are two models of what new computer technologies mean to constitutional democracy. The first is positive and the second is Orwellian. The positive model assumes that new technologies will enhance voter education, increase access to useful education, provide more rational decision-making abilities, and allow more feedback for ideas about political matters. The positive model assumes that computer networks will empower citizens. The Orwellian model assumes that computer networks will result in greater citizen disempowerment. The Orwellian model notes that governmental data bases on citizens are becoming increasingly centralized and cross-connected.

A theory of political interactivity may assume that either of the other two models is possible but that computer networks and new communication technologies can be used for citizen empowerment to the extent that they are designed and managed to. In other words, there is nothing inherent in the technologies themselves that make either model inevitable. The directions of development are dependent on how future design incorporates a model of political communication and democratic interactivity into its goals.

INTERACTIVE VS. MASS COMMUNICATION

Traditional mass communication provided channels for one-way dissemination of political information. It is fast and inexpensive. Mass communication is related to a linear view of communication. Many current discussions about networks and democracy also rely on a linear model of human communication. Computer networks, because of their two-way messaging abilities, are assumed to be something more than mass communication. However, in the absence of interactivity, these networks still serve as means of dissemination from one source (formal or informal) to many receivers.

Mass communication has transformed citizens and activists into consumers and spectators. American citizens watch American politics on television more than they actively engage in political activities. While they have representatives in Congress to propose and evaluate legislation, they have representatives in the media to articulate and defend what they supposedly think and are concerned about. Consumers of politics buy politicians and policies. They also critique the performance of leaders through media more than they evaluate issues and ideologies.

According to James Carey (1987, 14), "The public will begin to awaken when they are addressed as a conversational partner and are encouraged to talk rather than sit passively as spectator before a discussion conducted by journalists and experts." Carey makes a strong point about interactivity being necessary to making citizens out of consumers. Citizens are engaged in interaction about policies, issues, and leadership. Consumers simply respond to mediated messages in routine ways.

Gonzales (1989) notes that accurate feedback from those who are governed requires an encouragement from those who govern. This necessitates a divergence from laissez-faire assumptions about electronic democracy. Upward flows of negative information are not encouraged in organizations, in public debates, and even computer networks linked to the new presidential administration.

A move away from broadcasting or simply gaining information about citizens, toward interactivity, requires that new systems be grounded in principles of openness and feedback. Linear communication supports traditional power structures resting on active leaders and quiescent citizens. Interactive communication creates a symmetry of communication between leaders and citizens. This shifts the balance of power and is a threat to leaders who wish to remain elitist in their administration. Interactive approaches to political communication expand the public sphere and decrease the elite sphere of power and influence. Linear political communication, that which exists now despite computer networking, maintains unequal social and political relationships. To the extent that these relationships are maintained, democratization is stagnant.

CONNECTIVITY PLANS OF THE CLINTON ADMINISTRATION

Communication technologies and networks serve as systems of organization for corporations, military operations, educators, scientists, students, and others who work with information and seek new data and resources. Computer and communication networks are vital to law enforcement, government intelligence, military messaging, banking, revenue collection, accounting, and modern educational interactions. The question now is how important are these networks to political empowerment? If the past suggests anything about the future, caution is in order. The federal government itself reports that computer networks have created a morass of data storage, retrieval, and manipulation, in which "individual citizens have lost control of information about themselves" (OTA, 163). The function of computer networks, as related to government, like previous forms of communication in the past, is not to empower citizens, although such empowerment is certainly possible. Despite rhetoric about the enormous decentralizing effects of computer networks, there is always the possibility of governmental centralization of surveillance and analysis of what appears to be decentralized. Thus, computer networks can contribute to new and more subtle forms of citizen control (OTA, 1990).

Simply increasing the amount of exposure of political issues does not guarantee any form of empowerment. It has been noted that intense coverage of the student protests in China did more than stimulate concern for the students; it also make have provoked Chinese leaders to retaliate against the protestors in extreme ways (OTA, 1990).

Open communication is valued in American society. Having a voice is always important, but it is not enough for a system of democracy. Democratic communication provides the opportunities to persuade, not simply chances to be heard or counted. The Clinton administration may consider moving beyond the progress it makes with citizen connectivity to the White House to political interactivity with various computer networks. There appear to be signs that the planning is open to that direction.

CURRENT DATA ABOUT SYSTEM USE

Documentation from the Artificial Intelligence Lab at MIT shows key findings about the White House e-mail system so far. About 30,000 to 40,000 people access documents on nearly a daily basis. About 100,000 additional people receive documents or reports about the documents through e-mail, interpersonal conversation, phone, or hard copy. Document receivers are younger, more educated, and more male than the American population. Of those who use the system, 75 percent have college degrees and 50 percent have postgraduate degrees. Only 20 percent of the users are female. The ranked order of organizational affiliations are universities and colleges, government and military, high technology companies, advocacy groups, and economic interest groups. There are few users affiliated with elementary or high schools. Users are more politically involved than most Americans. Uses of the process include keeping informed, following issues, and getting closer views of political processes. Two-thirds of the users take information from the documents into political conversations (Hurwitz and Mallery, 1994).

THEORIES OF DEMOCRACY AND COMMUNICATION

Politics are everywhere in human communication. Conflict and power are part of ordinary human existence. Democracies do not simply arise in isolation. As political scientist Ian Shapiro (1994) notes, democratic movements often emerge in opposition to an existing order. They want more than participatory politics; they also want to limit or abolish unfair hierarchies of the past (Shapiro, 1994). Democracies therefore depend on conflict and change. With such changes are suspicions of experts who lay out blueprints for the future or presume to be able to impose reforms (Shapiro, 1994). Shapiro (1994) argues that expertise is important and valuable in a democracy but should not be allowed to monopolize key decision-making processes. Instead, experts should be required to persuade lay people about their analyses, in nontechnical terms. When this does not happen, political rhetoric may be disguised as technical rhetoric, and ordinary citizens are locked out of the decision-making debates that they should be involved in. As our culture does not allow final courtroom evaluations of guilt or innocence to rest with psychiatrists, fingerprint specialists, forensics experts, or lie-detector technicians, it should not allow domestic and foreign policy experts to make policies immune from public deliberation. A theory of democracy incorporates assumptions of the need for mechanisms that ensure public sovereignty, such as the jury system. Democracies cannot be installed by force. Rousseau was wrong when he assumed that humans can be forced to be free. As Shapiro (1994) notes, ''People will discover ways to democratize things for themselves'' (142). Examples of unsuccessful attempts to force democratic changes, as defined by elites, include the current Endara government, which replaced the Noriega regime in Panama.

What Shapiro describes, of course, is an empowerment theory of democracy. An alternative view of democracy is elite pluralism. Elite pluralists believe that there are well-defined interest groups that compete for power in a democracy. Therefore, it does not matter if average members of society are poorly informed or weakly involved, since their leaders will advocate on their behalf (Robinson and Levy, 1986). To the extent that one subscribed to an elite pluralist view of democracy, levels of political literacy in America are not at issue.

We must beware of undemocratic shortcuts to democracy. These include events such as the three-hour summary trial and execution of Nicolai and Elena Ceaucescu by a Rumanian military tribunal in 1989. Such fast justice, while done with justified hatred for the executed, is not harmonious with a theory of democracy. Another example is the kind of fast-change, ''get under the hood and fix it'' rhetoric of politicians like Ross Perot. Fast and undebated change is inimical to democracy. So are ideas such as teledemocracy and virtual candidacies and/or voting.

Working with a theory of democracy mandates that we be vigilant at attempting to empower the disempowered, extend the boundaries of political debate, make enfranchisement into the systems of political discourse easier, make political discourse more rational and informative, and bring citizens close to interaction with centers of power. These efforts are related to the need to limit technical blueprints for a better society, in favor of using technologies to remove impediments to the natural inclinations of our citizens to participate in governance. We face some mundane work to start with, such as working against the correlations of money and access and the professionalization of public service (Shapiro, 1994). When the CEOs of the Forbes top 500 corporations pay themselves as much as 157 times more than their average workers, there are clear reasons why Americans attach economic concerns to their political involvement (Sanders, 1994). Indeed, analysts working on the most recent Times-Mirror survey suggest that voters are angry today because of economic disappointment (Kohut, 1994).

DEMOCRACY AS DIALOGUE

Computer networks can foster discussions about political issues and also the exchange of resource information and data. Thus, it is clear that citizen-citizen communication can be enhanced through new communication technologies. Unlike mass communication, participants in computer-mediated communication can act more as their own gatekeepers and can also create new systems of gathering, editing, and disseminating news.

Democracy is sometimes thought of as a systems construct that names a type of political structure. In this structure, citizens are allowed to elect representatives to express their views and concerns. A competing view of democracy is that of a democracy as process, and more specifically, of democracy as a type of political communication. In this view, democracy is defined by free speech, active voices in decision making, and communication between leaders and citizens. The only connection that Americans have to government is through various forms of communication. To the extent that citizens have interactive communication with those who represent them, they have influence in the political system and function as system participants. To the extent that citizens view news and talk with peers who share a viewer's position in the system, they are spectators in the making of decisions and structuring of power.

POLITICAL INTERACTIVITY AND DEMOCRACY

Much of human communication theory is based on the observation that humans interact when they communicate. In other words, one action leads to another in a recursive pattern of message exchange. The construct of political interactivity is derived from the communication theory construct of interactivity formally defined by communication scientist Sheizaf Rafaeli. Rafaeli (1988) defines interactivity as message dependency or the extent that messages are done in direct or indirect responses to each other.

In conditions of high interactivity, communication roles are interchangeable. Thus, power is equal. In conditions of low interactivity, formal and rigid power relations are in place. One human may simply give commands to others. Power is skewed and privileged. Interactivity in human communication is part of the mutual determinacy that is possible in good conversation and negotiation.

It is essential to note that interactivity is not only a matter of message initiators getting some form of feedback. Concepts like bandwidth, fast response, personalness, and social presence do not explain interactivity. What is most defining about interactivity is how messages are related closely together in a sequence of message exchange. Sending e-mail notes to President Clinton is not interactive. Nor is getting a form letter stating that the president is glad to hear from you. Receiving a personal note (or other form of message) in which answers are given to questions and responses are made directly to assertions is interactive.

We are well past the day of assuming that free speech or the right to speak openly is all one needs to have power in modern democracies. We know that the ability to have access to communication networks is just as essential as the right of speaking openly. Without such networks, one is not likely to gain the significant audiences necessary for modern political discourse. However, the right to communicate is not adequate. Citizens need interactivity with each other and with leaders. The higher the political interactivity, the greater the democratic nature of political communication.

Information is withheld at times to maintain the advantage of information holders over people who do not have the information. Most people are familiar with the adage that knowledge is power. Ideas of free speech and a marketplace of ideas often guide consideration of how computer networks should be related to political communication. These ideas are useful but insufficient to relate democracy to forms of computer-mediated communication. The relationship of democracy to new media is best understood with a model of interactivity.

Gonzales (1989) proposes a model of interactivity. In this model, similar to Habermas' ideal speech situation, public decisions and policies are based on public argumentation. The model also assumes that senders of messages get feedback to comments and questions. There is no such thing as one-way messaging in this model.

In conditions of political interactivity, citizens may interact, discuss, debate, and argue about political matters. When applied to computer networks and society, political interactivity means two-way communication about issues raised at any level to any other level. Such interactivity is not a simply uncertainty-reduction mechanism. Nor does it exist to solely reduce equivocalities. Instead, its purpose is the co-creation of political perceptions and policies. In such communication, communicators work together to ask questions, find answers, and formulate policies and actions.

Gonzales (1989) observes that feedback is not solely generated by receivers of messages, that senders of messages can actively stimulate the receivers to provide feedback. Of course, for interactivity, feedback must be responded to as feedback, not simply as messages. As discussed here, political interactivity is a construct constructed from the work of Rafaeli and Gonzales. The key idea is that democratic communication involves message interdependence and systemic encouragement of accurate feedback.

To the extent that computer networks facilitate only informal discussions among citizens, there is no political interactivity in terms of the political system. For systemic interactivity, there must be informal, formal, and informal-formal exchanges of messages and message dependence. Gonzales (1989) notes that while face-to-face communication generally offers the greatest opportunities for fast and immediate feedback to messages, this advantage over other contexts declines as the number of communicators increases. This is a critical point for considerations of computer networking for political communication. While "town hall" depictions of computer conferencing seem shaky on the surface, if they in fact can facilitate interaction among large numbers of citizens and leaders, they may have certain advantages over face-to-face meetings that are so large that many citizens are inhibited from speaking and interacting.

Delays in message feedback are less important than the quality of the messages that respond to others and constitute what we call feedback. In other words, a face-to-face conversation may contain immediate feedback, but the feedback messages may have little analysis behind them. Computer-mediated messages may be less immediate but richer in content. This is never guaranteed, of course. Gonzales (1989) argues that cumulative feedback, that which is delayed intentionally across time, can have specific benefits that are not possible with discrete feedback messages, or those done at the moments of receiving other messages. Gonzales argues that cumulative feedback is valuable because the long-term nature of the communication exists as a social relationship.

A NEED FOR POLITICAL INTERACTIVITY THEORY

If political interactivity can enhance democracy as communication, there should be specific ways in which this can be accomplished. These ways can be tested empirically as a set of propositions. The list below is just a start:

1. Political participation can be quantitatively and qualitatively improved by increasing interactivity between leaders and citizens, as well as between various levels of society, media, and government.

2. Levels of citizen political knowledge can be increased by improving interactivity among citizens and expanding the range of social connections among classes, data sources, and political analysts.

3. Democracy can be enhanced by increasing political participation, active input into decision making, interactivity among all levels of the political system, and channels for those who normally do have avenues of discussing political matters.

Instead of assuming linkages between computer networks and citizen involvement, we need to test those assumptions to see which ones hold and which do not. Gina Garramone, Allen Harris, and Gary Pizante (1986) tested citizen motivation to use computer-mediated political communication systems (CMPCS). These researchers note how common it is to assume that interactive media release citizens from the constraints of mass media, but also how untested such an assumption is. Their study found that traditional political participation predicts motivation to use computers for political communication for computer owners. Another significant predictor is anticipated satisfaction. The researchers note that "rather than closing the gap between the politically active and the politically inactive, the CMPCS may widen the gap" (455).

INTERACTIVITY AND LIBERATION

Freedom and liberation are material realities that are attained through political struggles. Democracies are idealistic forms of governance that depend on democratic means of communication. Democracy involves communication processes and can never therefore be static. Interactivity allows people to create their own conditions of freedom and liberation. Information dissemination and channels for opinion-giving are important, but less important than dialectic and democratic praxis.

Americans still depend on presidents to save them from problems, when they should be working with presidents to solve problems as a total society oriented toward reforms. Liberation will not come through any form of communication technology. There is no embeddedness of empowerment in any communication technology or computer network. But communication technologies and computer networks may aid people who have engaged themselves in processes of liberation.

Democracy may be enhanced by new communication technologies and computer networks that are designed and used for purposes of high interactivity between and across levels of society. Political interactivity facilitates self-liberation and does so by empowering all levels of society to accept the basic premises of democracy, namely that citizens must be informed and citizens must participate in formulating political policies and actions.

Communication and political power have always been interrelated. The acquisition or the yielding power is closely related to speech, language, argumentation, media, and social interaction. In ancient civilizations, speech was related to acts of divine creation. Naming things was part of asserting power. Those who could communicate with natural or spiritual forces had power over those who could not. In time, political ideas and doctrines were formed through acts of story telling and the narration of myths. Covenants, social contracts, and rights evolved with political arguments and narratives. Today, we still tell stories about power democracy while continuing a mythology of empowerment through expanded communication channels. But for the kinds of plans we have looked at in this chapter to really contribute to democracy, we need to sort out what are social contrivances from what are technological enablements for more democratic communication.

Without a guiding theory of democracy and communication, the White House e-mail system could unwittingly serve rationalist and status quo functions that do little for empowering anyone. There are two types of political theory for the White House planners to consider. First, there are organic theories, and second there are social contract theories. The first type of political theory allows one to see natural and historical evolution to political systems. The second type is more about the social contract relationship between the State and its citizens. People give up some freedom to the State in exchange for the securities offered by the State. Organic theories of power have strong tendencies to evaluate government in terms of moral judgments. The other type of theories are more pragmatically oriented.

There is a common search for "technologies of freedom" in American history. Some thought radio, for example, would be a great liberator. Others saw great hope in television. Simply increasing the number of channels through which citizens can gain access to messages generated by their leaders is not enough to substantially improve democratic participation. Notwithstanding the increased access due to new communication technologies, electoral turnout in most Western democracies has declined (Forester, 1992). Some observers have suggested that when citizens are bombarded with an increase in messages, they are able to retain less of what they perceive (Forester, 1992).

DISCUSSION

The White House citizen e-mail plans are idealistically touted as a new set of efforts to provide connections for everyday people to the seat of power in Washington, D.C. There are realistic and practical ways of designing and evaluating new communication technologies. Wober (1988) notes that whenever any new communication arises, there are "priests" who worship the new medium and make utopian claims about its capabilities. On the other extreme, there are prophets of doom who see the new technology as threatening society in a multitude of ways. In between, Wober argues, are the scientists and historians who study the new technology and determine its advantages and disadvantages. Wober (1988, 99) argues that "in a morally neutral position between the prophets of doom and the priesthood of the message systems of the screen are a host of communication scientists."

So far, with political uses of computer networks, there is little theory, research, or data in this middle ground. A theory of political interactivity can only emerge in between the good and bad scenarios. The priests of communication technology wish us to believe that it will solve education problems as well as enhance our democracy by giving more access to citizens. It is assumed that new technologies will empower those citizens by helping them become more informed (Gleason, 1994). In fact, better means of access simply mean improved access. That is being accomplished by the White House planners and should be applauded. But hard realities fly in the face of the visionaries when one looks at the history of communication technology. The predictions in the 1960s for today gave a picture of us living in plastic houses, traveling in vertical take-off craft (like the Jetsons), farming ocean floors, and taking holiday time off on the moon (Forester, 1992). The reason for such inaccurate projections is simply that researchers listen to what manufacturers and vendors of technology say about new technologies, without critically assessing their claims (Forester, 1992).

There are differences between various concepts that require more attention by White House e-mail planners. First, information consists of messages or data that can reduce uncertainty and facilitate meaningful thought and decisions (Hacker and Monge, 1988). Wurman (1989, 38) notes that after World War II, the term ''information'' was a ''technological term to define anything sent over an electric or mechanical channel.'' Second, information and communication are not the same; information is the product that is produced in the process known as communication. Third, knowledge is not just another word for information. As Bacon said, ''Knowledge is power.'' Knowledge is information that can be used for more than simply making decisions, but can facilitate interconnections between concepts, for example (Wurman, 1989). Knowledge is closely related to meaningfulness of information. Wurman (1989) argues that information processing can speed the flow of data but cannot aid meaningful interpretation.

If the White House is simply providing data retrieval (speeches, papers, documents), it has not yet provided an information system. They will have reached the level of an information system when citizens can ask questions and get answers specifically directed to their questions. A communication system will exist when citizens have interactivity with government officials, staff, and employees.

American citizens do not just need access or information. More new information has been produced in the last thirty years than in the past 5,000 years (Wurman, 1989). The total of printed knowledge doubles every eight years (Wurman, 1989). In a likely environment of information overload and channel excess, it will be necessary for system planners to facilitate communication that helps citizens find answers to questions and ways of interacting with others about policy issues.

Some communication scholars argue that democracy can only be enhanced with the Internet if a national communication policy protects noncommercial interaction between a variety of institutions and segments of society (Gleason, 1994). But technologies of communication are probably not enough. Just as computers have not made students more intelligent or creative, CMC has transformed organizational structures, and information systems have not yet provided the long-awaited boosts in productivity for white-collar workers, new on-line political communication will do little for the causes of political alienation and its consequent low participation. It may be that schools need better support for better teachers as much as they need multimedia software and hardware. Organizations may need new methods of management and worker involvement as much as new means of data storage and retrieval. Our democracy may need as much attention to why citizens do not believe in leaders, journalists, and bureaucracy employees as much as we need to design new means of communicating with the White House electronically.

In September 1994 (C-SPAN, 9/24/94), Andrew Kohut spoke for the Times Mirror Center for the People and the Press, revealing the findings from their latest national survey. This survey and its analysis were designed to tap citizens' political beliefs and values. The center telephone surveyed 5,000 people in July and did follow-up interviews with 1,500 of the same respondents. Results were compared with the findings from a similar survey done in 1987. Like the Kettering Foundation studies, this one found that there is a strong anger in the American citizenry. It also found that most citizens have political opinions without ideological anchoring. Kohut surmises that the deep cynicism is related to the hard economic circumstances that people perceive for themselves. Americans are still angry at politicians and the news media. Distrust for both has increased since 1992. People are more unfavorable about their views of TV news and newspaper news. Over 70 percent say that news organizations get in the way of society solving its problems. The number one issue appears to be crime, followed by economy. Kohut argues that most of the survey data reflect concerns with jobs and the economy. He believes that the anger of the citizenry is related to the fact that gridlock still exists in federal government, that the middle class does not feel more prosperous, and there has been a lack of reforms that the public expected with the election of Bill Clinton. He suggests that the federal government needs to get more people to start feeling better about their personal prospects.

Despite honorable intentions, President Clinton has some strong communication problems now with the public. He is likely the most attacked president ever, not necessarily by his own fault, as there appear to be concerted efforts to obstruct and attack nearly everything he does. Still, when Reagan left office, he had an approval rating of 63 percent. FDR was at 66 percent, Eisenhower at 59 percent, JFK at 58 percent (Denton and Woodward, 1990). Clinton is currently behind these other presidents in approval rating. While President Clinton attempts to have dialogic communication with reporters and the public, some citizens perceive this as a weakness, not a strength. This can be understood only in light of our political culture and what citizens expect of their presidents. Ironically, the president who is doing the most at trying to create innovations in communication is perceived as having powerful problems with his communication with the American people.

Beyond theoretical issues of democracy and communication, there are simple practical matters that can hinder the White House e-mail efforts as well. For example, Rosen and Wail (1994) discuss various findings about how common ''technophobia'' or fear of using computers is among Americans. They argue that studies indicate that between 25 percent and 50 percent of Americans are technophobic. This means that they either have negative attitudes about computers or have anxiety about using them. These researchers say that no important gender or age differences are found with technophobia. While children or teenagers may like computer games, they may still fear other uses of computers. The bright side of their findings is that technophobia can be cured in a very short amount of time, with effective education and training. Some cases can be remedied in a matter of hours. About 45 percent of school teachers have technophobia. This indicates that much work toward building a national communication infrastructure must target schools and teachers.

More and more Americans are obtaining computers for home use. Experts estimate that by 1998 the home market will account for about half of all PC sales (Investor's Daily, 7/20/94, A5). Since June 1993, the White House e-mail system has received over 250,000 messages from around the world (White House e-mail Auto-Responder Message, September 24, 1994). The technologies of access to the White House are in place. The hard question is how those technologies will affect citizen desires to feel more involved with persuading their leaders to solve key problems.

The White House e-mail project will most likely be effective at (1) providing easier access to documents related to the presidency and to government policies and proposals, (2) making new contacts between citizens and government employees easier, (3) helping citizens find and use new forums for political self-expression, and (4) making it possible for everyone involved and interested in politics to disseminate their ideas to ever widening audiences.

However, there are problems that need to be addressed. These include: (1) the fact that most Americans are locked out of technical literacy (we should never forget the 20 percent who are functionally illiterate as well), (2) the fact that those people who now use political CMC are the same people who would use quills if that was the latest method of sending messages, (3) the fact that profit motivation narrows and does not expand the diversity of political views in political communication, and (4) that more fully informed consumers of political data are still consumers, and not citizens. With the likely accomplishments and the problems in mind, some debatable recommendations emerge.

As designers have learned with organizations, planners of new governmental communication practices need to learn that a key part of design success is user participation. How many average people know about the Clinton e-mail system plans and who is working on them? The typical designer-user chasms should be ended. Political interactivity should be facilitated by initiating more conversations and computer conferences between citizens and leaders. We need more dialogue more than we need more reports and position papers. The e-mail plans should be part of a much larger and ambitious project to get more people involved in policy discussions. The White House can help people understand issues and policies more; this was botched terribly with the universal health care plan. Communication theorists could have warned the president that when people cannot process arguments (National Health Security Act) they will process simple forms of heuristic thought (Harry and Louise). Something like a democracy test should be applied to all plans and implementations. The test is simply the act of ascertaining how many more people are not active with policy and government than were not before the changes. Instead of relying on un-realistic (and outdated) notions of direct democracy, we should think more in terms of making our representative democracy more representative and more responsive.

CONCLUSION

It is time to move beyond vague notions of democracy and communication and to give up the media metaphysics of computer network utopianism. It is possible, technically and socially, to reconstruct political communication through computer networks so that more people are not only connected, but are engaged in the conversations and debates that generate political policies and actions.

Democracy is a system of political participation that is dependent on informed citizens sharing power and having elected representatives who participate in the community of citizens and their public sphere of rational debate and policy making. Computer networks and new communication technologies offer impor-tant potential new means of enhancing democratic communication. These po-tentials, however, depend on the willingness and desire of designers and users to incorporate political interactivity into a new kind of political communication system.

The Clinton e-mail system was started with campaign communication objec-tives (i.e., persuasion of voters). It developed into an access-to-documents sys-tem. It presently offers ways for citizens to gain more access to documents as well as to send mail to the president and vice president about issues. Citizen empowerment will serve more as this system accounts for the following. First, democracy is never accomplished top-down only. Citizens must be involved in design thinking. Second, rather than mainly relying on theories borrowed from artificial intelligence and physics, designers of this system should read and use theories of democracy and democratic communication to guide their efforts to increase citizen involvement with White House communication.

We must remind ourselves how the Kettering research indicated that Ameri-cans in 1991 felt disconnected from power and how they wanted to have new means of two-way interaction with leaders (*Citizens and Politics,* 1991). In 1863, President Abraham Lincoln said that the American government was "of the people, by the people, for the people." By 1992, many Americans saw the government as remote, corrupt, and something to oppose. People in America want better political communication. They are weary of the negativism that characterizes much of current political discourse. When they converse, they learn new facts and viewpoints. They want more discussion and debates in which they can be participants. This is far different from any belief that there is a contri-bution to democracy from polling, presidential approval rating nonsense, 900 number measures, radio talk-show propaganda, mail questionnaires, and picnics with politicians. Citizens want more involvement. It is essential that we realize that they want (1) more issue substance in political discussions, (2) more citizen-leader interaction, and (3) more interaction of citizens with each other about issues.

When I did my interview in Washington, D.C., for this chapter, I remember looking over at the White House and telling Jock Gill that I would like to see Clinton succeed because I thought he had some good ideas for progressive changes. I still believe that, but I also perceive some strong problems with how his ideas are moving from the abstract to the concrete. In the final analysis, it seems to me that President Clinton's objectives of improving political community and political communication will happen at the point that he brings American citizens closer to the discussions which most affect them. There is relevant wisdom in the Chinese proverb that says, "Tell me, I'll forget. Show me, I may remember. But involve me and I'll understand" (Smith, 1984, iv).

REFERENCES

Arnal, N. 1990. "The Residential Uses of Teletel in France." Paper presented to the Human Communication Technology Division of the International Communication Association, Dublin, Ireland, May.

"Background on the Administration's Telecommunications Policy Reform Initiative." 1994. White House Press Release, January 11.

Baym, N. K. 1995. "The Emergence of Community in Computer-Mediated Communication." In *Cybersociety: Computer Mediated Communication and Community,* ed. Steven G. Jones. Thousand Oaks, Calif.: Sage.

Bertelsen, Dale A. 1992. "Media Forms and Government: Democracy as an Archetypal Image in the Electronic Age." *Communication Quarterly* 40, 325–37.

Boucher, Rick. 1994. "The Information Superhighway: Turning the Vision Into Reality." *National Forum* 74, 16–18.

Carey, James W. 1987. "The Press and Public Discourse." *The Center Magazine,* March/April, 14.

Citizens and Politics: A View from Main Street America. 1991. Report prepared for the Kettering Foundation by the Harwood Group. Washington, D.C.: Kettering Foundation.

"Clinton Administration Aims for Open Information Policy." 1993. White House Press Release, CRTNET #810, RPI-Bitnet-Comserve.

Curran, J. 1982. "Communications, Power and Social Order." In *Culture, Society, and the Media,* ed. M. Gurevitch, T. Bennett, J. Curran, and J. Woollacott (pp. 202–35). London: Methuen.

Denton, Robert E, Jr., ed. 1994. *The 1992 Presidential Campaign: A Communication Perspective.* Westport, Conn.: Praeger.

——— and Gary C. Woodward. 1990. *Political Communication in America.* Westport, Conn.: Praeger.

Didsbury, Howard F. 1994. "The Wolf Is Here: The Impact of Telepower." *National Forum* 74, 22–23.

"Electronic Communication at the White House." 1994. *Educom Review* (January/February), 16–18.

Entman, Robert M. 1989. *Democracy Without Citizens.* New York: Oxford University Press.

Flanigan, William H. and Nancy H. Zingale. 1991. *Political Behavior of the American Electorate.* Washington, D.C.: Congressional Quarterly Press.

Forester, T. 1992. "Megatrends or Megamistakes?: Whatever Happened to the Information Society?" *The Information Society* 8, 133–46.

Frederick, Howard H. 1993. *Global Communication and International Relations.* Belmont, Calif.: Wadsworth.

Gandy, Oscar H. 1994. "The Information Superhighway as the Yellow Brick Road." *National Forum* 74, 24–27.

Garramone, Gina M., Allen C. Harris, and Gary Pizante. 1986. "Predictors of Motivation to Use Computer-Mediated Political Communication Systems." *Journal of Broadcasting and Electronic Media* 30, 445–57.

Glance, Natalie S. and Bernardo A. Huberman. 1994. "The Dynamics of Social Dilemmas." *Scientific American* (March), 76–81.

Gleason T. 1994. "The Information Hypeway." *Oregon Quarterly* (Spring), 12–13.

Golson, B. and P. R. Range. 1992. "Clinton on TV." *TV Guide,* November 21, 18.

Gonzales, Hernando. 1989. "Interactivity and Feedback in Third World Development Campaigns." *Critical Studies in Mass Communication* 6, 295–314.

Gore, Al. 1992. *Earth in the Balance.* Boston: Houghton Mifflin.

———. 1994. Remarks to the International Telecommunications Union, March 21.

Graber, Doris. 1988. *Processing the News.* New York: Longman.

Hacker, Kenneth. 1993. "Dear President Clinton: The Construction of Electronic Citizen Access to the White House." CRTNET #X75, Comserve communication studies network, RPI.

——— and B. Goss. 1994. "Issues of Electronic Mail Management in Organizations." Working paper.

——— and L. Monge. 1988. "Toward a Communication-Information Model: A Theoretical Perspective for the Design of Computer-Mediated Communication Systems." In *Mathematical Modelling for Information Technology,* ed. A. O. Moscardini and E. H. Robson. Chichester, England: Ellis Horwood.

Hamelink, C. J. 1986. "Is There Life after the Information Revolution?" In *The Myth of the Information Revolution: Social and Ethical Implications of Communication Technology,* ed Michael Traber. London: Sage.

Heim, Michael. 1993. *The Metaphysics of Virtual Reality.* New York: Oxford University Press.

Hurwitz, R. and J. C. Mallery, 1994. "Survey Briefing Points for Busy Officials." MIT AI Lab.

Kohut, A. 1994. Times-Mirror Presentation, C-Span. Washington, D.C., September 24.

Jones, Steven G. 1995. "Understanding Community in the Information Age." In *Cybersociety: Computer-Mediated Communication and Community,* ed. Steven G. Jones (pp. 10–35). Thousand Oaks, Calif.: Sage.

Mallery, J. C. and R. Hurwitz. 1994. "The Digital Revolution in Political Communication: Some Hermeneutic Challenges of the Emerging Global Infrastructure." Paper presented to the Department of Political Science, MIT, April 18.

Markus, M. Lynne. 1990. "Toward a Critical Mass Theory of Interactive Media." In *Organizations and Communication Technology,* ed. J. Fulk and C. Steinfield (pp. 194–218). Newbury Park, Calif.: Sage.

"National Information Infrastructure: Agenda for Action." 1994. Washington, D.C.: National Telecommunications and Information Administration.

Nelkin, Dorothy. 1994. "Ironies in the Public Response to Information Technology."
    National Forum 74, 7–10.
Neuman, W. Russell. 1986. *The Paradox of Mass Politics.* Cambridge, Mass.: Harvard
    University Press.
Nimmo, Dan. 1994. "The Electronic Town Hall in Campaign '92." In *The 1992 Pres-
    idential Campaign: A Communication Perspective,* ed. Robert E. Denton, Jr. (pp.
    207–26). Westport, Conn.: Praeger.
OTA (Office of Technology Assessment). 1990. "Critical Connections: Communication
    for the Future." Washington, D.C.: U.S. Government Printing Office.
Rafaeli, Sheizaf. 1988. "Interactivity: From New Media to Communication." In *Ad-
    vancing Communication Science: Merging Mass and Interpersonal Processes,* ed.
    Robert P. Hawkins, John M. Wiemann, and Suzanne Pingree (pp. 110–34). New-
    bury Park, Calif.: Sage.
Robinson, John P. and Mark R. Levy. 1986. *The Main Source: Learning from Television
    News.* Beverly Hills: Sage.
Rogers, Everett M. 1986. *Communication Technology.* New York: Free Press.
Rosen, L. D. and M. M. Wail. 1994. "What We Have Learned from a Decade of Re-
    search (1983–1993) on 'the Psychological Impact of Technology.' " *Computers
    and Society* (March), 3–5.
Sakkas, L. 1993. "Politics on the Internet." *Interpersonal Computing Technology: An
    Electronic Journal for the 21st Century,* 1.
Sanders, Bernard. 1994. "Whither American Democracy?" *Los Angeles Times,* January
    16: A16.
Schiller, Herbert I. 1994. "Electronic Highway to Where?" *National Forum* 74, 19–21.
Shapiro, Ian. 1994. "There Ways to Be a Democrat." *Political Theory* 22, 124–51.
Smith, A. 1984. *The Mind.* New York: Viking Press.
Smith, R. L. 1972. *The Wired Nation.* New York: Longman.
Steffen, Jerome O. 1994. "Edenic Expectations of New Technology: A Recurring Pattern
    in American Culture." *National Forum* 74, 11–15.
Steinberg, Stephen. 1994. "Travels on the Net." *Technology Review* (July), 20–21.
"The New Citizenship: A Partnership between Citizens and Government White Paper."
    1993. Humphrey Institute of Public Affairs, University of Minnesota posting to
    Internet.
Traber, Michael. 1986. "Introduction." *The Myth of the Information Revolution: Social
    and Ethical Implications of Communication Technology.* London: Sage.
Westin, A. F. 1993. "Impact of Information Technology on American Democracy." In
    Demystifying Media Technology, ed. John V. Pavlik and Everette E. Dennis (pp.
    14–17). Newbury Park, Calif.: Sage.
"What It Takes to Make It All Happen: Key Issues for Applications of the National
    Information Infrastructure." 1994. Washington, D.C.: Committee on Applications
    and Technology, National Institute of Standards and Technology.
Wober, J. Mallory. 1988. *The Use and Abuse of Television.* Hillsdale, N.J.: Lawrence
    Erlbaum.
Wurman, R. S. 1989. *Information Anxiety.* New York: Bantam Books.

Chapter Four

"The Bad Days Are Part of It": Editorial Cartoonists on Clinton's First Year

Edward H. Sewell, Jr.

A new president was elected, and you expected everything to be better the day after the election. Sitting down for your morning coffee and newspaper, you scan the headlines only to find that *nothing* has changed. How should you react? Hide your head in the sand like the proverbial ostrich? Put on sack cloth and ashes like some biblical character? Perhaps even lament with Job's friends in the biblical story, "Curse God and die!"

No, wait. Please, turn a few more pages in the newspaper. Try to get past all the harsh reality of the news until you find a journalistic wardrobe door to a Narnia-newsland or a news-hole to journalistic-Wonderland. Look for the journalistic bard, the newspaper teller-of-tales who uses myth, fantasy, fairy tale, and exaggeration to interpret the world of politics through visual images. Turn to the editorial cartoon.

Editorial cartoons are a rhetorically and politically potent form of visual communication that operate within the context of communication-play and the public sphere of editorial journalism. After presenting several theories of communication and play and providing an analysis of the role of editorial cartoons in presidential politics, this chapter focuses on how editorial cartoonists "reported" the first year of the Clinton administration.

THEORIES OF PLAY AND COMMUNICATION

Editorial cartoons are communication-play. The editorial cartoonist, like the student who draws funny pictures during the worst of classes, plays with visual caricatures of politics and politicians, providing a seriously playful perspective on the issues that shape the news. Several theories have drawn a useful parallel between play and communication to help us understand the nature and role of the editorial cartoon (Sewell, 1986a).

Play is a serious topic in social science research. Johan Huizinga (1950) began the modern exploration of play-related research, and his work has provided a foundation for the development of a significant body of interdisciplinary research. According to Huizinga, play is *pretending,* which allows us to step outside the world of work and responsibility; it is an *interlude* in a stream of serious actions. It is *voluntary* and *temporary.* It is often *secluded* in that it takes place in special spaces such as a playground, sports field, or gameboard. It is, above all, *fun.* Each of these characteristics of play fits editorial cartooning. In the editorial cartoon, the cartoonist creates metaphors and images that, while bearing a clear relationship to reality, are also pretending or play because they take the serious actions of politics and place them within a context or interlude that invites readers to temporarily and voluntarily suspend their own belief and value system and enter into the world created by the cartoonist. Only in special parts of a newspaper, the editorial page and the comics pages, can such levity and fun be allowed, and once you leave the freedom of the editorial and comics pages, you reenter the world of real politics.

Another theory of play that relates specifically to communication was formulated by William Stephenson (1967, 151) who said, "Communication is carried out in play. The communication situation is not one in which information is passed from a communication source to a receiver; it is one in which the individual plays with communication." Stephenson's theory is based on the thesis that at its best mass communication allows people to become absorbed in *subjective* play, which reaches into myth and fantasy (Stephenson, 1967, 1–3). Most human activity, *work,* is subject to *social control.* Conformity and consensus are the outcomes of social control, informing us about work, teaching us literacy and technology, and developing economic infrastructures. Some human activity, *play,* is subject to *convergent selectivity,* a relative freedom from social control that tends toward individuality of choice and behavior. Convergent selectivity is more voluntary, often chaotic, sometimes ecstatic, and usually focused on individuality and self-existence. Play, a disinterested interlude from work, is distinguishable from work (i.e., social control), which is a form of communication-pain while play (i.e., convergent selectivity) is a form of communication-pleasure.

The mass media do not communicate truth or reality, but only a semblance of it. Truth and reality are the domain of science, technology, reason, and work. "[Reality] is so complex," says Stephenson (1967, 195), "that its symbolic representation is essential to give it meaning that ordinary people can appreciate. Politics is conversation about freedom, democracy, liberty, fundamental rights, and the like—issues which need bear little relation to ongoing real conditions or legislative actions. But all these can be good fun, that is, good communication-pleasure."

Significant symbols, myths, and fantasies provide the medium for people to experience communication-pleasure. It is not the problems of information theory, technology, or information diffusion that are of critical importance, but rather as Stephenson (1967, 198) concludes, "The problems of immediate importance concern the myths of man." Play in the media gives people something to talk to each other about (a form of play providing emotional release), or it can serve to "rock the boat" of the status quo (Stephenson, 1967, 64–65).

The editorial cartoon is subjective play that provides communication-pleasure because as a form of convergent selectivity there is an almost unconditional freedom from social control that allows the cartoonist to use images and metaphors to caricature politicians and politics in a manner that would never be acceptable in a news story or even an editorial. It is important to note that there has never been a successful suit against an editorial cartoonist for libel because the courts have interpreted the editorial cartoon as a protected and specialized form of rhetorical expression. According to Steve Barkin (1984), the role of the journalist as storyteller assumes that journalists do more than describe events. In writing about values, they act as reinforcers of specific views of social reality, and therein lies the role of storyteller for a particular social order. In a sense, editorial cartoonists are journalists since they work for a newspaper, but their freedom to express ideas and state opinions goes far beyond that of the journalist-as-reporter-of-events role of the more typical journalist.

A third perspective on play was provided by Victor Turner (1982, 23), who focused on the "ludic capacity" of symbol systems by "[catching] symbols in their movement, so to speak, and to 'play' with their possibilities of form and meaning." Play, or leisure-time activity, is associated with two types of freedom: first, *freedom from* institutional obligations and forced regulated rhythms of factory and office, and second, *freedom to* enter into and even generate new symbolic worlds that transcend structural limitations. This suggests a "freedom to play . . . with ideas, with fantasies, with words" (Turner, 1982, 37).

Turner developed the concept of *liminality* to describe cultural situations where a person moves from one social structure to another. The liminal person is "betwixt and between the position assigned and arrayed by law, custom, convention, and ceremonial" (Turner, 1977, 68). On the American college campus, fraternity pledging is a liminal phenomenon. There are, however, some situations that resemble liminality, but that are not equivalent to it. These events, which Turner called *liminoid phenomena,* take place in neutral spaces or privileged areas (e.g., laboratories and the editorial page) set apart from the mainstream. These privileged spaces within mainstream institutions provide for greater freedom allowing free-wheeling, experimental forms of symbolic action not permitted outside these privileged areas. Liminoid phenomena and persona are more characteristic of industrialized (and I would add information-rich) societies while liminal phenomena are more characteristic of primitive or traditional societies.

Liminoid phenomena tend toward an *individual product,* which may have a collective or "mass" effect, and they develop *apart from the central economic*

and political processes (i.e., on the margins, interfaces, and interstices of institutions). Liminoid phenomena tend to be *idiosyncratic,* leaning toward more
subjective symbols. Like Stephenson, Turner also formulated a work/play dichotomy in that "one *works* at the liminal, one *plays* with the liminoid" (Turner,
1982, 55).

Within the framework of Turner's theory of liminoid persona, the editorial
cartoonist is provided greater freedom to work and to play with ideas, to push
them to the margins of acceptable social commentary and criticism. Their work,
unlike that of the reporter, is characterized by great individuality, for while the
reporter has to follow established guidelines for accurate reporting of news
events, the editorial cartoonist sets rather than follows prescribed guidelines.
Cartoonists are the most idiosyncratic and playful employees of the newspaper,
and they operate not within the traditional liminal roles of custom and convention, but rather on the fringes of the symbolic and mythical in the privileged
spaces of the newspaper.

POLITICAL CARTOONISTS AS LIMINOID PERSONA AND STORYTELLERS

Cartoonists are unique people. They may be more psychotic and neurotic than
the average person (Pearson, 1983). Some seem to have a fetish-fixation such
as Jeff MacNelly's use of old cars, front porches, and dragon-like images of the
economy or political ideas, while others employ idiosyncratic devices such as
Pat Oliphant's use of Puck to comment on the content of the cartoon or Tom
Toles' habit of including himself in his cartoons, sitting behind his drawing
board offering personal commentary about the events in the cartoon.

Perhaps the best way to characterize cartoonists as liminoid persona is to let
a few of them speak on their own behalf. Tony Auth of the *Philadelphia In-
quirer* says:

There's something so satisfying about expressing your point of view about issues that
are current and that are monopolizing peoples' attention. I don't know if I ever thought
that I would be a catalyst for any change or not. I tend to think that all of us are
contributing one particle a day to a torrent of information, propaganda, analyses, lies,
truths . . . so that the effect of any one particle is greatly diminished. That's the way I
see the role of a cartoon. But I want my particle to be the best I can muster ("Politics
and Emotion," 1982, 14–15).

Jeff MacNelly ("MacNelly Returns," 1982, 12) of the *Chicago Tribune* says,
"I personally like to stick a knife in someone. Because it's that extra dimension
that makes a political cartoon a political cartoon and not a *Ladies Home Journal*
gag cartoon."

On the issue of objectivity versus subjectivity, Paul Conrad ("Conrad: Man
of Opinion," 1983, 9) of the *Los Angeles Times* says, "I'll be goddamned if

I'm going to be objective on a thing like that [abortion]! I'm going to be subjective! Any cartoonist has to be subjective on the questions he's addressing. The minute you become objective, all you're doing is illustrating what's going on. Subjectivity—that's when you state an opinion. It's that simple.''

Pat Oliphant (''Quintessential Cartooning: The Art of Pat Oliphant,'' 1982, 6) comments,

Political cartooning's too valuable to just be a vehicle for gags. Don't you agree? This is more than a column. Your name goes on it and you can't equivocate. You have to take a position on an issue. You have to come out and say, ''[Menachem] Begin is wrong. Begin's a sonofabitch. Begin is a nasty little fascist.'' And you are going to invite all sorts of shit, but you've still got to say it, because that's your job, that's what you're supposed to be doing, and that's what you believe.

Each of these quotations from editorial cartoonists clearly demonstrates their perception of themselves as liminoid persona within the context of newspaper journalism. Their free-wheeling, opinionated statements clearly separate them from their liminal counterparts, the reporters. The editorial cartoonist sees the function of the editorial cartoon as one of communication-pleasure or play mixed with a healthy dose of ''truth'' about political events and politicians.

THE MEDIA AND THE PRESIDENT

When the role of the media in presidential politics is discussed, the most frequent point-of-reference is television and news reports, usually overlooking the editorial cartoon or the comic strip. If, however, the media are ''a site on which various social groups, institutions, and ideologies struggle over the definition and construction of social reality'' (Gurevitch and Levy, 1985, 19), then the editorial cartoon provides a significant point of analysis. Within this context, the media provide ''a series of arenas in which symbolic contests are carried out among competing sponsors of meaning'' (Gamson and Stuart, 1992, 55).

Within the larger context of political communication, symbolic contests tend to focus on a few central issues or ''frames'' that define the parameters of the contest and create the metaphors that best help interpret the contest (Bennett, 1975; Tuchman, 1978; Gitlin, 1980). By analyzing the content of the media in terms of how symbolic contests are framed, we gain insights into the key issues of the event under study as well as an interpretation of the meaning of the event. From a cognitive perspective, metaphors are used in communication to facilitate the analysis, understanding, and interpretation of problematic situations in terms of images or contexts that are familiar and generally understood by the reader (Chilton and Ilyin, 1993). Metaphors, whether old or new, grow out of basic human concepts that are created by our interaction with the world around us, and metaphors often originate in liminoid phenomena.

The media provide a number of different arenas for both work and play, each with its own public sphere of influence. Some are focused more on reporting events in as objective a manner as possible (i.e., work) while other arenas focus more on the interpretation of events in terms of their derived meaning (i.e., play). News attempts to recount an event in a manner that comes as close as possible to recreating what actually happened. Editorial, on the other hand, attempts to put a "spin" on the event and provide an interpretation of how actions should be understood in relation to event. Still further down the spectrum from objective news and editorializing, the editorial cartoonist looks at an event for the unique purpose of finding a metaphorical or symbolic context within which to interpret the event. Little attention or care is given to objectivity; indeed, irreverence and joking are the primary tools of the cartoonist's trade.

The newspaper has a clearly defined public sphere, but within that sphere of influence there are sub-publics that seek different types of information and use it for different purposes. A casual observation on my part is that one seldom see news articles posted on office doors, but one often sees editorial cartoons posted. In a brief and precise statement, the editorial cartoon takes the content of the news article and with the scalpel of visual humor cuts directly to the marrow of the issues and events. The sub-public or readers of editorial cartoons is not large in terms of either size or the influence wielded. People do not come up with the same interpretation of an editorial cartoon as that intended by the cartoonist or implied by the symbols included in the cartoon (Carl, 1968; DeSousa and Medhurst, 1982; Bedient and Moore, 1985; Hunter, Moore, and Sewell, 1992). The cartoonist cannot impose a concept presented in metaphoric format on any audience and assume understanding by that audience. Chilton and Ilyin (1993) suggest that the role of metaphor in political discourse operates at two distinct levels: first at the macrolevel in which the standard language or symbol system is expected, required, and imposed on any individual who wishes to participate in the discourse; and second at the microlevel, which breaks down into the two substructures of (1) the level of the individual text or utterance and (2) the interaction between various political actors expressed in terms of conversational give-and-take.

At the macrolevel, most editorial cartoonists key into the same political events being covered in news articles. They all read the same newspapers and listen to the same national newscasts. Each of them, however, finds a unique way to express the issues. This variety of expressions, at the microlevel, makes up the content of the "conversation" that takes place as readers are presented with different visual approaches and interpretations of the same event. It is regrettable that most newspapers do not run multiple editorial cartoons and thus deprive their readership the opportunity to engage, along with the cartoonists, in a dialectic about political events. Some newspapers, such as the *Washington Post, New York Times,* and *USA Today* do run a weekly page with multiple editorial cartoons focused on the same issues, and the *Washington Post Weekly* edition, which primarily runs editorial content, includes a wide range of editorial cartoon opinion, but it is certainly an exception and has a significantly more limited readership than the daily newspaper. The *Washington Times* runs more editorial cartoons per day than most newspapers, but the cartoons are always on the conservative end of the political spectrum, thus short-circuiting a true dialectic on political issues. Only in specialized publications such as *Comic Relief, Witty World,* and the *Gallery of Cartoons* can a wide variety of editorial cartoons be found printed side-by-side addressing specific topics.

In the tradition of storytellers, editorial cartoonists do not create news or news stories as much as they tell the news in terms of the values and images of their culture that can be understood, thought about, and laughed at by the audience (Sewell, 1986b, 1987). The editorial cartoonist works to find images that can be related to the event under consideration and translates some thought or kernel of truth into a format that can be visually comprehended by the reader with as little effort on the reader's part as possible.

EDITORIAL CARTOONISTS AND PREVIOUS PRESIDENTS

Editorial cartoonists play no favorites when it comes to presidents (Sewell, 1992). They look at the person in the office and search for weaknesses—physical, emotional, ideological, and personal. They see the person in the office in much the same way Norman Mailer in *Cannibals and Christians* (1966) described President Lyndon Johnson: "Johnson had compromised too many contradictions and now the contradictions were in his face: when he smiled, the corners of his mouth squeezed gloom; when he was pious, his eyes twinkled irony; when he spoke in a righteous tone, he looked corrupt; when he jested, the ham in his jowls looked to quiver. He was not convincing."

In similar vein, editorial cartoonist Bob Gorrell (1981, 12–13) observed that images of the president are in the reader's mind, and the cartoonist simply calls to mind those common images:

Nixon wears a perpetual 5 o'clock shadow; Gerald Ford is an inept, uncoordinated simpleton; Jimmy Carter stands two-feet short; and Ronald Reagan is an elitist senile warmonger. All of these impressions reflect the cartoonist's emotional response to his subject, and contain, perhaps, a bit of truth. In their brutal simplicity, though, there lies a real hazard for the reader. While he laughs and snickers at our irreverent portraits, he is also being conditioned to perceive our subjects in dangerously simplistic terms. We reinforce his stereotypes and substantiate his misconceptions. And the individual who envisions issues in one-dimensional caricature has no true appreciation of the complexity of events.

How does the editorial cartoonist choose the caricature for each president? Thomas Griffith (1984) explored the cartoonists' dilemma of how to caricature presidential nominee Fritz Mondale. Pat Oliphant said, "I hate changes of Administrations. It takes six months to 'get' a new man." While most of the cartoonists interviewed found Mondale "dull," "boring," "bland," and "wimpy," and thus a difficult target to caricature, they found Ronald Reagan an easy target with his "pompadour and neck wrinkles," for as Mike Peters observed, "you can put a pompadour on anything and it becomes Reagan." Griffith concluded, "Undoctrinaire iconoclasm is their style. They think more in metaphors than in arguments and don't want to dull a witty simplicity with a weighty qualification."

Caricature is the first craft of the editorial cartoonist. British cartoonist Nicholas Garland (1988, 76–77) noted:

Caricatures are not static; they grow and evolve in the cartoonist's work, taking the readers with them. When a new political figure takes his or her place on the stage the cartoonists first of all carefully produce fairly academically accurate likenesses of the newcomer. Gradually, certain features become established as standing for the individual. . . . In its directness and simplicity, caricature does not allow for fine degrees of criticism. It has an awful bluntness. It cannot dilute its message to say, for example: "You are behaving like a fool." It says more succinctly: "You idiot!" It strikes at the most vulnerable and private sides of its targets.

Mike Peters (1985, 45) provided clear statements of how he caricatured several presidents. Of Richard M. Nixon he said:

As many times as I've seen Richard Nixon, I still save a picture that shows him from a different angle or captures something I've never seen in his face before. I guess I was lucky that when I began my career as a real life editorial cartoonist that the President of the United States was Richard Nixon. His every move offered such fertile drawing possibilities for a hungry cartoonist. Nixon's nose, his eyes and eyebrows, even his hunched posture offered such potential for editorial statements.

Of President Gerald Ford, Mike Peters says, "I realized immediately that I had been drawing Mr. Ford all my life. All I had to do was my basic Frankenstein without the scar and the neck pegs and give him wispy hair and a pipe. A perfect caricature of President Ford" (59).

Not all caricature is based on physical feature. Caricature, in its original meaning, was related to capturing the "character" or personality of a person. Perhaps physical features do capture personality, but often metaphor or setting offers a better format for caricature. Take, for example the concept of the "Imperial Presidency." What better way to capture the imperial desires of power than with the "King Andy" image in the first quarter of the nineteenth century. Thomas Nast cast President U.S. Grant in the role of a monarch with a less than loyal kingdom, and what better image for Richard Nixon than Shakespeare's "King Richard." With his ivy-league and wealth-endowed background, is it too difficult to picture George Bush as "King George" of the aristocracy?

When we consider the rhetorical dimensions of the editorial cartoon, we see the major role played by metaphor communicated via symbols that help us structure reality in terms we can understand and with which we can identify. Zarefsky (1986, 5) pointed out this relationship when he said,

Rhetoric involves the selection of symbols which will represent ideas, since those symbols evoke support or opposition by virtue of their association with an audience's prior experience and belief. Rhetoric includes the choices among possible appeals and arguments, since these choices influence whether audiences will be convinced that a proposal is in their interest. And rhetoric includes decisions about how to explain ambiguous situations, so that they may be taken as evidence for one's point of view rather than the opposite.

Take for example, President Bush's free use of "sound bites" to explain many policies of his administration. He was described as the "education president." Perhaps you can recall other images in cartoons based on one of the Bush policy statements qua sound bite and think of possible visual metaphors that bring the sound bite to life: "A thousand points of light," "A kinder, gentler nation," or "Read my lips." The importance of the sound bite and metaphor relationship was found by the University of Washington Discourse Analysis Group or WAUDAG (1990) to be the key to understanding President Bush's public discourse. The editorial cartoonist, like the television reporter, looks for the small metaphorically rich, but verbally or visually brief, expressions that characterize effective sound bites. It is this level of discourse that becomes the rhetorical fodder for the daily editorial cartoon.

CARICATURING CLINTON

Even before the election, editorial cartoonists began making decisions about how they would caricature Bill Clinton in the, some felt, unlikely event he won the race for president (Moore, 1992).

What did the cartoonists see in Clinton worth caricaturing? Chris Britt of the *Morning News Tribune* (Tacoma, WA) focused on the geometric in Clinton's body, or as Britt said, "I have focused on his roundness; he is round from hair to nose to belly." Other cartoonists' opinions highlight different approaches. Steve Benson of the *Arizona Republic* focused on the hair, which is "just like cotton candy you used to get at the county fair." Gary Markstein of the *Milwaukee Journal* moved beyond specific physical traits to see Clinton in the image of "a cross between a television evangelist and W. C. Fields."

The cadre of cartoonists making decisions about how Clinton would look, should he become the next president, provide visual flesh for dry political bones. Like God's question to the Hebrew prophet Ezekiel in his vision of the valley of dry bones (Ezekiel 37:3, NRSV), "Mortal, can these bones live?" the political cartoonist stands on the outside viewing a valley of dry political bones and is asked not *if* these bones can live but *how* they can be made to live.

The attitude of editorial cartoonists mirrors that of "spectator politics" as described by David Zarefsky (1992) in his formulation of five characteristics that describe the relationship between the media spectacle and the political process. The five characteristics are (1) the transience and volatility of events, (2) the avoidance of complex subjects, (3) the simplification of what cannot be avoided, (4) the magnification of the trivial, and (5) the debasement of political debate in favor of one-liners and canned minispeeches.

Zarefsky's five characteristics are an apt description of the normal way in which the editorial cartoonist operates. Each day a new cartoon must focus on the ever-changing and volatile issues that make the headlines. The more complex the event, the greater the difficulty of reducing it to a simple one-panel visual image. The easiest issues to cartoon about are those that lend themselves to simple metaphorical images that carry their own connotative values. The best way to draw attention to an issue is to focus on the most trivial aspects as a means of pointing out the important ideas that are being overlooked, and if a one-liner or sound bite is used, the work of creating the visual image is made much easier for the cartoonist.

CLINTON'S FIRST YEAR PORTRAYED IN EDITORIAL CARTOONS

Assuming all the foregoing discussion, let us turn our attention to President Bill Clinton's first year in office. Clinton summed up his first year in office ("Clinton Marks 1st Year as President," A2): "The bad days are part of it. It's humbling, and it's educational." When asked by a reporter if he was "happy," Clinton "somberly" replied, "Oh, yes. And grateful for the chance to serve."

How did the editorial cartoonists sum up the first year? Gary Brookins and Bob Gorrell of the *Richmond Times-Dispatch* illustrate their treatment of President Clinton in a simple visual metaphor that recalls the hunters bringing home the game after a successful hunt (see Figure 4.1). Rather than analyze and question the process and look for the good story or photograph, the editorial cartoonists simply take the bounty of the presidential game-hunt home for the roasting fires. Tied to the cartoonists' ink pen, the bewildered and perhaps unsuspecting and naive President Clinton is their hostage.

The spirit of the "president-as-hostage" metaphor is captured by Jeff Koterba of the *Omaha World-Herald* in the image of a "Presidential Basic Training" course in which Clinton has made it over the first, and largest, obstacle of the course ("The First 100 Days"), but in less than good physical shape, and with the main course obstacles yet to come (Brooks, 1994, 19).

Herblock of the *Washington Post* visually summed up the first year in a cartoon that showed Clinton making a toast at an "Anniversary Party" with a "1 YEAR" birthday cake on a round table surrounded by empty chairs labeled "nominations withdrawn," "unfilled ambassador posts," "judicial vacancies," "Department of Justice vacancies," "State Department resignations," and "unfilled defense positions." Not a very "happy" birthday (see Figure 4.2).

Figure 4.1
Brookins and Gorrell Illustration

Gary Brookins and Bob Gorrell, *Richmond Times-Dispatch.* Reprinted with permission.

One image that has been the focus of many editorial cartoons about Clinton is his saxophone and his love for doing public performances on such unpresidential networks as MTV. The simple saxophone player as illustrated by David Donar (see Figure 4.3) has been transformed again and again into images such as that of Jim Morin of the *Miami Herald,* who caricatured Clinton standing with his sax between two sets of music. In good order is the simple "Rhetoric Waltz" of the campaign, but in disarray is the much more complicated "Reality Fugue in C Minor" with notes and pages falling unplayed to the floor. Paul Conrad (Brooks, 1994, 12) of the *Los Angeles Times* drew Clinton holding a sax in each hand, one labeled "Domestic Policy" and the other "Foreign Policy." The caption read, "And now, I'd like to play a duet . . ." Finally, Paul Szep (Brooks, 1994, 27) of the *Boston Globe* portrayed Clinton as "The Blues Player" wearing sunglasses and playing a bigger-than-life sax with keys labeled the "50 billion deficit reduction" producing a blues rendition of "unhappiness," "pain," "loss," "heartbreak," "hurt," "suffering," and "misery."

An analysis of Clinton's campaign in 1992 (Sewell, 1993) found that several themes dominated the editorial cartoons about the campaign, with the top four being images of (1) media and entertainment, (2) sport and games, (3) driver's seat, and (4) playing the saxophone. These four images accounted for a little over 68 percent of the sample of over fifty cartoons.

An analysis of editorial cartoons done for this chapter found that the same themes dominated the editorial cartoons of the first year of the Clinton administration with one major addition, Hillary Rodham Clinton. The sample for the current analysis was taken from Brooks (1994), an annual series to which car-

Figure 4.2
Herblock's "Anniversary Party"

ANNIVERSARY PARTY

Figure 4.3
Donar Illustration

David S. Donar. Reprinted with permission.

toonists are invited to submit several samples of their work. The justification for the use of this source is threefold: (1) it is the only established annual collection of editorial cartoons readily available to the general public, (2) it includes cartoonists from across the nation with reputations ranging from some who have won a Pulitzer Prize to others early in their careers, and (3) it includes cartoons chosen by each cartoonist from their own set of cartoons for inclusion in the anthology.

The sample included eighty-seven cartoons by sixty-six different cartoonists representing twenty-seven states as well as eight with syndication in specialized

Table 4.1
Summary of Content Analysis

Category/Subcategories	Category %	Cumulative%
Economics (19)	21.59	21.59
Taxes (8)		
NAFTA (6)		
Deficit (5)		
Foreign Relations (17)	1932.	40.91
General (8)		
Bosnia (3)		
Haiti (2)		
Somalia (2)		
Iraq (1)		
North Korea (1)		
Health Reform (12)	13.64	54.55
Hillary (10)	11.36	65.91
Health Reform (7)		
Power (3)		
Gridlock (7)	07.95	73.86
Gays in the Military (6)	06.82	80.68
Public Opinion (4)	04.55	85.23
GOP Problems (3)	03.41	88.64
Reinventing Government (3)	03.41	92.05
Appointments (2)	02.27	94.32
Social Security (2)	02.27	96.59
Personal Problems (2)	02.27	98.86
Haircut (1)	01.14	100.00

publications (e.g., agriculture) or national syndication without a newspaper base (e.g., NEA). The content analysis based on these cartoons is integrated with verbal descriptions of representative cartoons from each category. In some cases a cartoon included more than one topic, but each cartoon was placed in only one category that was most descriptive of its overall content. Table 4.1 is a summary of the categories, subcategories, category percentages, and cumulative percentages for the content analysis.

It is no surprise that economic issues top the agenda for editorial cartoonists, with over 21 percent of the cartoons falling into this category. There were three major subcategories: taxes, NAFTA, and the deficit.

There was no consistent theme in the taxes subcategory. Ed Gamble (Brooks, 1994, 13) of the *Times-Union* (FL) showed Clinton and Congress as two robbers holding up a "Mom & Pop Small Business" while one employee says to another employee, "No, it's the same gang . . . just a new leader!!" On the same theme, David Cox (Hardin) (Brooks, 1994, 84) of the *Northwest Arkansas Morning*

News (Rogers, AR) depicted a small businessman sweeping his porch at his small, but neat, establishment with Clinton in a bulldozer labeled "Taxes" about to destroy the unsuspecting small businessman.

Other cartoons in the taxes subcategory include a cartoon by Walt Handelsman of the *New Orleans Times-Picayune* (Brooks, 1994, 30) with Clinton tying and gagging two taxpayers while saying, "The budget process is finally over . . . just tying up the loose ends"; and a cartoon by Chip Beck (Brooks, 1994, 24) of the *Northern Virginia Sun* with Clinton standing behind a "TAX PLAN" cannon pointed at average "U.S. Tax-Payer," who is thinking, "So this is patriotism" while Clinton says, "Y'all stand by to bite the bullet, y'hear." Using a consumption metaphor, Joe Hoffecker (Brooks, 1994, 31) of the Cincinnati *Business Courier* depicted Clinton having dinner with "Gov't Spending" as they are about to dine on "Taxpayers" being served up by Congress. In this cartoon, government spending is drawn as a hog, and the taxpayers being served for dinner recall the biblical story of the head of John the Baptist being served up on a platter.

In a more humorous vein, Jim Berry (Brooks, 1994, 109) uses the image of Laurel and Hardy starring Clinton in the role of Laurel smiling brightly as Hardy holds the "Higher Taxes" bag and in the well-known cliché says, "This is another fine mess you've gotten us into!" Finally, Dick Locker (Brooks, 1994, 84) of the *Chicago Tribune* pictured the economy as a large eighteen-wheeler under repair at the starting line of an auto race. In the next lane, and ready to go, sits Clinton in a souped-up racing car labeled "Taxes." Not much of content will come out of this race.

Several of the cartoons about NAFTA used Perot as their focal point. Randy Bish (Brooks, 1994, 70) of the *Tribune-Review* (Greensburg, PA) depicted Perot as a "back pain" poking his head out of Clinton's collar, while Steve Scallion (Brooks, 1994, 72) of the *Democrat-Gazette* (AR) drew Clinton as a swimmer ready to head into the surf but being restrained by a small dog with "Perot" on its collar. One of the more interesting images of Clinton was done by Mike Peters (Brooks, 1994, 65) of the *Dayton Daily News,* who caricatured Clinton as a vacuum cleaner that had just sucked Perot in, and from the dusty insides of the vacuum cleaner Perot says, "Now . . . kin ah finish? Say . . . what was that giant sucking sound?" Other cartoons about NAFTA showed Clinton in bed with the GOP Elephant on "The Morning NAFTA" (Charles Fagan of Associated Features [Brooks, 1994, 2]); Clinton standing in the remains of a building labeled "Clinton's Trading Post & Gift Shop" beside his jar of "NAFTA Chits" in his underwear saying, "Boy . . . did I do some horse trading or what?" (Ed Gamble of the *Times-Union* [Brooks, 1994, 66]); and Clinton as the paleolithic inventor of the wheel (NAFTA) confronted by the irate neighbor saying, "Not having that was good enough for our ancestors—and what was good enough for them is good enough for us!" (Art Henrickson of the Illinois *Daily Herald* [Brooks, 1994, 71]).

Cartoons about the deficit used images of a pig pulling an ornate carriage of

"Big Plans" driven by Clinton (Jeff MacNelly of the *Chicago Tribune* [Brooks, 1994, 18]), and of a pit bull tearing up "Campaign Promises" as its owner, Clinton, comes into the room (Ben Sargent of the Austin [TX] *American-Statesman* [Brooks, 1994, 26]).

The second major category was foreign relations, representing slightly over 19 percent of the cartoons. Almost a third of the cartoons placed Clinton in a military role as a tank driver (Dana Summers of the *Orlando Sentinel* and Ed Gamble of the Florida *Times-Union* [Brooks, 1994, 97 and 17]), airplane pilot (Mark Cullum of the *Birmingham News* and Jeff MacNelly of the *Chicago Tribune* [Brooks, 1994, 99 and 23]), and as a platoon leader (George Danby of the *Bangor Daily News* [Brooks, 1994, 32]). All these images depicted Clinton as inept and confused. The most visually interesting of these images is Mac-Nelly's cartoon that recalls the bombers of World War II. Pilot Clinton looks back to see navigator Christopher using a square globe and bombadier Aspin fishing out the bomb door. The caption reads, "Thirty Seconds over Haiti, Somalia or Possibly Bosnia."

Several classical images or metaphors were used to represent Clinton's failures in the area of foreign policy. He was drawn as Rodin's "Thinker," who could not move beyond thinking into action on Bosnia (Rex Babin [Brooks, 1994, 102] of the *Times Union* [NY]); as the damsel in distress who cries out "STOP! . . . or I'll SCREAM!" while watching two ruffians fighting one another in the mud puddle of Bosnia (Jon Richards [Brooks, 1994, 104] of the *Sun Mount Syndicate*); and finally by Mark Streeter of the Savannah [GA] *Morning News* (see Figure 4.4) as Winnie-the-Clinton stuck in the "Foreign Policy" hole with Christopher, Aspin, and Lake trying to pull him out.

Health care reform, while perhaps most hotly debated, was represented by only 13.64 percent of the cartoons in the sample, but it also, excuse the pun, bled over more than any other category into other areas such as the economy, Hillary, and reinventing government. Dick Wright (Brooks, 1994, 46) of the Providence (RI) *Journal-Bulletin* represents big government as a dinosaur trying to carry the wheel-less ambulance of the Health Care System driven by the Clintons, both Bill and Hillary. Larry Wright (Brooks, 1994, 31) of the *Detroit News* shows Clinton as a surgeon with saw and cleaver calling the next patient (U.S. Health Care System) into the operating room as the first patient, now legless (U.S. Economy) leaves. Also using the surgeon image, Ed Fischer (Brooks, 1994, 14) of the Rochester (NY) *Post-Bulletin* shows both Clinton and Gore bending over the patient (AMA) telling him to "trust us." Brookins (Brooks, 1994, 48) of the *Richmond Times-Dispatch* depicts Clinton as the driver of Health Care Reform ambulance (see Figure 4.5). Out of the back come all the clowns of the "bureaucracy" that will be a part of the final package. Finally, Walt Handelsman (Brooks, 1994, 39) of the *New Orleans Times-Picayune* portrays Clinton as a sinister physician putting on the latex examination glove of "health reform" and telling you the patient (he's looking right at you the reader)

Figure 4.4
Streeter's "They're Doing the Best They Can"

Mark Streeter, courtesy *Savannah Morning News*. Reprinted with permission.

Figure 4.5
Brookins' "Health Care Reform"

Gary Brookins, *Richmond Times-Dispatch*. Reprinted with permission.

Figure 4.6
Handelsman's "Bend Over America"

Walt Handelsman, *New Orleans Times-Picayune*. Reprinted with permission from Tribune Media Services.

to "bend over America" in an image quite too familiar to all male readers (see Figure 4.6).

Hillary was the primary subject of 11.36 percent of the cartoons. Most of the cartoons depicted Hillary as the "real" president, or at least as the person getting most of the publicity. Gary Brookins (Brooks, 1994, 35) of the *Richmond Times-Dispatch* showed the U.S. Health Care System (in the metaphor of an ambulance) pulling into "Billary's Garage" for repairs. Hillary is the mechanic while Bill stands looking on as she works to repair the ambulance. In a similar image, William Costello (Brooks, 1994, 43) of the *NEA Syndicate* drew Hillary as the driver of an ambulance labeled "Hillary's Health Care Package." She has just crashed into the rear of a car, the "Economy," and seeing the damage says, "Whooaa . . . look at the damage!! Good thing I'm here to HELP . . ." Drawing on the classic Disney image of the wicked witch in "Sleeping Beauty," Jim Berry (Brooks, 1994, 47) of NEA caricatures Hillary as the evil witch who offers us the box of "Socialized Medicine" locked with a sword and snake parody of the caduceus of medicine. Rather than a wicked witch, Jack Higgins (Brooks, 1994, 45) of the *Chicago Sun-Times* drew Hillary as an evil physician or nurse preparing to give the AMA a giant injection. Using an image from Norman Rockwell (with appropriate apologies cited), Higgins has the AMA (a male) pulling down his pants, but looking at the diploma on the wall, obviously to check on the credentials of his health care provider. The smile on Hillary's face clearly suggests that she is enjoying the experience of giving the shot.

In three cartoons that focus on Hillary, there is a clear comparison of her role to that of her husband-president. Mike Ramirez (Brooks, 1994, front cover) of the *Memphis Commercial Appeal* had Hillary sitting on a high stool behind Bill's back, looking over his shoulder as he examines papers. Two of the presidential staff come into the room and one whispers to the other, "It still unnerves me a bit . . ." Even more critical was the cartoon by Jeff Stahler (Brooks, 1994, 25) of the *Cincinnati Post* that showed Bill Clinton having his portrait painted with Hillary sitting at the desk in the background. Then we notice that the painter is painting Hillary, not Bill! Of course, the role of the First Lady is not unique to the Clinton administration (Nancy Reagan also was often in the editorial cartoons during her husband's administration). In true mythic imagery, Bob Gorrell (Brooks, 1994, 14) of the *Richmond Times-Dispatch* presents Hillary as Wonder Woman walking, briefcase in hand, with President Clinton, papers in hand, who asks "Hillary . . . are you sure all this new power isn't going to your HEAD?! . . ." (see Figure 4.7).

While perhaps the most global of issues surrounding the first year of the administration, gridlock represented only 7.95 percent of the sample. We have already referred to Paul Conrad's cartoon that showed Clinton with a saxophone in each hand trying to play a one-man duet on "Domestic Policy" and "Foreign Policy." The theme of indecision or gridlock is presented by Lambert Der (Brooks, 1994, 17) of the *Houston Post* as a "holding pattern" airport tie-up (see Figure 4.8). The president's plane sits on the tarmac with other aircraft trying to make landings. The aircraft caught in the holding pattern include "the economy," "Middle East," "crime," "the deficit," "Iraq," "Serbs," and, of course, "health-care." Oh yes, the problem is caused by the vanity of the president, who "SNIP . . . SNIP . . ." is getting a haircut. Art Wood (Brooks, 1994, 25) for the Farm Bureau News drew Clinton-as-Magician announcing, "Now for my next trick . . ." as all the rabbits are jumping out of the hat at the same time. The rabbits are "Health Care Tax," "Middle Class Tax," "Energy Tax," " 'Sin' Tax," and "Sales Tax." Hugh Haynie (Brooks, 1994, 16) of the Louisville *Courier Journal* drew Clinton riding a donkey through a swamp while holding a sign ("It's the economy, stupid!") with which he is trying to beat off an alligator ("Foreign Crises") that already has Clinton's foot in its mouth. The inscription reads: "When you're up to your donkey in alligators, it's difficult to remember that you were elected to drain the swamp." Finally, Bubba Flint (Brooks, 1994, 26) of the Ft. Worth (TX) *Star-Telegram* caricatured Clinton as a fireman trying to put out a dog house fire ("Military Ban on Gays") while the larger house ("Federal Budget") is belching the smoke of "Deficit" as it is being consumed by the fire.

Figure 4.7
Gorrell's "Hillary . . . Are You Sure"

Bob Gorrell, *Richmond Times-Dispatch*. Reprinted with permission.

Figure 4.8
Der's "Tower, This is Air Force One"

Lambert Der, *Houston Post*. Reprinted with permission.

Flint's cartoon about the debate over the role of gays in the military is a nice transition to the series of cartoons dealing specifically with the theme of gays in the military (6.82%). John Trevor (Brooks, 1994, 143) of the *Albuquerque Journal* drew Clinton holding a hand grenade labeled "Gays in the Military" while being advised by both his civilian and military staff to be "careful now, Mr. President. . . . Just grasp it firmly . . . with your teeth, pull out the pin, then throw it!" With the pin pulled and the grenade still in his mouth, Clinton runs forward while his staff scrambles in all directions. The president is thinking, "Hah! Who said I needed experience serving in the military?!" In a visually very simple cartoon, Paul Conrad (Brooks, 1994, 149) of the *Los Angeles Times* depicted President Clinton saluting a passing military officer, who rather than returning the standard salute is thumbing his nose at the president. Clinton carries the brief case "Order lifting ban on gays." In a similar three-panel cartoon, Dick Wright (Brooks, 1994, 144) of the *Providence Journal-Bulletin* drew a military officer in panel one saluting Clinton; in panel two Clinton turns the corner and the officer has a sour look on his face; and in panel three, both Clinton and the officer, now out of sight of one another, turn and give one another a thumb of the nose.

Seven other issues accounted for less than 5 percent each and less than 20 percent of the total. Public opinion about Clinton (4.55%) primarily on keeping campaign promises, such as in the cartoon by Dale Stephanos (Brooks, 1994, 78) of *USA Today,* who drew Clinton having a conversation with Pope John Paul II. Clinton, reading a newspaper with the headline "Many U.S. Catholics at Odds with Pope–Low Approval Rating," asks "Wow, what did you do, break some campaign promises?" With a smug smile on his face, the Pope replies, "No, I kept them."

Problems with the Republicans, especially Dole, accounted for 3.41 percent of the sample. Dick Locher (Brooks, 1994, 107) of the *Chicago Tribune* focused on Clinton's problem of dealing with a powerful Republican Party in a cartoon that caricatured Clinton as the big game hunter holding an ivory tusk on his shoulder while trying to leave the carcass of the GOP elephant, badly wounded but perhaps not dead, only to find that his coat is snagged by the remaining tusk labeled "Dole." A cartoon by Joe Majeski (Brooks, 1994, 108) of *The Times-Leader* (PA) depicted Clinton asleep while fishing with Dole in the creek about to snip the fishing line with a pair of scissors, and Gary Thomas (Brooks, 1994, 108) of the Des Moines *Business Record* caricatured Clinton as suffering from apnea caused by Dole standing on his neck. An insert has the definition "Apnea: A sleep disorder caused when a lump of excess tissue blocks the breathing passage forcing the dreamer to snap back into reality."

Cartoons on reinventing the government (3.41%) used mythical or literary images to question the validity of the exercise. Jack Jurden (Brooks, 1994, 24) of the Wilmington (DE) *News Journal* caricatured Clinton as Batman in the pumpkin patch on Halloween. The government as Frankenstein was being uncooperative as Clinton pulls the lever to transform the monster in a cartoon by

Ed Stein (Brooks, 1994, 32) of the *Rocky Mountain News* and NEA. The assistant warns, "It doesn't *want* to be reinvented!" Finally, Jeff MacNelly (Brooks, 1994, 15) of the *Chicago Tribune* has a very small Clinton on his horse trying to tame a giant oversized alligator ("Gov't") with the obvious conclusion that it will not work.

Cartoons about Clinton's family in the form of the unknown half-brother was treated with humor by Jerry Holbert (Brooks, 1994, 28) of the *Boston Herald,* who used Charlie Brown as a half-brother while Charles Daniel (Brooks, 1994, 29) of the Knoxville (TN) *News-Sentinel* depicted Clinton introducing Chelsea to her "Uncle Sam" with her response, "Oh, No!! Not another half-brother!"

Cabinet appointments and failures took on the theme of sacrifice and suicide. Mike Thompson (Brooks, 1994, 31) of the Springfield (IL) *State Journal-Register* drew Les Aspin ready to jump from the bridge in a scene from "It's a Wonderful Life" while Clinton advises from the sideline "Don't jump! Think what things would be like if you'd never been born. . . . On second thought— jump! JUMP!!!" Paul Duginski (Brooks, 1994, 20) of *McClatchy News Service* treated Clinton's Supreme Court nomination failure as a witch burning. An evil GOP elephant stands by with gas can and torch in hand while Lani is tied to the stake with law reviews as the fuel for a witch-burning. Clinton, reading a law review, says "Gee, Lani, I wish I'd read some of these articles before now. . . ."

Finally, one cartoon by Randy Wicks (Brooks, 1994, 33) of the Valencia (CA) *Signal* treated Clinton's haircut as an issue in itself, unlike several other cartoons referred to earlier where it was used as a means to talk about more significant issues. Two trucks are waiting for a jet to land. One is "jet fuel" while the other contains "styling mousse." A ground worker says, "That's the ground crew for Hair Force One!"

CONCLUSION

On a range of issues from those of international and national significance to those of no serious importance, the editorial cartoonists took Clinton hostage and held him accountable for every blunder and inadequacy of his first year in office. Of course, they were no meaner to Clinton than to those who have occupied the Oval Office before him. The cartoonists stood on the political sidelines and commented on the game-plan, coaching, fumbles, and even on the cheerleaders. Their commentary was biased against the coach-as-president and found fault with any and all players and plays in the game-plan. The coach-as-president should expect no less from the liminoid quasi-journalists who each day take pen in hand and with little sympathy critique our political system and those with leading roles in its day-to-day operation and management.

The editorial cartoonist serves as a form of vox populi in the newspaper, saying what the public might want to say if given the power and the resources. And so, as President Clinton in his anniversary appearance on CNN's "Larry

King Live'' said, ''The bad days are part of it. It's humbling, and it's educational.'' If the news reporter can take some credit for the ''educational'' days, surely some of the credit for ''humbling'' the president goes to the editorial cartoonists.

REFERENCES

Barkin, Steve M. 1984. ''The Journalist as Storyteller: An Interdisciplinary Perspective.'' *American Journalism* 1: 27–33.

Bedient, David O. and David M. Moore. 1985. ''Student Interpretations of Political Cartoons.'' *Journal of Visual/Verbal Learning* 5(2): 29–35.

Bennett, W. Lance. 1975. *The Political Mind and the Political Environment.* Lexington, Mass.: Heath Publishing.

Brooks, Charles, ed. 1994. *Best Editorial Cartoons of the Year.* Gretna, La.: Pelican Publishing Company.

Carl, Leroy M. 1968. ''Editorial Cartoons Fail to Reach Many Readers.'' *Journalism Quarterly* 45: 533–35.

Chilton, Paul and Mikhail Ilyin. 1993. ''Metaphor in Political Discourse: The Case of the 'Common European House.' '' *Discourse and Society* 4: 7–31.

''Clinton Marks 1st Year as President.'' 1994. *Roanoke Times & World-News* (from AP report), January 21, A2.

''Conrad: Man of Opinion.'' 1983. *Target: The Political Cartoon Quarterly* 7 (Spring): 4–10.

DeSousa, Michael A. and Martin J. Medhurst. 1982. ''The Editorial Cartoon as Visual Rhetoric: Rethinking Boss Tweed.'' *Journal of Visual Verbal Languaging* 2: 2.

Gamson, William A. and David Stuart. 1992. ''Media Discourse as a Symbolic Contest: The Bomb in Political Cartoons.'' *Sociological Forum* 7: 55–86.

Garland, Nicholas. 1988. ''Political Cartooning.'' In *Laughing Matters: A Serious Look at Humour,* ed. John Durant and Jonathan Miller (pp. 75–89). New York: John Wiley & Sons, Inc.

Gitlin, Todd. 1980. *The Whole World Is Watching.* Berkeley: University of California Press.

Gorrell, Bob. 1981. ''A Responsibility to Fairness.'' *Target: The Political Cartoon Quarterly* 1(1): 12–13.

Griffith, Thomas. 1984. ''Finding a Face for Fritz.'' *Time* (October 8), 86.

Gurevitch, Michael and Mark R. Levy, eds. 1985. ''Preface.'' *Mass Communication Review Yearbook 5.* Beverly Hills, Calif.: Sage.

Huizinga, Johan. 1950. *Homo Ludens.* Boston: Beacon Press.

Hunter, John Mark, David M. Moore, and Edward H. Sewell, Jr. 1992. ''The Effects of Teaching Strategy and Cognitive Style on Student Interpretations of Editorial Cartoons.'' *Journal of Visual Literacy* 11(2): 35–55.

''MacNelly Returns.'' 1982. *Target: The Political Cartoon Quarterly 3* (Spring): 4–12.

Mailer, Norman. 1966. *Cannibals and Christians.* New York: Dial Press.

Moore, W. John. 1992. ''Cartoonists Train Pens on Clinton.'' *National Journal,* July 18, 1697.

Pearson, Paul. 1983. ''Personality Characteristics of Cartoonists.'' *Personality and Individual Differences* 4: 227–28.

Peters, Mike. 1985. *The World of Cartooning with Mike Peters: How Caricatures Develop.* Dayton, Ohio: Landfall Press.

"Politics and Emotion: The Art of Tony Auth." 1982. *Target: The Political Cartoon Quarterly* 2 (Winter): 11–17.

"Quintessential Cartooning: The Art of Pat Oliphant." 1982. *Target: The Political Cartoon Quarterly* 5 (Autumn): 4–12.

Sewell, Edward H., Jr. 1986a. "Taking Aim—The Liminality of Political Cartoonists." In *Communication as Performance,* ed. Janet L. Palmer (pp. 125–34). Tempe: Arizona State University.

———. 1986b. "Rhetorical Analysis of Visual Discourse: A Defense of the Study of Cartoons as Speech Communication." In *Miteinander sprechen und handeln: Festschrift für Hellmut Geissner,* ed. Edith Slembek (pp. 279–87). Frankfurt am Main, Germany: Scriptor Verlag.

———. 1987. "Narrative Communication in Editorial Cartoons." In *On Narratives,* ed. Hellmut Geissner (pp. 260–68). Frankfurt am Main, Germany: Scriptor Verlag.

———. 1992. *Mr. President: Presidential Image in Political Cartoons.* Paper presented at the Speech Communication Association, October.

———. 1993. *Editorial Cartoon Images of Bill Clinton in the 1992 Presidential Campaign.* Paper presented at the Speech Communication Association, November.

Stephenson, William. 1967. *The Play Theory of Mass Communication.* Chicago: University of Chicago Press.

Tuchman, Gaye. 1978. *Making News.* New York: Free Press.

Turner, Victor. 1977. "Process, Systems, and Symbols: A New Anthropological Synthesis." *Daedalus* 106: 61–80.

———. 1982. *From Ritual to Theatre.* New York: Performing Arts Journal Publications.

WAUDAG [University of Washington Discourse Analysis Group]. 1990. "The Rhetorical Construction of a President." *Discourse and Society* 1: 189–200.

Zarefsky, David. 1986. *President Johnson's War on Poverty: Rhetoric and History.* University: University of Alabama Press.

———. 1992. "Spectator Politics and the Revival of Public Argument." *Communication Monographs* 59: 411–14.

Chapter Five

Media Conflicts over Clinton Policies: Political Advertising and the Battle for Public Opinion

Lynda Lee Kaid, John C. Tedesco, and Julia A. Spiker

In its first two years the Clinton presidency faced a number of serious challenges over policy initiatives, beginning almost immediately with the discussion of "gays in the military" and escalating to the crisis over health care reform as the midyear elections neared in the fall of 1994. Battles such as these are common for any administration, but the conflicts over Clinton policy initiatives have taken on a new dimension with the evolution of new uses of media advertising on both sides of the issues. This new use of political advertising, to compete for public support on issues normally decided by the interplay of executive and legislative forces, has added an entirely new element to the policy environment and changed forever the ways in which policy issues may be decided in the American governmental process. This chapter analyzes the usage of this new element in the policy process, political advertising, to influence the policy debate over two important issues in the first half of the Clinton presidency, the debate over the North American Free Trade Agreement (NAFTA) and the legislation to reform health care.

ISSUE ADVERTISING AND THE POLITICAL PROCESS

While the most common usage of the term "political advertising" applies to the use of paid advertising in various media during political campaigns, the use of advertising to advocate issue or policy positions or to support or enhance a corporate image or policy preference has a long history in the United States (Paisley, 1981). Such advertising goes by many names, including corporate advocacy advertising, editorial advertising, issue advertising, and nonproduct advertising and has many purposes.

Advertising sponsored by public or private entities and designed to influence public opinion on policy questions has occupied an unusual place in the American political system because it often blurs the line between commercial and political speech. While, on the one hand, the purpose of the advertising can be seen as offering information and viewpoints on a political issue, it is also often the case that such advertising has the ultimate purpose of influencing policy that may have economic implications for the advertiser. Early in this century the courts clearly held that purely commercial speech (or advertising) was not protected by the First Amendment but that editorial advertising could be interpreted as political or ''protected'' speech (Meeske, 1973).

Issue advertising first drew the serious attention of scholars in the mid-1970s when corporate advocacy advertising became salient (Sethi, 1976), primarily as a result of the outspoken and aggressive attempts of Mobil Oil to gain public exposure for its own viewpoint on energy concerns (Crable and Vibbert, 1983). Corporations looked to advocacy advertising for several reasons, including the desire to clarify issues and to respond to perceived adverse criticism in the news media (Meadow, 1981). Such advertising also offers another distinct advantage for the corporate entity, and that is the ability to *control* the content of the message conveyed to the public, thus escaping the gatekeeping function of news media outlets (Salmon et al., 1985).

Most of the research on issue advertising has focused on print advertising, partly because until very recently that has been the dominant channel for such messages. This preference for the print channel was not so much a matter of choice on the part of the corporate message sources, but was due to the unwillingness of broadcast outlets to provide access to issue advertising messages. Unlike the situation with Public Service Announcements (PSAs), where the broadcast media donate time for nonprofit, governmental, and even business entities to provide ''propaganda'' on issues of public concern (Paletz, Pearson, and Willis, 1977), broadcast media have refused to sell time to corporations or other entities to advocate on behalf of public policy issues. Their right to reject such time requests has been upheld in the courts, although some have suggested that such refusals threaten the free marketplace of ideas (Gwyn, 1970; Meeske, 1973).

A good example of a well-developed analysis of corporate advocacy in the print media is Dionisopoulos' (1986) analysis of the strategies used by the nuclear power industry in trying to recapture ''favorable public opinion'' (84) in the aftermath of the Three Mile Island disaster. Meadow (1981) has provided a broader overview by developing a typology of the purposes and categories of nonproduct advertising, although his typology has been criticized for placing too much emphasis on the implied purpose of the message and giving too little recognition to the notion of multiple outcomes and to the notion that issues of fact, value, policy, and control may converge in the ads (Heath and Nelson, 1983).

EFFECTIVENESS OF ISSUE ADVERTISING

Scholars and researchers have also been concerned with the effectiveness of issue advertising. Atkin (1981), in an early review of the effectiveness of mass media information campaigns, points to findings that suggest public information campaigns often have their greatest success in affecting public knowledge levels, and Heath (1988) cites several examples of situations where public opinion and beliefs have been influenced by issue advertising. A few researchers have attempted to test the effectiveness of specific message and source strategies in issue advertising. For instance, a special concern has focused on whether the *source* of the advertising affects audience evaluations. Salmon and his colleagues (Salmon et al., 1985) compared the message effects of an issue advocacy print ad with the presentation of the same message via print news. They concluded that advocacy advertising can be effective and may be as persuasive as news in the presentation of some information. In other research that parallels the findings of the superiority of independent sources in negative political advertising (Garramone, 1985), Hammond (1987) found that nonprofit sources had greater credibility in issue advertising than did those perceived as having a profit motive.

Message characteristics have also been a concern in studies of advertising effects. Interest has often focused on whether rational/logical or emotional appeals work best in public information campaigns. Atkin (1981) summarizes this research with the conclusion that emotional appeals have the "advantage of attracting the interest of indifferent persons and are best suited for broadcast channels, dynamic sources, and affective change" (276). A specific type of emotional appeal, the fear appeal, is frequently employed in public issue campaigns, as one or both sides attempt to convince the public of the dangers of success if the opposition's policy initiative is enacted. Pratkanis and Aronson (1992) note that fear appeals in propaganda messages have proven effective, particularly when the threat is very strong, offers a specific recommendation for overcoming the threat, and seems *doable*. Fear appeals have been found to "play a central role in health campaigns" (Atkin, 1981, 276), which makes such research especially relevant when considering Clinton's health care reform package.

Against this backdrop of potential success for corporate advocacy advertising and the general success of political advertising in political campaigns, it is not surprising that those on both sides of highly visible policy debates might turn to advertising as a way of gaining public support. The NAFTA and health care reform issues provided particularly fertile ground for such political advertising use. They offered, of course, situations that could capitalize on the usual advantages recognized by issue advertising advocates (ability to clarify viewpoints through direct public communication, ability to combat media viewpoints, and ability to control message characteristics). However, the political advertising would occur in a situation much more like a traditional political campaign setting in that the policy at stake would be decided by specific congressional votes on policy legislation. Unlike the molding or remolding of a longterm corporate image or the attempt to shape overall public opinion on an issue of public concern, NAFTA and health care reform would be decided in a finite time span under controlled conditions.

THE ISSUES AT STAKE AND THE ADVERTISING CAMPAIGNS

NAFTA

The North American Free Trade Agreement issue was an important test for the Clinton presidency, coming as it did at the end of the first presidential year after several tough fights on gays in the military and the president's economic package.

NAFTA eliminates most trade barriers between the United States, Canada, and Mexico. Originating in Mexico as a result of an economic crisis in the early 1980s, NAFTA took form in May 1991 when formal negotiations began between the Mexican government and then President Bush. By August 1992, a deal was made. However, by the time NAFTA came to Congress for a vote, it was the fall of 1993 and the president was Bill Clinton.

While any president would like to win majority support for all issues before Congress, NAFTA became a crucial battle for the Clinton administration due to the timing of the vote. Health care reform was at the top of Clinton's wish list. A vote on health care was slated for 1994. Even though winning the vote on NAFTA would not necessarily ensure success of the health care plan, losing the battle on NAFTA might provide negative momentum and hurt the chances for later success in health care legislation. It was politically necessary for the Clinton administration to fight for and win NAFTA.

An easy passage for NAFTA was not guaranteed. Support was divided in Congress and in the public viewpoint. According to a September 16, 1993, *Wall Street Journal*/NBC News Poll, 36 percent of the public was opposed to NAFTA while 25 percent supported it. A large number, 34 percent, felt they did not know enough about the agreement to make a decision. A media battle for NAFTA support ensued in the fall of 1993.

Supporters of NAFTA included the Clinton administration, USA*NAFTA, retired Chrysler Corporation Chairman Lee Iacocca, three former U.S. presidents, and the Mexican government. Neither the Clinton administration nor the three former U.S. presidents were directly involved in the pro-NAFTA advertising campaign. The business-backed group, USA*NAFTA, included member corporations of Citibank, Allied Signal, Mobil, the Automobile Manufacturers Association, Toys R Us, Merrill Lynch, and Coopers & Lybrand. Lee Iacocca became the television pitchman for USA*NAFTA. Opponents of NAFTA included Ross Perot, the Citizen's Trade Campaign, and the AFL-CIO, with Ross Perot as the central figure of the anti-NAFTA campaign. The Citizen's Trade Campaign was a grassroots movement comprised of consumer, labor, family farm, and other organizations. The AFL-CIO labor organization included over 14 million members from eighty-six unions.

The campaign to win support was expensive. Public relations and lobbying efforts to win NAFTA support cost the Mexican government approximately $30 million since 1989. Both sides favored the use of unfiltered media. Their campaigns utilized television commercials, print advertising, talk radio, debates, thirty-minute infomercials, letters, phone calls, and petitions. The three major networks refused to air NAFTA advertising, so the advertising budgets were spent in local markets and on cable. USA*NAFTA spent between $5 and $8 million. The advertising agency of Grunwald, Eskew & Donilon managed the campaign for USA*NAFTA. The AFL-CIO spent approximately $3 million, and Ross Perot spent between $1.5 to $2 million. The anti-NAFTA campaign relied on media consultant Frank Greer, Grunwald's former partner.

The anti-NAFTA campaign took the lead in television advertising, beginning over the Labor Day weekend in 1993. Thirteen states were blitzed, including markets of Springfield, Missouri, St. Louis, and Detroit. The advertising campaign sent the message that NAFTA would hurt the American economy and workers by sending U.S. factories and jobs to other countries. The anti-NAFTA supporters portrayed themselves as the underdogs in the battle.

The pro-NAFTA campaign began its television advertising campaign in the middle of September 1993. It targeted a local market, Washington, D.C., and the national market using the Cable News Network (CNN). The campaign's message was that NAFTA would increase U.S. jobs by creating new markets for U.S. products. The pro-NAFTA supporters countered the opposition's underdog portrayal by noting the extensive campaigning, which required a great deal of money.

After a battle fought through the media, NAFTA passed in Congress and in the public viewpoint. According to a January 1994 Gallup poll, 53 percent of the public supported NAFTA, 38 percent opposed it, and 9 percent had no opinion on NAFTA. The passage of NAFTA was considered a much-needed success for the Clinton administration. It provided a testing ground for the use of political advertising in the battle over public opinion on issues. NAFTA set the stage and provided a positive momentum for the number-one item on President Clinton's wish list, health care reform.

Health Care Reform

The lobbying efforts for the health care reform issue are developing as one of the most costly in our nation's history. Nearly fifty different interest groups are spending an estimated $50 million on television and print ads on the health care issue (Feeney, 1994). The cast of characters participating in the health care debate includes several powerful lobbying groups with impressive resources. The battle lines were drawn early for this heated debate, and each side is gaining strength as negotiations for the issue continue. Groups included in the pro–health care reform side include the Health Care Reform Project, the League of Women Voters, the California Wellness Foundation, the Henry J. Kaiser Family Foundation, and the Democratic National Committee. Groups against the Clinton-proposed plan include the Health Insurance Association of America, the National Restaurant Association, the Project for the Republican Future, and the American Medical Association.

The Health Care Reform Project is a coalition formed to pool the resources of such groups as the American Federation of Labor and the Congress of Industrial Organizations (AFL-CIO), the American Association of Retired Persons (AARP), Consumers Union, and the Children's Defense Fund. The Health Care Reform Project has spent upwards of $5 million on an advertising campaign consisting of ten specific ads. This group's campaign was directed at states whose members of Congress hold key committee seats, such as Ways and Means and Energy and Commerce in the House and the Finance committee in the Senate. Jerry Shea, head of AFL-CIO employee benefits, has argued that, although difficult to trace because of the number of coalitions and groups formed to pool resources, about $10 million in union resources have been dedicated to the health care reform issue (Salwen, 1994).

In addition to contributing to the health care reform project, AARP used direct mail to reach a million of its constituents and ran print ads that were produced by W. B. Doner & Co. of Baltimore (Colford, 1994). The National Association for the Advancement of Colored People also contributed to the proreform side with radio ads that targeted the southern states of Alabama, South Carolina, and Louisiana. Their ads, produced by McKinney & McDowell and Chlopak Leonard Schechter and Associates, endorsed universal coverage and shared responsibility (Colford, 1994).

The Henry J. Kaiser Family Foundation teamed up with the League of Women Voters in a $4.1 million campaign that included town hall meetings in addition to television and print ads (Toner, 1994). The Kaiser Foundation also paired with the California Wellness Foundation for a campaign targeting issues specific to California.

The Democratic National Committee has produced thirteen television ads. Eight of their ads are two-minute public address format ads in which Clinton is shown sitting at his desk addressing the public about American public policy. The ads were produced to counter the fact that the major networks said that they would not cover a public address speech about health care reform.

Perhaps the most controversial of all the ad campaigns is the Health Insurance Association of America's Harry and Louise ads. In a series of ads meant to depict the average American couple, Harry and Louise illustrate the pitfalls of Clinton's health care plan. The Health Insurance Association of America, a trade group that represents more than 300 health insurance companies, spent $10.5

million in 1993 and an additional $3.5 million in the first two months of 1994 to identify their points of disagreement with the Clinton plan: mandatory insurance through state alliances and insurance premium price caps (Toner, 1994).

The National Restaurant Association has spent an estimated $500,000 to oppose the health care reform legislation. Their ad campaign hit twelve states and the Washington, D.C., area. The Federation of Health Care Systems spent an estimated $400,000 to show their ad campaign, which ran on CNN during August 1994. Two additional groups on this side of the issue are the American Medical Association (AMA) and The Project for the Republican Future, which is headed by former Bush administration official William Kristol. The AMA print campaign weighs in at about $1.6 million, an investment that is the group's largest since fighting Medicare almost thirty years ago (Span, 1994). In October 1994, the AMA made the decision to begin a $500,000 advertising campaign. The AMA's campaign questions whether doctors will take a back seat to bureaucrats in the proposed health care reform legislation. The Project for the Republican Future, which aired their ad on CNN and in five major markets, emotionally argues that lives will be in danger under the proposed Clinton plan.

In addition to the pro/con debate, the Pharmaceutical Manufacturers Association (PMA) has been running ads that extol their work. The ads are neither for reform nor against reform, yet the PMA has invested $13 million in their nationwide ad campaign (Span, 1994).

Confusion about the plan remains high a year from its introduction. The informational campaign about the planned legislation, mainly grass roots, failed miserably compared to the barrage of information in the advertising arena. The purpose of this chapter is to explore the trends in the NAFTA and health care reform advertising.

METHODOLOGY

Public policy televised ads for the issues of NAFTA and health care reform legislation were explored by combining content analysis and interpretive analysis of all the spots that were available from the Political Commercial Archive at the University of Oklahoma. The ad sample consisted of seventy-two ads; nine were NAFTA ads and sixty-three were health care reform ads. Ads were also classified by the policy position that the ad advocated. "For the issue" ads are ads that support Clinton's policy on the issue. "Against the issue" ads were classified as those ads that are against Clinton's proposal for the issue. "Informational" ads were ads that did not take a specific pro/con stance but instead provided information about the issue. The content analysis was designed to analyze the ads in terms of appeals and proofs, production techniques, values, and strategies. Rokeach's (1971) value dimensions were used to identify the types of values that are appealed to in the ads. Using Holsti's formula (North et al., 1963), intercoder reliability between the two

Table 5.1
Policy Ads Content Analysis Results

	Health care reform (n=63)	NAFTA (n=9)
Position		
For the issue	49%	78%
Against the issue	27%	22%
Informational	24%	0%
Appearances or speaking role		
Bill Clinton	22%	22%
Hillary Clinton	2%	0%
Other famous people	6%	44%
Production techniques		
Still pictures	43%	22%
Moving or live seeming video	81%	89%
Music	67%	67%
Head-on style	40%	22%
Graphics	91%	78%
Issue Dramatization	24%	11%
Testimonial/Endorsement ad	30%	44%
Voice-over	82%	78%
Male	64%	78%
Female	18%	0%
Appeals	70%	56%
Dominant Appeal		
Emotional	62%	33%
Logical	22%	33%
Ethical	16%	33%
Proofs		
Statistics	33%	67%
Experts	33%	67%
Past presidents	2%	22%
Newspapers/Journals	13%	11%
Call for Action		
Call your congressman	62%	33%
give money	2%	0%
aimed at congressperson's vote	3%	0%
Does the ad offer a solution?	22%	0%
Is the ad a response ad?	13%	0%

trained graduate student coders averaged +.94 across all categories with a range of +.80 to +1.00.

ANALYSIS OF THE ADS

The content analysis of the NAFTA and health care reform advertisements points to some interesting results. Table 5.1 compares the results of the health care reform ads to the NAFTA ads. Comparison shows several interesting similarities and differences between the two types of ads. The findings regarding the ratio of pro to con spots reveals that ads "for the issue" outnumber ads "against the issue" by a ratio of 2 to 1: thirty-eight spots "for the issue" and nineteen spots "against the issue." Also of interest is the percent of the ads that were "against the issue." In both areas under analysis, the ads "against the issue" comprise about one-quarter of the total ads for the particular issue; 27 percent for health care reform and 22 percent for NAFTA. Table 5.1 shows the percent of ads that were "for the issue," "against the issue," and "informational." The health care reform ads against the proposed presidential plan result from five organizations. These organizations include Coalition for Health Insurance Choices, Citizens for a Sound Economy, Empower America, Health Care Reform Offer, and American Council for Health Care Reform, whereas the anti-NAFTA ads were sponsored by the AFL-CIO.

The typical strategy for the anti-Clinton proposed health care reform ads is to address the points of disagreement that the sponsoring organization has with the Clinton plan. For example, the Harry and Louise ads produced under the Coalition for Health Insurance Choices and the Health Insurance Association of America focus their ads on the spending caps built into the plan. Suggesting that "there's got to be a better way" than the Clinton plan, the ads use a fear appeal to point out that the government may run out of money to treat patients if the plan is not run effectively. Similarly, the Empower America ad called "EKG" uses a fear appeal in both verbal and visual form. Their ad reads as follows:

Bill Clinton Wants to Socialize Health Care.

Small Business Will Pay the Bill.

The Largest Government Bureaucracy in History.

The Bureaucracy Will Decide.

The Bureaucracy Will Never See You.

The Bureaucracy Will Never Examine You.

Never Talk To You.

Never Even See You.

Limit Your Choice of Doctors.

The Bureaucracy will Dictate.

The Bureaucracy will Decide.

You Will Lose Choice and Control.

It's Your Health Care They're Socializing.

The above script is read aloud and printed on the screen while the sounds of a heartbeat and the visual line of an EKG monitor appear on the screen. The ad ends with the statement "It's Your Health Care They're Socializing" as the EKG line goes flat, implying that death will result from the implementation of the Clinton proposed plan.

The remaining 73 percent of the health care reform ads includes 49 percent (n = 31) "for the issue" ads and 24 percent (n = 15) "informational" ads. This compares with 78 percent (n = 7) of the NAFTA ads that were "for the issue." None of the NAFTA ads were coded as "informational."

Ads that were pro-NAFTA were sponsored by USA*NAFTA and the Mexican Business Council. The strategy for the pro-NAFTA ads sponsored by USA*NAFTA was to establish credibility for support of NAFTA. This is evidenced by the use of a large number of famous Americans who support NAFTA. One strategy that was used for the NAFTA ads that was not used to the same magnitude in the health care spots was the use of famous people to endorse or discredit the issue. Every living former president, all Nobel Prize–winning American economists, Lee Iacocca, Bill Gates, Colin Powell, and all secretaries-of-state were used as supporters of NAFTA in an attempt to establish credibility for the issue. While supporters for NAFTA included members listed above, opponents of NAFTA used in the USA*NAFTA spots included Pat Buchanan, Ross Perot, Jesse Jackson, and Jerry Brown. Buchanan, Perot, Jackson, and Brown were used in such a way that suggested that alignment with them on any issue is undesirable, thus, NAFTA must be a good thing.

The Mexican Business Council's ads attempted to show a modern Mexico, one with an advanced technology prepared to offer fertile ground for America. The argument for the Mexican Business Council ads was "Together We're Stronger," suggesting that Mexico and the United States will each experience growth and strength with NAFTA.

An additional interesting result of the content analysis of the ads regarding both issues is the use of Bill or Hillary Clinton. For both NAFTA and health care reform ads, the president appeared or spoke in 22 percent of the total ads. Table 5.2, which breaks down the results of the content analysis by stance on the issue (either pro, con, or informational) shows that neither the president nor his wife appeared in any of the "informational" or "against the issue" ads. Since it is common for advertisements in candidate campaigns to use the opposing candidate's words or image in some way, usually negatively, this result is somewhat surprising. It is also surprising that Hillary Clinton is used in only 3 percent of the health care reform ads. Hillary's position as head of the Health-care Reform Task Force would lead one to expect that she would be a greater presence in the health care reform ads. The ad that Hillary does appear in is a Democratic National Committee–sponsored ad entitled "Fighting for

Table 5.2
Position Breakdown of Policy Ads

Issue	Pro	Con	Informational
Health Care Reform	n=31	n=17	n=15
NAFTA	n= 7	n= 2	
Appearances or speaking role			
Bill Clinton	42%	0%	0%
Hillary Clinton	3%	0%	0%
Other famous people	16%	11%	0%
Production techniques			
Still pictures	32%	47%	53%
Moving or live-seeming video	90%	84%	60%
Music	61%	58%	93%
Head-on style	37%	37%	40%
Graphics	87%	95%	87%
Issue Dramatization	16%	37%	20%
Testimonial/Endorsement ad	37%	37%	13%
Voice-over	64%	100%	94%
Male	58%	95%	47%
Female	8%	5%	47%
Appeals			
Emotion or Fear	47%	95%	87%
Dominant Appeal			
Emotional	37%	90%	73%
Logical	29%	10%	27%
Ethical	34%	0%	0%
Proofs			
Statistics	29%	47%	47%
Experts	42%	16%	53%
Past presidents	8%	0%	0%
Newspapers/Journals	16%	5%	13%
Call for action			
Call your congressman	61%	79%	27%
give money	3%	0%	0%
aimed at congressperson's vote	0%	11%	0%
Does the ad offer a solution?	16%	42%	0%
Is the ad a response ad?	21%	0%	0%

Seniors.'' Hillary is shown briefly during two portions of the ad; first on a podium next to the president and then in a receiving line shaking hands with some older members of the audience. Perhaps this ''presidential'' absence was due to the declining general popularity of Clinton as the health care issue progressed.

Production Techniques

Production techniques used in the ads are fairly similar. Table 5.1 identifies the percent of the ads for each issue that uses a particular production technique. Of particular note is the high percentage of the health care ads that use still pictures. Forty-three percent of the health care ads used still pictures, as compared to 22 percent of the NAFTA spots. A breakdown (Table 5.2) of the production techniques used by position of the ad (pro, con, informational) reveals that informational ads relied more on still pictures than either pro or con ads.

Ads for both issues used a great deal of moving or live-seeming video, music, graphics, and voice-overs. Although the percent of voice-overs used in the ads is nearly the same, 82 percent for health care reform and 78 percent for NAFTA, only the health care reform ads employ the voice of a woman. Of the 82 percent of the health care ads that use a voice-over, 18 percent is female voice-over and 64 percent is male voice-over. The breakdown of voice-over use by ad position provided in Table 5.2 shows even greater disparity in the use of a female voice. Of the 64 percent of the pro ads that employ a voice-over, 58 percent is male voice-over and 8 percent is female voice-over. All of the con ads used a voice-over, and only 5 percent were the voice of a woman. When the same analysis is applied to the "informational" ads, the results change dramatically. Of the 94 percent of the "informational" ads that have a voice-over, 47 percent are female and 47 percent are male. This result indicates that female voice-overs were used sparingly in ads that were attempting to persuade the audience either positively or negatively toward a particular issue. When the ad was not attempting to persuade, but rather to inform, the use of female voice-over was equal to that of male voice-over. While testimonial or endorsement ads were used more frequently in the area of NAFTA, issue dramatization ads were used more during health care reform ads. The "against the issue" side of health care reform used dramatizations to show what they believed the health care situation would look like under Clinton's plan. The health care reform project decided to counter some of the drama created by their opposition in a dramatic ad of their own entitled "Rain." In "Rain," a man is shown standing in a rain storm as thunder and lightning pound and illuminate the area around him. The man is rescued by a car driving by, saving him from being "left out in the cold." The implication of the ad is that the Clinton-proposed plan will rescue those that are currently left out in the cold, unprotected by the current health insurance system.

Appeals

The appeals used in the ads and the subsequent proofs supplied for some of the appeals reveal the greatest difference for the two types of ads. Although both types of ads rely on some form of emotion or fear appeal in over half the ads, 70 percent for health care reform and 56 percent for NAFTA, the dominant type of Aristotelean appeal in health care reform ads are emotional (62%). Thus, the majority of the health care reform ads attempt to persuade the viewer by using a dominant emotional appeal, as compared to 22 percent of the ads using a dominant logical appeal and 16 percent using a dominant ethical appeal. Although over half of the NAFTA ads also used an emotion or fear appeal, only one-third of the ads coded had a dominant emotional appeal. The dominant appeal used in the NAFTA ads was evenly split between emotional, logical, and ethical appeals, each dominant in one-third of the ads.

Because the dominant appeals used in the two types of ads differ a great deal, it is not surprising that the types of proof used in the ads also differ. One-third of the health care reform ads used either statistics or experts as a form of proof for the claims in the ads, whereas two-thirds of the NAFTA ads relied on statistics or experts to support the claims in the ads. Both issues relied on newspapers or journals as a source of support for the appeal made in the ad. Newspapers or journals were used as supporting evidence in 13 percent of the health care reform ads and 11 percent of the NAFTA ads. USA*NAFTA used the power in numbers strategy by using past presidents to support the argument for NAFTA. Reference to past presidents was used in 22 percent of the NAFTA spots and 2 percent of the health care spots.

When appeal strategies of the ads are analyzed by position of the policy ad, an interesting development occurs. ''Informational'' ads and ads ''against the issue'' use emotion or fear appeals in 87 percent and 95 percent of their ads, respectively. The percent of ''for the issue'' ads that use emotion or fear appeals is not nearly as large (47%) as ''informational'' or ''against the issue'' ads. The dominant appeal used in the ads is also very different depending upon the stance of the ad. Of the ads ''against the issue,'' 90 percent used an emotional appeal as the dominant form of appeal. Logical appeals were used in 10 percent of the ads ''against the issue.'' The ''informational'' ads are similar to the ads ''against the issue'' in that they do not use an ethical appeal as the dominant appeal in any of the ads. For the ''informational'' ads, 73 percent used a dominant emotional appeal and 27 percent used a dominant logical appeal. The emotional nature of the ''informational'' ads is most commonly used in such a way as to stress that this issue is too important to your family for you to be unaware of the facts. The pro ads, or ads ''for the issue,'' use all three appeals in their ads. Emotional appeals are dominant in 37 percent of the pro ads, while logical appeals constitute the dominant appeal in 29 percent of the ads, and ethical appeals dominate in 34 percent of the ads.

A breakdown of proofs used in the ads based on the position the ad takes reveals that ads ''against the issue'' use experts a lot less frequently than either ads ''for the issue'' or ''informational'' ads. Ads ''against the issue'' relied on experts in 16 percent of the ads as compared to 42 percent for ads ''for the issue'' and 53 percent for ''informational'' ads. Despite failing to use an ethical appeal, statistics were used in ads ''against the issue'' and ''informational'' ads at a greater percentage than ads "for the issue," 47 percent for both "informational" and ads "against the issue" and 29 percent for ads "for the issue."

Call for Action

It is clear that with 62 percent of the health care reform ads asking the viewers to call their congressperson, the strategy was to send Congress a message. This strategy was also used in 33 percent of the NAFTA ads. Seventy-nine percent of the ads "against the issue" asked the viewer to call his or her congressperson, compared to 61 percent of the ads "for the issue."

Very few of the ads asked the viewer to do anything else; 2 percent of the health care reform ads asked the viewer to send money to the interest group, and 3 percent of the health care reform ads were aimed at a congressperson's vote. However, all the ads that were coded as "aimed at a congressperson's vote" were on the "against the issue" side; comprising 11 percent of the "against the issue" ads. Clearly, a strategy of the ads that were "against the issue" was to bypass the ordinary viewer and target the congressperson.

Solution/Response

Of the ads that were "against the issue," 42 percent were coded as providing some form of solution to the issue. None of the anti-NAFTA ads were coded as providing a solution to the proposed legislation. This was different for the health care reform ads. Nearly half (eight of seventeen) of the anti–Clinton proposed health care reform ads offered some alternative solution to the plan.

It also appears from the results that the "for the issue" side was put on the defensive during the rivaling ad campaigns. None of the "informational" or "against the issue" ads were coded as ads that appear to be in response to another ad. Twenty-one percent of the "for the issue" ads were coded as response ads.

Values

A group of Rokeach's value dimensions was also used as a mode of comparison for the two types of ads. Rokeach (1971, 70) argued that these values are among those terminal values that "transcend and dynamically determine" attitudes. Values coded include freedom, equality, family security, happiness, a comfortable life, wisdom, self-respect, and social recognition. The results shown in Table 5.3 indicate that health care reform ads were more likely to appeal to all of the values. Health care reform ads were most likely to appeal to wisdom (68%), equality (65%), and self-respect (64%). In both "for the issue" ads and "against the issue" ads, wisdom was used in a high percentage of the ads; 68 percent to 74 percent, respectively. These results suggest that logical appeals to wisdom of the viewer were made in the ads. A typical strategy in the ads was

Table 5.3
Rokeach's Value Dimensions in Health Care Ads and NAFTA

American values	Health care reform		NAFTA
Freedom	51%		33%
Equality	65%		11%
Family security	43%		0%
Happiness	24%		11%
A comfortable life	45%		44%
Wisdom	68%		56%
Self-respect	64%		56%
Social recognition	51%		44%

American values	Pro	Con	Informational
Freedom	55%	47%	33%
Equality	61%	53%	60%
Family security	32%	16%	80%
Happiness	16%	21%	40%
A comfortable life	47%	26%	60%
Wisdom	68%	74%	53%
Self-respect	68%	47%	67%
Social recognition	55%	42%	47%

to argue that to agree with the claims in the ads is the only "smart thing" for the viewer to do.

Of the three ad types, "informational" ads resulted in the greatest percent of use of any one of Rokeach's dimensions. In 80 percent of the "informational" ads about health care reform, a concern for family security was addressed or implied. For example, the Pharmaceuticals Research and Manufacturers Association ad entitled "Pamela and Claudia" shows a researcher searching for a cure for breast cancer and a mother afflicted by the disease. A boy is shown in the background of the ad as the mother watches him play. The ad suggests that Pharmaceuticals Research and Manufacturers Association is responsible for 90 percent of the research discoveries that help keep families together.

DISCUSSION

The results of the content analysis and interpretive analysis are interesting when one looks at the change in public opinion poll results that address NAFTA and Clinton's health care reform proposal.

Since appearing on Gallup's "Most Important Problem" list at the end of 1990 with a 1 percent rating, health care has skyrocketed into salience. From January 1992 to January 1993, the percent of Americans listing health care as the "most important problem today" jumped from 6 percent to 18 percent. By September 1993, health care became the second most important issue facing more than one out of four Americans (28%), second only to the economy. Thus, all the attention that health care reform received during the presidential election of 1992 and the debates that have ensued since the Clinton plan was unveiled have increased the salience of the issue dramatically.

The release of Clinton's plan to revamp the health care system did not alleviate the concern that the public has about health care. A September 1993 Gallup Poll conducted shortly after the release of the health care plan showed that 59 percent of those polled supported the plan and 33 percent opposed the plan.

Despite overall support for the plan, several aspects of the plan held very weak support. For example, 84 percent of those polled said that Clinton's plan to finance the health bill would not be adequate and that other sources of funding would be needed. Moreover, 65 percent of those polled thought that the plan would create an additional government bureaucracy that would have too much control over health care. These specific points of concern about the plan were used in the Health Insurance Association of America's ad campaign to raise doubts about the Clinton plan. Shortly after the HIAA's ad campaign began, support for the Clinton plan dropped to 45 percent and opposition was up to 45 percent, an even split. Thus, the strategy of the HIAA appears to play on the skepticism that surrounded the Clinton plan.

Skepticism and doubt were also part of the public opinion about NAFTA. In August 1993, Gallup reported that support for NAFTA was at 41 percent and that opposition was at 44 percent. Once again, questions geared toward the aspects of NAFTA revealed some areas of cynicism. Over two-thirds of the public (68%) thought that the United States would lose jobs to Mexico, and only 22 percent thought that the United States would acquire more jobs.

The pro-NAFTA ad campaign sponsored by USA*NAFTA started in October 1993, shortly before the Gore-Perot debate on NAFTA. The Mexican Business Council was also running ads in October and November of 1993. Their ads mentioned the fact that Mexico spends $41 billion on U.S. goods, is the fastest growing U.S. importer, and spends more per person on U.S. goods than Japan or Europe. By early November, just prior to the debate, evidence showed that the pro-NAFTA arguments were winning public support. Those who thought that Mexico would benefit from more jobs was down to 47 percent (from 67% in September) and those who thought the United States would receive more jobs was up to 46 percent from 22 percent in September. But even after an astounding victory for NAFTA in Congress, public support for NAFTA was split, 43 percent in favor and 41 percent in opposition (Gallup, November 25, 1993). By January 1994, the poll results regarding NAFTA began to swing, indicating that the advertising may have had a positive effect. The approval rating for NAFTA jumped to 53 percent and the disapproval rating was down to 38 percent.

What these results reveal is that the public was split on these two important public policy issues and that there were particular aspects of the issues that made the public skeptical. It is not surprising that the NAFTA and health care reform ads used the points of skepticism to their advantage. Neither side of either issue offered comparison of the proposed legislation and the alternative solution. Although 42 percent of the anti–health care reform ads offered an alternative solution to Clinton's plan, the ads did not reveal how the alternative solution would work or how the alternative solution compared specifically to the Clinton plan. Thus, it appears that the ads did little in the way of helping to inform the public about the issue. Instead, the ads were all-out attempts to persuade the public.

Consistent with findings from previous research on public policy advertising, a great deal of emotion and fear appeals were used in an attempt to persuade the public. Statistics and experts were occasionally used in the ads, but the major battles were fought on emotional grounds. This strategy, used more often in the opposition ads than in the support ads, appears to have worked, since the poll results indicate that neither issue has gained much in the way of increased approval ratings. As is the case with negative ads in political campaigns, emotion and negative claims seem to be effective in policy advertising.

What is surprising about the health care ads and the NAFTA ads is the virtual nonexistence of the two individuals that were a real force on the issues, Al Gore for NAFTA and Hillary Clinton for health care reform. Despite a very successful televised debate with Ross Perot on NAFTA, Gore was not used in the pro-NAFTA ads. Hillary, head of the Health Care Reform Task Force, was only used in one ad and her appearance in that ad was nonsubstantial. Considering that Mrs. Clinton was used by the administration in many other channels, it is surprising that she was not used in televised ads. Could these two individuals have helped push the president's agenda via advertising?

Also worthy of discussion is the lack of the use of women in voice-overs by the pro and con sides of the issue. The virtual nonexistence of a female voice-over in the ads suggests that a female voice is not perceived as persuasive. It is surprising that the pro–health care reform side did not use a female voice more, particularly with the recent attention to women's health needs. Perhaps a female voice-over would prove more trustworthy when used with such an emotional issue as health care.

The interplay between the pro and con sides of the health care reform debate is also noteworthy. The "against the issue" side used the strategy of attacking the claims of the pro-Clinton side. This strategy put the "for the issue" side at a disadvantage and required that they spend money and time responding to the attacks. The response ads comprised nearly one in four of the health care ads. With all the attacks and refutations that entered the policy arena, it is surprising that no systematic checks on the truth of the claims in the ads were made. It has become customary for media sources to dissect the contents of candidate-sponsored political ads, but that analysis seems less apparent when the ads are about public policy.

This analysis of the health care reform and NAFTA issue advertising raises many questions about the effects of the ads on the public. Additional research in this area should be done to measure whether issue advertising helps viewers to learn about the issues, shapes or reaffirms public opinion, or makes the viewer become skeptical. Since research on ads has found that ads have a great potential to influence votes in candidate ads and opinions in public policy ads, a systematic check on the claims in the ads should be made so that the public will be deciding policy based on accurate information.

Regardless, however, of the trends in academic research on such issues, it is clear that public policy proponents and opponents have found a direct and highly visible battleground for influencing public opinion. Political advertising on policy issues will surely continue to play an important role in the American policy process.

REFERENCES

Arndt, M. 1993. "NAFTA Foes Holding Their Own in Battle." *Chicago Tribune,* September 21, C1–2.
Atkin, Charles K. 1981. "Mass Media Information Campaign Effectiveness." In *Public Communication Campaigns,* ed. Ronald E. Rice and William J. Paisley (pp. 265–79). Beverly Hills, Calif.: Sage.
Cloud, D.S. 1993. "The History of the Deal." *Congressional Quarterly,* November 20, 3,180.
Colford, Steven W. 1994. "Millions for Healthcare." *Advertising Age,* August 15.
Crable, Richard E. and Steven L. Vibbert. 1983. "Mobil's Epideictic Advocacy: 'Observations' of Prometheus-Bound." *Communication Monographs* 50, 380–94.
Dionisopoulos, George. 1986. "Corporate Advocacy Advertising as Political Communication." In *New Perspectives on Political Advertising,* ed. Lynda L. Kaid, Dan Nimmo, and K. R. Sanders (pp. 82–106). Carbondale: Southern Illinois University Press.
Fenney, S. 1994. "Polls: Few People Trust DC to Fix Health Care." *Dallas Morning News,* August 5, 1A, 22A.
Garramone, Gina M. 1985. "Effects of Negative Political Advertising: The Role of Sponsor and Rebuttal." *Journal of Broadcasting and Electronic Media* 29, 147–59.
Goldman, Kevin. 1993. "NAFTA Friends, Foes Blitz Public With Ads." *Wall Street Journal,* September 16, B6.
Gwyn, Robert J. 1970. "Opinion Advertising and the Free Market of Ideas." *Public Opinion Quarterly* 34, 246–55.
Hammond, S. L. 1987. "Health Advertising: The Credibility of Organizational Sources." In *Communication Yearbook 10,* ed. Margaret L. McLaughlin (pp. 613–28). Newbury Park, Calif.: Sage.
"Health Care: Clinton Supports Mitchell and Gephardt Plans." 1994. *Hotline Weekly,* August 8.
Heath, Robert L. 1988. "The Rhetoric of Issue Advertising: A Rationale, a Case Study, a Critical Perspective—and More." *Central States Speech Journal* 39(2), 99–109.
——— and Richard A. Nelson. 1983. "An Exchange on Corporate Advertising." *Journal of Communication* 30(4): 114–18.
Kamber, Victor. 1993–1994. "How to Win and Really Lose in Washington." *Public Relations Quarterly* 38(4): 5–7.

Meadow, Robert G. 1981. "The Political Dimensions of Nonproduct Advertising." *Journal of Communication* 31(3): 69–82.

Meeske, M. D. 1973. "Editorial Advertising: A New Form of Free Speech." *Free Speech Yearbook* 12, 51–59.

North, Robert C., O. Holsti, M. G. Zaninovich, and D. A. Zinnes. 1963. *Content Analysis: A Handbook with Applications for the Study of International Crisis.* Evanston, Ill.: Northwestern University Press.

"Opinion of Clinton Administration's First-Year Achievements." 1994. *The Gallup Poll Monthly* (January): 10–11.

Paisley, William J. 1981. "Public Communication Campaigns: The American Experience." In *Public Communication Campaigns,* ed. Ronald E. Rice and William J. Paisley (pp. 15–40). Beverly Hills, Calif.: Sage.

Paletz, David, Roberta E. Pearson, and Donald L. Willis. 1977. *Politics in Public Service Advertising on Television.* New York: Praeger.

Pratkanis, Anthony and Elliot Aronson. 1992. *Age of Propaganda.* New York: W. H. Freeman Co.

Priest, Dana. 1994. "Health Groups Launch Ad Blitzes Criticizing Increased Federal Role." *Washington Post,* January 25, 8A.

Rokeach, Milton. 1971. "Persuasion that Persists." *Psychology Today* (September): 68–71, 92.

Salmon, Charles T., Leonard N. Reid, James Pokrywczynski, and Robert W. Willett. 1985. "The Effectiveness of Advocacy Advertising Relative to News Coverage." *Communication Research* 12, 546–67.

Salwen, Kevin G. 1994. "Unions Consider How to Spend Funds in Drive for Health-Care Reform." *Wall Street Journal,* February 22, 22A.

Sethi, Suresh P. 1976. *Advocacy Advertising and Large Corporations.* Lexington, Mass.: D. C. Heath.

Span, Paula. 1994. "Ad Ventures in Health Care: Supporters and Opponents of President's Plan Slug It Out in the Media." *Washington Post,* January 31, 1D.

Toner, Robin. 1994. "Ads are Potent Weapon in Health Care Struggle." *New York Times,* February 1, 14A.

Chapter Six

The Compromising Clinton: Images of Failure, A Record of Success

Rita K. Whillock

There is a story reporters frequently tell that provides anecdotal evidence for the power of images to shape the news. According to the story, a reporter was assigned to cover President Ronald Reagan's media tour of child care facilities. The reporter, rather than merely covering the event, informed the audience of Reagan's poor record on child care and child welfare issues. After the story aired, Reagan aide Michael Deaver congratulated the reporter for an excellent job. The reporter was dumbstruck. "Didn't you hear the story?" "Yeah," said Deaver, "but the pictures were great!"

The contrast between the record of an event and the image the media conveys of that event has been the subject of political anecdotes for years. Underlying the humor, however, are serious issues for those who study political communication. Do the images of an event overpower the record of that event? Are people persuaded by these images? What is the role of the press in selecting and magnifying such images? How do images affect what we believe?

Scholars who investigate these issues overwhelmingly conclude that images of people and events are compelling, stimulating interest and increasing recall (Hart, 1994; Abramson, Arterton, and Orren, 1988; Altheide, 1985; Berman and Kitch, 1986). Images are important, in part, because they affect a person's perceived credibility. This may account for studies that indicate voters rank personal characteristics (or character traits) as important to their political decisions (e.g., Conover and Feldman, 1989; Graber, 1988). The overwhelming research in this area leads researchers to conclude that "the politician's ability to govern is increasingly intertwined with his or her public image" (Ansolabehere, Behr, and Iyengar, 1993). Given this perspective, it is little wonder that television, a major repository for images, is the preferred medium of news for most Americans. Seven in ten Americans—regardless of age, income level, or educational background—say television provides most of their news information (Roper, 1993; Graber, 1988). Most certainly, televised images with their repetition and dramatic effect make an impression on voters.

Because of the power of images—of personally "seeing" events—television has become a powerful medium of political persuasion. Noted media expert Tony Schwartz (1994) uses a slightly different version of the old adage when he says that for audiences today "believing is seeing." People tend to believe things they see for themselves, whether in person or on the television screen. As a result, Rod Hart (1994) argues that television "encourages an arrogance of the eye" (61). What we see, we believe. A 1993 Roper study supports Hart's assessment: "In the event [the public] heard conflicting news reports on each of the various media, a majority (56%) would believe the television account over the newspaper (22%), radio (7%) and magazine reports (4%)" (Roper, 1993, 3). Clearly, people prefer a visual medium with "self-authenticating" pictures.

Yet for all the importance scholars attach to images, the public pays little attention to the way media images can be manipulated, whether intentionally or not, or for what purpose. Thomas Patterson (1994) argues that, in fact, the way news organizations select and cover news can skew the public's interpretations of events. News organizations inherently look for a story that is dramatic or appealing. That alone is nothing particularly new to the field of journalism. According to Patterson, however, the drama captured in today's headlines is more likely to be found in stories about strategy. Descriptions of a news event are often the wallpapering behind the strategy story. He argues that when the press covers a story with such strategy emphasis they fail to adequately report the substance of what was said or done. Moreover, the public begins to question the motives of the players rather than focus on their actions. No wonder researchers have discovered that people who receive political information from television news sources (remember that is seven out of ten of us) are increasingly cynical about politics (e.g., Robinson, 1975, 101).

When we evaluate the images of the president, this climate of cynicism must be taken into account. I do not mean to argue that people are completely susceptible to what they are told by the media, but they are cynical when it comes to accepting good news about a person they once vilified. In this chapter, I have been asked to evaluate the emerging image of the Clinton presidency. What is it that Americans have come to see in Bill Clinton? Is he a "New Democrat," and if so, what does that mean? Did he keep faith in his word to the American people? Has he delivered on campaign promises?

Depending on what you know and where you turn for information, the answers to these questions can be quite different. Moreover, I should add that we should not accept any of these images as historically fixed. Few people recall, for example, that Ronald Reagan entered office with one of the lowest approval rates of any president in recent history. Today, it is his image as a strong and successful leader that dominates Americans' image of him. Similarly, we cannot forget that just after the Gulf War, President Bush had one of the highest approval ratings in history. Yet he was unable to sustain those favorable images in his quest to retain the presidency in the 1992 election. With the notation that images are fluid, this chapter examines the Clinton image. Based on my assessment of the news coverage during Clinton's first two years in office, I argue that the images of Clinton show a failed and struggling president. The record of his legislative accomplishments, however, paints quite a different picture.

PRESUMPTIONS OF SUCCESS

Two presidents are notable for their media skills: Kennedy and Reagan. Both seemed comfortable in front of the camera. Each of them developed personalities that made them more interesting and more human to the camera. While Kennedy is immortalized for his rhetorical style, Reagan's success has often been attributed to his media style. As the only two-term president since Eisenhower, and the only president to be reelected in the television era, Reagan was a tough act for any president to follow. Bush's major weakness may have been that he could not fill the media void left by his predecessor.

Many people believed Clinton had the potential to set a new standard for media handling. He entered office as the first president to be raised in the age of television. His media-age predecessors—Kennedy through Bush—were products of the radio era. People wondered if Clinton would use the media differently, if he would learn to capitalize on more visual forms of persuasion.

In the past, Clinton demonstrated a degree of media prowess, particularly in his ability to overcome negative images left from his devastating performance at the 1988 Democratic National Convention. He was able to laugh at himself. In fact, many argue that his saxophone playing, relaxed performance on the "Johnny Carson Show" in 1988 saved his political career.

Clinton seemed to understand the power of images. During the 1992 presidential campaign, Bill Clinton was depicted as a young and vigorous leader. His campaign worked to draw favorable comparisons to John F. Kennedy. Certainly, a campaign video used widely during the campaign showing a young Clinton shaking hands with President Kennedy helped link these perceptions. Both were young leaders. Both were depicted as members of a "new generation" coming to political power. In fact, this link to Kennedy may have helped him overcome the infidelity issue raised by the Gennifer Flowers story. Few people thought Kennedy's infidelity interfered with his ability to govern the nation (Whillock, 1994a). Unlike Gary Hart, the infidelity issue did not scare voters away from Clinton.

Similarly, Clinton demonstrated skill in controlling his image in a variety of media formats (e.g., Whillock, 1994a). He handled public forums well, seeming relaxed and comfortable when asked direct questions by audience members. He played well with the MTV crowd. In a slightly more relaxed version of his Carson-show appearance, Clinton's performance as a saxophone player in sunglasses on the "Arsenio Live" show furnished images that helped a younger audience explore another aspect of his demeanor. Early in the primary season when his campaign seemed gasping for its last breath after breaking stories of infidelity and draft dodging, Clinton found a way to make a compelling case to the American people. He broke with tradition by addressing serious news issues through alternate media such as "60 Minutes." Unlike the press conference format where the candidate's statements are reduced to eight-second sound bites, Clinton demonstrated an ability to fit the message to the medium. The "60 Minutes" format, for example, provided ample time for the Clintons to make their case to the public.

Clinton's media skill was also demonstrated during the general election period. He performed well in each of the presidential debates, handling a variety of formats with skill. He was particularly effective in more relaxed, unstructured formats.

Importantly, throughout the campaign Clinton played well in media interviews with local reporters. He made even better impressions on members of the public who heard him speak or watched him interact with other citizens on call-in shows.

Clinton seemed to be developing a powerful media instinct during the campaign. Yet Clinton never trusted the national press. They were kind to him when he made his initial announcement to run. But he also felt that they abandoned him when things got rough during the opening months of the campaign. This explains, in part, why the Clinton campaign developed an alternate media strategy during what insiders called "the dark days" of the campaign. The strategy was to bypass the national press altogether. He used narrowcasting rather than broadcasting. He chose media that would allow him access to specific audiences in particular locations. He spoke to the needs of local communities in town hall meetings where he met face to face with citizens, not national reporters. He made appearances on MTV and found himself in discussions with people on popular talk shows. This strategy proved successful in courting voters. However, Clinton's media handling isolated the national press, in effect preventing them from getting the stories they needed to maintain their prestige.

The result was that hostility dominated the administration's relationship with the national press as Clinton took office. Veteran reporter Ann Compton said, "I've only covered [the White House] under five presidents, but this is the only one who did everything in his power to go around, over, under, and away from the White House press corps" (Compton, cited in Vanocur, 1994).

Clinton's relationship and ability to work with the national press is important. It profoundly affected his first term in office. As Brit Hume, ABC news correspondent, remarked, "There really was no honeymoon between this Administration and the media, no attempt by this remarkably personable President to schmooze or buddy-buddy with reporters" (Hume, May 7, 1993, cited in Vanocur, 1994).

Certainly, an early failing of this administration was its lack of ability to use the power of the office to create news at the national level. This, coupled with a disdain for the press, prevented the Clinton administration from exercising more influence in the way intricate issues were presented to a public only marginally aware of the complexity of day-to-day legislative tasks and executive decisions. A year into his term, Clinton remarked: ''I did not realize the importance of the communications and the overriding importance of what is on the evening television news. If I am not on there with a message, someone else is with their message'' (Woodward, 1994, 313).

This failure is particularly significant to a public who had placed such high hopes upon the election of someone they hoped would be different. Expectations for a successful Clinton presidency were very high. A poll at the beginning of his presidency showed that ''Americans [are] generally confident that he will be successful in meeting many of the nation's most pressing challenges. Large majorities are very or somewhat confident that the president-elect can handle an international crisis (70%), make health care available for everyone (68%), create an economic recovery (65%), keep the United States out of war (61%), and secure the nation's long-term economic future (61%)'' (Gallup, 1994, 19). Few people should realistically expect that a president could be successful in all of those areas. Yet those were the expectations as Clinton took office in 1993. Clinton needed public support to succeed. What he found upon entering office was that the office of the president could not bypass the national media. Additionally, heavy demands on the president's schedule did not permit him to access small-town newspaper reporters or schedule town hall meetings in local communities. Clinton's narrow-casting successes gave way to broadcast failures. The national press is the president's bedfellow, and this marriage was a rocky one.

Did Clinton receive bad press during his first days in office? Indisputably, yes. Did it influence voter perceptions? Of course. As Thomas Patterson explains in his book, *Out of Order,* the press has taken a decidedly negative role in politics, one that has affected Americans' attitude toward government. Patterson claims that ''voters begin each campaign without a firm opinion about the candidates, but after months of news that tells them over and over again that their choices are no good, they believe it'' (Patterson, 1994, 24). Clinton was no exception to Patterson's rule. Yet by alienating the national press, Clinton lost the opportunity to take advantage of the traditional honeymoon period with the press and the chance that comes with it to rebuild a positive public image. Clinton never got (or earned) the benefit of the doubt.

COMPLEXITY IS CONFUSING

How did Clinton fail in utilizing the press and taking control of his administration's image? The first, and most obvious, answer to this question is that people are rarely as simple as they are portrayed and issues are rarely as uncomplicated as they are depicted in two minute news stories. Multifaceted issues and complex people do not play well in eight-second sound bites.

If Bill Clinton is anything, he is an enigma to the public, a mass of contradictions. Consider these examples:

- He is a country boy raised in Hope, Arkansas. Yet he is also a Rhodes scholar who graduated second in his law school class behind Hillary Rodham.

- He talks about his belief in traditional values, yet he seems anything but traditional. He married a strong-willed, out-spoken woman who maintained her maiden name for a number of years after they were married and her voice even after her husband became President (Goodall, 1994). So strong is public opinion about the First Lady that *Newsweek* reporters Peter Goldman and Mark Miller (1994) noted that "a sizable number of voters . . . see her as the yuppie wife from hell, all career and no home life; the impression was widespread that she and Bill were childless" (39). Assigning his wife the task of health care reform did not make life easier. The Clintons defied traditional First Couple definitions. The change was discomforting to many Americans.

- Like many other young people in the 1960s and 1970s, Clinton questioned our government's involvement in Vietnam and rebelled against military service in a war he considered unjust. Yet Clinton defeated a war hero who had been credited with exemplary foreign policy leadership. Moreover, as Clinton took office, the public was confident of his ability to handle a foreign crisis and keep the nation out of war. Once in office Clinton received positive marks for most of his foreign policy achievements. In fact, *Time* reports that overall "both well-wishers and critics—some almost reluctantly—sight a surefootedness in Clinton's approach to overseas affairs" (Church, 1994, 30). Later, when Senator Jesse Helms made negative comments about Clinton's suitability to lead the nation's military, 70 percent of the American people said Helms was "wrong" (CBS, 1994, 3).

- Young leaders often have difficulty establishing strong identification with the elderly. Yet Clinton was the youngest governor in Arkansas history, a state second only to Florida in the number of elderly per capita. Clinton's success in breaking the perceptual link between his youth and inexperience enabled him to win and maintain their support.

- Clinton openly proclaims his personal faith in God and is a Southern Baptist. Yet he is publicly pro-choice and contends that gays deserve to live their private lives free from state control or judgment. So volatile is his stance within the Baptist church that the Southern Baptist convention tried to keep delegates from his home church in Little Rock from attending the 1993 annual meeting. They argued that his home church should have expelled Clinton for views that contradicted church beliefs.

No doubt, Clinton is a complex person. As one writer describes him, "He's Elvis Presley with a calculator on his belt, an outsized candidate with a drawl as big as his brain, a would-be president of both pie charts and Moon pies" (von Drehel, 1992, A1).

Images are often contradictory. At times, they can be used to divert people from more substantive issues of governance. Sometimes, they are reported and magnified in ways that damage a leader's ability to govern. Walter Lippmann (1914) claimed that "religion, patriotism, race, and sex are the favorite red herrings of foul political method—they are the most successful because they explode so easily and flood the mind with those unconscious prejudices which make critical thinking difficult'' (250). Yet they are also a political staple. Modern political strategists know that dealing with the images is as critical as dealing with the substance of issues.

The fact that Clinton is viewed as a mass of contradictions, however, may also help to define him as a product of his age. Rather than the strict, prescriptive rules that dictated citizenship and behavioral roles accepted by older generations, Clinton was a member of a generation faced with dynamic choices and empowered like no other generation before it. Sociologists argue that the sixties was a time for breaking the rules. Whether experimenting with drugs or advocating free love, the generations that grew up in the post–Annette Funacello baby-boom period were disgusted with capitalism, greed, and government, themes that emerged as mainstream thought by the 1990 election. Additionally, Clinton had the benefit of MTV with its mix of images and emotions. Disparity between word and image are commonplace to a generation raised in videospeak.

To many of his generation, Clinton's seeming contradictions are no more than phases of growth sprinkled with an attitude of tolerance for others who have made different choices. Yet for others, these contradictions are evidence of a valueless leader who acts out of political expediency and who is not strong enough to put his beliefs into action. These seeming contradictions demonstrate the difficulty of dealing with complex issues through the news media.

How do you explain a complicated issue or decision? Some scholars suggest that it cannot be done given the current news climate. Patterson, for example, contends that the current style of reporting emphasizes images of handling issues more than progress on resolving the issue itself. The impact of this type of reporting is that ''when candidates speak out on the issues, the press scrutinizes their statements for an ulterior motive. Most bad-press stories criticize candidates for shifting their positions, waffling on tough issues, posturing, or pandering to whichever group they are addressing'' (Patterson, 1994, 8). Certainly, press coverage of the Clinton administration has fallen prey to this type of reporting. Clinton himself recognizes the problem: ''The longer you're around, you understand the difference between what you do and how you're perceived'' (Goodgame and Duffy, 1994, 36).

THE WAFFLE IMAGE

Grappling with a media image is difficult under favorable conditions, but Clinton not only alienated the national press corps but failed to unite a divided public. The 1992 election was similar to the one in 1980 when Anderson's third-party candidacy prevented Reagan from entering office with a majority mandate. The president's first task should have been to find some grounds for unity. Perhaps, though we will never know, the president planned to do just that. Because Clinton relinquished control of the press, opposing forces were able to dominate the news agenda and control the message coming out of the White House.

Moreover, since 1980 the presidency had been dominated by ideological leadership. Both Reagan and Bush held absolute positions on issues ranging from national defense to a woman's right to choose. They often conveyed a definition of moral leadership by viewing issues through the prisms of right or wrong, black or white. Even when people disagreed with their edicts, both presidents commanded a certain level of respect. Americans assessed their motives to be honorable, even if they also found them to be misguided. Moral leadership is, after all, defined by its consistency. As the saying goes, we always know where the minister stands on sin.

Perhaps Reagan's experience as an actor gave him an understanding of simple story lines and plot structures that mark news treatments. When Reagan was asked what kind of governor he would make, his answer was instructive: "I don't know. I've never played one." Reagan may have developed his presidential character, but he always seemed to understand the one rule that has to be followed: characters have to be consistent to be believable.

By contrast, Clinton is a pragmatist (Whillock, 1994b). What he brought to office was a markedly different style of leadership. He saw politics as compromise. He recognized that people will rarely get everything they want but that through compromise and negotiation, they could improve their position. To Clinton, politics works because it permits a path of cautious, steady progress and change.

One of the major failures of Clinton image-makers is that they allowed the terms compromise and inconsistency to become synonymous. Communication studies are replete with examples of how people who are viewed as inconsistent have negative images (see Allgeier et al., 1979; Bostrom, 1983, 88–107).

Could Clinton convince the American people that he would follow through on his campaign promises? Could he make them believe that they made a good choice? In the first two years, the answer to that question is "no." Here's why.

Political images are ethereal. They are guided by impressions, selected and magnified by the press (Patterson, 1994). Moreover, they are often constructed on the basis of a single event. The events that initially defined Clinton's presidency set a negative tone. Though the timing was not of his choosing, Clinton fulfilled one of his campaign pledges almost immediately upon taking office. He ended—or at least lessened—discrimination policies against gays in the military. He was also immediately branded for his action as the Liberal the Far Right always claimed him to be. The issue made news headlines and sparked endless hours of talk radio pseudoanalysis. In theory, one good action or one bad action should not be the measure of leadership. Yet single events affect images by impressing upon the imagination an issue that can be retrieved for anecdotal support of future claims. Spiro Agnew once remarked that "a raised eyebrow, an inflection of the voice, a caustic remark dropped in the middle of a broadcast, can raise doubts about the veracity of a public official or the wisdom of a public policy'' (Agnew, cited in Vanocur, 1994).

As a result of Clinton's action on gays in the military, the initial days of his presidency were marred by negative impressions. The gay issue should not have taken the public by surprise. It was, after all, a position that Clinton had taken during the campaign. But it had divisive overtones. First, conservatives had warned that Clinton was a ''Liberal'' despite the fact that his public pronouncements during the campaign positioned him as a centrist, a New Democrat. Forced to deal with the gays-in-the-military issue in the opening days of his administration, Clinton provided them the fuel to support their claims. Second, the resulting ''Don't Ask, Don't Tell'' policy was far from the absolute edict the gay community expected from Clinton. Failing to understand the art of compromise, both sides of the controversy were unsatisfied with Clinton's position. Third, and perhaps most important, the fact that the issue surfaced so quickly in the new administration gave the appearance that it was a priority. The fact that the timing was not of Clinton's choosing did not penetrate the debate.

One of the divisive aspects of the image of a compromiser is that those who hold more rigid value systems interpret the compromiser's actions as a sellout of values. Commentator Rush Limbaugh expressed this sentiment in his November 1, 1994, television program when he attacked a fellow Republican for his compromising stance on issues: ''We don't get anything done in politics by getting along. . . . The aggressor always sets the rules for the game.''

The aggressors clearly intended to control the game—and Bill Clinton's image. Clinton opponents had dubbed him ''Slick Willie'' during the campaign. Once in office, the clamor did not end. Moral crusaders who attacked Clinton continued to press the use of simple decision rules as a framework for decisions. More extreme factions depicted him as the anti-Christ. In a video widely circulated and advertised among Radical Right groups as the ''real story'' about Bill Clinton, *The Clinton Chronicles* accused Clinton as the kingpin of a drug smuggling operation in Arkansas, the person responsible for the deaths of people who got in his way, a womanizer, and a governor whose abuse of authority brought Arkansas to its knees.

For those who entertained negative stereotypes of Clinton, his actions could not be viewed in a total package of who he is and what he stands for. The record was picked apart for specific, supporting evidence. Gays in the military, the death of Clinton confidant Vincent Foster, Hillary's remarkable success in the stock market, each served as evidence to support claims of immorality and valueless leadership.

To make matters worse, failure to meet—or to control—the public's expectations became crippling. Clinton began his administration with approval rankings similar to other presidents. By the time of the first public measurement after one hundred days in office, Clinton's approval rating was the lowest of any president since this type of poll was conducted.

With negative images dominating the news, it would be easy to think of the Clinton administration as a failure. Yet during his first two years, Clinton fulfilled a number of his legislative objectives. He began by fulfilling his promise to institute stronger ethical standards for presidential appointees and by significantly cutting the size of White House staff. Legislatively, he increased taxes on the wealthier citizens who he claimed were better suited to bear the burden. In a tough legislative battle, he was able to execute broad-based spending cuts and pass an economic stimulus package. He signed the family leave act, instituted a job training program, restored abortion counseling as an option at family planning centers, instituted banking reforms, strengthened the college loan program, and passed NAFTA. Clinton was highly successful in passing the elements of his campaign promises. By the end of Clinton's first two years in office, change was evident. The jobless rate dropped to a four-year low and over 194,000 jobs were added. In addition, hourly wages rose at their fastest pace in eleven years (Dodge, 1994, 1A). Yet, as Patterson argues, "Press accounts of Clinton's early months in office made it appear otherwise. The news focused on the promises he broke and, more so, on the instances where he was forced to negotiate with Congress. Each compromise was reported as a headlong retreat from principle" (Patterson, 1994, 14).

After twelve years of ideological leadership during the Reagan-Bush years, the American people had lost their understanding of politics as an art of compromise. In part, people were unsure whether Clinton, this child of the media age, was pulling the wool over their eyes or if he was "the real thing." Press coverage of his early days in office permitted the interpretation to exist. Political cartoonist Gary Trudeau even depicted Clinton as a waffle, a reference to the fact that people viewed Clinton as capable of being on every side of an issue. The waffle image is now part of the news lexicon. For example, in an article assessing Clinton's foreign policy success, *Time* reporter George J. Church (1994) noted that when Clinton responded to another threat by Saddam Hussein "he did it so rapidly and decisively as to appear anything but the waffler of the political cartoons" (29).

Clinton failed to get credit for many of the campaign issues he enacted into law during his first two years in office. Rather than impress upon the American psyche the difficulty of the task and the achievements he made, Clinton is depicted as the model for failure. Perhaps no issue demonstrates this as clearly as the health care debate. And perhaps no issue did as much to divide the nation.

FAILURE AND ALIENATION

If compromise is an indictment, then Clinton is in good company. Walter Lippmann, referring to Theodore Roosevelt, once said:

Many people say he has tried to be all things to all men—that his speeches are an attempt to corral all sort of votes. That is a lefthanded way of stating a truth. A more generous interpretation would be to say that he had tried to be inclusive, to attach a hundred sectional agitations to a national program. . . . Inconsistent: yes, he tried to be the leader of factions at war with one another . . . he is a statesman and not an agitator—his business was to meet demands when they had grown to national proportions. . . . He has said some silly things. He has not been subtle. But his success should be judged by the size of his task, by the fierceness of the opposition, by the intellectual qualities of the nation he represented. (Lippmann, 1914, 99)

Clinton was not able to enjoy such a "generous interpretation" of his struggle to address some of the nation's pressing problems. What the health care debate did to the image of Clinton is as important to perceptions of Clinton as any event in his presidency thus far.

Health care was one of the major issues Clinton pressed in the presidential campaign. It is an area of the budget that has been growing exponentially during the last two decades and, according to numerous pundits, is a real threat to the economic stability of the nation. Clinton attached a great deal of significance to the issue, as he demonstrated by putting his most reliable advisor at its helm, Hillary Rodham Clinton.

Hillary Rodham Clinton successfully led a smaller but similar effort while serving as First Lady in Arkansas. The issue then had been school reform. Hillary learned from her experience there. She was convinced that there was much to be gained from listening to the people who were struggling with the issues on a day-to-day basis. So, in like manner to her Arkansas endeavor, Hillary hit the road conducting meetings across the nation to take the pulse of the American people on health care reform. Opinion polls consistently ranked health care as a concern of the American people. Heartrending testimony put a face on the data. Hillary was moved and motivated to stimulate action.

At the heart of her efforts was a desire to remove abstract labels and get those involved in the decision-making process to remember the people for whom they were working. Doing this, she believed, would add the force of public pressure and moral decency to the reform effort (Woodward, 1994, 99).

The strength of the opposition and the depth of their commitment against proposed reforms are notable. The issue, discussed in more detail elsewhere in this book, permeated media coverage for weeks. Each trial balloon floated to gauge public or congressional reaction regarding issues ranging from methods of financing to what kind of coverage should be offered to who evoked hostile reactions. These were not the reactions of lunatics or fringe groups. They were the reactions of decent people, many of whom saw their livelihood threatened.

Many people who opposed specific reforms worked in industries known to contribute to health risks. The tobacco farmers, for example, were in danger of losing their livelihood if the proposed Clinton reform measures were adopted. Hillary Clinton's antismoking stance and her proposal to pay for health care, in part, by a tax on tobacco products engendered wide criticism. So deep was the emotion on this issue that the First Lady was burned in effigy by Kentucky tobacco farmers.

Everyone wanted reform, but no one could agree on how to achieve it. When the Congress voted down health care reform, the public again saw a chance for real reform slip away. Everyone wanted a solution. Despite Clinton's other successes, the fact that a salient issue, one that the public cared deeply about, failed to pass was viewed as a clear example of failed leadership. No one seemed to consider that health care reform efforts in the past had also failed miserably. Nor did the public care that the issues were terribly complex and opposing forces were well financed. Clinton failed the American public, if in no other way, by encouraging them to believe that success was possible. Health care reform failed, and Clinton failed to live up to expectations, however lofty those expectations may have been. In the process, Clinton was accused of selling out, of compromising to the point where reform was meaningless. The image of Clinton the statesman did not emerge.

What did surface was an unusual coalition of voters opposed to Clinton and Democratic policies. Clinton reform measures, including health care issues, stressed the plight of the middle class. But the fear of a health care crisis was not as salient as the fear of an economic crisis.

Researchers advise us that a person's experiences carry a great deal of weight in the decision-making process. The experiences of the middle class during the last decade resulted in economic insecurity. (Remember that it was the economy that served as the issue that propelled Clinton to victory.) After a decade of downsizing and right sizing by big business, people felt threatened by economic conditions that resulted in numerous layoffs. Many, many families were touched by the economic downturn. The fear that government programs might cause even more layoffs presented more of a threat than a potential health care crisis. Clinton's opposition understood that. They played upon fears convincing small businesses that they would be saddled with the burden of paying for health care.

While Clinton tried to be inclusive, the image that dominated was of a president who supported one constituency over another. The needs of the poor and the middle class seemed to be consistently ranked over the needs of wealthier Americans. True to his promise, Clinton raised taxes on the wealthy. This, he said, was necessary in order to control an ever-mounting national debt. So they pay more, okay. But then they were told that there are more expenses that will result from other programs, specifically health care for all workers in America. And guess who has to pay again? Many white males came to believe that they were the only people who were not in a protected class, the only ones singled out for more burdens with fewer benefits. As Lerner (1992) points out, "The ultra rightists have learned how to appeal to many decent Americans by speaking to real and legitimate needs, to acknowledge the pain in their lives, and to give them the sense that they are being recognized and respected" (37). That was certainly true in 1994.

Over the last three decades, the underclass learned to justify entitlements based on what sociologists have defined as "special victim status." Using this line of argument, certain groups of people claim they are "special" victims of an imbalanced society in order to get special favors out of the system. Leo (1989) notes that the use of such a strategy is indeed widespread: "More and more aggrieved groups want to magnify their victim status. . . . The more victimized you seem, the more political leverage you have" (24).

Both David Duke and Patrick Buchanan adopted such arguments in their 1992 presidential bids, arguments that resonated with many voters. They claimed that the real victims are the citizens who have to pay for the favors these "special victims" receive. The result is that "they resent them as a special interest group that gets special favors" (Goodgame, 1991, 44). As Teun van Dyke contends, pitting class against class enables economic hatred that is just as compelling as hatred of race, gender, or sexual preference (Van Dyke, 1995, 7–45). Indeed, rather than bringing the country together, the Clinton policies tore the nation apart.

The result was an attitude that permeated the 1994 elections. White males felt that in the competition for government benefits and entitlements, they had no voice. Accordingly, they came to believe that health care reform only meant that the new entitlements would be paid by only a few Americans but enjoyed by everyone without consideration of other values. "Does the work ethic mean anything?" they asked. "Are we now to be punished for our success and they rewarded for their laziness?"

In an age of political correctness, white males embodied the image of success and bore the brunt of attacks that claimed their success was made at the expense of—and to the exclusion of—other classes of people. In a best-selling book entitled *Politically Correct Bedtime Stories,* fairy tales have been rewritten to reflect this cultural attack. In the stories, the white male is always to blame and is always the one out of touch with the needs of others. Perhaps its best-selling status is also a reflection of the fact that people sensed some ironic truth in the satire.

Two images emerged as a direct result of the health care debate. First, Bill Clinton was viewed as a leader who promised more than he could deliver. Inadvertently, he fueled the cynicism already infecting the American public. Second, in the process, an alienated group found their voice, rebelling against political correctness and taking back their voice.

RHETORICAL RESIDUE: HOW IMAGES WILL AFFECT CLINTON'S FUTURE

Whatever Clinton's legislative successes or failures may produce in the next two years, it will be difficult to overcome the images created by the "Slick Willie" label. Through this prism, every compromise can be easily interpreted as inconsistency. During the campaign, analysts noted that "his character problem no longer had much to do with the particulars of the case against him. It was the residue of all those things, and it was worse than any of them. Clinton was, in the public mind, a politician—one more smiling hustler who would promise anybody anything to win and could not be trusted thereafter'' (Goldman and Miller, 1994, 40). This is what Tony Schwartz calls ''evoked recall'': it is what people remember while they watch. Slick Willie is the image many people will recall as future events unfold.

During his first two years as president, Clinton produced a strong record of legislative and foreign policy achievements despite continual attacks on his character. At times, he changed his position on issues. He responded to public opinion and reasoned judgment. For many, this leadership style is prudent. Federal Reserve Chairman Alan Greenspan noted that such behavior indicates merely that Clinton is ''afflicted with the problem of the thoughtful'' (Woodward, 1994, 70–71). It is a style that obviously works for Clinton in many ways. According to the *Congressional Quarterly,* Clinton was able to win the support of the Congress on 88 percent of the contested votes during the 1993 legislative sessions. Only two other presidents (Eisenhower and Johnson) have had more successful records. Yet those are not the images that he retains.

Clinton's image will not be viewed in isolation from others in government service. We should also take note of the fact that those who attacked Clinton also paid a heavy price. Rather than demonstrate an ability to govern, gridlock continued to dominate the images of elected leaders in Washington. While Clinton was being attacked, many Americans believed no one was doing the job they were elected to do. Walter Lippmann (1914) opined that: ''If one half of the people is bent upon proving how wicked a man is and the other half is determined to show how good he is, neither will think much about the nation. . . . If politics is merely a guerilla war between the bribed and the unbribed, then statecraft is not a human service but a moral testing ground. It is a public amusement, a melodrama of real life, in which a few conspicuous characters are tried, and it resembles nothing so much as schoolboy hazing. . . . The angels are largely self-appointed, being somewhat more sensitive to other people's tar than their own'' (2–3). Lippmann's scenario was certainly the case in 1994.

Both Clinton and his detractors have much to lose by sustaining the negative images the public holds of them. The 1994 off-year elections proved that once again as it did in 1992 when Clinton was elected—the public wants its elected leaders to get on with the business of governing, to rise above personal interests to serve the public interests. It is just as compelling to note that the Republicans swept the off-year elections as it is to take note that after two years of investigations, the American people are also tired of paying for the Whitewater investigation. According to a CBS news poll conducted during the same time frame as the elections, two out of three Americans say it is not necessary to hold more hearings on Whitewater (CBS, 1994, 2). As with the other issues that have been deflected, many Americans have come to believe that the hunt for misconduct is a political ruse that has little bearing on the president's ability to govern.

Both Clinton and his detractors have a need to revise their negative perceptions. With the Republican majority holding legislative seats, there is a decided pressure to get things accomplished. Passing the elements—or at least many of the elements—in the Contract with America is critical to Republicans' continued success. But they cannot do it alone. They need a partnership with the president.

Pushing past the images requires supplanting them with a new set of images, using the power of the presidency—our one nationally elected position—to set the agenda for the American people. If he can do that successfully over the next two years, he may still be reelected to office. If he does, it will be partly attributable to the fact that Clinton will learn to work with the press, to tell a simple story, to explain complicated issues clearly, and to facilitate reform as the public demands. As Clinton notes: "I think I've learned that . . . explaining to the American people what our interests, our values and our policies are requires more systematic and regular explaining. In a time when the overall framework is not clear and when people are bombarded by information, I think a President has to do that with greater frequency and to try to make a continuing effort not only to shape a new world but to find ways to explain the world to the American people" (Goodgame and Duffy, 1994, 35). Should people write off Clinton as a failed, one-term president? No. Images are fluid. New situations and events can change public perceptions. If the voters come to believe that the change they want is being implemented, both Clinton and the Republican majority may retain their seats. According to Texas political lore, Lyndon Johnson was once asked how he got so much congressional support for civil rights legislation in the face of what seemed overwhelming negative reaction. His answer here is instructive: "Sometimes you get people to do the right thing. In the end, the reason they did it is less important." If Clinton is successful in reforming government in partnership with the Republican majority, how they did it will also fade from memory. The image of success will remain.

REFERENCES

Abramson, Jeffrey B., F. Christopher Arterton, and Gary G. Orren. 1988. *The Electronic Commonwealth: The Impact of New Media Technologies on Democratic Politics.* New York: Basic Books.

Allgeier, A.R., D. Byrne, B. Brooks, and D. Revnes. 1979. "The Waffle Phenomenon: Negative Evaluations of Those Who Shift Attitudinally." *Applied Social Psychology* 9: 170–82.

Altheide, David L. 1985. *Media Power.* Beverly Hills, Calif.: Sage.

Ansolabehere, Stephen, Roy Behr, and Shanto Iyengar. 1993. *The Media Game: American Politics in the Television Age.* New York: Macmillan.

Berkman, R. and L. Kitch. 1986. *Politics in the Media Age.* New York: McGraw-Hill.

Bostrom, Robert N. 1983. *Persuasion.* Englewood Cliffs, N.J.: Prentice-Hall.

CBS. 1994. "The Republican's Honeymoon." November 2. New York: Polling data.

Church, George J. 1994. "Taking His Show on the Road." *Time,* October 31, 28–34.

Conover, Pamela J. and Stanley Feldman. 1989. "Candidate Perception in an Ambiguous World." *American Journal of Political Science* 33(4) (November): 912–29.

Dodge, Robert. (1994). "U.S. Jobless Rate Drops to 4-Year Low." *Dallas Morning News,* November 5, 1A.

Edelman, Murray. 1977. *Political Language: Words that Succeed and Policies that Fail.* New York: Academic Press.

Gallup, George, Jr. 1994. *The Gallup Poll: Public Opinion 1993.* Wilmington, Del.: Scholarly Resources.

Goldman, Peter and Mark Miller. 1994. "The Message Struggle." *Newsweek,* November 7, 38–40.

Goodall, Sandra. 1994. "De/reconstructing Hillary." In *Bill Clinton on Stump, State, and Stage,* ed. Stephen A. Smith (pp. 163–86). Fayetteville: University of Arkansas Press.

Goodgame, Dan. 1991. "Why Bigotry Still Works at Election Time." *Time,* November 25, 44.

Goodgame, Dan and Michael Duffy. 1994. "Blending Force With Diplomacy." *Time,* October 1, 35–36.

Graber, Doris. 1988. *Processing the News: How People Tame the Information Tide.* New York: Longman.

Hart, Roderick. 1994. *Seducing America: How Television Charms the Modern Voter.* New York: Oxford University Press.

Leo, John. 1989. "The Politics of Hate." *U.S. News & World Report,* October 9, 24.

Lerner, Michael. 1992. "Stopping David Duke and Patrick Buchanan." *Tikkun,* January/February, 37–42.

Lippmann, Walter. 1914. *A Preface to Politics.* New York: Mitchell Kennerley.

Patterson, Thomas E. 1994. *Out of Order.* New York: Vintage Books.

Robinson, M. 1975. "American Political Legitimacy in an Era of Electronic Journalism: Reflections on the Evening News." In *Television as a Social Force: New Approaches to TV Criticism,* ed. Douglass Cater and Richard Adler. New York: Praeger.

Roper Organization. 1993. *America's Watching: Public Attitudes Toward Television.* New York: Roper Organization.

Schwartz, Tony. 1994. Presentation at the Speech Communication Association National Convention, November, New Orleans, La.

Van Dyke, Teun. 1995. "Elite Discourse and the Reproduction of Racism." In *Hate Speech,* ed. Rita Whillock and David Slayden. Newbury Park, Calif.: Sage.

Vanocur, Sander. 1994. *Television and the Presidency.* Nashville, Tenn.: The Freedom Forum at Vanderbilt University.

Von Drehel, David. 1992. "Letter from the Campaign Trail: Clinton's Political Persona Blends Redneck, Policy Nerd." *Washington Post,* March 7, A1.

Whillock, Rita Kirk. 1994a. "Easy Access to Sloppy Truths." In *Bill Clinton on Stump, State, and Stage,* ed. Stephen A. Smith (pp. 292–314). Fayetteville: University of Arkansas Press.

———. 1994b. "Dream Believers: The Unifying Visions and Competing Values of Adherents of American Civil Religion." *Presidential Studies Quarterly,* 375–88.

Woodward, Bob. 1994. *The Agenda: Inside the Clinton White House.* New York: Simon & Schuster.

Chapter Seven

Redefining the Role of the First Lady: The Rhetorical Style of Hillary Rodham Clinton

Janette Kenner Muir and Lisa M. Benitez

The election of Bill Clinton as president of the United States brought much speculation and concern about his wife's role as First Lady. Hillary Rodham Clinton, a formidable politician and thinker in her own right, did not appear to fit the image of a Barbara Bush, a Nancy Reagan, or even a Rosalynn Carter. As a successful Arkansas lawyer, Clinton had already made a name for herself, leading many to speculate that she would break the traditional mold regarding expectations for the wife of the president. While she "stood by her man" in the primaries and offered assurances that she, indeed, liked to bake cookies with Chelsea, many people wondered what role she would undertake as she moved into the White House.

The role of the First Lady has long been a perplexing one. To survive the long campaign year, doggedly trudging from state to state, meeting to meeting, requires a great deal of fortitude. Private lives are open to public scrutiny; media representatives look for every opportunity to exploit one's vulnerabilities and show the public how the candidate and his or her family *really* lives. As Ann Grimes reports in *Running Mates: The Making of a First Lady,* a profile of candidates' wives campaigning in 1988, great dilemmas exist for political wives:

When times get tough she becomes a cheerleader rallying demoralized staffers. Like a den mother urging unhappy campers to put up tents in the rain, she perseveres even in races everyone knows are shot. When she is in trouble, she can't—or doesn't—retreat into the privacy of her bedroom and quietly sing the blues. When her husband loses, she too is abruptly forgotten. When he wins, she takes on what *Time* magazine once called an "ill-defined, unpaid job," one that forces her to dance and dodge, "the many conflicting notions Americans hold about women as mothers, wives, lovers, friends, colleagues." And leaders. (1990, 16)

In many ways the campaign wife is being prepared for the criticism that she will face should she move into the White House. Though women have evolved into political leaders and executives of large corporations, the specific duties of the president's wife often seem limited and provincial. Many Americans believe that the First Lady should support her husband, oversee stately parties and banquets, find a social cause to support, and ultimately, serve as the identifying symbolic focal point for women, both young and old.

Scholars who have studied the lives of past presidential wives argue that this is a narrow and limited view of this important role. Many past wives did exercise political power as Edith Mayo, Smithsonian director of the exhibit "First Ladies: Political Role and Public Image," notes:

It's very sad but very telling that the media and the public are so pathetically ignorant of women's history that they don't realize that presidential wives since Abigail Adams have been wielding political influence. It's a long-standing, red-blooded American tradition. . . . Every First Lady who has used her position in this way has been ridiculed or vilified as being deviant from women's proper role or feared as emasculating. (Qtd. by Anthony, 1991, F1)

Because a lot of the First Lady's political muscle is often flexed privately, behind closed doors, the role of the president's wife often remains elusive.

Past presidential wives have been as varied in their impact and approach to their expected roles as their husbands have been in governance. There are, however, some historical examples that stand out. Carl Sferrazza Anthony, author of two volumes on the history of First Ladies, argues that prior to Hillary Clinton, Rosalynn Carter had one of the most active roles of any First Lady. Serving as the honorary chair of a presidential commission on mental health reforms, she oversaw thirty separate task forces, conducted national meetings, and testified before Senate subcommittees. The result of her efforts was a 1,000-page document arguing for radical changes in the way the government handled mental health concerns. Carter's work eventually won the passage of the Mental Health Systems Act of 1980 and a $47 million increase in funding, though later these efforts were reversed by the Reagan administration (Anthony, 1993, F4).

Ellen Wilson, the spouse of Woodrow Wilson, was the first presidential wife to have a project turn into federal legislation. Focusing on public housing issues, she assumed a semiofficial post as the honorary chair of the National Civic Federation, which drafted a law to renovate or demolish Washington slum dwellings. She also edited her husband's speeches, frequently inserting common touches to make his philosophical ideas about governance clearer for his public audience. On August 7, 1914, Ellen Wilson's housing bill passed; that afternoon she died from a terminal illness (Anthony, 1993, F4).

Eleanor Roosevelt has often been cited as an activist First Lady and as the presidential wife with whom Hillary Clinton most identifies. Roosevelt worked as the unsalaried deputy director of the Office of Civilian Defense, an agency established by Franklin D. Roosevelt at the beginning of World War I. Mrs. Roosevelt was particularly concerned about the prejudice against married working women. Immediately after she became First Lady she began to hold news conferences with women reporters that served as forums for her to speak out on a woman's right to work (Caroli, 1987, 191). Roosevelt's insistence on speaking her mind throughout her husband's years in office led to a great deal of negative press, including negative political caricatures and hostile media attacks (194–95). Despite these attacks, however, there was also talk of Eleanor Roosevelt succeeding her husband in 1940, and the following year she was selected as one of the ten most powerful people in Washington, D.C. (195).

Throughout history, presidents' wives have taken active roles in their husbands' affairs of state. The evolution of these roles often seems to parallel the changes in society. As the role of women in the public arena has evolved, so has the role of the First Lady. Unfortunately, many people have trouble accepting this natural evolution and the idea that women can be powerful people. Blanche Wesson Cook, a biographer of Eleanor Roosevelt, argues that "we have yet to enter the 20th Century when it comes to recognizing that women can be leaders and have ideas" (qtd. by Judy Mann, 1994, B8).

Into the fray of discussion about the role of the First Lady enters Hillary Rodham Clinton, a well-educated, politically active career woman who has long had a vision of making a difference in society. Curious about the specific role she might undertake should Bill Clinton win the presidency, political pundits speculated about changes in the White House management. With the numerous responsibilities of running the White House—"a household, a symbol, a source of potential good"—Meg Greenfield predicted that as Hillary Clinton would be more engaged in her husband's work compared to other past presidents' wives, in turn, Bill Clinton would assume more of the responsibilities "conventionally associated with First Ladies only" (1993a, A7). Suzanne Fields suggested that Hillary Clinton's intelligence and experience in legal issues would represent a significant shift from the social emphasis long equated with the First Lady role. "Maybe in this transitional year of the woman," she writes, "we should rethink her office. We might hire a first hostess for the White House, and eventually let the first lady get a life—with pay—somewhere else" (January 28, 1993, G1).

Amidst concerns about a "copresidency" between husband and wife (a term mentioned for the first time in presidential politics), and comments that Hillary might be better suited for the presidency than her husband, the election of Bill Clinton ushered in a new way of looking at the presidential First Wife. Given her background experience and interest in issues concerning women and children, it was not surprising that the president would select his wife to head the task force on health care reform—a major concern expressed during his campaign, as well as a political quagmire for anyone taking on the task. By serving as an advisor to the president, Hillary Clinton's role as First Lady could take on an unprecedented course in the political arena (Lawrence, September 22,

1993, sec. 2, 5). Questions of accountability, experience, and her ability to handle the complexity of the issue were raised about her viability in this role. If successful, Mrs. Clinton could be recognized as making a major contribution to one of the messiest and most complex issues to face the American public. If she failed, many would question Bill Clinton's judgment in giving her this role and challenge the idea that a First Lady could handle the important policy issues of the day. Failure could, ultimately, mean a backward step in the evolution of expectations for the president's wife.

While health care reform did prove to be unsuccessful for Hillary Clinton, the issue is far from over and it seems to have had little devastating results on Clinton's persona. This is due, in large part, to the way she handled herself during the entire process and to the natural evolution of ideas and debates in Congress. It also has much to do with how Hillary Clinton addressed the issue as she engaged in her own various roles over the past two years. The remainder of this chapter will explore these roles and then consider some implications for Clinton's future as well as the future of the First Lady in the White House.

THE ROLES OF HILLARY CLINTON

One of the expectations of a First Lady is to make numerous public appearances, delivering speeches with poignant messages, and focusing attention on specific causes. In Hillary Clinton's initial two years as First Lady she delivered hundreds of speeches in a variety of settings. As she interwove the complex issue of health care reform with stories of ordinary people facing difficult situations, Hillary Rodham Clinton demonstrated her understanding of the power of words, her capacity for expressing emotions, her ability to provide logical, well-grounded arguments for her cause, and her overwhelming sense of purpose. This section considers five ways Clinton engages her audiences, suggesting how she envisions her role as First Lady and exploring the rhetorical strategies that enable her to manifest these visions.

Hillary, the "Average Person"

Whether speaking to the American Medical Association, to a group of Democratic women, or even to college graduates, Hillary Clinton uses identification as a way to engage her audience with the ideas she wishes to communicate and to show that she, in many ways, is an average citizen. The use of identification stands out in two dominant strategies, identifying common values and recognizing a common enemy.

In Kenneth Burke's discussion of identification, he uses the term "consubstantiality" to suggest that humans strive to "share substance" with one another while, at the same time, retaining their own "locus of motives." In acting together, Burke notes, humans have "common sensations, concepts, images, ideas and attitudes that make them consubstantial" (1969, 21). Identification through a sharing of common substance has long been an important way to reach audiences, a way to convince listeners that the rhetor recognizes their experience and understands their sorrows and frustrations.

In her role as head of the task force on health care reform, Hillary Clinton made many speeches across the country about the problems surrounding health care in America. Her use of identification seems a natural part of her rhetorical repertoire. In a speech to the American Medical Association (AMA) Clinton attempts to establish nonadversarial, common ground with health care providers. She begins by recognizing the elementary school children in the audience, then segues into her own childhood experiences and the lost optimism that many in the audience may be feeling:

Much has changed since those days. We have lost some of the hope and optimism of that earlier time. Today, we too often meet our greatest challenges, whether it is the raising of children or reforming the health care system, with a sense that our problems have grown too large and unmanageable. And I don't need to tell you that kind of attitude begins to undermine one's sense of hope, optimism, and even competence. (June 13, 1993, 581)

Clinton's identification of common experiences, along with traditionally inclusive pronoun usage such as ''we'' and ''our,'' attempts to persuade the audience that she understands their specific needs and concerns.

The First Lady also demonstrates the use of identification as a means to an end—persuading the medical establishment of the need for health care reform—when she speaks of her father's hospitalization and the attention he received from health care professionals:

I witnessed firsthand the courage and commitment of health care professionals, both directly and indirectly. I will always appreciate the sensitivity and the skills they showed, not just in caring for my father, not just in caring for his family—which, as you know, often needs as much care as the patient, but in caring for the many others whose names I will never know. (581)

By recognizing the commitment of the professionals, Clinton seeks to create an atmosphere of understanding and support rather than antagonism. These strategies are seen in numerous speaking situations where Clinton talks about health care reform. Whether speaking to union workers, the American Pediatric Association, or the American Hospital Association, she seeks to establish common ground by recognizing the commitment and hard work audience members put into their profession.

Another way that people identify with one another is by sharing a common enemy or scapegoat. Burke writes, ''To begin with 'identification' is . . . to confront the implications of *division*,'' and humans are ''brought to that most tragically ironic of all divisions, or conflicts, wherein millions of cooperative acts go into the preparation of one single destructive act'' (1989, 181). It is the division of humans that enable them to identify with one another by recognizing a "scapegoat" or "representative" of "certain unwanted evils, the sacrificial animal upon whose back the burden of these evils is ritualistically loaded" (Burke, 1973, 40).

In the case of Hillary Clinton's rhetoric, she is not one to regularly identify a particular person as a common enemy, but she will speak out against an idea or a larger association. For example, in her speech to the American Pediatrics Association, she attacks the insurance industry, accusing the industry of lying in its television advertisements. Insurance companies "like being able to exclude people from coverage because the more they can exclude, the more money they can make," Clinton claims, and "Now they have the gall to run TV ads . . . the very industry that has brought us to the brink of bankruptcy because of the way that they have financed health care" (Qtd. by Bruck, May 30, 1994, 87).

Many audience members attending Clinton's health care speeches could easily identify with her against the insurance industry, seeing this industry as responsible for the excessive paperwork, restrictions, and high costs that have come to represent health care in America. In a significant way, the entire health care industry becomes a scapegoat, representing a system that has strayed far from meeting the needs of American citizens.

Hillary, the Storyteller

In her role as the chair of the health care reform task force, Hillary Clinton spent a great deal of her time reading letters and listening to the stories told by thousands of Americans regarding their own struggles with the health care system. Clinton's attempt to personalize the issue of health care was dramatically seen in the appearance of several American citizens at a Rose Garden session where each talked about his or her particular problems with the system (C-SPAN, 1993). The stories told cast an emotional pallor on the issue, because they tended to express the fears and anxieties many Americans feel about health care reform.

Hillary Clinton told stories in many of her speeches. Whether speaking to union workers, to a hairdressers' convention, or to lawyers' wives, Hillary Clinton interwove many powerful narratives about people she had talked to around the country who were suffering because of inadequate health care coverage. In the telling of these stories, Clinton was able to present a compassionate argument for restructuring the health care system. Usually one or two narratives would serve as "representative anecdotes" to clarify a particular argument or to instill a more dramatic sense of pathos into her speech. For example, in her AMA speech, Clinton uses many examples to underscore the need for reform and reminds her audience about the numerous stories she has heard around the country. One story, in particular, stands out for her:

[T]he most poignant that I tell because it struck me so personally was of the woman with no insurance; working for a company in New Orleans; had worked there for a number of years; tried to take good care of herself; went for the annual physical every year; and I sat with her on a folding chair in the loading dock of her company along with others—all of whom were uninsured; all of whom had worked numbers of years— while she told me at her last physical her doctor had found a lump in her breast and referred her to a surgeon. And the surgeon told her that if she had insurance, he would have biopsied it but because she did not he would watch it. I don't think you have to be a woman to feel what I felt when that woman told me that story. And I don't think you have to be a physician to feel what you felt when you heard that story. We need to create a system in which no one ever has . . . to hear it ever again. (Clinton, June 13, 1993, 584)

The story, like many of the others she integrates in her speeches, presents a human side to the massive health care debate and provides an emotional clincher for Clinton's appeals. She thereby lends power to her role by serving as a master storyteller—*retelling* people's stories in a national forum. The narratives she uses, along with identification strategies, serve to balance her more logical, lawyer-like manner of speaking.

Hillary, the Lawyer

Clinton's background as a lawyer naturally shapes much of her approach to dealing with issues. Some people note that she can easily argue both sides of an issue, therefore making it difficult to assess what she really believes. Whether or not these perceptions are accurate, it is important to realize that often what makes Clinton so impressive is her ability to conceptualize the complexities of a problem and clearly explain them to her audiences. This has certainly been the case in addressing health care reform.

In many of her speeches on health care reform, Clinton presents her ideas in a logical progression, reflecting a lawyer-like manner for detail and organization. She begins with some form of identification with her audience, moves to a problem-solution format, interweaves poignant stories to emphasize her point, and concludes with a positive vision of the future with a new health care system. While seemingly formulaic in its approach, this structure serves to provide clarity to the complex issues and, at the same time, allows her to use important emotional appeals.

An example of Clinton's problem-solution format is clear in her speech to the Service Employees International Union on May 26, 1993. In this speech she details the problems facing the country concerning the rising costs of health care, the excessive paperwork that took up valuable time, and the overwhelming bureaucracy that directly affect the employees. After defining the problems of health care, she moves on to call for members of the audience to discuss the health care crisis with others in order to ensure support for comprehensive health care reform. By providing a clear solution, she enables the audience to visualize what a better health care system can provide—good information for good choices among health care plans—and a more "secure and healthier" American citizenry.

In keeping with the lawyer mode of presentation, Clinton also presents a number of "preemptive" arguments in her speeches. Given that many in her audiences will be skeptical of her plans to dramatically transform the health care system, she presents the other side of the issue and attempts to answer the argument before the audience has the opportunity to respond. In her speech before union workers she acknowledges that some people feel "if we change the system it will get much worse," and responds that it's "hard to imagine" how a proposal to stay with the status quo could be successful (Clinton, May 26, 1993). Clinton also acknowledges in the AMA speech the difficulty of reaching consensus, since not everyone "will agree with every recommendation the President makes." However, she implores the group to understand and support the solution proposed by the administration:

I suppose that if everybody's not a little put out that means we probably haven't done [the work] right. But I do hope and expect that this group, as with other groups representing physicians and nurses and other health care professionals, will find in this plan much to be applauded and supported. And I also believe that given the complexities of the problem we face, it would be difficult to arrive at a solution that was universally accepted. (Clinton, June 13, 1993, 582)

By acknowledging the perspectives some audience members may have regarding health care reform, and attempting to recognize that another side of the issue exists, Clinton presents a seemingly reasonable approach to understanding the problem. In turn, by presenting both sides of the issue, and admitting that many would not agree with the plan brought forth, she supplies a stronger persuasive argument, particularly suited for an educated or even hostile audience.

Repeating the promises of the Clinton health care reform plan, including universal health care coverage, Hillary Clinton spoke about a body of information in which she was well informed, often speaking eloquently without any notes. Her testimony before the congressional committees in September 1993 was the climax of nine months of task force meetings, public speeches and hearings, and strategy sessions. The Clinton plan was still in progress, the 1,300-plus–page tome did not reach completion until the end of November. Having courted a number of senators and representatives prior to her meetings on Capitol Hill, Clinton was well prepared to face her supporters and adversaries.

Many political pundits noted that Clinton's presentations on Capitol Hill marked a turning point in perceptions of the First Lady. Increased approval ratings and positive headlines proved that Hillary Clinton could easily handle the rigorous appearances before five House and Senate committees over a three-day time span. Without asking for help from the passel of aides who accompanied her, Clinton fielded tough questions smoothly and with confidence, even injecting moments of humor as she bantered with some committee members.

While downplaying her career as a lawyer, it was clear that Hillary Clinton's training prepared her well for the Hill appearances. Her ease with complex details, and her handling of difficult questions, directly contributed to the perception that she clearly grasped the difficulties of the health care issue. Her ability to manage this discussion, and her subsequent popularity ratings, is what led, perhaps, to the disappointment many Americans felt when listening to the Whitewater allegations and Hillary Clinton's specific role in the affair.

The Clintons' handling of the controversy surrounding their investment in the Whitewater real estate development, and Hillary Clinton's representation of a savings and loan run by her Whitewater partner, brought widespread suspicion about their innocence in the dealings. Some believe Hillary Clinton played a larger role in the affair than did her husband, hence offering a rationale as to why she would oppose the special investigation (Kranish, January 22, 1994, 8).

As one of the first real challenges to her credibility, the Whitewater controversy escalated when Hillary Clinton tried to ignore it. Her reactions to the unfolding drama, many argue, were politically flawed. Opposing the special investigator, refusing to turn over tax documents, fighting to keep White House counsel Bernard Nussbaum on board, all served to question her character as well as to affect the president's. Some of the criticism went back to Clinton's expected role as the First Lady. Paul Greenberg, editorial page editor of the *Arkansas Democrat and Gazette,* noted that "Whitewater makes me yearn for the good old days of Bess Truman and Grace Coolidge . . . spouses of presidents who have stepped in and done important work. But they did not step in in their own right" (Qtd. by Wolf and Edmonds, March 8, 1994, 2A).

After many months of speculation about Hillary Clinton's role in the Whitewater incident, and the investments that profited her close to $100,000, the First Lady finally broke her silence and held a press conference to answer media questions on the Whitewater investigation and several other issues. During the press conference, Clinton admitted that "we never should have made the investment. But, you know, those are things you look at in retrospect. We didn't do anything wrong. We never intended to do anything wrong" (Clinton, April 22, 1994). Nancy Gibbs, a reporter for *Time Magazine* observed that "the First Lawyer came well prepared; to even the softest questions she had a hard boiled answer" (March 21, 1994, 28). Specific topics Clinton dealt with included the circumstances surrounding the profits gained from her commodity trades, her view of Whitewater's impact on the state of Arkansas, her reluctance to release tax documents, the circumstances surrounding the death of Vincent Foster and, of course, health care reform.

Ultimately, it was beneficial for the First Lady to discuss this controversy. The press conference provided answers to some of the pressing questions surrounding Whitewater. While Clinton's responses did not completely exonerate her involvement in Whitewater, they did assuage some public concern about her role. While her position as a lawyer led to problems in this controversy, her ability to handle difficult questioning, in essence, her legal training, helped Clinton to convincingly present her case.

Hillary, the Good Methodist

Long before Hillary Clinton was a Democrat, a mother, or a presidential wife, she was a Methodist. Kenneth L. Woodward argues that for those who know her well, this perspective is the way to best understand Hillary Clinton: "She thinks like a Methodist, talks like a Methodist, and wants to reform society just like a well-Sunday-schooled Methodist churchwoman should" (October 31, 1994, 23).

Since her childhood, the tenets of Methodism have been a formative element in Clinton's identity and have played important roles in her political choices. Her call for a "new ethos of individual responsibility and caring," for "remodeling what it means to be human in the twentieth century" directly reflects the Methodists' liberal social creed (24). Likewise, her sense of obligation, of responsibility for making the United States better, is an undercurrent in many of Clinton's speeches and provides justification for her ongoing efforts on behalf of health care reform. "The one thing that motivates Hillary Clinton," notes Rev. Ed Matthews, Clinton's Methodist minister in Little Rock, "is that we are to make this world a better place" (Qtd. by Carol Jouzaitis, May 23, 1993, sec. 6, 1).

Recognized by many people as one of her more powerful public addresses because of its spiritual grounding, Hillary Clinton's "Politics of Meaning" speech was given at the University of Texas, April 6, 1993, the day before her father died. Speaking from a few notes she had scribbled on the plane while traveling to Austin, Clinton delivered a passionate call for national spiritual renewal (Kelly, 1993, 25).

In *The Agenda*, Bob Woodward believes that this speech "had been germinating for a long time" (160). Arguing that the country was facing a "crisis of meaning," Clinton called for "new acts of kindness" to address the alienation, despair, and hopelessness of the nation. The speech, while not particularly well organized, "was an outpouring of religious ideas and 1960s concepts, full of better-world rhetoric that reached beyond politics to the spiritual" (160). As Clinton interwove a deeper sense of personal meaning with the redesigning of the health care system, she called on Americans to "summon up what we believe is morally and ethically and spiritually correct and do the best we can with God's guidance" (Clinton, April 6, 1993, 8).

Clinton's focus on things spiritual, and her perception that the country's morality was weak, brought much scrutiny from the press. Some writers were left to wonder what Clinton, and other advocates, were really talking about (Leo, 1993, 20). Others criticized her for embracing the family values theme of the Republican convention, which she had eschewed at the time. The *New York*

Times Magazine ran a cover article titled "The Politics of Virtue: Saint Hillary" that featured a cover photograph of Hillary Clinton in a pure white satin suit. *Tikkun* (1993), a liberal Jewish magazine edited by Michael Lerner, the scholar who first coined the term "politics-of-meaning," featured a copy of Clinton's speech in a subsequent article.

John Leo, writing for *U.S. News & World Report,* contends that Clinton's speech, and the profile written by Kelly, may have changed public perceptions of the First Lady. He writes:

Just when much of the nation has settled into a general view of Clinton as a hard-edged, rights-oriented liberal activist, she reveals herself as heavily concerned with the spiritual realm and many of the themes sounded by social conservatives. (June 7, 1993, 20)

Clinton's spiritual commitment, while particularly evident in this speech, provides an underlying philosophy in many of her speeches. Donnie Radcliffe, a Hillary Clinton biographer, argues that this speech gives a major clue to who Hillary Clinton is and what she believes.

[Hillary Clinton's] friends had always known about her spiritual quest but the death of her father on the eve of the health care challenge seemed to provide new meaning. Still, just as religion had defined Hillary's life, and change had provided the direction hers took, politics had shaped it ever since her Goldwater Girl days. (1993, 254)

The Austin speech stands out as one of those pivotal moments when the First Lady's political philosophy and religious spirit coalesced to provide a poignant picture of her vision of and commitment to America.

Hillary Clinton's assessment at midterm comes full circle to the philosophy articulated early on in her "Politics of Meaning" speech, when she is interviewed by *Newsweek* in October 1994. In this interview, Clinton talks about her spiritual grounding, her belief that abortion is wrong, and admits to being uncomfortable about passing out condoms in public schools. One would think that Hillary Clinton's sense of spirituality and the confessions made in this article would dampen the distrust of those representing more fundamental religious viewpoints. In a *Washington Post* editorial, David Walsh, a professor at Catholic University, ponders the lack of attention given to Clinton's important *Newsweek* confessions, observing that:

It is one thing to give voice to one's inner ambivalences, but to express publicly their religious setting just about insulates them from all further examination. Within the public arena, we lack even a rudimentary sense of how religiously grounded opinions might even begin to be considered. . . . The result, as Mrs. Clinton's interview illustrates, is to explode the myth that the social conflicts are partisan issues. They are moral conflicts that arise because we emphasize different aspects of the various problems. (1994, A19)

Walsh argues that Clinton should be applauded for the "courageous character of her profession of faith" and implores the public to take up the many controversial social issues that ultimately come down to a debate over morality and values (A19). It is Hillary Clinton's testimony, he believes, that could lead the way to an honest discussion.

Yet, a tension exists in the believability of Clinton's spiritual grounding and the strategic choices used for political gains. Clinton's *Newsweek* interview was published the weekend prior to midterm elections and represented a stark contrast to the aggressive, shrewd, and financially minded woman characterized during the Whitewater controversy. This softer image of the First Lady serves essentially neither to win the hearts of the religious right nor to support liberal policies. It does serve, however, to remind readers of her spiritual grounding and her sense of obligation in making the country a better place to live.

Hillary, the "First Woman"

As the role of the presidency embodies the inhabitant of the office as well as larger symbolic meaning (Denton and Woodward, 1990), so does the First Lady, who serves as a synecdochic representation of American women. Given Clinton's strong sense of identity as a woman, however, the term "First Woman" seems much more appropriate in comparison to the more restrictive and "appropriate" manner of behavior implicit in the current label for the president's wife.

Indeed, Clinton's identity as a woman is an all-encompassing one that enlarges the understanding of what it means to be a modern-day woman. In her appearance before the House Ways and Means Committee Clinton begins by identifying herself as "a mother, a wife, a daughter, a sister, a woman" and interweaves these identities with her particular understanding of the health care crisis. She does not come before the group as "First Lady," or even as a "working woman" but rather, draws on those identities that most women share. In many of her speeches she talks about her father's guidance and advice, and she speaks of her relationship with her own daughter. As she interweaves her identity with the identity of women across the nation, she provides a strong sense of the perspective a woman brings to the issue.

Her role as a *woman* has also had significant implications in the policy-making arena. A number of writers noted the deference committee members showed the First Lady as she argued about health care reform. Observing her exceptional gift for mastering details and complex subject matter, Meg Greenfield also remarked about Clinton's ability to adapt to her audience, in this instance, the House Ways and Means Committee:

The horn-helmeted Valkyrie, the wicked witch, the intellectual ax murderess of conservative Republican theology could not be assaulted because nothing even remotely resembling such a creature was present. Hillary Clinton was the model of modesty, civility, family-minded understanding and concern, willingness to listen and learn—a gaggle of virtues that made her infinitely more invulnerable to attack than any well-armed Valkyrie, witch or ax murderess ever could be. She disarmed the guys. The only thing many of them could think to do was burble on about how much they admired the work she had done on the health care project. They then half apologized and half asked permission for expressing, ever so gently, just a few doubts. (October 4, 1993, A19)

As it was the first time a First Lady had ever testified before this committee, great interest was focused on the reactions of the members. Greenfield criticized the "excessive gallantry" demonstrated by the men as evidence that Hillary Clinton could not be seen as a "working official" but only as a First Lady. This was an unfortunate stereotype because, as Greenfield notes, Hillary Clinton had surpassed all her modern predecessors. "She is a strong, separate source of power inside the administration with a mandate of authority from the president and an operational base from which to carry it out" (A19).

Clinton's perspective as a mother is a significant part of her persona and is emphasized on numerous occasions. In a commencement speech at George Washington University, delivered on Mother's Day, Clinton pays a wonderful tribute to mothers, talks of her own accomplishments, and embraces the larger American community. "Our community must be a family," she declares, "We must find balance in individual life and find balance in community life. We must take care of the larger extended family" (Clinton, May 8, 1994).

Some might argue that Clinton's sense of nurturance and motherhood went too far in her sense of responsibility over health care reform, only adding to the difficulty of successfully arguing for the president's package. Her refusal to support health care proposals provided by moderate Democrats created tension and frustration, underscoring difficulty in developing a working relationship with Congress on the issue. In some ways, Clinton's "overprotectiveness" of universal coverage and her lashing out at the insurance industry served to create a great amount of tension that, in the end, affected the proposal's ability to make it through congressional channels.

This overprotectiveness perhaps can be seen in Hillary Clinton's handling of the health care issue after her appearance on Capitol Hill. Health care was put aside so that all focus could be placed on passing the North American Free Trade Agreement (NAFTA), much to the First Lady's consternation (Bruck, 1994, 87). Despite the fact that President Clinton was trying to win crucial votes in the NAFTA debate, Hillary Clinton spoke against an alternative health care plan proposed by Rep. Jim Cooper (D-Tenn.), when the president most needed his support. At the same time, she openly criticized the health insurance industry, upsetting health care opponents who were NAFTA proponents. Both of these attacks, Bruck argues, "underscores the seeming autonomy with which Hillary made moves that could affect contemporaneous and critical White House initiatives; if she needed to be reined in, and prevented from following her instincts, there appeared to be no one up to the job" (87).

Though Hillary Clinton chooses to primarily identify herself as a wife, mother, and daughter, the power she has brought to her position, based on her own career and agenda, has played an important role in the public debate about gender roles and feminism. Though "feminist" was not a term Clinton used when facing congressional members on the Hill, she is still embraced as feminism's "first mainstream icon—a powerful, smart woman" who is able to combine feminine charm and the confidence often associated with "powerful and persuasive men" (Lewin, October 3, 1993, 4:1).

Judy Mann (October 6, 1993) observes that Hillary Clinton's approach to health care reform epitomizes the "female management style" characterized by employee clusters, a sharing of responsibility, an emphasis on consensus, and a reaching across divisions to find common ground (E15). Clinton's 500-member task force talked to thousands of people, listened to personal experiences, sought opinions, and tapped into various expertise. "It was a process of breathtaking comprehensiveness and inclusiveness," writes Mann, "She maintained that style during her appearances before Congress, giving us the most visible demonstration of the female style of leadership that we have ever witnessed" (E15).

Clinton has been criticized for presenting too positive of a feminist image, emphasizing what women *can* do rather than what they are *kept from* doing, or their victimization (Lewin, 1993, 1). Some argue that Clinton's feminism is "a thing she has made acceptable to different political audiences" (Wills, 1992, 4), conveniently adopting the feminist mantle when its seems politically prudent to do so. What seems to be clear is that Clinton chooses to celebrate women's successes rather than their struggles. She still refuses to talk about women-as-victims, rarely talks about the women's movement, and ignores the largely feminist issues of abortion, equal pay, and domestic violence (Lewin, 3). She does, however, recognize powerful, successful women who have made a difference in politics and in society by mentioning and celebrating their achievements in many of her speeches.

Yet many feminists embrace Hillary Clinton because she serves as a symbolic focal point for women. Feminist writer Katha Pollitt notes: "Whatever you think of the health care plan or the Clintons' politics, it's very good to see a First Lady living the life millions of American women live, breaking down the mentality that says there's a contradiction between being a warm, fuzzy mom and being an expert on health care" (qtd. by Lewin, 1). The image of a woman who can balance both aspects of her life is particularly important for many women, young and old alike, who struggle with the difficult decisions related to their gender.

In this light, Clinton addresses the criticisms against her, and refers to herself as a "transition figure," a "gender Rorschach test" where people are not necessarily reacting to her as much as they are "reacting to their own lives and the transitions they are going through" (Qtd. by Stout, September 30, 1994, A1). Clinton deflects criticism by arguing that much of the negative feeling the public has about her comes down to struggles with gender constructions in individual homes. Men come to resent her because their daughters' lives are now different or their wives have decided to go back to school; women challenge men in the workplace and hostility is transferred to Clinton (A1). As "First Woman," the persona Clinton projects redefines the very nature of expectations regarding women, particularly those in the White House, but more generally, the expectations for women in public life.

What becomes clear in observing these roles played by Hillary Clinton during her first two years in the White House is that health care reform served to frame most of her public appearances. Even when speeches did not directly deal with the issue, she still managed to interject her concerns about the need for a better health care policy in the United States. The personal crises she experienced, such as the death of her father and mother-in-law, only served to underscore the importance of good health care coverage. As she identified with her audiences as an average American, told compassionate stories about those who suffered because of inadequate health care, presented logically developed arguments for change, called for a spiritual renewal for America, and embraced the qualities of womanhood as her mantle, Hillary Clinton challenged many assumptions about the job of a First Lady. It is interesting to consider the overall impact these roles have had on changing perceptions and what this may say about the evolving nature of the president's spouse.

IMPLICATIONS: HILLARY CLINTON'S RHETORICAL STYLE

As a president establishes a sense of ethos with the American public, so too does the First Lady. The expectations and responsibilities that come with this position are so varied and open for scrutiny that a constant struggle exists to present a strong sense of oneself. At the same time, it is important to balance this sense with an understanding of the various perceptions of being feminine. While this is challenging, it is not impossible to achieve.

At a traditional level, where style is considered in the elocutionary sense of good delivery and language use, Hillary Clinton's style is powerful and engaging. On many speaking occasions she uses few notes, maintains eye contact with audience members, and exhibits animated facial expressions. Her nonverbal cues tend to support her verbal commitments and passionate pleas. Her voice level increases as she emphasizes those issues she most cares about, softening as she turns to a story of someone who cannot afford adequate health care coverage. In the verbal stylistic sense, Clinton employs repetition of words to create momentum, uses pauses for emphasis, and incorporates humor when appropriate. Much of the positive response to Clinton often comes down to the charismatic nature of her interactions with audiences. This charisma was particularly true on Capitol Hill, and may be what led many to remark about Clinton's "charming" manner.

Style, however, needs to be considered on a larger scale, as a representation of a more powerful sense of one's identity and purpose. Modern notions of rhetorical style acknowledge that this element can serve an important function in shaping the rhetor, creating his or her image. In the case of the presidency, Rosenman and Rosenman's (1976) observation that a president's style "delineates his personality and influences his achievements and failures" suggests a more wholistic approach to understanding style, essential to understanding the creation of one's persona (Muir and Muir, 1992). Hence, one's rhetorical style may be equated with a larger sense of ethos.

Despite her continual efforts to keep health care reform at the forefront of public awareness, the issue eventually died in a congressional tug-and-pull. Though she handled the issue with competence and grace, Clinton's critics believed she demonstrated too much control. Ruth Marcus, writing for the *Washington Post*, notes the tension that emerged and the challenge to the credibility of the entire administration: "In her work on health care, [Clinton] has been praised as a brilliant public ambassador and a dazzlingly effective messenger to Capitol Hill but also has been burned in effigy, vilified as the architect of a secretly crafted and dangerously bureaucratic plan, and personally identified with the administration's most searing defeat" (September 30, 1994, A26).

So what does one make of the First Lady's persona? Hillary Clinton has forged a new path in shaping and redefining the First Lady's role in the White House and has also suffered much criticism along the way. While not unlike the negative reactions directed at other presidential wives such as Eleanor Roosevelt, Doris Kearns Goodman, a Roosevelt biographer, notes that the criticism leveled against Hillary Clinton may be more a reflection of the times than of the woman herself. She draws an interesting parallel with Eleanor Roosevelt, but notes an important difference:

When a first lady is speaking out and is independent and powerful, there is some strain in the country that is touched forever. . . . Franklin Roosevelt would get letters saying "Can't you muzzle that wife of yours?" or "Can't you at least chain her up?" There seems to be an anger toward Hillary that wasn't even present toward Eleanor. Because she was so far ahead of her time, she wasn't representing, as Hillary is, the change that is taking place in this country between men and women. (Qtd. by Stout, 1994, A7)

Yet many of Clinton's critics disagree with this depiction, arguing that it is not her role as a strong woman that people disagree with but, rather, her arrogance in communicating this strength to the public. In a series of letters to the editor of the *Wall Street Journal,* several people attacked Hillary Clinton as a "demagogue," who uses her power to conceal information, to shift positions, and to manipulate the truth (October 17, 1994).

The disparities in the public's response to Hillary Clinton speak to the larger issue of the tension between expectations and roles the First Lady must perform, and the expectations for Clinton specifically. David Maraniss refers to Clinton as "the First Lady of paradoxes," noting that she is seen as both "old-fashioned and postmodern, prone to remodeling and redefinition, revered by some as the epitome of modern womanhood and equality in marriage and reviled by others as arrogant and domineering'' (January 15, 1995, A1). Hillary Clinton is feared by some people in the White House as the tensions within her role are faced by people in her own immediate context. She is a bitch according to Newt Gingrich's mother, and many feel she has played a significant role in the president's decreasing popularity.

On the other hand, Clinton admits to inherent contradictions in her handling of her role as First Lady. While driven to public service, she does not like public scrutiny. She is straightforward and aggressive, while at the same time, inherently shy (A26). Realizing that there are image problems, she invites Newt Gingrich and his mother to the White House for tea, she appears in a forum on First Ladies at George Washington University, and in various interviews, acknowledges the criticism leveled against her:

You can be involved and on the front lines like Mrs. Roosevelt and be criticized. Or you can be totally concerned with your family and not venture forth and be criticized. It is a no-win situation. I don't mind criticism that will come to me from people who honestly disagree about the President's health-care plan. I think that is what we should be arguing about in our country. But like every other woman who has been in this position, it hurts when people make up stories or say things that aren't true in order to get at you. (Qtd. by Landon Y. Jones, April 11, 1994, 40)

The contradictions in Hillary Clinton's role as First Lady speak directly to the dialectical tensions between the rational/discursive style in which she operates and her more spiritual, family-oriented rhetorical style. Clinton faces a great dilemma precisely because of who she is and the spirit of the times she faces. Given her experience level, if she comes across as too polished and prepared she is viewed as arrogant and insincere. If, on the other hand, she exposes her more spiritual side she is seen as deceitful, and her motives are called into question.

Some women believe that Clinton's negative reactions come primarily because she is a woman with power in the White House. Edith Mayo claims that ''the furor over Hillary Clinton is but the latest chapter in a theme that runs throughout First Lady history. It is much less about Hillary herself than it is about America's deep-seated ambivalence, even hostility toward power in the hands of women'' (Qtd. by Anthony, 1993, F1, F4).

Blanche Wesson Cook concurs with this claim, noting that media coverage has much to do with the treatment of women. ''The most provocative woman in the country is Hillary Clinton, but I don't think there is a First Lady who has been treated as rudely and meanly, except for Eleanor Roosevelt,'' Cook notes, and further speculates that ''[I]t has everything to do with the fact that she's a woman, a woman with power, vision and dignity'' (Qtd. by Judy Mann, March 14, 1994, B8).

How Hillary Clinton handles that power during the remainder of her time in office will play an important part in predicting the role of future presidential spouses. Some people see Clinton at a crossroads in her journey as First Lady. Now that health care reform has been defeated and Congress is controlled by Republicans, Clinton may model her role after Eleanor Roosevelt's, traveling as a public ambassador throughout the country, continuing to listen to the people's concerns about public policy issues. On the other hand, knowing that her activist nature plays a large part in who she is, and that she is not the kind of person to take failure lightly, it is conceivable that health care reform will remain an important issue on the Clinton agenda into the next election. Like it or not, Hillary Rodham Clinton is not one to deny who she is, and she will continue to forge new ground in her role as the president's spouse. Most likely, those women and men who come after her will have a much easier road to travel.

REFERENCES

Anthony, Carl S. 1991. *First Ladies: The Saga of the Presidents' Wives and their Power, 1961–1990.* Vol. 2. New York: William Morrow and Company, Inc.
————. "First Ladylike, after All." 1993. *Washington Post,* January 31, F1, F4.
Bruck, Connie. 1994. "Hillary the Pol." *The New Yorker* 70(15): 58–96.
Burke, Kenneth. 1969. *A Rhetoric of Motives.* California Edition. Berkeley: University of California Press.
————. 1973. *The Philosophy of Literary Form: Studies in Symbolic Action,* 3d ed. Berkeley: University of California Press.
————. 1989. *On Symbols and Society,* ed. Joseph R. Gusfield. Chicago: University of Chicago Press.
Caroli, Betty B. 1987. *First Ladies.* Oxford: Oxford University Press.
Clinton, Hillary R. April 6, 1993. "The Politics of Meaning: Remarks of the First Lady at Liz Carpenter's Lectureship Series. The White House, Office of the Press Secretary, 1–10.
Clinton, Hillary R. September 28, 1993. Appearance before the House Ways and Means Committee. Videotape provided by Public Affairs Video Archives, the C-SPAN Networks, West Lafayette, Ind. ID: 50894.
Clinton, Hillary R. May 8, 1994. Commencement address: George Washington University. Videotape provided by Public Affairs Video Archives, the C-SPAN Networks, West Lafayette, Ind. ID: 56645.
Clinton, Hillary R. May 26, 1993. Health care reform speech to service employees international union. Videotape provided by Public Affairs Video Archives, the C-SPAN Networks, West Lafayette, Ind. ID: 41087.
Clinton, Hillary R. June 13, 1993. "Health Care: We Can Make a Difference." *Vital Speeches of the Day,* vol. 59: 580–85. Videotape provided by Public Affairs Video Archives, the C-SPAN Networks, West Lafayette, Ind. ID: 42946.
Clinton, Hillary R. April 22, 1994. Whitewater investigation. Videotape provided by Public Affairs Video Archives, the C-SPAN Networks, West Lafayette, Ind. ID: 56307.

C-SPAN Program. September 16, 1993. Citizens on health care reform. Taped off-air.

Denton, Robert E., Jr., and Gary C. Woodward. 1990. *Political Communication in America,* 2d ed. New York: Praeger.

Fields, S. 1993. "First Lady Adds a First." *Washington Times,* January 28, G1.

Gibbs, Nancy. 1994. "The Trials of Hillary." *Time,* March 21, 28–37.

Greenfield, Meg. 1993a. "First Ladyhood." *Washington Post,* January 11, A17.

———. 1993b. "Did She Take the Hill?" *Washington Post,* October 4, A19.

Grimes, Ann. 1990. *Running Mates: The Making of a First Lady.* New York: William Morrow and Company.

"Hillary, You're Not Listening." 1994. "Letters to the Editor." *Wall Street Journal,* October 17.

Jones, L. Y. 1994. "Speaking Out: An Interview with Hillary Clinton." *People* 41(13): 39–41.

Jouzaitis, Carol. 1993. "First Lady is Gaining New Respect." *Chicago Tribune,* May 23, 6:1.

Kelly, Michael. 1993. "The Politics of Virtue: Saint Hillary." *New York Times Magazine,* May 23, 22–25, 63–66.

Kranish, M. 1994. "Clintons' Marriage: A Powerful State of Union." *Boston Globe,* January 22, 1, 8.

Lawrence, J. 1993. "First Lady Rises to President's Challenge on Health-care Reform." *Chicago Tribune,* September 22, Sec. 2, 5.

Leo, John. 1993. "Hillary, from the Pulpit." *U.S. News & World Report,* 114(22): 20.

Lerner, Michael. 1993. "Hillary Clinton's Politics of Meaning Speech." *Tikkun* 8(3): 7–9.

Lewin, Tamar. 1993. "A Feminism that Speaks for Itself." *New York Times,* October 3, sec. 4, 1, 3.

Mann, Judy. 1993. "A Triumph of Style and Substance." *Washington Post,* October 6, E15.

———. 1994. "A Lesson for First Ladies." *Washington Post,* March 14, B8.

Maraniss, David. 1995. "First Lady of Paradox." *Washington Post,* January 15, A1, A26.

Marcus, Ruth. 1994. "Hillary Clinton Soldiers On." *Washington Post,* September 30, A1, A26.

Muir, Janette K. and Star A. Muir. 1992. "Closing the Gap between Tropal Theory and Rhetorical Practice: The Presidential Style of George Herbert Walker Bush." In *Foundations of Public Communication Workbook,* ed. Janette K. Muir and Star A. Muir. Dubuque, Iowa: Kendall/Hunt.

Radcliffe, Donnie. 1993. *Hillary Rodham Clinton: A First Lady for Our Time.* New York: Warner Books, Inc.

Rosenman, Samuel I. and Dorothy Rosenman. 1976. *Presidential Style: Some Giants and a Pygmy in the White House.* New York: Harper & Row.

Stout, Hilary. 1994. "Hillary Clinton Looks at Her Strange Role: Gender Rorschach Test." *Wall Street Journal,* September 30, A1, A7.

Toner, Robin. 1993. "Hillary Clinton Seeks to Assure Hospitals." *New York Times,* August 10, A14.

Walsh, David. 1994. "Did Anyone Hear Mrs. Clinton?" *Washington Post,* November 15, A19.

Wills, Garry. 1992. "H. R. Clinton's Case." *The New York Review,* 39: 3–5.

Wolf, R. and P. Edmonds. 1994. "Furor a Sign of First Lady's Changing Role." *USA Today,* March 8, A1–A2.

Woodward, Bob. 1994. *The Agenda: Inside the Clinton White House.* New York: Simon & Schuster.

Woodward, Kenneth L. 1994. "Soulful Matters." *Newsweek,* October 31, 22–25.

Chapter Eight

The Clintons and the Health Care Crisis: Opportunity Lost, Promise Unfulfilled

Rachel L. Holloway

In 1992, Bill Clinton promised change. The litany of issues was long, but two headed the list—economic recovery and health care reform. Throughout his election campaign, Clinton argued that health care reform was necessary to American economic competitiveness and to the security of individuals and their families. Health care stories filled town hall meetings around the nation. Clinton asked about deductibles and hospital stays and prognoses. He reported that the nation faced a "health care crisis" and promised to do something about it. As he began his presidency, over 68 percent of Americans said they were "very or somewhat confident" that Bill Clinton could make health care available and affordable for all Americans. When asked to predict what issue would bring the president his greatest success, the people said "making health care affordable" (Gallup, 1994, 19). But by year's end, after months of talk and a proposed reform plan, confidence had dropped dramatically. Equal numbers favored and opposed the Clinton plan. Thirty-seven percent reported they would be a "little worse" or a "lot worse" off under Clinton's reform. Only 8 percent said they would be a "lot better." Fifty-six percent said the costs of their care would go up (Gallup, 1994, 190–91).

The more the Clintons worked on the problem, the worse the public response. By July 1994, only 17 percent of people surveyed believed that Clinton's plan would produce major improvements. Another 43 percent believed they would receive worse care. By September 1994, a year after he officially launched the debate, President Clinton's health care reform had failed. A combination of poorly conceived issue definitions and a badly designed policy process resulted in cumbersome and complicated legislation, a plan so comprehensive and complex that the Clintons and journalists found it difficult to explain to the American people. Skillful and motivated opposition took advantage of the weaknesses in the Clintons' strategies through a well-planned and well-financed negative campaign and, in the end, won the day.

In order to offer a communication-based analysis of why things turned out as they did, a general perspective of the role of communication in the management of issues is necessary. David Zarefsky (1986) defined the overall rhetorical perspective on issues this way: "To view a question of public policy as a problem of rhetoric, then, is to focus on the creation and exchange of symbols through which issues are perceived, defined, addressed, and resolved" (5). The stages in that process of persuasion are detailed in the next section.

INFLUENCING PUBLIC ISSUES

As the Clinton administration took office, health care costs had been rising well ahead of the rate of inflation for some time. An August 1991 Gallup Poll reported that 91 percent of Americans answered "yes" when asked "Is there a crisis in health care today?" (Newport and Leonard, 1991, 4). Many people were uninsured. Others paid more for less care, less choice of doctor, and limited treatment. Emergency rooms overflowed with problems that could have been prevented with earlier treatment by a primary care physician. None of these problems were new, but the issue did not produce full-scale national debate until President Clinton placed it at the center of his political agenda. What had changed was the issue's status.

Richard E. Crable and Steven L. Vibbert (1985) argue that an issue "is created when one or more human agents attaches significance to a situation or perceived 'problem' " (5). People, literally, "make an issue of something" by challenging others to see a situation as somehow in need of their interest and attention. People give a "situation" the status of an "issue" by identifying something in the situation as problematic and in need of some response. In the opposite direction, sometimes a person or group is asked "not to make an issue" out of some situation, signaling that increased attention and discussion is unwarranted or inappropriate and not worthy of others' energy or action. In either case, the "status" of the situation is negotiated through the symbolic interaction of involved parties. Not all situations are issues for all people, nor are all issues of equal importance to all people. The issue's "status," or the degree of significance attached to the issue and the numbers and identities of people attaching significance, varies and is influenced through argument and experience (Crable and Vibbert, 1985).

When this understanding of an "issue" is applied to political life in America, "issue management" encompasses attempts of involved parties "to understand the 'perceived' level of status that the issue holds for important publics and to move judges toward the 'desired' level of status by communicative intervention" (Crable and Vibbert, 1985, 15). What an issue manager hopes to do is to anticipate and build a strategy that moves the issue through its "life cycle" to a preferred resolution. Those in opposition to the "preferred resolution" use competing strategies to either move toward a different resolution or to quash the issue's momentum. Throughout its life cycle, the issue is shaped by a range of communication efforts and public responses (for additional discussions of issue management, see Heath and Nelson, 1986; Heath, 1990; Hainsworth, 1990).

The first stage in the issue's movement toward public policy is "potential" status. A person or group has expressed interest in the situation, identified what is problematic in the situation, and then advocates some "resolution" to the problem as defined. The essential elements of potential status are the questions raised about the "perceived problem," arguments that define that problem, and the proposed resolution of the issue. The problem may be the "cost" of health care or "access" to health care. Quality may be excellent but not available equally to all citizens. The issue may be purely an economic one—the financial burden that health care places on individual families and the nation as a whole may be intolerable. Having chosen an analysis of the problem, what should be done to resolve the issue is narrowed around some appropriate resolution. Definitions embody evaluations and direct actions. As Zarefsky (1986) notes, "to choose a definition is to plead a cause" (8).

An issue definition not only inherently advocates what should be done but who is to blame and who should respond. Definitions call forth friends and foes simultaneously. If medical mismanagement, greed, and fraud are the causes of escalating health care costs, then the medical institutions are to blame and are opponents of the people and of reform. They are part of the problem and must be changed. If, however, the burden of government regulation causes gross inefficiency and thus limits care, then medical institutions, the people, and reformers are aligned against government interference. Definitions identify who holds a stake in the issue's resolution and begin to align those groups either for or against change. Such "stakeholders" may bring a range of resources to an issue's development—credibility, expertise, political access, influence, money—that are critical to the issue's movement to the next status level, "imminent" status.

An issue moves to imminent status when the "potential" of the issue is accepted by others and thereby legitimized beyond its mere "potential" as an issue. The increased "significance" or status of the issue may be created by increasing numbers of people attaching significance to the issue or the significance of the people who endorse the issue's potential. Strategies for increasing the issues status include endorsement of the issue-as-defined by influential or important people; legitimization of the issue based on historical tradition and societal values; and symbolic linkages with other already legitimate issues or publics. Interested individuals also may organize their efforts to convey institutional legitimacy to their actions. Mothers Against Drunk Driving (MADD) carries more influence than individual mothers; numbers of people organized by structure, strategy, and commitment of resources all suggest "there's something important here" and level of motivation and a level of commitment that won't go away. At imminent status, the base of support is increasing and the issue is gaining momentum. A sense that individual interests are organizing into influential forces gains further attention for the issue.

The issue moves to its third stage, current status, when it becomes a topic of "current" interest and is "currency," an honored topic of conversation and concern, among widespread publics. In other words, the issue is on the public agenda. A primary, and sometimes essential, means to achieve current status is mass media attention. Crable and Vibbert (1985) define a current issue as "one which can be spent or purchased readily as part of the social agenda; its widespread distribution, due to the intervention of (usually) popular media, makes it known to (or 'honored' by) increasingly greater, but more remote, publics" (6). The issue's status is heightened by the increasing numbers of people attaching significance across a broader spectrum of public life. When the media places an issue on the national political agenda, policy-makers and stakeholders previously merely watching the situation from afar may feel pressure to become actively involved.

The practices and routines of the media shape the issue at current status. Mass media coverage tends to polarize and dramatize the issue, shaping the "story" of the issue around traditional American themes of appearance versus reality, efficiency versus inefficiency, good against evil, the routine versus the unique, big guys versus little guys (Jamieson and Campbell, 1992, 39). The news story identifies who is important and who is not, what is good and bad, advantageous and disadvantageous, and creates a dramatic narrative designed to capture and hold the reader's or viewer's attention. The news tells the audience what to think about and, to some degree, shapes the boundaries of what the public thinks by the selection of what is presented and the context into which those facts and ideas are placed. The journalists and analysts take control of the issue. Because those outside the media have limited ability to change news coverage, they may attempt to influence public opinion by going directly to key constituencies through advertising, direct mail, and direct organizing strategies. The issue's physical boundaries are expanded as increasingly distant audiences become interested and involved in the issue (for discussion of role of the media in politics, see also Denton and Woodward, 1990, 143–87).

The last issue stage, critical status, is the point of decision at which interested people identify either for or against the issue resolution and are actively concerned that *some* resolution take place. Issue managers may leave the timing open or may use institutional schedules to "force" the issue decision—for example, legal appeal procedures on the abortion issue; congressional recesses and elections for the health care issue. Of course, the issue's momentum may move more quickly or more slowly than desired and fail to match those deadlines. "No action" is also a resolution, if only for a time. Whatever resolution results, the issue drops to dormant status, where it rests until someone brings the issue's potential to life again (Crable and Vibbert, 1985, 6–7).

This understanding of how issues are created, gain status, and move toward resolution recommends several strategies for a president's attempts to "manage" an issue. He should define the issue with terms ambiguous enough to create a broad base of support but not so broad that they do not guide public evaluations toward his preferred resolution of the issue. The proposed definitions must carry enough symbolic force to arouse and sustain public attention through a long legislative battle (for examples of the role of definition in presidential influence, see Bennett, 1975; Crable and Vibbert, 1983; Zarefsky, 1980, 1986).

The chosen definition should also create strategic alliances on the issue, ideally giving rise to coalitions that preempt anticipated opposition and form a majority opinion around the president's proposal. Special interest and grassroots support shapes the range of options for congressional action, the timing of action, and usually prevents elected officials from simply avoiding an issue.

A president's resources to manage issues are exceptional. He can simultaneously define and legitimize issues-as-questions and bring the expertise of the office of the president to bear on any problem. His speaking about any issue places it on the agenda of the national news media. Because the president, unlike most political actors, can generally assume media coverage, he must establish a clear, personal voice on the issue, one not easily misrepresented by the media or opponents. The president's "message" should fit the themes of news whenever possible, knowing that their routines and values will not change, but merely be applied to the issue at hand. Once the media attends to the issue, the president must reiterate the central definitions offered and "stay on message" until the issue is resolved. Given his guaranteed access to the media, he should make issue statements in coordination with other communication efforts and in a way that maximizes the timing of the political forces throughout the year (for examples of presidential timing and media influence, see Bennett et al., 1976; Zarefsky, Miller-Tutzauer and Tutzauer, 1984).

At critical status, the president may use the bully pulpit to build momentum toward resolution outside Congress while he employs his political skill behind the scenes to gather the necessary votes. He can issue public challenges to Congress and attempt to force action. The sheer power of the office gives the president opportunities not only to shape the nature of the debate but its timing of resolution as well.

On health care, President Clinton had public opinion weighing in his favor, had key special interests in business and state government already in his corner, and showed early talent as the "new media" president who was "in touch" with America's domestic concerns. That a president with so much already in his favor failed to enact the legislative centerpiece of his "change agenda" reveals much about the early Clinton administration and the political art of issue management.

TAPPING INTO THE ISSUE'S POTENTIAL

Health care reform was a key component of Clinton's 1992 campaign for "change." The famous, "the economy, stupid" sign on the war room wall actually encompassed broader themes—"Change vs. more of the same. The economy, stupid. Don't forget about health care'' (Drew, 1994, 189). Harris Wofford's surprising election in Pennsylvania a year earlier demonstrated the "potential" of health care as a campaign issue, and the Clinton campaign embraced it with calls for insurance reform, elimination of medical fraud, malpractice reform, emphasis on primary and preventive care, increased access in rural communities, and a system of managed competition to control costs and maintain quality. Candidate Clinton said, ''It's a big human problem and a devastating economic problem for America, and I'm going to send a plan to do this within the first 100 days of my presidency'' (Presidential Debate, 1992, 44). Within the first five days of his administration, Clinton acted quickly to keep his campaign promise by appointing the President's Task Force on National Health Reform.

Appointing a task force is a frequent presidential strategy used pragmatically to develop policy and symbolically to lend the president's endorsement to an issue's status. A task force confers institutional legitimacy on the issue, brings the credibility of systematic study to the problem, and draws public attention through the president's personal endorsement. The issue is instantly legitimized because the president can report he has taken action on the issue.

Clinton added a new twist to the strategy by appointing First Lady Hillary Rodham Clinton as the chair of the task force. Already under Republican criticism and a lightening rod during the campaign, Hillary Clinton's ethos brought mixed symbolic trappings to the issue. President Clinton said, ''I think that in the coming months the American people will learn, as the people of our State did, that we have a First Lady of many talents, that who most of all can bring people together around complex and difficult issues to hammer out consensus and get things done.'' The president talked about the many people struggling with health care problems, especially the cost of health care, and the importance of health care reform to businesses of all sizes. The president's directive to the task force was to ''build on the work of the campaign and the transition, listen to all parties, and prepare health care reform legislation to be submitted to Congress within 100 days of our taking office'' (Clinton, 1993b, 96).

Mrs. Clinton had her work cut out for her. The health care system, in and of itself, was highly complex and involved every segment of American life. The Congressional Budget Office reported that health care accounted for one-seventh of the economy in 1992. For businesses, big and small, health care benefits were a growing influence in the bottom line. For health care professionals and related industries, reform could change the way they worked, their personal compensation, and organization profits. For insurance companies, the reform could mean fundamental, and potentially devastating, changes in the ways they did business.

Such special interests surround all issues, but this issue in particular gathered stakeholders far beyond businesses, associations, and lobbyists. Health care reform would affect literally every American, so consequences of reform were personal and personalized from the start. Throughout the campaign, President Clinton listened to and shared the stories of people across the nation. He asked about deductibles and copayments, about diagnoses and treatments. The same personal investment that reached them in the campaign and proved he was "in touch" would be critical to the issue's eventual resolution. One grassroots campaign strategist said, "On health care, the interest level is immediately there, and it is very deep. You don't have to explain to people why they should care" (Rubin, 1993a, 1,084).

In theoretical terms, "health care" as an "issue" had achieved somewhat "permanent" legitimacy and easy movement to current status, due to the "medical beat" in national news organizations. "Health care *policy*" easily fit within those broader boundaries and could be moved swiftly to current status when proposed, especially by a president. The Clintons' challenge was not a need to build interest in the issue. They were, to the contrary, overwhelmed with broad-based, diverse, and intense interest. Their challenge was to shape those interests into constituencies that would support their version of health care reform.

Unfortunately, the task force alienated many of the people whom the Clintons needed in order to succeed. Although the task force staff met with over 572 organizations before its work was over and was comprised of over 500 people from various areas of expertise, its meetings were not open. Worse yet, the task force subgroups included no Republican committee staff, and Republican legislators were only brought up-to-date infrequently by Ira Magaziner, the chief task force policy advisor (Drew, 1994).

The secrecy of the task force process not only failed to build the important relationships with legislative and committee staff needed for the crafting and passage of policy, but it also provoked a suit by Association of American Physicians and Surgeons, the American Council for Health Care Reform, and the National Legal & Policy Center. GOP Senator Charles Grassley called the task force a "dangerously secretive 'shadow government' " (Clift, 1993a, 20). The official justification of the closed process was to "stop reporters and lobbyists from badgering the staff" (Priest, 1993b, A1). The "unofficial" analysis was to protect the administration from the potential fallout of work performed by "amateur policymakers" (Drew, 1994, 192).

The task force was criticized by those inside the administration as well, both for its process and the policy developing out of it. Behind closed doors, Donna Shalala, Secretary of Health and Human Services, warned that the plan was "developing a negative coalition. This program will turn off liberals and conservatives; no one will be enthusiastic. All the interest groups will be mad—the doctors, the hospitals, the labs. You're building on all the negatives" (Drew, 1994, 306). Apparently the controversy was ignored because the task force charged ahead with the same process and in April presented the president with 1,100 individual decisions to be made before the task force could move ahead. The plan, clearly, would be all-encompassing and complex, dealing with every possible aspect of health care reform, from medical education to specific benefits to be included in a comprehensive insurance package.

During this time, not only interest groups but the press became increasingly alienated from the work of the task force. Several professional media organizations, including the American Society of Newspaper Editors and the Associated Press, joined in the legal action against the task force and offered an amicus curiae brief to the U.S. Court of Appeals, hoping to gain access to the task force meetings and its documents. Reporters were having trouble covering the issue without adequate information and were not developing the expertise needed to cover the issue effectively. They often resorted to the administration's "trial balloon du jour" syndrome to explain the issue to the public (Morganthau, 1993, 36) or they spent their words covering political process rather than substantive issue controversies, an issue which developed throughout the campaign. Eleanor Clift called the task force a "covert operation" and said in March 1993 that their process was "making people angry now" (Clift, 1993a, 37).

Despite the negative process, some groups began to line up behind the Clintons. The Business Roundtable and the U.S. Chamber of Commerce endorsed Clinton's position of "managed competition." The AFL-CIO called for a broad-based consumption tax to pay for a reformed system. Over 184 consumer, religious, social, labor, and health industry groups signed a letter in support of "guaranteeing health coverage with comprehensive benefits for all Americans" (Priest, 1993a, A5). Business leaders, *in general,* supported the concept of "managed competition." Insurance companies, *in general,* supported "universal coverage." While a broad consensus seemed possible, neither the detailed requirements of legislation or the means to finance health reform had been proposed.

The task force disbanded in April, partly due to legal and political pressures, partly because they had done all they could without more direct involvement of the administration. The legislative package was far from complete, and the Clintons and top advisors continued to craft a plan. The introduction of reform also had to be timed with the administration's other initiatives. Advisors Bentsen, Panetta, and Stephanopoulos wanted to keep health care reform off the public agenda while they concentrated on the budget battle (Drew, 1994, 189). The "gay ban in the military" debate had already intruded unexpectedly upon the president's attention and headlines (see Bostdorff, chapter 9). Events in Bosnia could not be controlled or postponed. Given the crowded agenda, the administration announced in May that they would address health care reform in June. Then, in June, a meeting between the administration and Congress produced yet another delay, this time until September. The issue the president had identified as critical to economic recovery and American domestic security slipped further and further down the agenda. The administration appeared to be struggling.

The delay had other important long-term consequences. It gave special interest groups time to develop alternative plans and to prepare and launch massive grassroots campaigns that redefined public perceptions about the president's plans. Throughout the summer, the communications industry exploded around the health care issue. The Pharmaceuticals Manufacturers Association hired the Sawyer Miller Group, a Washington lobbying firm. The Medical Rehabilitation

Education Foundation, a group of rehabilitation organizations and hospitals, hired Hill and Knowlton to represent its interests. The Consumers Union commissioned a Gallup Poll (Rubin, 1993a). Health care reform took the lead as *Congressional Quarterly*'s largest advertising category (Starobin, 1993).

The most noted of the opposition groups was the Health Insurance Association of America (HIAA). A group representing small- and mid-sized insurance companies, HIAA hired former Congressman Bill Gradison to lead its efforts and launched the first phase of print advertising for the "Coalition of Health Insurance Choices" in the summer of 1993. Before it was all over, the HIAA would spend $17 million on its "Harry and Louise" advertising campaign. Less visible, but equally important, the HIAA launched grassroots efforts nationwide and made several public relations firms wealthier in the process. They hired field directors in six key states, sponsored a grassroots program in fifty states, hired a firm for telephone contact, another for direct mail, a third for opinion leader grassroots organizing, and a fourth firm for public opinion polling (Faucheux, 1995).

The lack of access to the administration heightened the relationships between and among lobbyists, interest groups, and the press. TJFR Publishing created *The Health Care Reporter,* a newsletter devoted to analysis of health care reporting. As a special service, they sold reporter profiles to assist those hoping to gain access to the key journalists in health care coverage. Speakers' bureaus representing journalists reported booming business. One agent said that "virtually every pharmaceutical company desperately is trying to line up press speakers." Health Speaker's Inc. sponsored a two-day conference on health care at the National Press Club with health economists, journalists, and government officials sharing their insights, for only $635 per person (Starobin, 1993). Information was flowing in all directions, except directly from the administration. Because the White House could not legally participate in high-cost advertising and lobbying strategies, the Democratic National Committee originally took the lead in the public campaign for the president's plan, but the DNC could not attract the bipartisan support (basically, money) needed to launch the campaign. Finally, much later than their opponents, health care reform supporters organized "The Health Project" and worked in conjunction with the DNC (Priest, 1993d, A10.)

While the Clintons crafted their plan and their supporters floundered in disorganization, others used the time to develop competing proposals. As the September 1993 "launch date" for the Clinton plan neared, 137 House Republicans announced a plan of "incremental" change to the existing system. Then, Senator Don Nickles introduced a bill drafted by the conservative Heritage Foundation with twenty-four Republican cosponsors. A third Republican plan, closest to Clinton's, was introduced by Senator John Chaffee along with nineteen cosponsors.

The president's own party produced its alternatives. Representative Pete Stark (D–Calif.), Chair of the House Ways and Means Committee, attacked "managed competition'' early in the summer. After the task force "leaked" a general outline of its recommendations, Senator Daniel P. Moynihan, a key player in the reform debate, called the president's plan a "fantasy." Liberal Democrats offered two proposals patterned after Canada's single-payer systems, with ninety cosponsors in the House. The most threatening of all alternatives, proposed by Representative Jim Cooper (D–Tenn.), was sponsored by nearly equal numbers of Democrats and Republicans. Cooper's plan incorporated managed competition and insurance reform without employer mandates to finance the plan or mandatory participation. The plan would not "guarantee" universal coverage.

The delay shifted the terms of the debate. One analyst observed: "The debate is starting to get focused on whether the solution is worse than the problem, not how to solve the problem. If people don't think they're getting something else— security, better care, something—then the plan will be in trouble" (Morin, 1993, A4). Moreover, instead of moving toward a clear choice between alternatives, a "for or against" vote around which people could rally, the competing plans complicated and confused the issue. Robert Blendon, a professor of public health at Harvard University, said, "By waiting, it will no longer be his [Clinton's] plan versus the status quo, which everyone agrees is terrible. It's his plan versus the simple-payer plan, versus the tax-credit plan, and it will be harder to get a consensus when there are these other plans on the table" (Morin, 1993, A4). The president's base of support, and his ability to control the definition of the health care issue, was slipping away before his plan was even made public.

CLINTON OFFICIALLY LAUNCHES HEALTH CARE REFORM

Finally, on September 22, 1993, President Clinton launched the "official" health care debate with a special address to a joint session of Congress. The speech centered around a central theme of "security": "If Americans are to have the courage to change in a difficult time, we must first be secure in our most basic needs," the most "critical" of which was health care. Clinton proposed "health care that can never be taken away" (Clinton, 1993d, 1,837).

He defined the issue not as one of quality of technology, knowledge, or the skill of the medical professionals who provide care but a "broken" insurance system that sometimes does "take away" insurance or is so expensive as to offer no protection at all. He said the American health care system itself "is too uncertain and too expensive, too bureaucratic and too wasteful. It has too much fraud and too much greed" (1,837), a system for which there was "no excuse" (1,838).

He used the speech not to introduce specifics of policy, for in fact they were not yet totally compiled, but to offer six principles to guide the reform effort— security, simplicity, savings, choice, quality, and responsibility. "Security" was defined as a "comprehensive package of benefits over the course of an entire lifetime" guaranteed for every American (1,839). "Comprehensive" included preventive care, coverage for the cost of prescription drugs, and long-term care for the disabled and elderly, programs especially important to the large and politically active senior citizens lobby.

Late in the speech, Clinton tied security to its strong political roots in America. He linked "domestic security" to the "security" won in the cold war:

Just a few days ago we saw a simple handshake shatter decades of deadlock in the Middle East. We've seen the walls crumble in Berlin and South Africa. We see the ongoing brave struggle of the people of Russia to seize freedom and democracy. And now it is our turn to strike a blow for freedom in this country. The freedom of Americans to live without fear that their own nation's health care system won't be there for them when they need it. (1,845)

The psychological connections between "security" and "freedom" were made explicit. Health care reform was a matter of American pride and could be accomplished with American know-how.

The second principle, "simplicity," specifically addressed the burden of paperwork that prevented doctors from spending time with their patients. The proposal called for one standard insurance form and easing the regulatory burden to promote efficiency and better care. "Savings" returned Clinton to his campaign theme that linked health care reform to economic security. He said, "Our competitiveness, our whole economy, the integrity of the way the government works and, ultimately, our living standards depend upon our ability to achieve savings without harming the quality of health care" (1,840). To address the savings issue, Clinton proposed managed competition, "a combination of private market forces and a sound public policy," coverage for all citizens, and the simplification of the insurance procedures. He also called for elimination of waste and fraud. "Choice" of doctors and health care plans, Clinton asserted, was already slipping away. Clinton wanted to guarantee choice both for doctors and for consumers. Present high "quality" in health care was to be preserved.

The final principle, "responsibility," was all-encompassing. Insurance companies and laboratories had to adopt more responsible practices. Responsibility also required curbing violence, "higher rates of AIDS, of smoking and excessive drinking, of teen pregnancy, of low birth-weight babies" (1,843). Re-sounding a campaign theme, Clinton reminded Americans that responsibility "isn't about them. It's about you, it's about me, it's about each of us." He argued that "if we're going to produce a better health care system for every one of us, every one of us is going to have to do our part" (1,843). And "all of us" and "each of us" would pay for these reforms, through a combination of employer and employee contributions to health care insurance, new savings, taxes on tobacco, corporate contributions, and small business subsidies.

Clinton's principles were "goods" in and of themselves. The ambiguity of the terms created a strong presumption for the president's plan and stifled criticism. Who would argue against "simplicity," or "choice," or "savings" per se? The term, "responsibility" echoed Clinton's vision for the role of government shared in his campaign—a partnership where government created a system of opportunity and security and citizens took individual responsibility for the quality of their lives. "Security," as the central principle in Clinton's analysis, resonated with the public's sense of uncertainty and anxiety in tough economic times. It tapped both individual motivations and political tradition. The insurance industry exploited the desire of people to protect themselves from the normal risks of life and unpredictable loss, except people who *had* insurance no longer felt "secure" about its permanence or coverage. Many others had already lost their insurance. Their "insecurity" fueled reform. Moreover, in a society built on productivity, economic security requires a physical capacity to work. The connections between and among "security," "health," and "work" are strong in American culture. The fact that "insurance" no longer contributed to the connection between "health" and "economic security" was a trend well worth exploiting rhetorically.

General reaction after Clinton's speech was positive. *Congressional Quarterly* reported that "for the first time in years, it seemed as if Congress was filled with a sense of the possibility of enacting a piece of sweeping social legislation" (*Congressional Quarterly Almanac,* 1993, 338). Representative Thomas Bliley's response signaled both the strength and weakness of Clinton's opening in the debate: "The public wants us to work something out. Of the six goals the president laid out, I don't think any Democrat or any Republican disagrees with any of them. It is how you get from A to B that there is disagreement on" (*Congressional Quarterly Almanac,* 1993, 338). The need for change and reform was a source of general agreement. The devil would be in the details as the public waited for specific reform proposals.

Clinton (1993d) signaled that a lively debate would follow, some of it genuine and some by people "motivated by the self-interest they have in the waste the system now generates, because that waste is providing jobs, incomes and money for some people" (1,845). He asked the public to ask one question when the information started flowing: "Ask yourself whether the cost of staying on this same course isn't greater than the cost of change" (1,845). But the president's attempt to inoculate the public against "motivated self-interest" arrived after they had already contracted a strong case of suspicion of government.

The battle to come was quickly revealed. In his town hall meetings on health care, almost every question related a personal experience with health care and asked how the president's plan would help individual situations (Clinton, 1993e). Clinton's ability to answer those questions, to show empathy and understanding of the individual's situations, to explain and interpret each situation within the overall health care system, and to express how comprehensive reform would address the public's needs seemed to reenergize the public's support for a while. His job approval rating climbed from 46 percent a week before his speech, to 50 percent the day after, and 56 percent four days later, after he'd barnstormed around the country doing what he did best—talking to Americans about their problems and articulating the broad concepts of his plan to address their needs (Schneider, 1993). He was initially successful in reinvigorating the polarization of the campaign: change versus more of the same, linking "change" to positive outcomes for most Americans. He was perceived as active, committed, and in touch with the day-to-day concerns of the American people. Hillary Clinton took the lead with Congress through a week of testimony. Her performance was described as "marvelous" and "outstanding" (Rubin, 1993b, 2,640). The First Lady's approval ratings were at 60 percent.

Not until a month later did Clinton finally deliver the specific proposal to Congress and the story shifted dramatically. The 1,342-page document looked anything but a model of "simplicity" as promised. The financial side quickly came under criticism. The media repeated Senator Moynihan's statement that Clinton's plan was a "fantasy." Tom Foley called it a policy "Godzilla." Representative Pete Stark of California said, "His bill is so complex and convoluted, we'll have to go through it a section at a time and just redo it" (Rubin and Connolly, 1993, 2,969).

Committees wrangled for who would draft health care reform legislation, and ultimately five committees won the honor: House committees on Ways and Means, Energy and Commerce, and Education and Labor and the Senate committees on Finance and Labor and Human Resources (Rubin, 1993b). Critics began speaking of "entitlements" and "bureaucracy," "rationing" and a loss of "choice." The polarizations were shifting from Clinton's preferred "change versus more of the same" or "Clinton's plan" versus "the status quo" to a fractionalized and confusing discussion among many plans in several committees with diverse membership and concerns.

While Congress started working "line by line" through Clinton's plan, the HIAA again attracted media attention, this time with the help of Hillary Clinton. The HIAA released the first among the "Harry and Louise" advertisements in September that ended with the tag line, "There's Got to Be a Better Way." In early November, Hillary Clinton responded strongly to the HIAA campaign, saying the industry had "brought us to the brink of bankruptcy because of the way that they have financed health care" (Priest, 1993e, A1). The clash gave the HIAA's message extensive free time on the network news programs. HIAA president Bill Gradison said, "All this gives us a degree of visibility way beyond what we would have achieved by the [advertising] markets we're involved in. I'm delighted at the things they've done to make it possible to reach a larger audience" (Weisskopf, 1993b, A8).

The Clintons' response to critics only strengthened the opponent, while the "positive" campaign designed by the Democratic National Committee to support the Clintons' efforts was floundering from limited funding and poor planning. "National Health Care Awareness Day" was canceled. Speakers sent out by the White House faced open opposition from the public and interest groups. The HIAA had already spent $3.7 million on grassroots lobbying before the DNC did anything.

Stakeholders outside government began to fractionalize into many diverse interests as the details of reform plans and their consequences reached the public. The HIAA represented the majority of the insurance industry. The five largest health insurers split with the HIAA to form the Alliance for Managed Competition, a group more favorable to Clinton's reforms. The Council for Affordable Insurance represented smaller insurers who feared they would be eliminated in Clinton's move to large insurance pools. The issue also generated new coalitions.

Business fractured along similar lines. The National Association of Manufacturers (NAM), representing 12,000 companies, predicted that any health care reform would "contain some bitter medicine for individual companies." The major divisions in business were between "big versus small, older work force versus younger, service versus manufacturer, union versus nonunion" (Day, 1993, D1). General Motors, for instance, favored a single-payer system with employer mandates, arguing that the companies that do not insure their workers were driving up costs for everyone without paying their fair share. GM maintained that the present system discriminated against companies with older workers and retirees. Marriott Corporation, another NAM member, wanted government out of the system. The Small Business Legislative Council, a coalition of 100 trade and professional associations, favored price freezes. The National Federation of Independent Business opposed any government interference (Day, 1993). The Business Roundtable had initially endorsed "managed competition," a balance of market and government forces used to reduce cost.

As the debate continued, delays, fractionalized interests, confusion, active opposition, and competing issues all slowed the momentum for health care reform in 1993. The overall good news was that Clinton was able to report continued economic improvement throughout 1993—job creation, relatively low interest rates balancing reasonable inflation, spending cuts, and movement to lower budget deficits. The economic upturn produced yet another "downturn" for health care reform because the "insecurity" at the heart of Clinton's reform momentum was improving on its own.

Self-imposed reforms in segments of the health care industry also showed improvement. Managed competition, consolidation of health care organizations, bargaining of large voluntary health care alliances, and increased use of generic drugs all produced decreasing costs (Hilzenrath, 1994). Citizens were also shown evidence that the health care industry was, to some degree, fixing itself without government interference. At the winter meeting of the Republican National Committee in January, Senator Robert Dole announced, "There isn't any crisis in American in health care" (Balz, 1994). Given that the public generally distrusted government's ability to "fix anything," presumption moved back to the status quo.

At the end of 1993, the plan for health care reform was months behind schedule, with vocal opposition having developed during the delay. Clinton's plan met with immediate challenges inside Congress, on both sides of the aisle. Its sweeping scope and complexity appeared to be much different than he promised—neither simple nor affordable. If he were going to succeed, Clinton needed to regain control of the debate.

CLINTON'S ATTEMPT TO RECAPTURE MOMENTUM

President Clinton tried to refocus the health care debate with his State of the Union on January 25, 1994, exactly a year after he commissioned the health care reform task force (Clinton, 1994a). Instead of looking back on the momentum lost, Clinton predicted an end to the debate, "This year, we will make history by reforming the health care system." He responded to opponents "who say there's no health care crisis" with a litany of statistics—"tell it to the 58 million Americans who have no coverage at all for some time each year. Tell it to the 81 million Americans with those preexisting conditions. Tell it to the small businesses burdened by the skyrocketing costs of insurance" (152). Clinton highlighted the "insecurity" in the present system: "It means every night millions of well-insured Americans go to bed just an illness, an accident, or a pink slip away from having no coverage or financial ruin." He reiterated the goal of "health insurance everybody can depend on" and "guaranteed health security" and reaffirmed the principles of reform. Finally, he attempted to assert some final authority on the issue: "I want to make this very clear. I am open, as I have said repeatedly, to the best ideas of concerned members of both parties. I have no special brief for any specific approach, even in our own bill, except this: If you send me legislation that does not guarantee every American private health insurance that can never be taken away, you will force me to take this pen, veto the legislation, and we'll come right back here and start all over again" (Clinton, 1994a, 153). Clinton hoped to challenge Congress, but the problems with health care reform had only barely begun.

In the Republican response to the State of the Union, Senator Robert Dole said "President and Mrs. Clinton deserve credit for starting the debate. It has been very helpful. Now, nearly a year later, we better understand this important issue." What we understand, Dole said, was that "America has the best health care system in the world" and that while "our country has health care problems," there was no "health care crisis." He argued that the Clintons' "massive and complex program" would create the very crisis it was designed to overcome. Dole turned Clinton's discourse against him, summing it up as "more cost. Less choice. More taxes. Less quality. More government control. Less control for you and your family" (Dole, 1994). In the most memorable moment, Dole displayed a complex chart of 200 or so boxes representing Clinton's plan and the "new bureaucracy" it would create. He described some of the plan's provisions and then pointed to the bottom of the chart and said, "You and I are way down here, somewhere. The president's idea is to put a mountain of bureaucrats between you and your doctor" (Dole, 1994). The House Republican Policy Committee said, "Only in ivory tower isolation could academic ideologues create a plan to take over 14% of the economy, cripple job creation, hinder technological and pharmaceutical breakthroughs and ration health care" (Eaton, 1994). Clinton's plan was not yet even moving through congressional committees and it was labeled as "bureaucracy, rationing, crippling, hindering."

Dole's speech, and especially his chart, hit a nerve. Over 2,000 phone calls blocked the switchboards in the office of Senator Arlen Specter, the creator of the chart. Over 24.7 million homes saw Clinton and Dole polarize the debate for the coming year (Grove, 1994, C1). The sides from which to choose were Clinton's growing bureaucracy versus more of the same, a status quo that middle-class Americans were embracing more strongly by the month. A new blitz of advertising built on the negative force of Dole's analysis. The American Medical Association asked, "Would you rather trust your life to an M.D. or an MBA?" The HIAA's Harry and Louise complained about the plan "that forces us to buy our insurance through these new, mandatory government health alliances." The Health Care Reform Project attempted to counter the HIAA but again came up short. They flashed across the screen: "The Republicans. They just don't get it" (Kurtz, 1994, A3). But increasingly the "out of touch" message was sticking to the Clintons. While they still said the nation was in a "health care crisis" and the majority of Americans agreed, they were no longer sure that the Clinton plan would end the crisis.

On February 3, 1994, the Business Roundtable, part of the early "reform coalition," announced their break with the Clintons and support of the Cooper Plan (Priest and Devroy, 1994, A1). The next day, the U.S. Chamber of Commerce withdrew its support from the Clinton plan. Only a few days later, the National Association of Manufacturers and Ross Perot announced their opposition. Then, the Congressional Budget Office reported that the Clinton plan cost estimates were severely underestimated. As their plan moved to Congress, the Clintons focused on the elderly, but despite much improved coverage for long-term care and medicines, senior citizens were reluctant to support the plan. With the policy finally being hammered out, no coalition of public support was available to assist Congress in its work.

Of course, other issues distracted the public and the media from health care reform. The upheaval in Bosnia, Iraq, Rwanda, North Korea, and eventually Haiti reminded the nation that some of their problems were not domestic. The Whitewater scandal, Hillary Clinton's cattle futures, and Paula Jones' sexual harassment charges shifted the White House focus to damage control for much of the summer. The O.J. Simpson case captured the media's attention. The Brady bill and the crime bill took congressional time away from health care.

But while Congress and the president dealt with other issues, during the Easter and Memorial Day recesses, senators and representatives learned that the public, still under a barrage of grassroots lobbying, had not forgotten health care reform. Public opinion was becoming increasingly skeptical about the ability of government to address their health care problems. In June, 74 percent of Americans approved of "universal coverage" but only 33 percent supported the Clinton plan (Waldman, 1994a, 28). By July, public opinion stalled.

As six committees struggled to develop workable legislation, other obstacles developed. In June, Dan Rostenkowski, chairman of the House Ways and Means Committee, left his key position amidst charges of corruption. By July, Energy and Commerce gave up, Ways and Means produced a 20–18 bill including many of Clinton's key components. House Education and Labor and Senate Labor and Human Resources both produced bills too liberal to achieve support. The Senate Finance Committee finally brought a bill forward, but only after lengthy battles about "hard triggers" and "soft triggers" and many amendments to Chairman Moynihan's draft (Alter and Waldman, 1994, 14–15).

Hillary Clinton hit the road again in July, hoping to support representatives as they returned home for the July 4 recess. The central component of the campaign was a revival of the campaign bus caravan, this time called the Health Security Express. But Mrs. Clinton quickly ran into trouble. Media coverage focused on poor planning and problems of the caravan and on the anti-reform protesters who greeted the caravan all along its route (Clift with Waldman, 1994, 21). Mr. Clinton himself responded to protesters directly in New Jersey (Clinton, 1994c). Again, the Clintons' message was met only days before the congressional debate with vocal public opposition.

As momentum seemed to fail, President Clinton appeared to be looking for compromise. He went back to his former colleagues at the National Governors' Association and began at talk compromise on his "universal coverage" standard, saying he could accept in the "ballpark of 95 percent" coverage, if it meant getting reform (Clinton, 1994b). But he quickly returned to his original standard. Was it a "waffle"? A compromise? That work was finally left to Congress. Opinion polls already reported that the people wanted Congress to take the lead, and many wanted everyone to give up for 1994 (Samuelson, 1994b, 51). If anything positive happened, the president probably wouldn't get much credit. If nothing happened, he'd probably receive significant blame.

Democratic leaders Gephardt and Mitchell struggled to craft a compromise before the looming recess. Floor debate in the Senate began on August 9. (The House delayed action until the Senate made some move.) Majority leader George Mitchell proposed a package of insurance reform to achieve 95 percent coverage, guaranteeing a minimum package of benefits and cap on costs. The changes would be financed by a cigarette tax and cuts in Medicare and Medicaid. Mitchell worked to create bipartisan support through a compromise with the supporters of the Chaffee plan ("Issue," 1994, 53–54).

Meanwhile, the Senate was also engaged in delicate negotiations to win the crime bill. On August 25, the democrats squeaked to victory with a 61–39 vote at 11 P.M. The next day, with a need to regroup (and not to push their luck), Mitchell called a halt to health care debate until after the Labor Day recess.

In September, a few glimmers of hope launched a "last ditch effort." Bob Dole signaled Republican willingness to continue discussions. Clinton endorsed the less than "universal" Mitchell plan and silenced his threats to veto. But in reality, the fight was over. Senator Phil Gramm said, "These guys have got to accept the fact that for two weeks they've been dragging a dead body around" (Lacayo, 1994, 41). Finally, on September 27, Senate majority leader George Mitchell conceded and ended the debate: "The insurance industry on the outside and the majority of Republicans on the inside proved to be too much to overcome" ("Health Care: Dead," 1994). Health care reform was a "promise unfulfilled" in 1994.

WHAT HAPPENED: ISSUES ABOUT THE "ISSUE"

The "health care crisis," as defined by Clinton, was problematic from the start. Because Clinton moved from a broad description of the problem and principles of reform to detailed commitments to "universal coverage," and "guaranteed health insurance that can never be taken away," accomplished through a system of "managed competition" and "employer mandates," he defined the issue in a way that eventually splintered potential constituencies, moved away from the important middle-class constituency and toward what was perceived as a "big government," liberal position that met the needs of the under class at the expense of the middle class.

The "comprehensive" nature of the proposed reform set boundaries for the issue that included literally every American citizen, every business and industry, and every aspect of the health care system from direct costs to the medical education system and distribution of doctors throughout the nation. Nothing was left untouched. Traditional interests fractured along the aspects of the policy most central to their particular identities. Business splintered according to size, employee demographics, and product or service offered. Even the insurance industry divided. What started out as a public mandate for change soon disintegrated along politically partisan lines (Democrat versus Republican, state versus federal control) and according to individual circumstances: the young versus senior citizens, employed versus unemployed, those trying to preserve the health care they enjoyed versus those without adequate health care, and on and on.

Without either strong consensus among special interests or a mandate of public support, the issue followed its involved publics: change versus more of the same splintered into multiple plans with multiple provisions. Confusion and disintegration characterized the debate and outcome. Thomas Mann, director of governmental studies for the Brookings Institution, summarized the "stakeholder" problem: "You can legislate health care form in the absence of public opinion as long as you have the support of interest groups. But with a divided, skeptical public and no interest group support, you haven't got a chance" (Cloud, 1994, 18).

Clinton's "crisis" rhetoric made the whole situation worse in the end. Declaring a crisis can be a powerful rhetorical strategy for presidents. A "crisis" demands public and congressional attention . . . immediately. The "crisis" moves quickly to the national agenda through instant media analysis, and the sense of urgency "legitimizes the issue, the need for quick action, and any sacrifices citizens may be asked to make" (Bostdorff, 1994, 5). A declaration of "crisis" also usually polarizes rhetoric between the "threat" and the "threatened." What is needed in a crisis is swift action to fend off the threat.

Clinton's response to the "crisis" was neither immediate nor a clear source of unity. He embraced a slow, cumbersome process that produced an inscrutable and complex policy that squelched any urgency or momentum created by the "crisis." If there were a crisis, how could the delays be justified? If there were a "crisis," why wasn't health care pushed to the front of the agenda? Again, Clinton's rhetoric and his actions were inconsistent. Worse yet, two years later, nothing had changed. Are the problems still there? Does the crisis still exist? If so, Clinton failed. If not, Clinton exaggerated the nation's conditions for political purposes. Either way, he lost credibility and missed the momentum generated by the recession.

Clinton also failed to clearly define and personify the "threat" posed by the "crisis." The intangible threat was the anxiety and insecurity of not knowing if you would be taken care of, if and when you would become ill. Late in 1993, the Clintons attempted to make the policies of the insurance industry the "enemy," but in their own rhetoric, the industry's threat was to the Clinton's reform plan, not to the American people. Had Clinton defined the crisis more specifically, as others suggested, as an "insurance crisis," short-term action could have been passed almost immediately and the industry could have been the personified "enemy." Ironically, insurance reform is *still* viable and received bipartisan support throughout the debate. Clinton could have addressed the immediate "crisis" for the middle class, removed the threat to those already insured, and then undertaken long-term study and significant change necessary for remaining health care issues. Daniel P. Moynihan asserted all along that the health care issue for the uninsured was a "welfare reform issue." Again, that shift in the boundaries would allow for bipartisan support, would limit the special interests involved, and would reshape public opinion. A "health care crisis" was unmanageable. An "insurance crisis" as separate from a need to address the "failing welfare system" would realign the public's involvement in the issues' resolution.

Clinton also failed to consider the full implication of his terminology when "universal coverage" became the ultimate legislative "line in the sand." He moved the issue away from the centrist economic message that made it a positive for middle-class Americans in Clinton's election. Throughout the campaign, Clinton argued that health care costs needed to be reigned in because of the effects on individuals and on the nation. Universal coverage was needed to eliminate cost shifting from those with insurance to those without and to distribute risk across all Americans, thus reducing costs. Covering the uninsured was an essential component to middle-class relief. Universal coverage was the means to achieve the desired end. As the debate developed, the emphasis of the reform message focused on "universal coverage" as an end in itself, ultimately creating a "right" of health care, without articulation of the connections to the middle class, who already had health care but were discouraged by escalating costs.

The stakes in "universal coverage" were high from the start. "Universal" still means 100 percent. "Guaranteed" means that *any* exception to the plan uncovers a disingenuous commitment, a false "security." The terms of the debate made the president politically vulnerable to any compromise plan. He would be settling and waffling. For a president accused of having no core principles, abandoning or fudging on the central principle of his most central issue position was untenable symbolically, but necessary politically. It was a self-imposed lose/lose proposition.

"Universal coverage" that "can never be taken away" also sets up the "rights" argument that was never addressed openly. While the American public likes "rights," they do not like the "entitlements" rights create. The dominant "undertow" of public opinion on *all* issues, and evidenced strongly in the Republican triumph in the midterm elections, was "a lack of faith in government, ... pulling against doing anything at all" on health care (Rubin, 1994c, 16). Presidential scholar Jeffrey Tulis warned in 1993 that "[Clinton] will have to be careful to demonstrate that what he is trying to secure is conditions for the free exercise of rights, not the actual exercising of those rights" (Barnes, 1993, 2,496). One of Clinton's promises as a "new" democrat was to balance "rights" and "responsibilities" as the nation moved to reform the "failed welfare state" and rejected "big government" solutions to social problems. Democratic pollster Celinda Lake said, "The energy for reform was around cost containment and health security. Voters were always very clear about what they wanted. The administration misread the answers." The administration's rhetoric originally was addressed to middle-class issues but the plan itself focused elsewhere. *Congressional Quarterly*'s analyst Alissa Rubin said: "The deepest flaw may have been that while Clinton and the democrats aimed their rhetoric at the middle class, the plan's clearest benefits went to a minority of the public, the 15 percent of Americans who are uninsured. And the biggest concern of the middle class—rising insurance costs—was rarely emphasized" (Rubin, 1994c, 13). Like it or not, on health care, even motivated voters had little ability to gather and process all information necessary to make an informed choice. In such a case, when the simplest analysis reveals inconsistency between words and policies, the level of trust and faith required for voters to support a plan is undermined.

All of these definitional factors opened the door to the negative campaign launched against the Clintons. They lost on the principle of "simplicity" when their huge plan thudded onto congressional desks. Accusations of unwieldy, inefficient, and costly bureaucracy were backed up with memorable charts and examples of minutiae. Discussions convinced people that they would have less rather than more "choice." "Managed competition" was redefined as "rationing." While Americans wanted reduced costs, they wanted unlimited access to the very best care of the very best medical system in the world.

Such negative messages were clearly and concisely communicated to carefully targeted publics by a series of advertising and direct mail strategies. The opposing messages were critical to the Clintons' failure. One analyst said, "This legislative battle was just like a political campaign, and I don't think the White House realized that. Whoever spends the most money in politics usually wins" (Scarlett, 1994, 37); Research has shown that negative messages are weighed more heavily than positive messages, are more influential in formation of judgments, and exhibit a great capacity to alter already existing impressions (Johnson-Cartee and Copeland, 1991, 15–16). In short, it's easier to argue against something than for something. The many negative ads, thus, may have had an impact. Kathleen Hall Jamieson argued vigorously that the HIAA ads in particular actually were highly overrated by the administration, Congress, and the Clintons. She reported that focus groups made "no sense at all" of one HIAA ad, and the minority who recalled the ads an hour after watching them remembered only vague appeals (Jamieson, 1994, A19). Jamieson also noted that "unless you are a CNN junkie or live in the hometown of a pivotal member of Congress on a health committee," you probably didn't see the ads. Of course, that was the point. The messages were carefully targeted to opinion leaders (a.k.a. CNN news junkies), the media, and Congress to build just the kind of debate that ensued. The ads also were only part of a savvy and expensive grassroots campaign. The ads were reinforced by more direct, specifically tailored messages. Unless the focus groups reproduced those conditions, they "tested" the ads out of the context of preexisting attitudes and behaviors of targeted publics and out of the context of the total campaign. What if face-to-face information sessions explained "community rating" and then the ad was shown? Chances are the second strategy would be only as good as the first.

Be that as it may, and despite the extensive media discussions of the HIAA campaign, advertising alone probably does not account for the Clintons' failure. While advertising should get its due, political advisors are clear: "Despite early support in opinion polls for the Clinton plan, . . . it was inevitable that the American people would turn against this proposal. It wasn't the ads that killed the Clinton plan; it was the contents of the plan itself" (Scarlett, 1994, 37). The ads took advantage of the policy's weaknesses.

All of these conclusions point to alternative strategies for health care reform. The differing "issues" within health care suggest breaking the issues on those lines. Had Clinton taken on welfare reform first and succeeded, he would have enhanced his credentials as a "New Democrat," built important alliances with Republicans, and separated the "uninsured" issue from the concerns of the middle class. Welfare reform, based on a principle of moving people from the welfare rolls to work, would have then reinforced the urgency of health care reform for "working" America. Reversing Clinton's equation, to complete welfare reform and then not to move directly to health care reform would only push people back to the welfare system and set the nation back. Clinton argued that a reformed health care system was needed prior to welfare reform. A more strategic move would have been to use welfare reform to push the more difficult health care issue through Congress.

Having addressed some of the needs of uninsured Americans, Clinton then could say the "short-term" fix needed to stabilize health care costs, the most pressing part of the health care crisis, was insurance reform, the middle-class issue that received strong bipartisan support. The insurance industry, when isolated from other special interests, also wields less influence. Welfare reform and insurance reform could have broken gridlock, brought meaningful change, and built a moderate bipartisan coalition to then take on the further challenges of broader health care reform.

What else should the Clinton White House and others learn from the failed health care reform initiative? The president should embrace the issue and generate momentum but maintain some distance from the practical process of hammering out policy details and the symbolic association with the outcome. Two factors contributed directly to the president's inability to manage his involvement on this issue. The first was appointing the First Lady as the "point person" on health care. Whatever the task force recommended, it immediately became the "Clinton plan," without any distinction between Hillary and Bill Clinton. Not only would the success or failure be his personally *by name,* but the ups and downs of his personal leadership would be tied directly to the policy. Consider the different symbolic and political possibilities if the plan were the "Shalala plan" or the "Magaziner plan." Symbolically, the possibility for yet another Clinton plan would still exist. And those plans could be challenged without a direct, personal challenge to the president. With Hillary Clinton in charge, such symbolic movement was cut off.

Moreover, the president's options for responding to "his" task force were also limited. A task force or commission is a typical presidential strategy used to legitimize an issue and gain expert advice. But the president usually has a range of *public* options when the task force reports. He may reject the findings of the task force, ask the task force to go back to consider additional issues, or ask some other group to take the task force recommendations and mold them to meet other interests. He might also "fire" or openly disagree with the leader of the group to separate himself from the group's recommendations, and literally or figuratively reassert control of the direction of policy through such a symbolic move. With Hillary Clinton in charge, the president was stuck. He could not create distance or "fire" his wife. Although it might have been somewhat suspect, the Clintons had a possible "out" when Hillary Clinton left Washington for several weeks to attend to her father as he died. Mrs. Clinton could have gracefully stepped aside as someone else carried on task force leadership and could have used her personal situation to drive home the underlying truth of the issue: sooner or later, everyone would deal with the health care system. She could then have stepped back into the role of advisor and spokesperson for the issue, but not necessarily as policy-maker. Her immense contribution as an advocate could be sustained without the many negatives that were eventually attached to her role.

A change in Hillary Clinton's role might have been important internally to the process because advisors and congressional leaders had to "manage" the First Lady differently than Cabinet officers, staffers, and other experts. Elizabeth Drew (1994) reported that the First Lady stifled discussion within the White House and that the praise received early from Congress created a false sense of support. Congress questioned other witnesses on health care with more vigor and more searchingly than they questioned Mrs. Clinton. But Mrs. Clinton captured media coverage. Later, Hillary Clinton's determination to establish the "right" of health care, which was not the president's stated objective, prevented important compromises with Democratic leaders at key points in the debate (Drew, 194). Of course, the ultimate outcome might not have been different but the president would have had more options at several points in the debate.

Another problem attached to the task force was its apparently closed process. Although the task force gathered information through many methods and many sources, what was missing was a sense of two-way communication and consultation. The body was more than an information gatherer and sorter. It formulated policy. That the group produced a plan that had no hope of gathering bipartisan support should not have been surprising, given that Republicans were totally excluded from the process. At a symbolic level, the president who *said* he would stay "in touch" and open and would work with Congress acted otherwise.

The closed process and the complexity of the plan, and then later competing plans, made the issue especially difficult for news organizations to cover. When they had no substance to consider, they turned to the process. The complexity also encouraged "horse race" coverage of the political process, highlighting who was winning or losing in the debate over health care reform, not the substance of the competing plans or interests. One journalist said, "Much of the frustration with press coverage of health care reform stems from the unwieldy nature of the issue and public ambivalence over the proper course of action. Too often, calls for a journalistic 'truth squad' are really pleas by advocates who want reporters to sell their worldviews or programs. In a debate that is complicated and value-laden, journalists have their heads full just ascertaining the facts. Ascertaining the truth is another matter, best left to our audiences" (Kosterlitz, 1994; 748).

As mentioned earlier, this process fostered interest groups unprecedented advocacy advertising, a controlled and highly effective communication strategy perfected by corporations in the 1980s, and sophisticated grassroots action typical of political election campaigns. This time, Clinton's "war room" was on the inside of the beltway, constrained by law and politics. His opponents were many, with skill, motivation, and deep pockets. *Campaigns and Elections* noted that "while media campaigns to affect legislative battles have been seen before in Washington (during the NAFTA debate, for instance) never before have private interests spent so much money so publicly to defeat an initiative launched by a President'' (Scarlett, 1994, 34). Clinton's response to the ad wars was limited but should not have been especially important. The president and Mrs. Clinton command free media time, time unavailable to their opponents. The real problem was that the Clintons seemed unable to articulate their message consistently and then shared their air time through attacking the ads of their opponents.

Hillary Clinton, the task force, and the media aside, the whole process Clinton followed was probably not advisable and was at the heart of all the other problems that emerged. Early on, White House advisors tried to get the president to go no further than his broad statement of philosophy and goals presented in September 1993 and then work with skilled and experienced congressional leaders to draft policy that would pass their respective committees and ultimately both Houses. President Reagan used the strategy successfully for his tax reform in 1986 and President Bush in the Clean Air Act. In these two successes, Reagan and Bush set broad parameters, generated public pressure for action, and then used the veto as leverage. Neil Brown, at the start of the debate, advised Clinton to ''create the climate for action; state a clear set of priorities, then as Congress hashes it out, move in—and out—of the debate as needed to keep his goals on track.'' He advised Clinton's opponents not to underestimate the ''vision thing'' (Brown, 1993, 2,602). In the end, it was Clinton who misused the ''vision thing'' by going beyond the strategic public boundaries of the bully pulpit and by choosing the wrong standard for his veto threat. Had he demanded health care reform that ''reduced costs'' and ''increased security,'' his strategic ambiguity would have positioned him for multiple outcomes. He could use the veto to protect the middle class *and* the uninsured and could take some credit for effective legislation, if passed and signed. Now, to be fair, Reagan and Bush both had the advantage of an opposing party in control of Congress. Clinton could not demonize the ''do nothing Democratic Congress'' in 1993 and 1994. But he removed the possibility of merely shaping the debate when he put forward a monstrous legislative proposal, apparently unwieldy and poorly crafted, with the Clinton name attached, and the full authority of his administration pushing for its passage. The Clintons' late statements of openness and willingness to modify their proposal only made the situation worse. Bill Clinton's saying he was open to compromise was like throwing raw meat to wolves. His greatest weakness was that he was perceived to lack focus, direction, and principle. To spend an entire year in an elaborate policy process and then to appear ''soft'' on the plan only played into his critic's hands. The party faithful in Congress had no good choice—to support a policy they felt was poorly conceived, undercut the president on a central legislative initiative, or evade the issue. Many groups outside of Washington that wanted to support the president were in a similar position. They could not support the president's plan but did not want to openly challenge him. Not only was the issue personal, but the process was made personal as well.

EPILOGUE

In the end, the failure to pass health care reform in 1994 contributed significantly to the lack of confidence in the Clinton White House and, generally, in the ability of a Democratic Congress to develop policies to solve problems. Newt Gingrich asked pollsters in May 1994 what it would take for the Republicans to capture Congress. The answer? Not having health care reform pass (Toner, 1994, A14). Apparently, the polls were right.

But the underlying problems have not changed. Insurance rates continue to go up. Preexisting conditions still preclude millions of Americans from insurance coverage. Many citizens are uninsured or underinsured. Paperwork still burdens doctors and nurses. Managed competition limits choice of doctors and treatments. Insurance companies ration care. Most other advanced nations have universal health coverage and spend a smaller part of the nation's economy on health care. The health care system and the costs of health care still affect the lives and livelihoods of all Americans. Robert Blendon, professor of public health at Harvard, said, "This issue is not event-driven. People are anxious about their insurance, and that won't disappear. People are worried about costs, and that won't disappear. The underlying object—the need for reform—is not going away" (Morin, 1993, A4). At the same time, the insurance industry still has millions to lose if health reform succeeds and therefore millions to spend to prevent change. What remains to be seen is if Clinton and a Republican Congress will try again, and if they do, what will they have learned from the eighteen months of hard-earned experience in the first two years.

REFERENCES

Alter, Jonathan and Steven Waldman. 1994. "Progress, Sort Of." *Newsweek,* July 11, 14–15.

Balz, Dan. 1994. "Dole Urges GOP Unity on Health Plan." *Washington Post,* January 23, A8.

Barnes, James A. 1993. "Reaching for the 'Security' Blanket." *National Journal,* October 16, 2,496.

Beck, Melinda, 1994. "Rationing Health Care." *Newsweek,* June 27, 30–35.

Bennett, W. Lance. 1975. "Political Scenarios and the Nature of Politics." *Philosophy and Rhetoric* 8: 23–42.

Bennett, W. Lance, Patricia Dempsey Harris, Janet K. Laskey, Alan H. Levitch, and Sarah E. Monrad. 1976. "Deep and Surface Images in the Construction of Political Issues: The Case of Amnesty." *Quarterly Journal of Speech,* 109–26.

Bostdorff, Denise M. 1994. *The Presidency and the Rhetoric of Foreign Crisis.* Columbia: University of South Carolina Press.

Broder, David S. 1994. "Upstaging the President." *Washington Post,* February 3, A1.

Brown, Neil. 1993. "Clinton, Health Care and the Long View." *Congressional Quarterly,* September 25, 2,602.

Clift, Eleanor. 1993a. "Health Care: Covert Operation." *Newsweek,* March 15, 37.

———. 1993b. "Hillary's Hard Sell." *Newsweek,* March 29, 20–21.

Clift, Eleanor with Steven Waldman. 1994. "All or Nothing on Health Care." *Newsweek,* August 8, 21.

Clinton, William J. 1993a. "Inaugural Address." *Weekly Compilation of Presidential Documents,* January 20, 75–77.

———. 1993b. "Remarks on Health Care Reform and an Exchange with Reporters." *Weekly Compilation of Presidential Documents,* January 25, 96–98.

———. 1993c. "Address Before a Joint Session of Congress on Administration Goals." *Weekly Compilation of Presidential Documents,* February 17, 215–24.

———. 1993d. "Address of the President to the Joint Session of Congress." *Weekly Compilation of Presidential Documents,* September 22, 1,836–46.

———. 1993e. "Remarks in the ABC News Nightline Town Meeting in Tampa, Florida." *Weekly Compilation of Presidential Documents,* September 23, 1,850–70.

———. 1993f. "Remarks and a Question-and-Answer Session on Health Care Reform in New York City." *Weekly Compilation of Presidential Documents,* September 26, 1,885–95.

———. 1993g. "Remarks at a Town Meeting in Detroit." *Weekly Compilation of Presidential Documents,* February 10, 171–84.

———. 1994a. "Address Before a Joint Session of the Congress on the State of the Union." *Weekly Compilation of Presidential Documents,* January 25.

———. 1994b. "Remarks and a Question-and-Answer Session with the National Governors' Association in Boston." *Weekly Compilation of Presidential Documents,* July 19, 1,511–22.

———. 1994c. "Remarks at a Health Care Rally in Jersey City, New Jersey." *Weekly Compilation of Presidential Documents,* August 1, 1,597–1600.

———. 1994d. "The President's News Conference." *Weekly Compilation of Presidential Documents,* August 3, 1,614–25.

Cloud, David S. 1994. "Clinton's Quandary." *Congressional Quarterly Special Report,* September 10, 17–19.

Congressional Quarterly Almanac. 1993. September 25.

Connolly, Ceci. 1993a. "DNC Aims to Approach Hill from Ground Up: Army of Democrats Mobilizes to Build Grassroots Support for Clinton Plan." *Congressional Quarterly,* October 16, 2,809–13.

———. 1993b. "The Health-Care Battlegrounds." *Congressional Quarterly,* October 16, 2,810.

Crable, Richard E. and Steven L. Vibbert. 1983. "Argumentative Stance and Political Faith Healing: 'The Dream Will Come True.' " *Quarterly Journal of Speech,* 290–301.

Crable, Richard E. and Stephen L. Vibbert. 1985. "Managing Issues and Influencing Public Policy." *Public Relations Review* 11: 3–16.

Day, Kathleen. 1993. "Corporate America at Odds over Curing Health Care System." *Washington Post,* April 13, D1.

Denton, Robert E., Jr., and Gary C. Woodward. 1990. *Political Communication in America,* 2d ed. New York: Praeger.

Devroy, Ann and Helen Dewar. 1994a. "Administration Opens Talks with Chief Rival on Health Compromise." *Washington Post,* January 29, A9.

———. 1994b. "On Health Plan, Clinton Is Back Where He Was When Year Began." *Washington Post,* February 6, A6.

Dole, Robert. 1994. "Dole: Nation 'Has Health Care Problems, but No Health Care Crisis.' " *Washington Post,* January 26, A13.

Drew, Elizabeth. 1994. *On the Edge: The Clinton Presidency.* New York: Simon & Schuster.

Eaton, William J. 1994. "Dole, in GOP Response Jabs at Health Care Plan." *Los Angeles Times,* January 26, A18.

Faucheux, Ron. 1995. "The Grassroots Explosion." *Campaigns and Elections,* December/January, 20–67.

Gallup, George, Jr. 1994. *The Gallup Poll: Public Opinion 1993.* Wilmington, Del.: Scholarly Resources.

Germond, Jack W. and Jules Witcover. 1993. "Getting It Right on Health Care Plan." *National Journal,* October 16, 2,497.

Ginzberg, Eli. 1994. "Dissatisfaction Guaranteed." *New York Times,* November 9, A27.

Goodgame, Dan. 1993. "Ready to Operate." *Time,* September 20, 54–58.

Grove, Lloyd. 1994. "Getting a Second Opinion: GOP's Health Care Maze Doesn't Amuse Democrats." *Washington Post,* January 27, C1.

Hainsworth, Brad E. 1990. "The Distribution of Advantages and Disadvantages." *Public Relations Review,* 33–39.

"Health Care: Dead." 1994. *Time,* October 10, 19.

"Health-Care Debate Takes Off: Congress Gets Up to Speed on the Complex Economics and Policies Driving the U.S. Health-Care System." 1993. *Congressional Quarterly 1993 Almanac,* 335–47.

"Health-Care Hucksters: What Their Ads Say—And Don't Say." 1994. *Consumer Reports,* February, 116–117.

Heath, Robert L. 1990. "The Study of Corporate Issues Management: Rhetorical Underpinnings." In *Public Relations Research Annual,* ed. James E. Grunig and Larissa R. Grunig, vol. 2 (pp. 29–65). Hillsdale, N.J.: Lawrence Erlbaum.

Heath, Robert L. and Richard Alan Nelson. 1986. *Issues Management.* Beverly Hills: Sage.

Hilzenrath, David S. 1994. "Trends Cost Health Plan Some Political Punch." *Washington Post,* January 25, D1.

"Issue: Health Care Overhaul." 1994. *The Final Stretch: Congressional Quarterly Special Report,* September 10, 53–54.

Jamieson, Kathleen Hall. 1994. "When Harry Met Louise." *Washington Post,* August 15, A19.

Jamieson, Kathleen H. and Karlyn Kohrs Campbell. 1992. *Interplay of Influence: News, Advertising, Politics and the Mass Media,* 3d ed. Belmont, Calif.: Wadsworth.

Johnson-Cartee, Karen S. Copeland and Gary A. Copeland. 1991. *Negative Political Advertising: Coming of Age.* Hillsdale, N.J.: Lawrence Erlbaum.

Klein, Joe. 1994. "Chafee at the Bit: How Clinton Squandered the Chance for Universal Coverage." *Newsweek,* August 1, 23.

Kosterlitz, Julie. 1993a. "Hiring Spree." *National Journal,* September 4, 2,120–25.

———. 1993b. "Health Lobby Cranks up Its Postage Meter." *National Journal,* October 16, 2,486–88.

———. 1994. "Journalist, Heal Thyself." *National Journal,* March 26, 748.

Kurtz, Howard. 1994. "Company for 'Harry and Louise' in Debate on Health Care Reform." *Washington Post,* February 13, A3.

Lacayo, Richard. 1994. "Checking Out: With All Hope Vanished for Universal Health

Care, Bill Clinton Will Settle for Less. But How Much Less?" *Time,* September 5, 40–41.

Lewton, Kathleen Larey. 1994. "The Death of Health Care Reform." *Public Relations Tactics,* December 1, 13, 29.

Morganthau, Tom. 1993. "Down to Brass Tacks: Hillary's Plan Is Delayed—but the Elements Are Coming into Focus." *Newsweek,* May 17, 36–37.

———— and Mary Hager. 1993. "The Clinton Cure." *Newsweek,* October 4, 37–49.

Morin, Richard. 1993. "Survey Finds Doubt About Costs, Quality Under Health Reform." *Washington Post,* July 7, A4.

———— and David S. Broder. 1993. "Health Plan Doubts Abound." *Washington Post,* October 12, A1.

Newport, Frank and Jennifer Leonard. 1991. "The Crisis in National Health Care." *The Gallup Poll Monthly,* August 4–17.

Pfau, Michael and Henry C. Kenski. 1990. *Attack Politics: Strategy and Defense.* New York: Praeger.

Presidential Debate. 1992. President George Bush, Republican Candidate; Governor Bill Clinton, Democratic Candidate; Ross Perot, Independent Candidate (Richmond, Virginia). *Federal News Service,* October 15, 31–58.

Priest, Dana. 1993a. "Diverse Group Endorses Universal Health Coverage." *Washington Post,* March 21, A5.

————. 1993b. "Health Reform Fever? Pollsters Take the Public's Temperature on Various Proposals as the Debate Progresses." *Washington Post,* April 6, WH 7–8.

————. 1993c. "Putting Health Care Under a Microscope." *Washington Post,* April 16, A1.

————. 1993d. "Groups to Promote Clinton's Health Plan." *Washington Post,* July 1, A10.

————. 1993e. "First Lady Lambastes Health Insurers." *Washington Post,* November 2, A1.

————. 1994a. "Health Groups Launch Ad Blitzes Criticizing Increased Federal Role." *Washington Post,* January 25, A8.

————. 1994b. "With Its Omissions, Cooper's 'Tennessee Solution' Fills Some Bills." *Washington Post,* February 3, A12.

———— and Ann Devroy. 1994. "Business Leaders Split With Clinton." *Washington Post,* February 3, A1.

Quinn, Jane Bryant. 1994. "Taking Back Their Health Care." *Newsweek,* June 17, 36.

Rubin, Alissa J. 1993a. "Special Interests Stampede to Be Heard on Overhaul." *Congressional Quarterly,* May 1, 1,081–84.

————. 1993b. "Mrs. Clinton Conquers Hill, Sets Debate in Motion." *Congressional Quarterly,* October 2, 2,640–43.

————. 1993c. "Members' Health Concerns Now Center on Turf Wars." *Congressional Quarterly,* October 9, 2,734–37.

————. 1994a. "Deadline Pressure Forces Talk of Compromise." *Congressional Quarterly,* June 18, 1,611–21.

————. 1994b. "Big Decisions Now on Shoulders of House, Senate Leaders." *Congressional Quarterly,* July 9, 1,866–72.

————. 1994c. "A Salvage Operation." *Congressional Quarterly Special Report,* September 10, 11–16.

————. 1994d. "An Opportunity Lost?" *Congressional Quarterly Special Report,* September 10, 13.

———— and Ceci Connolly. 1993. "Clinton Delivers Health Bill, All 1,342 Pages of It." *Congressional Quarterly,* October 30, 2,968–69.

———— and Janet Hook. 1993. "Clinton Sets Health Agenda: Security for Everyone." *Congressional Quarterly,* September 25, 2,551–59.

Samuelson, Robert J. 1994a. "On Health Care: Start Over." *Newsweek,* July 18, 39.

————. 1994b. "Will Reform Bankrupt Us?" *Newsweek,* August 15, 50–54.

Scarlett, Thomas. 1994. "Killing Health Care Reform: How Clinton's Opponents Used a Political Media Campaign to Lobby Congress and Sway Public Opinion." *Campaigns and Elections,* October/November, 34–37.

Schneider, William. 1993. "Health Care Reform: What Went Right." *National Journal,* October 2, 2,404.

Solomon, Burt. 1993. "Clinton's Inscrutable Health Plan . . . May Be No One's Fault But His Own." *National Journal,* September 18, 2,260–61.

Span, Paula. 1994. "Ad Ventures in Health Care." *Washington Post,* January 31, D1.

Starobin, Paul. 1993. "The Big Story." *National Journal,* October 9, 2,420–23.

Thomas, Rich. 1993. "A Walk in Space." *Newsweek,* October 4, 46.

Toner, Robin. 1994. "Pollsters Say Health Care Helped Sweep Away Democrats." *New York Times,* November 16, A14.

Waldman, Steven, with Bob Cohn and Eleanor Clift. 1994a. "How Clinton Blew It: What Happened to the Grand Hopes of Last Fall, When the Country Seemed Ready for Massive Health Care Reform?" *Newsweek,* June 27, 28–29.

————. 1994b. "Winners and Losers." *Newsweek,* July 25, 19.

Weisskopf, Michael. 1993a. "Grass-roots Health Lobby Financed by Insurers." *Washington Post,* October 20, A1.

————. 1993b. "Health Reform Advocates Add Visibility to Insurance Industry Group's Message." *Washington Post,* November 4, A8.

Zarefsky, David. 1980. "Lyndon Johnson Redefines 'Equal Opportunity': The Beginnings of Affirmative Action." *Central States Speech Journal,* 85–94.

————. 1986. *President Johnson's War on Poverty.* Tuscaloosa: University of Alabama Press.

————, Carol Miller-Tutzauer, and Frank E. Tutzauer. 1984. "Reagan's Safety Net for the Truly Needy: The Rhetorical Uses of Definition." *Central States Speech Journal,* 113–19.

Chapter Nine

Clinton's Characteristic Issue Management Style: Caution, Conciliation, and Conflict Avoidance in the Case of Gays in the Military

Denise M. Bostdorff

Americans profess to admire people of principle, yet public figures who are too ideologically pure—be it Pat Buchanan or Madelyn Murray O'Hare—tend to make the populace nervous. Perhaps for this reason, American politicians have, in Hart's words, "normally balanced ideals and practicality for their constituents" (1984, 759; see also Arnold, 1977; Bormann, 1985). Citizens like to hear that their government's policies are consistent with higher principles, but they also desire relatively quick, concrete results and discourse about those results (Bostdorff, 1994, 170; see also Bostdorff, 1992).

At first blush, Bill Clinton would seem to exemplify this desired balance of principles and practicality. His appeals to ideals during the 1992 campaign portrayed him as a "New Democrat," firmly situated in the mainstream of American values, thereby inspiring the electorate to make him the first Democratic president in over a decade. Since entering office, Clinton also has had a number of successes: He obtained approval for NAFTA, passage of his budget, ringing Senate endorsements for his Supreme Court nominees, and lived up to his promises to provide more money for Head Start and to sign both the Brady and family leave bills into law.

Despite this blend of principle and practicality, however, Clinton has faced nonstop questions about his leadership. He has been besieged by allegations of scandal—from Whitewater to Paula Jones—with the Republican opposition fanning the flames, aided by right-wing critics (for example, see Hosenball, 1994; Isikoff and Hosenball, 1994a, 1994b). On other occasions, as with the nomination of Zoe Baird for Attorney General and the furor over his $200 haircut, the president seemed to violate the moral principles of the "New Covenant" he had espoused. Clinton also has had to battle the persistent charge that he made shameless promises to get elected and then proceeded to break them. After the president-elect backed away from several pledges, one reporter asked if there were any campaign promises he wouldn't break (Duffy, 1993a, 28). Perceptions of Clinton as "Slick Willie" continued to dog the president after his inauguration, prompting columnist Charles Krauthammer to dub Clinton "a prisoner of his promises" (1993, A21).

As a case in point of the president's difficulties in this regard, one need only look to how he handled the issue of gays in the military. Clinton came out against the ban as early as October 1991 and, though it received relatively little attention at the time, he repeated his pledge to issue an executive order to lift the ban on a number of occasions during the 1992 campaign (Clinton, 1993oo, 1,370; Duffy, 1993b, 27). Days after Clinton's victory at the polls, he was asked by a reporter if he intended to keep his campaign promise to end discrimination against gays in the military. The president-elect responded that he had every intention of doing so (Gellman, 1992, A1, A11). With those words, Clinton set off a major controversy.

For eight months, from November 1992 through July 1993, the newly elected president and his emissaries coped with the recalcitrant Joint Chiefs of Staff, who were vehemently against the lifting of the ban; a defiant Senator Sam Nunn, the Democrat who headed the Armed Services Committee and who opposed any change; and vocal gay rights leaders, who pressed the president to keep his promise and were all too happy to point out the amount of money and votes they had contributed to his electoral victory. In the end, Clinton emerged with what he called a compromise: a puzzling policy, nicknamed "don't ask, don't tell," which allowed homosexuals to serve in the military as long as they did not reveal their sexual orientation, remained celibate, and refrained from a "pattern" of behavior (i.e., reading gay magazines, frequenting gay bars, *and* participating in gay pride marches) that indicated homosexuality (Devroy, 1993b, A1; Lancaster, 1993, A4). The policy gave the Joint Chiefs most of what they wanted, but the controversy itself further undermined Clinton's relationship with the military, which was already rocky due to his plans to cut defense spending and accusations that he had dodged the draft during the Vietnam War (Krauthammer, 1993, A21; Hackworth, 1993, 24–25). Moreover, the high profile of the issue damaged the president's credibility as a "New Democrat" with many voters, while his backing of the "don't ask, don't tell" policy hurt his support among gays (Klein, 1993, 35; Van Biema, 1993, 29–30; Bull, 1993, 24).

In many ways, Clinton's handling of the controversy over the gay ban is an example of how the president's characteristic issue management style has repeatedly undermined public perceptions of his leadership and opened him to charges of hypocrisy. First, Clinton appealed to campaign audiences through transcendent, moralistic rhetoric that magnified the public importance of issues, raised expectations that he would do something to resolve them, and encouraged citizens to judge him by a higher standard than is often applied to other politicians. Second, the president appears to have a personal predisposition for avoiding conflict and, when he does deal with it, relies almost exclusively upon a conciliatory, rather than confrontational, leadership style. While Clinton's tendency to engage in broad-based, strategically ambiguous appeals and to mediate among interested parties often has provided him with short-term benefits, it also has proven to be his greatest liability as a leader. The president's ambiguity allows different groups to read their own preferred meanings into his language choices, but also paves the way for feelings of alienation and betrayal when a specific Clinton policy turns out to violate the position that supporters assumed he had taken. Once the president has elevated an issue to one of national importance, his inclination to downplay and avoid the controversy such questions naturally spawn gives the appearance that he is unable to resolve the issue or unwilling to fight for his ideals. Hence, Clinton fails to provide citizens with the blend of practicality and principle they desire. In the pages that follow, I first explain the president's characteristic issue management style and then examine the rhetorical context of the gay ban controversy. Finally, I show how Clinton's rhetorical predispositions were exemplified in his discourse about the gay ban.

CLINTON'S CHARACTERISTIC ISSUE MANAGEMENT STYLE

As a politician, Bill Clinton has typically situated himself as a moderate in order to gain and maintain needed support. Larry Sabato, professor of political science at the University of Virginia, says the key defining event in Clinton's political life was the embarrassing defeat he suffered in 1980 when he ran for reelection after his initial term as governor. According to Sabato, the loss taught Clinton to restrain his progressive impulses, making him "much more cautious" politically. Hastings Wyman, Jr., editor of the *Southern Political Report,* concurs. He says that when Clinton regained the governorship of Arkansas, he "worked carefully with the legislature to get just enough of what he wanted to maintain his support among liberals and not create a backlash among conservatives" (Gallagher and Bull, 1993, 36).

Clinton continued to assume this centrist posture when he ran for president in 1992. To attract a broader spectrum of registered voters, Clinton depicted himself as a "New Democrat" who would bring much-needed change to a White House that had, for the last twelve years, pampered corporations and the wealthy at the expense of everyone else. The candidate made specific appeals and promises to attract particular voting blocks—he declared his support for the death penalty, promised the middle class a tax break, and vowed to allow the discussion of abortion at federally funded family planning clinics, for example— but wrapped all these specific entreaties in a more transcendent, moralistic rhetoric that appealed to all. Clinton presented a vision of America in which the government would "offer opportunity" to citizens, but "demand responsibility" on the part of individuals, as well. His campaign discourse emphasized community, unity, progress, work, faith, and "putting our people first." In a dig at

Bush's broken "read my lips" promise about taxes, Clinton pledged, "These commitments aren't just promises from my lips." Instead, he described his plans for the country as a "New Covenant," a solemn agreement or sacred contract with the American people that he planned to fulfill. As Clinton stated in his nomination acceptance speech, "Responsibility starts at the top; that's what the New Covenant is all about" (Goldman and Mathews, 1992a, 42, 43; Goldman and Mathews, 1992c, 78; Clinton, 1992, 642–45).

Clinton's rhetorical strategy worked. In November 1992, he won the presidency as the result of a broad-based coalition that included a significant number of born-again Christians, a plurality of Reagan Democrats, and the majority of senior citizens, women, African Americans, Hispanics, gays, military veterans, young, and first-time voters (Fineman, 1992, 8; Masters 1992, B3).

Despite the happy outcome, this turn of events posed a problem for Clinton. He had won the presidency with an impressive 357–168 electoral college victory, but his actual share of the popular vote was only 43 percent (Fineman, 1992, 8). To govern effectively and ensure his reelection in 1996, Clinton needed to protect and—if possible—expand the fragile coalition behind him.

The rhetoric that had helped him win the White House, however, now boxed him in politically. Through his transcendent campaign appeals, Clinton had raised expectations, now difficult to fulfill, that change would come quickly. The president also found it difficult to please his various constituencies—let alone those on Capitol Hill, in the State House, the Pentagon, and elsewhere with whom he had to work—once he began to translate transcendent principles into policies. People may find themselves in agreement on the former, for the strategic ambiguity of broad principles allows individuals to interpret them in light of their own preferred meanings, but be in volatile disagreement on the specific policies appropriate to carry out such principles. Although this is a problem that elected leaders commonly face, the fragility of Clinton's coalition made the dissension particularly dangerous for him. Clinton also had made specific promises without giving adequate thought to how easily he could fulfill them. In the first few weeks of his presidency, this led to a retreat on several high-profile promises of his campaign, such as plans to cut the deficit in half by 1996, to give the middle class a tax break, and to reverse the U.S. policy of returning Haitian refugees to their homeland (Duffy, 1993a, 25).

Clinton's moralistic campaign rhetoric, with its talk of a "New Covenant" and pledge to take personal responsibility, also may have set the standard by which he later would be judged. Shortly after Clinton's election, columnist Jonathan Alter presciently warned that because Clinton had voiced lofty ideals and promised that members of his administration would be held to a stringent code of ethics, journalists would scrutinize him more closely for perceived transgressions than they had Reagan and Bush. Alter (1992) added, "The more you sound accountable, the more you will be held accountable" (29). For his part, President Clinton argues that "the knee-jerk liberal press" holds him and his administration to "an impossible standard and never give us any credit when we're moving forward" (Wenner and Greider, 1993, 81). He says reporters do not understand that democracy works only through principled compromise (1993qq, 1,391). In a much more cynical explanation, White House Communications Director George Stephanopoulos complains, "We have become hostage to Lexis-Nexis," which allows the press to compare what Clinton says now to what he said earlier. The problem, according to Stephanopoulos, is "an excess of literalism." Voters, apparently, should not have taken everything the candidate said to heart (Krauthammer, 1993, A21). Journalists and citizens may, indeed, unfairly hold Clinton to a higher moral standard; nonetheless, the responsibility for voter expectations on specific campaign promises rests squarely upon the president's shoulders.

In 1992, Bill Clinton situated himself on the middle ground of American politics through transcendent, moralistic appeals, interspersed with specific promises to specific groups, and thereby constructed a heterogeneous but tenuous coalition to win the presidency. Once in office, however, his campaign rhetoric posed obstacles to his governance, for he had led members of a diverse coalition to believe that they agreed more than they did on what Clinton's policies should be. His discourse also had escalated expectations for change and raised the standards for ethical judgment of his performance to heights that were difficult to reach. As if this were not enough, the president's tendency to avoid conflict and, when forced to deal with it, to rely almost exclusively upon a conciliatory leadership style, made matters even worse.

In an editorial on the Clinton administration, Jonathan Alter writes that the president "often governs with only half the tools available to a politician. He's a gifted carrot man, proffering it with a deftness that even his enemies admire, but the stick has never rested comfortably in his paws" (1993b, 32). Clinton himself admits that growing up with an abusive, alcoholic stepfather led him to shy away from direct conflict. According to the president,

I grew up in an environment in which either nothing happened or all hell broke loose, so that the ordinary confrontation and conflict of daily life was not contained. . . . I do think it was one of my weaknesses. As a young man in politics I was trying to figure out how to reconcile my natural desire to have people be on good terms with one another and the need to stake out your ground and be in opposition. (Alter, 1993b, 32; also see Goldman and Mathews, 1992a, 55)

The president's mother, Virginia Kelley, shed additional light on Clinton's character when she observed that she and her sons, Bill and Roger, shared a mutual need for affirmation from others. According to Kelley, "Roger says the three of us, if there are 100 in a room and 99 of them love us and one doesn't, we'll spend all night trying to figure out why that one hasn't been enlightened" (Kelly, 1994, 25). As a result of these personal predispositions, the president prefers to please—to avoid conflict altogether or to serve as a mediator among the parties involved rather than to enter the fray himself. The advantage of his conciliatory approach is its potential to allow Clinton to compromise and to arbitrate when appropriate and thereby to break through the ideological gridlock that so often impedes legislative progress.

There is a dark side to the president's predilection to eschew conflict for conciliation, though. First, Clinton is often indecisive and prone to changing his mind (Woodward, 1994). This gives him the image of a "waffler" who does not stand his ground,[1] and it also has hurt the president in his working relationship with Congress, even among members of his own party. In June 1993, for example, Clinton convinced reluctant House Democrats to vote for his budget package, including its unpopular Btu-based tax, with the promise that he would go "out on a limb" to fight for the measure in the Senate. After his fellow Democrats had supported him, though, he gave into pressure in the Senate and dropped the controversial tax proposal; House Democrats were livid (Hilzenrath and Pianin, 1993, A1, A8).

During his term in office, Clinton also has developed a reputation for what columnist Joe Klein calls "the policy tease." He meets with legislators about policy matters, leaves the impression that he agrees with them, and then undercuts them by publicly denying that he has taken the position on which they assumed agreement. In such situations, Klein says, Clinton appears to change his mind and "the staff rushes to pull him back" (1994b, 23). As a result of such vacillation, the president has hurt his public credibility and undermined his ability to work effectively with Congress.

A second danger of Clinton's desire to please, rather than to confront, is that he not only does harm to would-be allies, but also fails to punish those from his own party who thwart him. In fact, Clinton frequently seems to reward political insurgents. When Democratic Senator Bob Kerrey actively opposed the president's spending programs, shouting and cursing at Clinton as he tried to talk to Kerrey by phone, the president responded by making him chairman of a panel on deficit reduction (Wines, 1994, D1, D5). Democratic Senator Sam Nunn of Georgia has been an even bigger thorn in Clinton's side. The Georgia primary was critical to Clinton's chances at the Democratic nomination in 1992, but Nunn abandoned the candidate when his public support was most needed. Once Clinton had won the nomination, Nunn embarrassed him by introducing his own budget plan. He also led the charge on the issue of gays in the military. Nonetheless, Clinton has consistently gone out of his way to praise Nunn (Alter, 1993a, 29; 1993b, 32). As Alter comments, "That's Clinton, always assuming the best about the other guy's motives. It's a strange habit of mind for someone in such a cynical business" (1993b, 32). The problem with the president's endless attempts to mollify renegades within his ranks is that he only encourages them to rebel again.

The combination of Clinton's tendency to change positions and to reward his opponents is particularly deadly. Perhaps journalist Michael Wines explained the phenomenon best when he wrote that "the President gets snubbed for two reasons that ring true to any parent of an unruly child. One is that Mr. Clinton often leaves it unclear where he stands, and stays rooted to the stand de jour even less often. The other is that nobody ever gets punished for sassing him. So there is no reason not to" (Wines, 1994, D5).[2]

A third hazard of Clinton's penchant for conflict avoidance and conciliation, rather than confrontation, is that his predispositions encourage him to act in ways that are less than courageous. When pressed by opposition, the president is too quick to back down on positions of principle. For instance, Clinton nominated Lani Guinier, a friend and esteemed law professor, to be the assistant attorney general of the Civil Rights Division, but withdrew the nomination without a fight when it sparked controversy. Guinier and others contend that her writings were not conducive to sound bites and were misrepresented by those out to sink her nomination, but the president did nothing to come to her aid. As Guinier recalls, "My opponents were busy deriding me falsely as a Quota Queen. My friends, including the president, were silent." Guinier observes that the administration seemed to "equate avoiding controversy with governing by consensus" (Guinier, 1994, 41–42). Herein lies the danger. To avoid conflict, Clinton rapidly accedes and attempts to cut off any discussion of issues on which disagreement might exist, which is certainly not healthy for the polity. His willingness to give in so easily, especially on questions that he himself has depicted as matters of principle, is also unhealthy for him politically, for it raises questions about the sincerity with which he made his commitments (see, for example, "The Gay Ban," 1993).

This is not to say that Clinton, or any president for that matter, should always dismiss negotiation and refrain from ever changing his mind. Nevertheless, the consistency with which Clinton has embraced compromise or, depending upon one's perspective, abandoned his positions under the guise of compromise, has tarnished his image and caused many to ponder his political courage. After Clinton promised to lift the military ban on gays through an executive order, but settled for "don't ask, don't tell," Torie Osborn, executive director of the National Gay and Lesbian Task Force (NGLTF), reflected: "We must recognize that the president sparked a very important debate that helped move the country out of the monumental state of denial that surrounded gays and lesbians in the military. . . . But it says something about his character that he sparked the debate and then ran" (Bull, 1993, 26).

In many ways, Bill Clinton is no different than the presidents who preceded him. All presidents make promises as candidates that they cannot keep. Upon entering office, they may find that their bold public declarations of policy are politically impractical, or new circumstances may arise that cause them to alter their earlier positions (Bostdorff and Vibbert, 1991). What sets Bill Clinton apart from his predecessors is the degree to which he has been attacked for failing to uphold campaign pledges and for compromising on other principles. The source of his difficulties is Clinton's characteristic issue management style that strives to position him as a moderate through transcendent moral appeals and specific promises to specific groups, coupled with a preference for conflict avoidance and conciliation. As the case of gays in the military demonstrates, in his unrelenting attempts to seek agreement with all, Bill Clinton often finds himself pleasing no one.

THE RHETORICAL CONTEXT OF THE GAY BAN CONTROVERSY

Homosexuality first became a major issue in the U.S. armed forces at the dawn of the McCarthy era. A headline in the *New York Times* on April 19, 1950, reflected the climate of the period quite well when it blared "Perverts Called Government Peril" (Schmalz, 1992, A22). As a result of such concerns, the Uniform Code of Military Justice was adopted, which made sodomy— whether homosexual or heterosexual—a felony. The Defense Department, under the auspices of the Reagan administration, instituted its own ban on homosexuality in 1982 as a means to expel military personnel who were suspected of homosexuality but who had not been caught engaging in forbidden sexual acts (Bush, 1993, A25). In the years that followed, the armed services enthusiastically implemented the ban, even though its financial cost, not to mention its cost in talent, was formidable. In 1990 alone, the U.S. government spent $27 million to discharge and replace approximately 1,000 individuals who were thought to be homosexuals (Lancaster, 1992, A12).

It was in this context that Bill Clinton first stated his opposition to the gay ban during a presentation at the Kennedy School of Government at Harvard in October 1991 (1993oo, 1,370; Duffy, 1993b, 27). He repeated his public declaration of principle and policy on a number of occasions in the year that followed. In response to a January 1992 questionnaire, for instance, the candidate promised that he would sign an executive order as president to overturn the ban because "patriotic Americans should have the right to serve the country as a member of the armed forces, without regard to sexual or affectional orientation" (Gellman, 1992, A1). Likewise, Clinton told *The Advocate* in February 1992, "If elected, I would reverse the ban on gays and lesbians serving in the United States armed forces. People should be free to pursue their personal lives without government interference." At a fund-raiser with gay leaders in May, Clinton repudiated the ban and declared, "We can't afford to waste the hearts and minds of gays and lesbians" (Bull, 1993, 24). The Democratic nominee broadened this appeal slightly for a larger audience in an interview on August 20, reported by the *New York Times*. He discussed the expense—$500 million during the 1980s—involved in expelling gays from the military and then made clear that cost was not the only factor behind his position; principle also was at work, for "I believe the real issue is . . . we don't have a person to waste" (Schmalz, 1992, A22). Clinton restated his pledge to repeal the ban through an executive order in his book, *Putting People First,* in a position paper issued by his campaign, and on at least two other public occasions during the 1992 election (Bull, 1993, 24; Schmalz, 1992, A22).

Despite the clarity with which Clinton spoke of his intentions, his plan to lift the gay ban did not become a major source of dispute until after he won at the polls. Members of the Joint Chiefs of Staff began lobbying Clinton through intermediaries within days of his election. In response, the president-elect told reporters at a news conference that he was "not going to change my position" on the issue; he hedged slightly on the idea of an immediate repeal, though, by stating that he planned to "consult with a lot of people" about "what our options are" (Gellman, 1992, A1, A11). A few days later, both Senate Armed Services Committee Chairman Sam Nunn and Senate Minority Leader Bob Dole publicly urged Clinton to keep the current policy. They argued that the president-elect should study the matter thoroughly first, the implication being that if he did so, he would decide not to overturn the ban (Kenworthy, 1992, A11).

During this time period, Clinton came face-to-face with one of the consequences of making a specific promise without sufficient thought to how easily it can be implemented: The president-elect discovered that he could quickly reverse the Defense Department ban through an executive order, but he would need congressional approval to revise the Uniform Code of Military Justice so that it conformed to the new policy, approval that seemed rather unlikely with leaders from both parties opposing Clinton's proposal (Kenworthy, 1992, A11). Despite this major obstacle, Clinton told reporters on November 16 that he had every intention of pressing ahead with his plans to lift the ban, but added that he had no "timetable" for doing so (Friedman, 1992, A18). A public furor ensued.

On January 29, 1993, Clinton announced a compromise that he hoped would reduce tensions and, temporarily at least, resolve the matter: He set a July 15 deadline for a draft of an executive order that would overturn the ban, thereby allowing Congress and the Defense Department time to study the issue. During the interim period, the military would refrain from asking recruits about their sexual orientation and stop investigating allegations that personnel were gay. As a concession to his opponents, though, Clinton also agreed that the military could proceed with separation hearings against openly gay members of the armed services and have them transferred to standby reserve, where they would lose all pay and benefits (Marcus and Dewar, 1993, A1, A12). Although no one was completely pleased with the compromise, it helped defuse the situation. For the president, the interim policy provided the possibility that he now could turn his attentions—and those of the nation—to other issues that he was more anxious to tackle, like the economy and health care.

In the months that followed, though, questions about the gay ban continued to torment Clinton. Cases of individuals kicked out of the armed services or moved to the standby reserves because of their homosexuality received widespread media attention, particularly those instances where the personnel involved were highly decorated and/or had decided to reveal their sexual orientation on the basis of Clinton's campaign promise (see, for example, McAllister, 1993; Niebuhr, 1993b; Smolowe, 1993; "Army Gives," 1993; Cary, 1993). During the same time period, a U.S. sailor was found guilty of murdering a homosexual shipmate, while three U.S. Marines in North Carolina beat up a young gay man as they shouted slurs against homosexuals and made references to the president's proposed policy (Reid, 1993; "A Few Bad Men," 1993).

Clinton fared even worse in March. Randy Shilts' book, *Conduct Unbecoming: Gays and Lesbians in the U.S. Military,* was released with great fanfare, and the president visited the *U.S.S. Roosevelt,* where sailors openly mocked him before his arrival ("And More Good News," 1993; Clinton, 1993o, 469). During a news conference that month, Clinton suggested publicly for the first time that he might consider job restrictions on gays in the military; the angry response from gay advocates quickly caused him to back away from the position (Berke, 1993; Schmitt, 1993b).

In April, gay and lesbian Americans again focused attention on the ban when they marched on Washington, D.C., to appeal for civil rights (Schmalz, 1993). The spring also brought Sam Nunn's much-vaunted congressional hearings on the ban, which grabbed headlines on a daily basis and most often favored retention of the policy. Particularly memorable was a widely published photo of Nunn and Senator John Warner kneeling in the cramped quarters of the nuclear attack submarine *Montpelier* while crew members lay on their bunks to demonstrate how closely they had to sleep to one another (Jenkins, 1993).

As Clinton's July 15 deadline drew nearer, it became more and more apparent that he would not have the congressional support needed to sustain an executive order repealing the ban. Representative Barney Frank of Massachusetts offered a compromise whereby gay military personnel could serve provided they kept their private conduct to themselves. He explained, "The rule would be: on duty, in uniform, on base, in effect you're asexual," a proposal that President Clinton intimated he might accept. Sam Nunn quickly shot down Frank's recommendation, however, condemning it as a policy that would create a "safe haven" for illegal behavior (Lippman and Marcus, 1993, A1, A14).

Faced with continuing opposition, Clinton set about negotiating with Nunn and the Joint Chiefs for a policy that would be acceptable to all. The end result was basically a proposal that Nunn had made earlier, dubbed "don't ask, don't tell." The policy required that gay soldiers remain celibate and forbade them from revealing their sexual orientation or engaging in a "pattern" of behavior that might indicate homosexuality (Van Biema, 1993). In remarks announcing the new guidelines, the president called them "a substantial advance" over the rules in place when he took office. He pointed out that an open statement of one's homosexuality would not automatically result in separation hearings but create "a rebuttable presumption" that the service member intended to engage in homosexual conduct. Clinton also emphasized that the compromise policy would not single out gay personnel for prosecution under the Uniform Code of Military Justice; instead, the code's provisions "will be enforced in an even-handed manner as regards both heterosexuals and homosexuals" (1993oo, 1,372).

The president's assurances to the contrary, the new policy offered gay military personnel very little. As Kevin M. Cathcart of the Lambda Legal Defense and Education Fund explained, "Don't ask, don't tell" effectively forced gays to convince the military that "they do not have even a propensity for sexual behavior" (Lippman, 1993, A2). By the time Sam Nunn finished with the policy in committee, he had whittled away at other aspects of it, as well. The guidelines, as they were eventually adopted, said new recruits should not be asked about their homosexuality, but nevertheless allowed such questioning to resume if the Defense Secretary deemed it necessary. In addition, the clause providing "equal enforcement" of the Uniform Code of Military Justice was dropped, paving the way for the resumption of witch hunts against gay military personnel (Dewar, 1993; Van Biema, 1993).

Among members of the gay community, the overwhelming sentiment was that Clinton had betrayed them. The NGLTF's Torie Osborn condemned the new policy as "simply a repackaging of discrimination" (Bull, 1993, 24); outside the White House, protestors held aloft posters of Bill Clinton sporting a Pinocchio nose (Osborne, 1994). Joe Zuniga, a former "Soldier of the Year" and discharged gay Army veteran whose case had received a great deal of publicity, called Clinton's actions "a huge betrayal" ("Reaction to the Policy," 1993, 29). Shortly after the new guidelines were announced, six members of the military reserves and one active-duty Coast Guard medical corpsman filed suit, claiming the "don't ask, don't tell" policy erected "an arbitrary distinction between the speech or conduct permissible for heterosexuals and the speech or conduct permissible for plaintiffs or other gay men and lesbians in the armed services" (Lippman, 1993, A2).

Nor had Clinton's handling of the controversy won him any favors elsewhere. Senator Dan Coats, for instance, dismissed the new policy as "a muddy political compromise that any second-year law student could tear apart" ("Reaction to the Policy," 1993, 29). For many from the religious right, Clinton's attempts to open the armed services to gays was, in Randall Terry's words, a "godsend." Terry, an antiabortion activist and leader in the Resistance, an organization that fights gay rights, noted that the support Clinton had managed to build among evangelicals during the 1992 election was "shattering before his eyes" as a result of the issue (Niebuhr, 1993a, A11). The president's attempt to lift the ban had alienated the military, conservatives, and others who opposed the open acceptance of homosexuality; the failure to fulfill his pledge had angered gay activists.

In addition, Clinton's handling of the issue raised questions in citizens' minds about his trustworthiness and values. Surveys taken shortly before the president's announcement of the compromise policy showed that only 33 percent of Americans thought he had kept important promises he made during the campaign, and 56 percent thought he had spent too much time on gay rights issues (Carlson, 1993; Shapiro, 1993). Even though Clinton was unable to repeal the gay ban, many voters were no doubt struck with how the president freely broke other campaign pledges—particularly his promise of a middle-class tax break—

and then squandered so much political capital in his attempts to fulfill a promise
to gays. During the 1992 campaign, Clinton had successfully positioned himself
as a moderate with mainstream American values, but suddenly he seemed left
of center.

Several factors contributed to the gay ban's eruption as a major issue for the
Clinton administration. With his presidential campaign, Clinton became the first
candidate from a major party to court the gay community openly. Gays rewarded
him with 72 percent of their votes, $3 to $4 million in campaign donations, and
thousands of volunteers (Masters, 1992, B3). The candidate's messages to gay
voters emphasized his plans to increase funding for AIDS and to repeal the
military's ban on gays. By portraying his stance on the gay ban as a matter of
principles (the right of individuals to serve, the nation's need for all citizens to
contribute) and stating his position in the form of a promise, Clinton imbued
the issue with moral significance and raised expectations among his gay supporters. Indeed, when aides to the president-elect floated a plan in early January
whereby Clinton would instruct Defense Secretary Les Aspin to remove the ban,
rather than lifting it himself through an executive order, gay rights advocates
responded angrily, saying that an indirect recission of the policy would not
"carry the same kind of weight or symbolism" as an executive order and, hence,
would be a violation of Clinton's campaign promise. The president-elect's aides
were said to be shocked at the hostile reaction to their overture, especially since
either approach would lead to a repeal of the ban, and Clinton quickly backed
away from the trial balloon (Schmitt, 1993a, A1, A17). Nonetheless, the episode
was a vivid example of the challenge Clinton faced in dealing with sentiments
among gay voters that he himself had helped create.

The president's words and symbolic deeds had magnified the significance of
the gay ban for other Americans, as well. Under the rubric of a "New Covenant," he had made specific promises during his campaign and then proceeded
to break a number of them immediately after his election. The dilemma Clinton
faced was that if he failed to fulfill his promise to gays, it would stand as one
more example of his broken promises and reinforce concerns about his honesty.
If he did fulfill his pledge to lift the ban, after reneging on other vows, the
president left himself open to charges that he was beholden to special interest
groups and unwilling to fight for the middle class. Clinton found himself in a
conundrum he was unable to resolve, but it was a conundrum of his own making.

Another reason that the gay ban seemed to explode upon the scene after
Clinton's election was that, for all his discussion of the issue during the campaign, his expressed intention to repeal the policy received almost no public
attention outside the gay community, apparently lulling Clinton and his aides
into complacency. They were simply unprepared for the resistance his plans
would incur. In part, the candidate's statements were overlooked because of the
nature of the forums in which he spoke on the issue: to gay publications and
audiences and in a position paper that few voters actually read. Moreover, the
Republican Party was remarkably reticent about the matter, fearing a backlash

after the gay-bashing rhetoric of the Republican convention. Dan Quayle, for example, appeared on "Larry King Live" and insisted that the Bush administration had "a policy of nondiscrimination" toward gays and that President Bush "just won't tolerate discrimination of any sort or any kind" (Goldman and Mathews, 1992b, 68–69; Bull, 1992, 18–19). Later, Bush's deputy campaign manager Mary Matalin would complain that in the aftermath of the convention, the Republicans spent "our entire time denying that the Republican Party was a bunch of homophobic bigots" (Evans and Novak, 1992, A31). A few right-wing groups attempted to draw attention to Clinton's support for gay rights but, generally speaking, the issue was ignored. Whatever the reason, Clinton was clearly unprepared for the opposition he would face once he tried to enact his pledge. Author Randy Shilts, an expert on gays in the military, underscored this notion when he recalled his conversation with gay leaders who were working closely with the Clinton campaign:

I remember right after he got elected in November, I said, "Well, of course this is going to be a very big deal," and they said, "What he's going to do is to come in January and issue his five or six executive orders and sort of slip this [repeal of the ban] in the middle of the pile and nobody will notice." And I just thought, *My God, what planet are you people living on?* (Yarbrough, 1993, 36)

The administration's lack of preparation was further exacerbated by tactical errors on the part of Clinton and his staff. According to critics, the new president surrounded himself with too many FOBs (Friends of Bill), political outsiders inexperienced in dealing with Washington, D.C., whose advice led to silly mistakes and general chaos on a number of issues (Cohn and Clift, 1994; Klein, 1994a; Woodward, 1994). Within the context of the gay ban, Clinton made and reaffirmed his pledge to repeal the policy without ever consulting key members of Congress or the Joint Chiefs of Staff. Advisors to Secretary of Defense designate Les Aspin had suggested that Clinton meet personally with Sam Nunn, Senate Majority Leader George Mitchell, and Senator Edward Kennedy in order to formulate a strategy for congressional support. The recommendation went unheeded (Balz, 1993, A6). Furthermore, Clinton sent intermediaries to meet with Chairman Colin Powell and his Joint Chiefs of Staff three times before sitting down to talk with them himself (Mathews, 1993, 35–36; Balz, 1993, A6).

In late January, the situation grew even worse when someone managed to locate the memo Aspin staffers had written on the House Armed Services Committee computer network and proceeded to leak it to the press. The memo advised that the president instruct Aspin to "take the necessary administrative steps" to stop the military from asking recruits about their sexual orientation and from discharging gay personnel. If Aspin reviewed the new policy, the memo said that Clinton would appear sensitive to the military's concerns; the president then could safely issue an executive order and fulfill his campaign promise. According to the memo, the administration's meetings with the Joint

Chiefs of Staff were "not a negotiation" (Barr, 1993, A1, A11; Mathews, 1993, 35–36).

When news of the memo circulated, the Joint Chiefs and their allies in Congress were incensed, for the few overtures the administration had made to the military now appeared to be a sham. The new president, whom the armed services already viewed suspiciously because of his draft record and his plans to cut defense spending (Schmitt, 1993a), found his credibility further damaged by the episode. In Congress, Sam Nunn angrily restated his opposition to Clinton's proposed policy, while Senator Dan Coats of Indiana accused Clinton of taking an "in-your-face" approach toward Congress and the Joint Chiefs and made plans to introduce a resolution that would confirm the gay ban as law (Mathews, 1993; Devroy, 1993a, A1, A11).

A fourth factor that magnified the public visibility of the gay ban and, for the Clinton administration, the problems associated with it, was that his political opponents saw an opportunity and exploited it. Republicans may have ignored the issue during the campaign, but once the contentious nature of the president-elect's proposed policy became clear, they tried to use it to derail Clinton's presidency before the honeymoon had even taken place. Bob Dole, for example, attempted to attach an amendment barring any changes in the military ban to the family leave bill, a pet piece of legislation for Clinton; Dole declared that any vote against his amendment was "a vote to put homosexuals in our military" (Clymer, 1993, A14). Although the amendment was rejected, it was proof of what political analyst Kevin Phillips called the Republicans' "strategy-cum-hope": that there were more votes in attacking gays than in courting them (1993, C3). In a similar fashion, right-wing religious groups decided that Clinton's support for what Jerry Falwell ominously called a "new, radical homosexual rights agenda" was the perfect issue for mobilizing their followers against the president (Weisskopf, 1993, A1, A10).

Even Democrat Sam Nunn may have viewed the gay ban as a way to punish Clinton. In late November 1992, the *Washington Blade,* a gay newspaper, revealed that Nunn had once fired two aides because they were homosexuals. Other media quickly picked up the story, and the gay rights group, Queer Nation, held a "kiss-in" at Nunn's office to protest. Speculation was that gay opposition to Nunn cost him a cabinet position. Although he took himself out of contention for Secretary of Defense, Clinton insiders reported that the president had led Nunn to believe he might become Secretary of State and then failed to inform him that he had decided to go with Warren Christopher instead. The senator sincerely disagreed with Clinton about the gay ban, but his decision to take the unusual step of challenging a new president from his own party so vociferously, thereby helping to ignite flames of public opposition, may also have been fueled by a desire for revenge (McCombs, 1992; Mathews, 1993).

Although an amalgamation of several factors led to the gay ban's emergence as a major public issue, one cannot deny the central role that Bill Clinton played in many of these factors. His talk of a "New Covenant" and willingness to make promises without thought to their consequences raised expectations among gay voters and triggered questions about his character from the public at large. The president's lack of preparation and tactical errors exacerbated the situation further, providing his political opponents with the opening they needed. Clinton's rhetoric about the gay ban also exemplified his characteristic issue management style, along with its attendant strengths and weaknesses.

CLINTON'S RHETORIC ON THE GAY BAN: CAUTION, CONCILIATION, AND CONFLICT AVOIDANCE

Clinton's rhetoric about the gay ban typified his usual issue management style. After elevating the ban into a critical issue of principle, he adopted the discourse of one who eschewed conflict for conciliation. He downplayed the controversy by attempting to divert attention to issues like the economy, muting his public support for gay rights, minimizing the extent to which he and the Joint Chiefs disagreed, and other means. During the six months that his administration, the Pentagon, and Congress studied the gay ban, Clinton offered transcendent definitions of the issue that cautiously situated him on the middle ground between extremists from both ends of the political spectrum. The problem with these definitions, however, was that they raised expectations in one camp and did nothing to allay fears in the other. Finally, Clinton attempted to legitimize the "don't ask, don't tell" policy as an "honorable compromise," but his words were often contradictory and at odds with the realities of the policy.

Downplaying the Controversy

Because the public battle over the gay ban started before Clinton had even been inaugurated, he had a strategic, political reason for wanting to subdue the controversy: The president did not wish to spend his honeymoon period dealing with a potentially divisive issue that would dissipate his public credibility and hamper his efforts to get passage of his economic and health care programs. To avoid this possibility, Clinton attempted to downplay the dispute in a number of ways.

First, the president frequently deferred comment on the gay ban and tried to divert attention to other issues. On January 26, when reporters asked when Clinton would issue his policy statement on gays in the military, he replied that he was on his way "to talk to the leadership of Congress about our legislative agenda" (1993b, 99). Similarly, in an exchange with journalists prior to a meeting with Federal Reserve Chairman Alan Greenspan, the president avoided questions about the principles behind his plan to lift the gay ban when he said, "I came here to talk about the economy today with Mr. Greenspan. If he wants to express his opinion on that subject [the gay ban], I'll be glad to hear it. Most people with whom I talk, except you folks, never discuss that. We have other things we're trying to deal with" (1993c, 100). Upon announcing the interim policy on gays in the military, Clinton emphasized that it was a "step in the right direction" and would "allow us to move forward on other terribly important issues affecting far more Americans." He then discussed his administration's work on economic and health care reform (1993f, 109–10). On other occasions, the president tersely responded to reporters' questions with answers like: "You know what my position is. I have nothing else to say" (1993ee, 858); "I have no further comment on this" (1993nn, 1,170); and "I can't comment on the specifics [of the Pentagon's recommendation] until I see it" (1993mm, 1,156). Although Clinton surely was wise not to speculate about reports he had not read, the general tenor of his remarks suggested frustration over the media's obsession with the ban.

Indeed, when given a choice, the president preferred not to talk about the controversy at all. Clinton's comments on the gay ban, with three exceptions— two of which were his announcements of the interim and "don't ask, don't tell" policies—came directly in response to questions from reporters or from citizens at town hall meetings and similar forums.[3] In February, March, and April, for instance, Clinton gave three speeches about his administration's goals—an address before a joint session of Congress and two radio addresses—but not once mentioned his promise to repeal the ban (1993i; 1993q; 1993t). Before audiences that included military personnel, the president was even more circumspect. He occasionally alluded to how the armed services had "pioneered our Nation's progress toward integration and equal opportunity" (1993m, 410; 1993l, 407), but more often elected to avoid even ambiguous references to the gay ban issue (1993r; 1993aa; 1993bb; 1993gg; 1993ii; 1993jj; 1993kk; 1993ll). The administration apparently decided that Clinton's draft record and plans for defense conversion injected more than enough controversy into his remarks to military personnel without his discussing the civil rights of homosexuals in their ranks.

As part of the low profile the president maintained on the issue, he also muted his public support for gay civil rights. On April 16, Clinton met with gay leaders in the Oval Office, a presidential first, yet the White House chose not to publicize the historic meeting—George Stephanopoulos admitted that it would occur only when reporters pressed him—and closed the event to television cameras (DeWitt, 1993a; Clinton, 1993s).

When gay leaders invited Clinton to the gay march on Washington, he said travel commitments precluded his attendance, but that he would participate, perhaps via television satellite (DeWitt, 1993b). David Mixner, a friend of the president who had raised considerable money for him in the gay community, expressed the feelings of many gay Americans when he commented, "I find it sad that politicians feel it necessary to leave, and they don't have the courage to stay in town" (DeWitt, 1993c, A10). Clinton then disappointed gay advocates further by simply sending a brief letter to be read by a member of Congress at the march, rather than communicating with the audience via telephone or satellite (1993y, 685). When reporters asked him about his lack of involvement, the president declared, "I don't see how any serious person could claim that I have snubbed the gay community in this country, having taken the position I have not only on the issue of the military but of participation in the Government'' (1993s, 602). He also insisted that presidents, except under unusual circumstances, do not participate in marches (1993s, 602; also 1993u, 660). More than any of his predecessors, Clinton had welcomed gays into his administration and articulated his support for their civil rights; that notwithstanding, he was still not anxious to publicize his affiliations because it was politically dangerous to do so. On April 24, as the march on Washington was about to take place, the president gave a nationwide radio address in which he discussed the economy, but never once mentioned gay civil rights.

The following day, April 25, U.S. Representative Nancy Pelosi read Clinton's letter to gay Americans assembled in Washington, D.C., while the president made remarks to the Newspaper Association of America in Boston. Clinton devoted about half of his speech to gay civil rights and his proposed repeal of the gay ban. In his remarks, the president passionately declared that the larger issue was ''whether we are going to live in a country free of unnecessary discrimination.'' More often, however, Clinton seemed concerned with how the issue was affecting public perceptions of him. He bemoaned the ''terrible political price'' he had paid for his position and attempted to depict himself as a moderate who supported individual rights. When he was the governor of Arkansas, the president said, the left wing had attacked him for defending the individual rights of fundamentalist religious groups, just as the right wing now attacked him for defending the individual rights of gays (1993w, 678–79). Other than his announcement of the ''don't ask, don't tell'' policy, Clinton would never again choose to speak before an audience with prepared remarks on the issue.

To downplay the controversy surrounding the gay ban, the president deferred comment, diverted attention to other issues, and muted his public support for gay civil rights. Clinton also attempted to quell concerns about his priorities by emphasizing that he had not chosen to make the gay ban a primary issue and that he was spending very little time on it, in comparison to other issues. On January 29, a reporter inquired as to whether the president was concerned ''that this controversy this week has given the American people the wrong idea of what your priorities are?'' Clinton responded, ''Yes. . . . Of course, I didn't bring it up; people in the Senate did. I just tried—I have not, frankly, spent very much time on it compared to the time I'm spending on the economy, which is what I was elected to do'' (1993e, 102). At a news conference later that same day, the president again made clear that he had no way to ''control the timing'' of the gay ban dispute. He explained, ''This issue was not put forward in this context by me; it was put forward by those in the United States Senate who sought to make it an issue early on. I don't know how I could have stopped them from doing that'' (1993f, 111).

In his public statements, Clinton described the instigators of the issue as members of the Senate, ''foes of lifting the ban,'' Republicans, or a combination of all three (1993e, 102; 1993f, 111; 1993h, 173; Wenner and Greider, 1993, 43). He portrayed these villains as obstructive political forces who had pushed the gay ban to the forefront, either as a way to keep his repeal from taking place or as a means of "hurting the . . . efforts we were making" on other issues (1993h, 173). Nevertheless, the president asserted that he personally had "not placed a great deal of emphasis on it" and was concentrating, instead, on issues more crucial to all Americans (1993u, 654). Perhaps Clinton's approach was exemplified best in his answer to a question at a town meeting in Detroit about why he had chosen to tackle the gay ban first, rather than the economy:

Senators in the other party wanted it [the ban] dealt with now. They saw it as a way to delay family leave and to throw the whole Federal Government into debating that. I actually spent very little time on the issue myself. . . . I was, frankly, appalled that we spent so much time the first week talking about that instead of how to get the economy going again. It wasn't my idea. My agreement with the Joint Chiefs was to study the issue for 6 months, so we could focus immediately on the economy. Thank goodness that's what we're now doing. (1993h, 173)

In other words, Republicans had attempted to derail the president's economic program by forcing the gay ban issue, but Clinton had managed to get the government back on track.

Just as the president indicated that his priorities were those of most Americans, Clinton also used a fourth tactic to downplay the gay ban issue whereby he tried to show, on five different occasions, that his position on the gay ban was very similar to that of the conservative Joint Chiefs of Staff and average Americans. The president reminded journalists on January 28 that the Joint Chiefs had agreed with him that enlistees should not be asked about their sexual orientation and that he agreed with them that "any sort of improper conduct should result in severance." According to Clinton, "The narrow issue on which there is disagreement is whether people should be able to say they're homosexual without being—and do nothing else—without being severed" (1993d, 101). According to Clinton, his position was very similar to that of the Joint Chiefs (1993f, 109), "everybody else" (1993p, 485), and "[M]ost Americans" (1993ff, 970); hence, the difference of opinion consisted of "a very limited argument" (1993p, 485) over a "narrow" issue (1993ff, 970), a "very narrow issue" (1993f, 111), or "a very narrow category of people" (1993cc, 805).

So anxious was Clinton to subdue perceptions that a major controversy existed—and that the president of the United States' views were aberrant and in direct opposition to those of the military and other Americans—that he occasionally went overboard. At the Cleveland City Club, for example, Clinton posed the question of whether the armed services should stop asking new recruits about their sexual orientation. He then exclaimed: "They [the Joint Chiefs] say yes, and I say yes. So we solved most of the issues. They say yes, and I say yes. Should we change the code of conduct? They say no, and I say no, not at all, not on the base, not any way, no changes in the code of conduct'' (1993cc, 806). In his efforts to downplay the degree of disagreement that existed, Clinton sometimes inadvertently sent the opposite message: The president doth protest too much.

Defining the Issue: A Question of Individual Rights and Conduct, Rather than Status

During the gay ban controversy, Clinton's characteristic issue management style also could be discerned in his efforts to define the issue through broad, transcendent language that would appeal to both sides of the dispute and situate him in the mainstream of traditional American values. Specifically, the president defined the issue as a question of individual rights, rather than group rights, in which persons should be judged by what they do rather than by who they are.

From the time that Clinton first expressed his support for a repeal of the military's ban on gays, he depicted the issue as a matter in which individuals had a "right to serve" without regard to their sexual orientation (Gellman, 1992, A1). The president placed special emphasis upon this component of the issue in four public statements from April 23, 1993, up to and including his announcement of the "don't ask, don't tell" policy on July 19. In answering a reporter's question about the dispute on April 23 (1993u, 653), Clinton stressed, "I just have always had an almost libertarian view that we should try to protect the rights of American individual citizens to live up to the fullest of their capacities, and I'm going to stick right with that." Similarly, on April 25, he made an analogy between American immigrants, who had fled persecution in other countries, and gay Americans, who simply desired to live their lives free of discrimination. Clinton commented to members of the Newspaper Association of America, "But just remember this: A whole lot of people came to this country because they wanted a good letting alone. And that's what we ought to be able to do today" (1993w, 678). When announcing the "don't ask, don't tell" policy before military personnel at the National Defense University, the president likewise noted, "For me, and this is very important, this issue has never been one of group rights but rather of individual ones" (1993oo, 1,370).

By defining the gay ban conflict in this way, the president could potentially secure two advantages. First, he could portray himself as a leader with traditional American values, rather than as a left-wing Liberal who was beholden to special interests. Second, and related to the first advantage, the issue definition could allow Clinton to transcend partisan attacks from the right wing. The president told listeners on two occasions that he had been attacked in the past by the left for his support of individual rights, just as he currently was being lambasted by the right. At his April 23 news conference, for instance, Clinton observed, "Obviously, those who disagree with me here are primarily coming from the political right in America. When I was Governor, I was attacked from the other direction for sticking up for the rights of religious fundamentalists to run their child care centers and to practice home schooling under appropriate safeguards'' (1993u, 653). From the president's perspective, his previous defense of individual rights clearly showed that he was not ''a dangerous Liberal,'' as his conservative critics charged (1993w, 678). As he told reporters on June 22, ''I don't see this as a liberal-conservative issue.'' Clinton went on to explain that supporters of a repeal included members of the Reagan administration, members of Congress who had distinguished military records, and even former Senator Barry Goldwater (1993mm, 1,156). In his announcement of the compromise policy, the president continued this line of reasoning when he drew upon the legitimacy of Goldwater—''patron saint of the conservative wing of the Republican Party''—in order to transcend partisanship. Clinton asserted:

> Senator Goldwater's statement, published in *The Washington Post* recently, made it crystal clear that when this matter is viewed as an issue of individual opportunity and responsibility rather than one of alleged group rights, this is not a call for cultural license but rather a reaffirmation of the American value of extending opportunity to responsible individuals and of limiting the role of Government over citizens' private lives. (1993oo, 1,371)

The president's argument for individual rights was one that could appeal to audiences on both sides of the gay ban dispute. After all, freedom from government intervention was a basic tenet of both conservative doctrine and mainstream political thought. The definition likewise could appeal to those who supported a revocation of the ban; at the very least, it was unlikely to offend.

These advantages notwithstanding, Clinton's transcendent argument faced a number of obstacles, for he chose not to emphasize the nonpartisan nature of his principles until late in the controversy, once opinions were already well formed. Too, the president's attacks on Republicans and apparent concerns for the rights of a special interest group, particularly one that many citizens viewed as aberrant, undercut his efforts to portray himself as above typical conservative-liberal partisanship. Most problematic strategically—at least in the long term—Clinton had qualified his ''individual rights'' depiction of the gay ban issue with a definition of the conflict as one in which conduct, rather than status, should prevail.

In an August 20, 1992, interview that was printed in the *New York Times,* Clinton explained the issue of the gay ban this way: ''But what I think the rule ought to be is in the absence of some inappropriate behavior, if someone has been in the service and they're serving well, that alone [homosexual orientation] should not be grounds for dismissal. . . . There would have to be something besides the simple statement of status'' (Schmalz, 1992, A22). This was, apparently, the first time Clinton publicly voiced his ''conduct, rather than status'' argument.[4] It modified his initial definition of the gay ban issue as a matter of individual rights by arguing, in effect, that individuals had the right to serve—regardless of their sexual orientation—*provided that* their behavior was acceptable. Noteworthy here is the fact that Clinton embraced the "conduct, rather than status" issue definition prior to his electoral victory and continued to rely heavily upon it throughout the controversy. From November 13, 1992—the day the president-elect publicly vowed to uphold his campaign promise—through July 22, 1993—three days after his announcement of "don't ask, don't tell"— Clinton framed the issue in terms of conduct, not status, on at least twenty occasions (Gellman, 1992; Friedman, 1992; Clinton, 1993d, 1993f, 1993h, 1993j, 1993p, 1993s, 1993u, 1993w, 1993y, 1993cc, 1993ee, 1993ff, 1993mm, 1993oo, 1993pp, 1993qq, 1993rr, 1993ss). Equally interesting, Clinton's newly modified issue definition first appeared in the same interview where he revealed that he had been consulting with Senator Sam Nunn on the gay ban. These two factors provide needed context for understanding both the strategic appeal of the "conduct, rather than status" argument for Clinton and how the qualification implicit in the issue definition allowed the president to adopt the untenable policy position of "don't ask, don't tell," with its politically divisive consequences.

On its face, the definition of the gay ban as an issue in which conduct, rather than status, should take precedence was persuasively alluring. American culture—at least in principle—has always emphasized judging people upon the basis of what they do, rather than upon their socioeconomic or other status in society. In his public discourse on the gay ban, Clinton appealed to this value premise to make his case. He told reporters on January 28, 1993, that the "elemental principle" behind his desire to lift the gay ban was "that people should be disqualified from serving in the military based on something they do, not based on who they are" (1993d, 101). To buttress his argument further, the president repeatedly depicted gays as no different than other Americans and, thus, deserving of judgment based on their actions, rather than their orientation. In remarks at a February 20 children's town meeting, Clinton said, "There are citizens in the United States who are homosexual, who work hard, who don't break laws, who pay their taxes, don't bother other people, who ought to have a chance to serve." The president insisted that other Americans should give gays "a chance to be citizens as long as they're not doing anything wrong" (1993j, 262). On April 16, Clinton defended the depth of his commitment to gay rights when he told a journalist that he took his position on the gay ban long before there was organized support for him within the gay community. He emphasized that his pledge to revoke the ban "had nothing to do with politics and everything to do with the fact that I grew up in a segregated society and have very strong feelings about the right of everybody who is willing to work hard and play by the rules to participate in American life" (1993s, 602). Likewise, his letter to participants at the gay march on Washington read, "I still believe that every American who works hard and plays by the rules ought to be a part of the national community. Let us work together to make this vision real" (1993y, 685).

Clinton's rhetoric surely was appealing to gays, for it portrayed them every bit as worthy as other Americans. Additionally, the president's words attempted to transcend ban proponents' feelings about homosexuality by invoking a deeply rooted principle of American culture. More simply put, Clinton's "conduct, rather than status" issue definition seemed designed to appeal to various elements of the polity. The strategic value of the president's argument, however, was more than offset by its built-in capacity to self-destruct.

The flaw of Clinton's issue definition lay in the ambiguity with which he discussed conduct. On November 17, 1992, for example, Clinton simply said, "There is a big difference between someone doing something wrong and their condition in life" (Friedman, 1992, A18). He was equally vague at a February 10 town meeting in Detroit where he asserted, "This is not about conduct. This is about status. I believe there ought to be the strictest code of behavioral conduct applicable here. . . . If people do wrong, they ought to be gotten out" (1993h, 177). Although the president clearly differentiated between sexual orientation and one's conduct, he was not specific about what constituted behavior that was "wrong" or what "the strictest code of behavioral conduct" would encompass. This encouraged gay listeners to interpret Clinton's statements as signs that he would not renege on his campaign promise. Certainly, it would not have occurred to many gay Americans, or their supporters, that the president could be in favor of gay civil rights and, simultaneously, assert that homosexual sex constituted conduct that was "inappropriate" (Friedman, 1992, A18), "improper" (Clinton, 1993d, 101; 1993p, 485), "wrong" (Friedman, 1992, A18; Clinton, 1993h, 177; 1993j, 262; 1993cc, 805; 1993mm, 1,156), and "unacceptable" (1993oo, 1,372).

Yet, this was exactly what the president implicitly argued. This is not to say that Clinton provided no hints of his evolving policy predispositions. At his news conference announcing the interim policy on January 28, Clinton explained that the military necessarily had "a different and stricter code of justice" that included restrictions on one's behavior, "many of which would be intolerable in civilian society" (1993f, 109). He told journalist Dan Rather on March 24 that "any kind of improper sexual conduct should be grounds for dismissal or other appropriate discipline" (1993p, 485). The president also publicly declared that he would not propose any changes in "the code of military conduct" (1993cc, 805) or the "Uniform Code of Conduct" (1993ff, 970), but he never spelled out what this meant. Unless listeners knew that the Uniform Code of Military Justice forbade sexual relations between people of the same gender— gays in the armed forces obviously understood what the code entailed, but were in no position to challenge the president openly—they easily could have interpreted Clinton's typical "conduct, rather than status" arguments to disallow the possibility of a policy like "don't ask, don't tell." Clinton's campaign promise had raised expectations among gays, and his discourse leading up to the controversy did little to prepare them for the policy outcome. Small wonder that this constituency felt betrayed.

The president's "conduct, rather than status" issue definition, with its attendant ambiguity concerning unacceptable behavior, also served to alienate citizens who opposed homosexuality. In his efforts to reassure this audience, Clinton contended that conduct could be the criterion for judging homosexual military personnel "without the Government appearing to endorse a lifestyle" (1993ff, 970). The imprecision of the president's explanations, however, seemed to suggest something different. At a "CBS This Morning" town meeting on May 27 (1993ff), Clinton said:

My view is people should be judged on their conduct. I have not called for any change in the Uniform Code of Conduct. I simply believe that if people work hard, play by the rules, and serve, they ought to be able to serve. That does not imply that the rest of society agrees with the lifestyle, but you just accept as a fact that there are in every country and always have been homosexuals who are capable of honoring their country, laying down their lives for their country, and serving. And they should be judged based on their behavior, not their lifestyle. That's my view; it's a behavior test. (970)

The problem with the president's argument was that it completely contradicted the worldview held by many citizens adverse to gay rights. In a case study of pro– and anti–gay rights discourse, rhetorical critic Barry Brummett (1979) observed that those opposed to gay rights usually describe homosexuality "as an 'act,' a 'lifestyle,' or 'behavior,' rather than as a condition of being"; that is, they believe a person only becomes a homosexual when he or she commits homosexual acts (256, 255). For anti–gay rights adherents, then, Clinton's argument was unacceptable. A person was gay *because* he or she had engaged in sex with someone of the same gender, which meant that status (who the person was) could not be separated from conduct (what the person did). From this perspective, lifestyle and behavior could not be differentiated because gay men and lesbians *chose* to behave in particular ways. Had the president spelled out that same-gender sexual relations were forbidden by the Uniform Code of Military Justice, he may have enhanced his case somewhat with members of this audience unfamiliar with the code, but done so at the risk of estranging citizens who opposed the ban—or, more to the point, estranging them earlier than he did.

By qualifying his "individual rights" definition of the gay ban issue with "conduct, rather than status," Bill Clinton attempted a balancing act that was doomed to failure. He reinforced high expectations in one camp, only to dash them, and angered those already opposed to a repeal of the gay ban. In many ways, the downfall of the president's "conduct, rather than status" argument lay in the differentiations he attempted to make. Gays and their supporters could not comprehend the distinctions of the "don't ask, don't tell" policy; for this audience, individuals engaged in homosexual sex (behavior) *because* they were gay men or lesbians (status). On the other hand, those morally opposed to a lifting of the ban considered homosexuality or one's status as derived from freely chosen actions.[5]

The factors leading to Clinton's qualification of his "individual rights" definition are not completely clear, but certainly it is no coincidence that his "conduct, rather than status" modification first appeared when he began consulting with Sam Nunn. Once the president realized he lacked the political support in Congress for a repeal of the ban, he may have seen this approach as his only chance of resolving the conflict with a minimum of furor and of holding his coalition together. It may also be that Clinton himself held some of the naive notions implicit in the "don't ask, don't tell" policy that he eventually, albeit somewhat reluctantly, endorsed. In his announcement of the compromise measure, Clinton said, "The only part of this policy with which I do not agree is that the rebuttable presumption, in effect, puts the burden on the service member to demonstrate credibly that he or she understands the rules of conduct and is going to adhere to them" (1993pp, 1,374), rather than having the word of the individual suffice. Clinton did not seem to recognize, of course, that even his preferred policy would have forced homosexuals either to remain celibate—and therefore be treated differently than heterosexuals—or to lie about their sex lives. Whatever the reason behind the president's "conduct, rather than status" issue definition, the argument's natural conclusion was to open Clinton to charges of hypocrisy from one side in the dispute and to allegations of immorality from the other.

LEGITIMIZING "DON'T ASK, DON'T TELL" AS AN "HONORABLE COMPROMISE"

Once the gay ban issue had erupted into a major controversy, the president found it necessary to legitimize both the process by which a decision on the ban would be rendered and the eventual product of that process, the "don't ask, don't tell" policy. To do so, Clinton primarily relied upon two techniques: emphasizing the consultation process and depicting the policy as a principled compromise.

Because members of Congress and the Joint Chiefs were so angry over his early failure to confer with them, it is not surprising that the president accentuated the degree of consultation that took place. Clinton told reporters on January 25, for instance, that he was going to talk with the Joint Chiefs that afternoon (1993a, 94), and Stephanopoulos later issued a brief statement in which he described the meeting as "cordial, honest, and respectful" (1993, 98). On January 29 (1993f), the president mentioned that he had come quite close to an agreement with Sam Nunn on how to proceed. He also reassured those who opposed a recission of the ban that "the change cannot and should not be accomplished overnight. It does require extensive consultation with the Joint Chiefs, experts in the Congress and in the legal community, joined by my administration and others. We've consulted closely to date and will do so again in the future" (108, 109). Statements such as these signaled to the military and legislative establishment that Clinton had gotten their message about the need to seek counsel; in addition, his words encouraged public confidence in the administration's policy-making process as one that would be deliberate and informed.

Lest gay Americans feel left out, the president's letter to participants in the gay march on Washington reminded them that he had met with leaders of the gay and lesbian community in the Oval Office, "the first time in history that the President of the United States has held such a meeting." Moreover, Clinton added, "members of my staff have been and will continue to be in regular communication with the gay and lesbian community" (1993y, 685). Although the president muted public signs of his support for gay rights during the controversy, he was quick to emphasize his consultation with gays in a message targeted specifically to them.

Clinton's announcement of and subsequent statements on the "don't ask, don't tell" policy similarly paid homage to the various parties involved in the issue. He thanked Colin Powell, the Joint Chiefs, and the Commandant of the Coast Guard for their "good-faith effort." The president also recognized Congressman Barney Frank, Congressman Gerry Studds, and the Campaign for Military Service, who had "worked hard to come to grips with this" and deserved "a lot of credit" (1993oo, 1,373; also 1993rr, 1,399). Reflective of Clinton's tendency to shun conflict for conciliation, he went out of his way to praise Sam Nunn as one who "feels a special stewardship for the military" and who had "worked hard . . . to open his mind and heart to the arguments on both sides" (1993rr, 1,399).

In spite of these epideictic tributes, Clinton's effort to legitimize "don't ask, don't tell" as the product of thorough consultation was less than successful for two basic reasons. First, the president hurt his relationship with the Joint Chiefs and members of Congress by repeatedly showing a lack of regard for their advice on the proposed policy. When Clinton sent Washington lawyer John Holum to discuss the ban with the chiefs prior to his inauguration, Holum told them, "I am not here to advise the president-elect *whether* to end the ban on gays in the military. I am here to discuss with you *how* this policy change can be done in a way least disruptive to your military mission" (Mathews, 1993, 35). The leaked memo written by Aspin staffers, with its "no negotiation" argument, only worsened the situation, as did Clinton's insistence in November 1992 and again in January 1993 that he was not going to change his mind about lifting the ban (Gellman, 1992, A1; Stephanopoulos, 1993, 98). By March, the president seemed to recognize the folly of this position when he stated that he would consider any recommendation the Secretary of Defense made in conjunction with the Joint Chiefs of Staff. Clinton explained, "I mean, I asked them to study this. I can't refuse then to get the results of the study and act like my mind's made up. This is not an area where I have expertise. I have to listen to what people say. . . . I have presumption against any discrimination based on status alone, but I will listen to any report filed" (1993p, 485). The president's rhetorical shift may have resulted from the dual recognition that he could not afford to appear indifferent to the advice of the military leadership, particularly given his own lack of service background, and that he had little chance of sustaining a repeal of the ban in Congress and therefore needed some room to maneuver. The Joint Chiefs and Clinton's opponents in Congress may have felt satisfied that the president had given in, but it is doubtful that they felt appreciated.

Clinton's attempt to depict "don't ask, don't tell" as the result of wise counsel seems unlikely to have persuaded the gay community, either, albeit for a different reason: The president had consulted gay leaders, but he had not listened. In keeping with his campaign promise, they had argued for a repeal of the ban and, instead, Clinton had endorsed a policy not much different than that already in place when he took office.

No doubt gay Americans' displeasure with the president was heightened further by his insistence that not only was the process by which "don't ask, don't tell" evolved valid, but also the policy itself was legitimate. In his public comments, the president again demonstrated his characteristic issue management style, portraying himself as a moderate who had mediated among competing parties to craft what he called "an honorable compromise" (1993oo, 1,372). Clinton observed, for instance, that the policy "is not a perfect solution. It is not identical with some of my own goals. And it certainly will not please everyone, perhaps not anyone, and clearly not those who hold the most adamant opinions on either side of this issue" (1993oo, 1,372). The president's words indicated that the policy truly was a compromise, for no one group had gotten exactly what it wanted.

At the same time, Clinton was careful not to disparage the worth of the policy. Instead, he described it as "a real step forward" (1993oo, 1,369) that clearly fulfilled the demands of both principle and practicality. In his announcement of "don't ask, don't tell," the president declared:

The policy I am announcing today is, in my judgment, the right thing to do and the best way to do it. It is right because it provides greater protection to those who happen to be homosexual and want to serve their country honorably in uniform, obeying all the military's rules against sexual misconduct. It is the best way to proceed because it provides a sensible balance between the rights of the individual and the needs of our military to remain the world's number one fighting force. As President of all the American people, I am pledged to protect and to promote individual rights. As Commander in Chief, I am pledged to protect and advance our security. In this policy, I believe we have come close to meeting both objectives. (1993oo, 1,370; also see 1,371)

Clinton continued these themes elsewhere. For those who were angry or disappointed that he had not lifted the ban, he pointed out that Congress would have reversed any such action (1993oo, 1,371, 1,372; 1993pp, 1,375; 1993qq, 1,391; 1993rr, 1,399, 1,407; 1993ss, 1,427; 1993uu, 1,970). For those opposed to any change, he explained that homosexuals already served with distinction in the military and that the courts currently were considering the matter in ways that might support more extended civil rights for gay personnel (1993oo, 1,370, 1,372; 1993rr, 1,399). The "don't ask, don't tell" policy was practical.

The president also insisted that the compromise was principled, rather than a compromise of his principles. In a July 19 exchange with reporters, Clinton retorted, "First of all, I think I did stand by my principles. Under this policy, a person can say, 'I am a homosexual, but I am going to strictly adhere to the Code of Conduct.' If you go back through every statement I have made, I never said that I would be in favor of changing any of the rules of conduct" (1993pp, 1,374). What the president did not mention here was that if a gay member of the military made such a statement, it would immediately force the person in question to prove that he or she was disinclined to engage in sexual activity. In two other public statements, Clinton acknowledged the presumption placed on service personnel, but nonetheless insisted that he had been true to his principles. As he told members of the Georgia media, "I never said one word, not a word, about changing anything about the Code of Conduct" (1993tt, 1,470; also 1993rr, 1,399).

The president also argued that his support for "don't ask, don't tell" was principled because it provided much-needed incremental progress, even though such steps were not politically attractive. When a journalist questioned him about his leadership, Clinton indignantly replied:

I am the first President who ever took on this [gays in the military] issue. It may be a sign of madness, sir, but it is not a sign of weakness. And I think we need to get our heads on straight about what is strong and what is weak. When a President takes on tough issues, takes tough stands, tries to get things done in a democracy, you may not get 100 percent. Was I wrong to take 85? What would have happened if I had just put my campaign pledge into play? What would have happened? You know and I know and Les Aspin will tell you, the United States Congress would immediately have reversed it. So I would have the great good fortune of being able to say I'm "Simon Pure," and the people in the military who are serving well and honorably who happen to be homosexuals would not be one step further ahead than they were when I got elected. They're much better off today because we took an honorable compromise. (1993rr, 1,391)

According to the president, the compromise policy ensured recruits would no longer be asked about their sexual orientation, and it provided gay military personnel with greater rights of association. Clinton posed the question this way to reporters from the New York and New Jersey press: "Was it a good compromise or an abandonment of principle? Should I have made everybody feel better for a day and then watch their hopes dashed and see Congress maybe even return to the status quo ante. . . . I think it was an honorable compromise by honorable people, and we did the best we could" (1993ss, 1,427).

Any president would have found the repeal of the gay ban a formidable issue to tackle. Viewed from this perspective, Clinton's willingness to compromise and his depiction of the "don't ask, don't tell" policy as progress seem under-standable, almost laudable. For gay Americans, though, the president's efforts to legitimize "don't ask, don't tell" must have sounded ridiculous, if not in-sulting. First, Clinton had a tendency to oversell the advantages of the policy. He claimed that it not only met basic questions of principle and practicality, but also constituted "a substantial advance" (1993oo, 1,372), "a major step for-ward" (1993oo, 1,372), and "a big change" (1993rr, 1,406) that "goes well beyond anything I even talked about in the campaign" (1993tt, 1,470). The president's descriptions of "don't ask, don't tell" stood in stark contrast to what the policy stipulated, even before Nunn had further revised the bill in committee, a fact that could not have been lost upon gay citizens. If the military leadership had gotten almost everything it wanted, then "don't ask, don't tell" was neither a compromise nor honorable.

Second, Clinton's insistence that he had stayed consistent with his principles, since he had never promised to change the Uniform Code of Military Justice, sounded like a lawyerly appeal to technicality. The president's transcendent definitions of the issue had led many citizens to believe that he wanted gays and lesbians in the military to have the same rights as heterosexuals. When this turned out not to be the case, Clinton's justification for his apparent retreat raised the spectre of "Slick Willie," a fluent politician whose words would trick voters if they were not careful. Clinton's handling of the gay rights dispute fostered such perceptions for many citizens, regardless of their position on the ban, but especially raised questions for members of the gay community who had trusted the president to fulfill his commitment.

Indeed, gay Americans must have wondered why Bill Clinton promised to repeal the ban, yet—his protestations to the contrary—failed to fight for his principles. The president instead preferred to field questions from reporters, rarely choosing to address the issue in prepared speeches. Ironically, Clinton's most impassioned defense of gay rights may have come in his announcement of the "don't ask, don't tell" policy, for he thoughtfully discussed the emotions surrounding the issue and countered many of the arguments made by supporters of the gay ban (1993oo). If Clinton's promise to lift the ban was a product of his principles, desire to please, and political necessity, then his reluctance to take his case to the American people arose from overriding caution: To please gays, he would have to offend the military leadership, key members of Congress, important segments of his electoral coalition, and other voters whom he wanted to woo. The political cost of fighting for his principles was greater than the cost of conflict avoidance.

LEADING FROM THE MIDDLE

Bill Clinton's characteristic issue management style strives to position him as a moderate through transcendent moral appeals—attractive to all—interwoven with specific promises to specific groups. Moreover, his typical issue management style couples talk of principles and promises with the president's predisposition toward conflict avoidance and conciliation. As a result, President Clinton has earned a reputation as a waffler, hurt his relationship with allies, rewarded fellow Democrats who thwart him, played into his opposition's hands, and, at times, acted in ways that were less than courageous.

The president's handling of the gay ban controversy is a case in point. No one forced Clinton to make a repeal of the gay ban the cornerstone of his appeals to gay voters during the 1992 presidential campaign; rather, Clinton himself made the decision to imbue the issue with moral significance through his repeated public promises, giving little thought to how difficult such a policy would be to implement. Once the ban issue exploded into a major public controversy, Clinton attempted to resituate himself as a moderate by downplaying the conflict; defining the issue as a question of individual rights and conduct, rather than status; and legitimizing "don't ask, don't tell" as an "honorable compromise." The president's efforts succeeded only in alienating citizens from both sides of the controversy: Gays and their supporters felt Clinton had sold them out, while opponents of the ban reviled him as the advocate of a radical social agenda. On the heels of his other broken campaign pledges, the president's management of the gay ban demonstrated to members of both groups that Clinton's words could not be trusted: His appeals to ideals seemed disingenuous when he failed to follow through with pragmatic results.

Clinton's continuing leadership problems—the initial failure of his crime bill and his wavering commitment to health coverage for all Americans—stem, at least in part, from his characteristic issue management style. Although compromise can certainly play an appropriate role in politics. Clinton's young presidency shows that one cannot perpetually lead from the middle. Sometimes the dictates of conscience demand not only that the president voice support for a policy that fails to meet with widespread public support, but also that he use the power of rhetoric to convince the people as to the wisdom of that policy. While one may admire Clinton for his decision to court gay voters openly and to voice support for gay rights publicly, his lack of care and courage in seeing his promises through are cause for concern. In the realm of politics, the first casualty is often idealism.

NOTES

1. Political cartoonist Gary Trudeau recently went so far as to ask readers to choose between two "finalists" for a "new presidential icon" to represent Clinton: a flipping coin or a waffle. According to Trudeau, readers overwhelmingly supported the choice of a waffle (1994).

2. Wines was paraphrasing a line of thought articulated by Leslie Gelb, president of the Council on Foreign Relations.

3. In addition to these three occasions, Clinton made brief mention of the gay ban in his statement to participants in the gay march on Washington, but chose to have a member of Congress read his statement rather than making it himself.

4. In the preliminary search done for this study, Clinton's August 20, 1992, articulation of the issue as one of "conduct, not status" was the earliest that I could locate.

5. I do not wish to suggest, of course, that everyone falls into one of these two camps. For additional explanation of the rhetoric of pro– and anti–gay rights groups, see Brummett (1979).

REFERENCES

Alter, Jonathan. (1992, Nov. 23). The double bubba double standard. Editorial. *Newsweek*, 29.

———. (1993a, Feb. 8). The manic-depressive media. Editorial. *Newsweek*, 29.

———. (1993b, Feb. 22). Where are the bone-crushers? Editorial. *Newsweek*, 32.

Army gives honorable discharge to highly decorated gay soldier. (1993, May 11). *The Washington Post*, A6.

Arnold, Carroll C. (1977). Reflections on American public discourse. *Central States Speech Journal* 28 (1977): 73–85.

Balz, Dan. (1993, Jan. 28). A promise that held inevitable collision. *Washington Post*, A6.

Barr, Stephen. (1993, Jan. 25). Hill backs gay ban, Aspin says. *Washington Post*, A1, A7.

Berke, Richard L. (1993, Mar. 24). Clinton would consider segregating gay troops. *New York Times*, A1, A11.

Bormann, Ernest G. (1985). *The force of fantasy: Restoring the American dream*. Carbondale: Southern Illinois University Press.

Bostdorff, Denise M. (1992). Idealism held hostage: Jimmy Carter's rhetoric on the crisis in Iran. *Communication Studies* 43, 14–28.

———. (1994). *The presidency and the rhetoric of foreign crisis*. Columbia: University of South Carolina Press.

——— and Steven L. Vibbert. (1991). The language of political reversal. Paper presented at the annual meeting of the Speech Communication Association, Atlanta.

Brummett, Barry. (1979). A pentadic analysis of ideologies in two gay rights controversies. *Central States Speech Journal* 30, 250–61.

Bull, Chris. (1992, Aug. 25). Gays and lesbians fare well at Democratic convention, but will Clinton regret it? *The Advocate*, 18–19.

———. (1993, Aug. 24). Broken promise. *The Advocate*, 24–27.

Bush, James T. (1993, Jan. 14). Cancel Reagan's ban. Editorial. *New York Times*, A25.

Carlson, Margaret. (1993, May 31). Shear dismay. *Time*, 21–23.

Cary, Peter. (1993, April 5). Coming out too soon: hit by friendly fire. *U.S. News & World Report*, 31.

Clinton, William J. (1992, Aug. 15). Acceptance address. *Vital Speeches of the Day* 58, 642–45.

Clinton, William J. (1993a, Jan. 25). Remarks on the establishment of the National Economic Council and an exchange with reporters. *Weekly Compilation of Presidential Documents* (hereafter *WCPD*), 94.

Clinton, William J. (1993b, Jan. 26). Exchange with reporters prior to a meeting with congressional leaders. *WCPD*, 99.

Clinton, William J. (1993c, Jan. 28). Exchange with reporters prior to a meeting with federal reserve chairman Alan Greenspan. *WCPD*, 100.

Clinton, William J. (1993d, Jan. 28). Remarks honoring the school principal of the year and an exchange with reporters. *WCPD*, 100–101.

Clinton, William J. (1993e, Jan. 29). Exchange with reporters prior to a meeting with the Close-Up Foundation. *WCPD*, 102.

Clinton, William J. (1993f, Jan. 29). The president's news conference. *WCPD*, 108–11.

Clinton, William J. (1993g, Jan. 29). Memorandum on ending discrimination in the armed forces. *WCPD*, 112.

Clinton, William J. (1993h, Feb. 10). Remarks at a town meeting in Detroit. *WCPD*, 171–85.

Clinton, William J. (1993i, Feb. 17). Address before a joint session of Congress on administration goals. *WCPD*, 215–24.

Clinton, William J. (1993j, Feb. 20). Remarks at the children's town meeting. *WCPD*, 254–74.

Clinton, William J. (1993k, Mar. 12). Remarks to the crew of the U.S.S. *Theodore Roosevelt. WCPD*, 407.

Clinton, William J. (1993l, Mar. 12). Remarks to the crew of the U.S.S. *Theodore Roosevelt. WCPD*, 407–10.

Clinton, William J. (1993m, Mar. 12). Radio address to the armed forces. *WCPD*, 410–12.

Clinton, William J. (1993n, Mar. 13). Radio address to the nation on defense conversion. *WCPD*, 412–13.

Clinton, William J. (1993o, Mar. 23). The president's news conference. *WCPD*, 466–75.

Clinton, William J. (1993p, Mar. 24). Interview with Dan Rather of CBS News. *WCPD*, 479–87.

Clinton, William J. (1993q, Mar. 27). Radio address to the nation on administration goals. *WCPD*, 503–4.

Clinton, William J. (1993r, April 1). Remarks to the midshipmen at the United States Naval Academy in Annapolis, Maryland. *WCPD*, 507–8.

Clinton, William J. (1993s, April 16). The president's news conference with prime minister Kiichi Miyazawa of Japan. *WCPD*, 596–603.

Clinton, William J. (1993t, April 17). Radio address on administration goals. *WCPD*, 607–8.

Clinton, William J. (1993u, April 23). The president's news conference. *WCPD*, 650–60.

Clinton, William J. (1993v, April 24). The president's radio address. *WCPD*, 668–70.

Clinton, William J. (1993w, April 25). Remarks to the Newspaper Association of America in Boston, Massachusetts. *WCPD*, 670–79.

Clinton, William J. (1993x, April 25). Question-and-answer session with the Newspaper Association of America in Boston. *WCPD*, 679–85.

Clinton, William J. (1993y, April 25). Statement to participants in the gay rights march. *WCPD*, 685.

Clinton, William J. (1993z, April 29). Remarks prior to a meeting with members of the House Ways and Means Committee and an exchange with reporters. *WCPD*, 710–11.

Clinton, William J. (1993aa, May 5). Remarks welcoming home military personnel from Somalia. *WCPD*, 754–55.

Clinton, William J. (1993bb, May 6). Remarks on presenting the commander in chief trophy to the U.S. Air Force Academy football team. *WCPD*, 772–73.

Clinton, William J. (1993cc, May 10). Question-and-answer session with the Cleveland City Club. *WCPD*, 805–9.

Clinton, William J. (1993dd, May 11). Remarks to high school students and a question-and-answer session in Bensonville, Illinois. *WCPD*, 809–20.

Clinton, William J. (1993ee, May 14). The president's news conference. *WCPD*, 856–65.

Clinton, William J. (1993ff, May 27). Remarks in the *CBS This Morning* town meeting. *WCPD*, 957–74.

Clinton, William J. (1993gg, May 28). Teleconference remarks with veterans in VA medical centers. *WCPD*, 975–77.

Clinton, William J. (1993hh, May 29). The president's radio address. *WCPD*, 994–95.

Clinton, William J. (1993ii, May 29). Remarks at the United States Military Academy commencement ceremony in West Point, New York. *WCPD*, 995–99.

Clinton, William J. (1993jj, May 31). Remarks honoring the observance of the 50th anniversary of World War II. *WCPD*, 999–1,001.

Clinton, William J. (1993kk, May 31). Remarks at a Memorial Day ceremony at Arlington National Cemetery, Arlington, Virginia. *WCPD*, 1,001–2.

Clinton, William J. (1993ll, May 31). Remarks at a Memorial Day ceremony at the Vietnam Veterans Memorial. *WCPD*, 1,003.

Clinton, William J. (1993mm, June 22). Telephone conversation with the crew of the space shuttle *Endeavour* and an exchange with reporters. *WCPD*, 1,154–57.

Clinton, William J. (1993nn, June 25). Remarks on the appointment of Kristine M. Gebbie as AIDS policy coordinator and an exchange with reporters. *WCPD*, 1,168–72.

Clinton, William J. (1993oo, July 19). Remarks announcing the new policy on gays and lesbians in the military. *WCPD*, 1,369–73.

Clinton, William J. (1993pp, July 19). Remarks on the dismissal of FBI Director William Sessions and an exchange with reporters. *WCPD*, 1,373–76.

Clinton, William J. (1993qq, July 20). Remarks in an interview with members of the Wisconsin press. *WCPD*, 1,385–91.

Clinton, William J. (1993rr, July 20). Interview with Larry King. *WCPD*, 1,397–1,408.

Clinton, William J. (1993ss, July 22). Remarks in an interview with the New York and New Jersey press. *WCPD*, 1,423–28.

Clinton, William J. (1993tt, July 27). Interview with the Georgia media. *WCPD*, 1,466–73.

Clinton, William J. (1993uu, Oct. 3). Remarks in a town meeting in Sacramento. *WCPD*, 1,965–82.

Clymer, Adam. (1993, Feb. 5). Congress passes measure providing emergency leaves. *New York Times*, A1, A14.

Cohn, Bob and Eleanor Clift. (1994, July 11). Shaking up the snake pit. *Newsweek*, 16.

Devroy, Ann. (1993a, Jan. 26). Joint chiefs voice concern to Clinton on lifting gay ban. *Washington Post*, A1, A11.

———. (1993b, July 20). President opens military to gays. *Washington Post*, A1, A11.

Dewar, Helen. (1993, Sept. 10). Senate codifies policy on gays in the military. *Washington Post*, A18.

DeWitt, Karen. (1993a, April 16). Clinton to meet with gay groups. *New York Times*, A20.

————. (1993b, April 17). Clinton meets with gay groups but won't attend their march. *New York Times,* A9.

————. (1993c, April 24). To gay marchers' anger, Clinton plans to be absent. *New York Times,* A10.

Duffy, Michael. (1993a, Jan. 25). Ready or not. *Time,* 27–29.

————. (1993b, Feb. 8). Obstacle Course. *Time,* 26–28.

Evans, Rowland and Robert Novak. (1992, Dec. 4). Fear of the homophobic label. Editorial. *Washington Post,* A31.

A few bad men. (1993, Feb. 15). *Time,* 19.

Fineman, Howard. (1992, Nov./Dec.). The torch passes. *Newsweek,* 4–10.

Friedman, Thomas L. (1992, Nov. 17). Clinton and top legislators pledge amity on economy. *New York Times,* A18.

Gallagher, John. (1994, May 17). One year later. *The Advocate,* 39, 41–45.

———— and Chris Bull. (1993, Jan. 26). Washington's new attitude. *The Advocate,* 34–38, 40–41.

The gay ban. (1993, July 18). Editorial. *Washington Post,* C6.

Gellman, Barton. (1992, Nov. 13). Clinton says he'll "consult" on allowing gays in the military. *Washington Post,* A1, A11.

Goldman, Peter and Tom Mathews. (1992a, Nov./Dec.) "Manhattan project." *Newsweek,* 40–42, 55–56.

————. (1992b, Nov./Dec.) Rocky road to Houston. *Newsweek,* 65–69.

————. (1992c, Nov./Dec.) The war room drill. *Newsweek,* 78–81.

Guinier, Lani. (1994, Feb. 27). Who's afraid of Lani Guinier? *New York Times Magazine,* 38–44, 54–55, 66.

Hackworth, David H. (1993, June 28). Rancor in the ranks: The troops vs. the president. *Newsweek,* 24–25.

Hart, Roderick P. (1984). The functions of human communication in the maintenance of public values. In *Handbook of rhetorical and communication theory,* ed. Carroll C. Arnold and John Waite Bowers (pp. 749–91). Boston: Allyn and Bacon.

Hilzenrath, David S. and Eric Pianin. (1993, June 10). Senators rewrite energy tax plan. *Washington Post,* A1, A8.

Hosenball, Mark. (1994, May 16). No laughing matter. *Newsweek,* 22–24.

Isikoff, Michael and Mark Hosenball. (1994a, July 11). Why Vince Foster died. *Newsweek,* 17.

———— and Mark Hosenball. (1994b, July 25). Getting even with Hillary. *Newsweek,* 22.

Jenkins, Kent, Jr. (1993, May 11). Into troubled waters. *Washington Post,* A1, A6.

Judge orders the Navy to reinstate gay sailor. (1992, Nov. 7). *Washington Post,* A7.

Kelly, Michael. (1994, July 31). The president's past. *New York Times Magazine,* 20–29, 34, 40, 45.

Kenworthy, Tom. (1992, Nov. 16). Nunn, Dole urge caution on military gay policy. *Washington Post,* A11.

Klein, Joe. (1993, April 26). Clinton's values problem. Editorial. *Newsweek,* 35.

————. (1994a, June 20). The consultants. Editorial. *Newsweek,* 43.

————. (1994b, Aug. 1). Chafee at the bit. Editorial. *Newsweek,* 23.

Krauthammer, Charles. (1993, July 30). Prisoner of promises. Editorial. *Washington Post,* A21.

Lancaster, John. (1991, June 19). Hill study challenges military's exclusion of gays. *Washington Post,* A1, A12.

————. (1992, Nov. 11). Navy agrees to reinstate gay sailor. *Washington Post,* A1, A21.

————. (1993, July 22). Joint chiefs take hypothetical test on gay policy. *Washington Post,* A4.

Lippman, Thomas W. (1993, July 28). Suit attacks Clinton's policy on homosexuals in military. *Washington Post,* A2.

———— and Ruth Marcus. (1993, May 28). President seeks gan ban compromise; Nunn rules out a "haven" in military. *Washington Post,* A1, A14.

Marcus, Ruth and Helen Dewar. (1993, Jan. 30). Clinton compromise delays showdown over ban on gays. *Washington Post,* A1, A12.

Masters, Brooke A. (1992, Dec. 19). Gays hope for higher profile during inaugural week—and beyond. *Washington Post,* B3.

Mathews, Tom. (1993, May 3). Clinton's growing pains. *Newsweek,* 34–38, 40.

McAllister, Bill. (1993, April 2). Learning the cost of coming out. *Washington Post,* B1, B7.

McCombs, Phil. (1992, Dec. 23). Two gay men in the line of fire. *Washington Post,* C1–C2.

And more good news for the Pentagon. (1993, Mar. 1). *Time,* 9.

Niebuhr, Gustav. (1993a, Jan. 29). Push on gay ban roils religious community. *Washington Post,* A11.

————. (1993b, Feb. 10). Lesbian ousted from the military is hoping to return as a chaplain. *Washington Post,* A4.

Osborne, Duncan. (1994, Jan. 24). Betrayed. *The Advocate,* 50–55.

Phillips, Kevin. (1993, Jan. 31). Gay clout, political dynamite. *Washington Post,* C1, C3.

Reaction to the policy. (1993, Aug. 24). *The Advocate,* 29.

Reid, T. R. (1993, May 28). Sailor gets life term in murder. *Washington Post,* A31, A35.

Schmalz, Jeffrey. (1992, Nov. 15). Difficult first step. *New York Times,* A22.

————. (1993, April 26). Gay marchers throng capital in appeal for rights. *New York Times,* A1, B8.

Schmitt, Eric. (1993a, Jan. 13). Clinton aides study indirect end to military ban on homosexuals. *New York Times,* A1, A17.

————. (1993b, Mar. 26). Clinton tries to erase impression he would set gay troops apart. *New York Times,* A1, A15.

Shapiro, Joseph P. (1993, July 5). Straight talk about gays. *U.S. News & World Report,* 42–44, 46–48.

Shilts, Randy. 1993. *Conduct Unbecoming: Gays and Lesbians in the U.S. Military.* New York: St. Martin's Press.

Smolowe, Jill. (1993, Feb. 8). Sex, lies and the military. *Time,* 29–30.

Stephanopoulos, George. (1993, Jan. 25). Statement by the director of communications on the president's meeting with the joint chiefs of staff. *WCPD,* 98.

Trudeau, Gary. (1994, Aug. 22). "Doonesbury." *Akron Beacon Journal,* A7.

Van Biema, David. (1993, Aug. 2). See you in court. *Time,* 29–30.

Weisskopf, Michael. (1993, Feb. 1). "Gospel grapevine" displays strength in controversy over military gay ban. *Washington Post,* A1, A10.

Wenner, Jann S. and William Greider. (1993, Dec. 9). The *Rolling Stone* interview: President Clinton. *Rolling Stone,* 40–45, 80–81.

Wines, Michael. (1994, July 17). Talk often and be a soft touch. *New York Times*, D1, D5.

Woodward, Bob. (1994). *The agenda*. New York: Simon & Schuster.

Yarbrough, Jeff. (1993, June 15). The life and times of Randy Shilts. *The Advocate*, 32, 34–39.

Chapter Ten

"Rough Stretches and Honest Disagreements": Is Bill Clinton Redefining the Rhetorical Presidency?

Craig Allen Smith

"So far, under Bill Clinton's watch," wrote syndicated columnist Clarence Page (1994, F4), "the economy has recovered, deficit growth has reversed, NAFTA was passed, the crime bill was passed, Reaganomics has been reversed (tax credits have been expanded for the lowest-income workers and the tax burden has shifted to the upper-income brackets), peace has broken out between Israel and Yasser Arafat and health care has become a top priority of Congress. And what is his reward? A lousy 38 percent approval rating in a recent CNN/Gallup poll." Page might have added that the family leave and national service acts were also passed and that disapproval of Clinton reached 52 percent. Thus at twenty months, the state of the Clinton presidency invites two related questions. First, why has this relatively unpopular president been so much more effective than his recent predecessors in securing the legislative enactment of his agenda? And second, why has this legislatively successful president—elected to end gridlock and bring about change—languished in the public approval polls?

Traditional models of presidential leadership fail to explain the emerging Clinton presidency. One view fails to explain adequately a record of legislative success by a president who had neither a broad electoral mandate nor high levels of public support (Neustadt, 1960; Seligman and Covington, 1989); but Clinton was elected with only 43 percent of the popular vote, his highest approval ratings have barely exceeded 50 percent, and many 1994 Democratic candidates are distancing themselves from him. A second view can explain such a record if the president regularly addresses the American people on television to mobilize support for his agenda, but Clinton did so only four times other than his inaugural and State of the Union addresses. And many ideologues could explain such a record from a president with a tightly focused agenda, but Clinton seems interested in reforming and innovating in almost every policy area from an ideological perspective that is neither left nor right. What, then, is happening in the early 1990s, and what are the implications for our theories of presidential persuasion?

This chapter argues that Bill Clinton is engaged in a profoundly innovative approach to the rhetorical presidency and that his approach is working far more than most observers have yet realized, perhaps because they have yet to grasp its strategic logic. The chapter does not speculate as to whether the Clinton White House has been fully aware of the overarching logic of its innovative approach, but it will assume that particular rhetorical choices made sense to those who made them because of a series of strategic assumptions. To understand President Clinton's leadership we shall examine (1) the logic of the campaign that won him the presidency, (2) the nature of the rhetorical presidency awaiting him, (3) the strategic models available to him, and (4) his emerging approach to presidential leadership.

JEREMIADIC LOGIC AND CLINTON'S ELECTORAL COALITION

The sign in Clinton headquarters read, "It's the economy, stupid," and pundits used it to dramatize the campaign's focus on economic frustrations as their vehicle for unseating George Bush (Atherton, 1993; Holloway, 1994). But by emphasizing the substance of Clinton's appeal these commentators deflected critical attention from the logical form of Clinton's argument, and the logical form of his campaign message was profoundly important.

Clinton's campaign rhetoric was framed in a consistent logic that exhibited all the features of the modern political jeremiad (Bercovitch, 1978; Ritter, 1993; Smith and Smith, 1994; Smith, 1994). Candidate Clinton explained that a chosen people ("the forgotten middle class") was incurring tribulations in the forms of recession, crime, drug abuse, AIDS, riots, rising health care costs, and inadequate education because they had followed false prophets (Reagan, Bush, Quayle et al.) who had led them away from the "first principles" that had always made America great. Jeremiadic logic reasons that followers must heed their leader's call to fundamental principles and obligations so that the afflictions will be lifted by divine intervention.

Clinton's campaign jeremiad was based on a fundamental truth he had learned as a student of Professor Carroll Quigley at Georgetown University. That truth, articulated in at least six of his major campaign speeches, was this: America has always been the greatest country in the world because Americans [the chosen people] have always believed in two things: first, that tomorrow will be better than today; and second, that each of us has a personal moral responsibility to make it so. From these premises Clinton argued (1) that Reagan and Bush had been "afraid to change in a world that was changing so fast," (2) that they had consequently distracted Americans from our personal moral responsibilities to make tomorrow better than today, and (3) that Americans therefore needed new leadership (conveniently, his own) to "make change our friend" (Clinton, 1991; Smith, 1994).

Clinton's policy speeches advanced his logical framework by advocating health care reform, economic change, national service, community boot camps, and a host of other multipoint plans that differentiated his leadership style from Bush's and demonstrated his own commitment to make tomorrow better than today. Significantly, Bush and Perot could not attack Clinton's programs without admitting that he had programs more detailed than theirs, and even when they found flaws in his plans they failed either to engage or to refute the jeremiadic logic that framed his campaign.

Thus the key to Clinton's electoral victory was his ability to pull a wide range of programs together into a coherent agenda for action. For example, at Notre Dame University he responded to the Bush-Quayle "family values" motif by saying, "We don't need an administration that talks about *family values,* we need an administration that *values families*" and then launching into his plans for family leave, health care, welfare reform, job training, and the like (Clinton, 1992, emphasis added). His message was unmistakable: "family values" was an ill-defined noun but "valuing families" was an active process with operationally defined goals and policy proposals.

Perhaps Bill Clinton won the presidency simply because he was not George Bush, but he was only one of many such candidates. Clinton was the one candidate who used the campaign to dramatize four of the ways in which he differed from George Bush. First, Clinton used the politics of inclusion rather than division. His announcement speech of October 3, 1991, introduced his themes of change and inclusion. In this and subsequent speeches Clinton provided an umbrella for any citizens tired of the divisiveness of the Bush era and its legacy of Willie Horton, Clarence Thomas, lines drawn in the sand, and confrontations with the Congress. But others also did this; it alone cannot account for his success.

The second contrast concerned "the vision thing." Clinton's announcement speech presented his jeremiadic vision. It articulated the ancient truth, spoke to people's need for optimism, justified his life-long pursuit of the presidency, and challenged each citizen to assume more personal responsibility for the condition of life in America. This provided a marked contrast to Bush's admitted lack of an overarching vision.

The third contrast with President Bush was Clinton's tendency to answer questions with multipoint programs. In an era of policy generalities, Clinton provided enough specific policies to boggle most minds. His campaign team decided early that the public was more concerned with action than personality, so they took the unusual step of introducing their plan before introducing their candidate (Greer, 1993). Indeed, the language and logic of Clinton's policy discussions created for him an image of expertise that contrasted sharply with Bush's willingness to wait out the recession.

A fourth contrast between candidates Bush and Clinton was Clinton's ability to lend coherence to problems and solutions. Like Ronald Reagan and unlike George Bush, Clinton's jeremiadic logic helped his constituents to make sense of seemingly disparate problems, issues, and tensions. His speeches and his answers to citizens' questions lent coherence to otherwise confusing public and private matters. But where Ross Perot tried to provide that coherence with the principle that governing is not as complicated as "they" would have "us" believe, Clinton took the long way around to argue that governing is not as simple as "they" would have "us" believe. To oversimplify, Perot's approach worked for 20 percent of the voters and Clinton's for 43 percent; but whereas Perot failed to finish within 5 percent of second place in any state Clinton's votes were strategically distributed to finish first in states sufficient to deliver two-thirds of the electoral votes.

But although these points of contrast helped Clinton to win the presidency, they would constrain his rhetorical options as president. Ronald Reagan and Bill Clinton each rode into the Oval Office on the shoulders of 43 million voters, but Bush and Perot combined to amass 18 million votes more than had Carter and Anderson in 1980. Clinton therefore lacked any appearance of widespread public support, and his position was more analogous to Richard Nixon's after his 1968 victory over Hubert Humphrey and George Wallace. Moreover, Clinton had difficulty staffing his administration with experienced Washingtonians, both because Republicans had controlled the Executive branch for twenty of the past twenty-four years and because he had run against the Washington establishment. Thus, even though Clinton gave high priority to the transition, he took office with a very weak governing coalition and a campaign commitment to a dramatic first hundred days (Cohen, 1994).

THE RHETORICAL PRESIDENCY AWAITING BILL CLINTON

On January 21, 1993, Bill Clinton was inaugurated into the American presidency, a political role with a decidedly rhetorical job description. I have elsewhere set forth the conceptual approach to presidential leadership that frames this analysis of the emerging Clinton presidency (Smith and Smith, 1994). That approach rests on twelve propositions.

1. *Presidential leadership in the modern era entails persuasion.* Presidential candidates must develop and sustain electoral and governing coalitions (Edwards, 1983; Lowi, 1985; Seligman and Covington, 1989; Tulis, 1987). The political interests, issues, and adversaries around whom persons converge and diverge are defined and understood only through discursive practices (Billig, 1991; Edwards, 1983; Harre and Gillett, 1994; Popkin, 1991). Hence presidents must rely on persuasive communication if they are to lead in a system of separated institutions sharing powers (Neustadt, 1960).

2. *The presidential job description constrains every president's personal rhetorical flexibility.* Constitutional constraints and public expectations have combined to create a

twentieth-century rhetorical presidency that is a striking contrast to the Framers' presidency (Kernell, 1993; Lowi, 1985; Tulis, 1987). In the footsteps of Wilson and the Roosevelts, contemporary presidents have used fourteen distinct genres of discourse (Campbell and Jamieson, 1990) in which they use language that differs from that used by candidates, corporate executives, social activists, and religious leaders even though it evidences elements of each (Hart, 1984). In short, presidents speak because they are president, and they speak in ways that are characteristically presidential.

3. *Presidents create electoral and governing coalitions by helping others to interpret social and political realities.* As political parties have weakened, presidents have increasingly developed their own coalitions by "going public" to mobilize support. *The White House Speaks* (Smith and Smith, 1994) advanced an "interpretive systems" approach to explaining the rhetorical dynamics of the coalition-building process. Every individual has four innate, involuntary, interpretive processes—needing, symbolizing, reasoning, and preferencing—which we coordinate by adopting and creating four kinds of social interpretive frameworks: laws, languages, logics, and ideologies. As persons use these interpretive processes and structures in their communication with others they find moments of convergence and divergence that help them to feel themselves members of some interpretive communities rather than others. These overlapping, incongruent interpretive communities struggle for the right to interpret social and political realities for everyone else. Presidents use discourse to create and sustain interpretive coalitions, such that presidential rhetoric is a melting pot of needs, words, arguments, and priorities.

4. *The breadth and heterogeneity of presidents' interpretive coalitions impinges directly on their latitude to lead, and vice versa.* Theoretically, the broader one's coalition the more latitude one has to lead. But sociological and technological developments have diversified American society and facilitated the dissemination of all political messages. Consequently, broad electoral coalitions are necessarily heterogeneous with diverse interpretive communities selectively perceiving the messages of all presidents, candidates, and critics. Once elected, the president's latitude to lead is constrained by the heterogeneity of his electoral coalition because each community in that coalition has been primed for disappointment. It is one thing to appeal to a broad coalition of voters, it is something else to satisfy them.

5. *Presidential coalitions are built around both convergence and divergence.* Unity and division, identification and polarization are interdependent. They can best be understood as unifying *around* and dividing *from,* as identifying *with* and polarizing *against.* Presidents Roosevelt, Truman, Eisenhower, Kennedy, Johnson, Nixon, Ford, Carter, Reagan, and Bush had the rhetorical option of polarizing Americans against the common enemies of depression, fascism, and communism. But the end of the cold war changed American political rhetoric by denying rhetors a potent object of fear and hatred beyond our borders. The demise of the Soviet Union defused both the rhetoric of the Evil Empire and much of the fear of World War III, and the quick and easy defeat of Iraq made it even more difficult to arouse public passions with foreign policy rhetoric. Without external demons, the 1990s provide rhetors with only Americans converging and diverging from other Americans.

6. *Presidents can seek convergence and divergence on individual or community levels.* President Harry Truman's antifamine program succeeded partly because it offered a

wide variety of personal reasons for people to conserve food, and because it mobilized around existing interpretive communities such as business, labor, and schools. President Carter's attempts to persuade people to conserve energy failed largely because he ignored his citizens' personal needs and because he largely ignored existing interpretive communities in favor of new federal agencies.

7. *Presidential persuasion can succeed or fail because of its timing.* There are ample examples of each possibility. President Kennedy's June 1963 civil rights address worked, in part, because he spoke just hours after Governor Wallace had defied the federal mandate to desegregate the University of Alabama. Conversely, President Ford's surprise address pardoning Richard Nixon invited the judgment that he intended to avoid news coverage and to slip it past the public. President Carter's unexplained postponement of his energy address from July 5, 1979, to the fifteenth raised expectations for the address and nurtured the perception that he was indecisive. And his decision to delay from September until February an address about the Panama Canal treaties gave the New Right time to coalesce and to disseminate their arguments against the treaties. Each of these addresses either met, or failed to meet, a rhetorically opportune moment.

8. *Presidential persuasion is adversarial, and competing rhetors play important roles.* American presidents lead in relation to aspiring leaders with whom they jockey for support. Each presidential argument implies one or more opposing arguments with which it must cope. Kennedy tried to allay the fears of foreign policy conservatives in his American University commencement address, and he transcended the segregationists' response to his legal arguments by reframing civil rights as a moral issue. Although Presidents Ford and Carter both supported the renegotiated Panama Canal treaties, Ronald Reagan and Phillip Crane advanced a more compelling narrative that persuaded the Republican party to move toward an antitreaty position, partly to mobilize their resources to challenge Carter and the Democrats in 1980. By winning the narrative conflict the New Right won the right to interpret foreign policy for the 1980s. Nixon stonewalled the Watergate investigation effectively for several months, but he was unprepared simultaneously to protect himself in the courts, the Congress, and in the court of public opinion.

9. *The rhetorical form of a presidential address has political consequences.* President Reagan was a master storyteller who generally avoided use of propositional logic. His addresses helped to unify Americans with compelling narratives that invited us to perceive his policy proposals as reasonable and preferable to their alternatives. When he did use propositional arguments in response to the first Iran-Contra charges, his ineptitude with the form invited us to perceive him as utterly uninformed about the operation—a perception that worked to his advantage. The narrative form of the jeremiad merges presidential authority with the first American sermonic form to elevate presidents and to undercut their adversaries, to encourage social cohesion and optimism while undermining the Framers' checks and balances on the presidency, and to advocate social change in terms of historical continuity.

10. *Presidential language, especially self-references, can be crucial to effective leadership.* Because people think with symbols, a figure of speech is a figure of thought. Contemporary presidents have employed an unusually high frequency of self-

references (Hart, 1984). These self-references accentuate presidents' personal leadership, for which they receive blame as well as credit. Ford justified the Nixon pardon with a string of references to "my" responsibility, "my" decision, and "my" conscience when impersonal references to the presidential authority to pardon would have insulated him from unnecessary criticism. Nixon pledged personally to cooperate with those investigating the Watergate affair when he had no intention of doing so; a grammatical choice for which, it can be argued, he was driven from office. Carter's energy jeremiad spoke of a crisis of public confidence, then dwelled on what he personally would do to solve it. All three presidencies were injured, perhaps critically, by these language choices. On the other hand, Ronald Reagan avoided using any self-references when admitting that "mistakes were made" in the Iran-Contra scandal. Indeed, he even spoke about what "you" do when "you" have a problem.

11. *Successful presidential leadership requires presidential rhetoric that evolves to meet changing political circumstances.* Political situations invite rhetorical choices that have both political and rhetorical consequences. When presidents' rhetoric fails to adapt to evolving political situations, they are left behind. George Bush failed to adapt to changes in America and the world such that the problems and divisions around which Americans had diverged in 1988 were largely irrelevant by 1992. Nixon was able to sustain his electoral coalition throughout 1972 by avoiding and containing the Watergate scandal, but he devoted too little attention to the effects of his choices on his governing coalition and it collapsed. Reagan chose not to use his familiar rhetoric to justify Iran-Contra, so he changed abruptly both the language and the logic that had served him so well. These presidents might have recognized more clearly the ratcheting effect of their words on their political circumstances.

12. *The contemporary rhetorical presidency requires presidents to use public persuasion that often backfires.* Ford's speech justifying his potentially explosive decision to pardon some Vietnam-era draft evaders facilitated public acceptance, but his remarks justifying the Nixon pardon plague him still. George Bush's attempts to polarize Americans with combative rhetoric against congressional intransigence, liberal permissiveness, and Saddam Hussein helped him in the short term, but they invited the candidacy of Pat Buchanan, who argued for actions that matched Bush's rhetoric. Jimmy Carter went public to mobilize support for the Panama Canal treaties, and thus provided more words for the New Right to use in their critique of his interpretive vision. And as Richard Nixon talked more and more about his role in the Watergate case he gave his adversaries more and more ways to trip him. To these cases we should add the experiences of Woodrow Wilson and Lyndon Johnson, who found that rousing public rhetoric alienated important swing votes in Congress.

In short, modern presidential leadership entails persuasion, and it matters greatly who says what to whom, when, why, how, and with what evolutionary political results.

CLINTON'S AVAILABLE MEANS OF LEADERSHIP

Had President Clinton and his aides perused the research literature on presidential leadership, they would have seen four strategic alternatives.

Strategy #1: Institutional Pluralism

Samuel Kernell (1993) coined the term "institutional pluralism" to refer to a political order characterized by bargaining among elites. From this perspective, "The politician is, above all, the man [sic] whose career depends upon the successful negotiation of bargains. . . . Most of his [sic] time is consumed in bargaining. This is the skill he [sic] cultivates; it is the skill that distinguishes the master-politician from the political failure" (Dahl and Lindblom, 1953, 333 quoted by Kernell, 10). This strategy of presidential leadership is appropriate when the political elites speak for their core constituencies, when each elite can deliver its part of a bargain, when the bargainers have either a strong commitment to reciprocity or a well-developed sense of mutual trust, and when bargains can be consummated out of the limelight. This kind of presidency reached its zenith during the Roosevelt and Truman years when reporters interviewed FDR off the record, when congressional leaders could deliver their colleagues, and when political party loyalties and discipline affected nominating and election.

Bill Clinton is reputed to be a master of institutionalized pluralism, and it served him well in Arkansas. But by 1993 institutional pluralism in Washington had been relegated to the Smithsonian collection because (1) presidential selection reforms had undermined presidents' ties to their core constituencies, (2) reform of the seniority system in Congress had undercut party discipline, (3) investigative journalism and communication and transportation technologies had infringed on the bargainers' privacy, (4) voters' migration from parties to independent voting had weakened coalitions, (5) the proliferation of single-issue political action committees that contribute to multiple candidacies had clouded the role of elites, and (6) the tendency of vulnerable candidates to posture for their next campaigns had muddied the argumentative waters. Thus Clinton excels at a strategic approach that had become largely inappropriate for presidential leadership.

Strategy #2: Maximize Personal Popularity

As the problems of institutional pluralism began to appear, Richard Neustadt (1960) encouraged presidents to maximize their public approval ratings in order to enhance their political leverage. More specifically, he advised them to build their public prestige, to engender professional respect among Washingtonians, and to protect carefully their policy options. From this strategic perspective public approval is considered a leading, as opposed to a lagging, indicator of presidential success because popular presidents have clout and unpopular presidents are vulnerable to challenge. This strategy has been so popular in this century that Lowi (1985) warned of a plebiscatary presidency that emphasizes personal popularity over sound policy making.

Although this strategy is deceptively appealing in its apparent simplicity, it is fraught with difficulties. Are approval and disapproval ratings equally significant, and if not, which is the more important? How does a president go about maximizing his popularity in an increasingly pluralistic and fragmented society? How does one maximize one's personal popularity while tackling complex and divisive problems? When and how does one invest one's popularity in an important but unpopular policy? Is aggregate national approval/disapproval as important to legislators as the president's approval/disapproval among his own constituents? What happens when the technical and rational arguments capable of persuading swing legislators conflict with the popular and passionate arguments needed to win public support? What happens when it takes a populist, anti-Washingtonian rhetoric to curry public approval? Can the president be sure that he will be able to parlay his personal popularity into legislative support? After all, despite their legendary public approval ratings Dwight Eisenhower and Ronald Reagan left their most ardent supporters disappointed that they had achieved no more of their political agendas. More recently, President Bush failed to capitalize on his record 89 percent approval to deal with economic problems, the government went into gridlock, and Bush was soundly defeated in his quest for reelection only a year and a half later. If this strategy failed Bush with his 89 percent approval, it did promise much success to a president with an activist agenda and 43 percent of the popular vote.

Strategy #3: Going Public

The most notable innovation in twentieth-century presidential leadership has been the tendency of presidents to "go public" by taking their case to the people. Frustrated with congressional gridlock at the turn of the century, progressive reformers and their allies put their faith in strong executives who could clean house. Progressives Theodore Roosevelt and Woodrow Wilson began the practice of presidential involvement in the legislative process. Wilson established the policy address, the visionary speech, and the popular campaign against congressional intractability as presidential resources. Unfortunately for Wilson and several of his imitators, his innovations often contributed more to the glory of defeat than to victory.

Kernell (1993) identifies the strategic problem: "Why should presidents come to favor a strategy of leadership that appears so incompatible with the principles of pluralist theory? Why, if other Washington elites legitimately and correctly represent the interests of their clients and constituents, would anything be gained by going over their heads?" (9). Partial answers to his question abound. First, presidents are often unwilling to concede that the Washington elites do, in fact, represent the interests of their clients and constituents, and they use their bully pulpit to sound the alarm. Second, reforms in the selection process and in technologies have facilitated the election of candidates more skilled at campaigning than bargaining with elites. Third, the development of loudspeakers, radio, television, satellite feeds, and jets have made it easier for presidents to address their publics, and the refinement of public relations practices has helped them to address shrewdly those publics. Fourth, the aforementioned decline of institutional pluralism has made bargaining less efficient than it once was.

But this contemporary reliance on public persuasion, which Jeffrey Tulis (1987) has referred to as "The Rhetorical Presidency," is problematic. For one thing it makes the president seem to be each citizen's personal voice even though the president is structurally the least able to represent the variegated nature of public opinion. Second, it has encouraged presidents to cloak their positions in moral trappings and to ignore almost completely the constitutional underpinnings of presidential authority. Third, it has encouraged the impression that the president *is* the federal government, that he can command things to happen, and that unsatisfying developments indicate the president's personal failure. Fourth, it has contributed to a presidential preoccupation with messaging behaviors that has resulted more in the "sound of leadership" than leadership (Hart, 1987). Fifth, presidential addresses to the nation function to crystallize public opinion, which is helpful if the president wants to crystallize majority opinion. But they can also galvanize the president's opposition, leading to a hardening of the rhetorical arteries and an undermining of negotiations. Sixth, presidents who use the resource of public persuasion deplete its usefulness; as the "Great Communicator" Ronald Reagan found himself addressing smaller and smaller television audiences. Seventh, the rhetorical presidency that works so well in time of real crisis has contributed to the proliferation of pseudo-crises such that the most mundane issue can become a "crisis" requiring a "war on" it.

That Bill Clinton loves to speak was evidenced by his interminable speech nominating Michael Dukakis in 1988. He is good on television, better in person, and best when interacting personally with questioners. He might have chosen to address the nation with regularity, but that would have risked crystallizing the 57 percent of the voters who had preferred Bush and Perot, even as he wasted the novelty of such addresses. Indeed, Clinton was elected on a domestic agenda, and domestic issues are considerably more divisive than are foreign policy issues (Wildavsky, 1966), such that televised domestic addresses carry greater risks than do televised foreign policy addresses. In short, President Clinton was a ready and persuasive speaker, but there were important constraints on his ability regularly to "go public."

Strategy #4: The Ideological Presidency

If presidents are engaged simultaneously in policy making and in media politics they must necessarily employ a set of symbols and arguments to justify their policies. Such ideologies are part rationale and part rationalization, but they nevertheless facilitate presidential coalition building (Florig, 1992). Perhaps ideological purists such as Pat Buchanan, Pat Robertson, Jesse Jackson, and Edward Kennedy have a valuable resource in this regard. But it seems more likely that their ideologies foster vocal minority communities at various points on the political spectrum. None of these ideological aspirants to the presidency has yet been able to mobilize a sufficiently large coalition to challenge seriously for nomination, much less election. Indeed, there is ample reason to believe that Ronald Reagan's success was due not only to his conservatism but to his personal charm and charisma. On the other hand, a president who backs into an ideology to justify his policies runs the risk of having his adversaries propose better means of fulfilling that ideology's promise.

Bill Clinton's quest for the presidency was apparently helped by his reluctance to woo liberal Democrats. Unlike Dukakis, who won nomination in 1988 by battling Jackson to the left of center, Clinton dared to tell Jackson's Rainbow Coalition that rap singer Sister Souljah's comment that blacks should take a week to kill white people instead of each other was morally indistinguishable from the views of white supremacist David Duke. Part of his message seemed to be that the war between assorted ideological purists had contributed to gridlock by undermining rational compromise. This did not equip Clinton with a familiar, clear-cut ideology from which to lead.

Instead, the president achieved rhetorical coherence during the campaign by linking his policy proposals together into a jeremiadic package. He continued to do this in his major addresses of the first hundred days. But each bill required separate legislative action. Thus, precisely because his proposals on taxing, spending, health care, national service, education, and the environment were interconnected he could not press for one without undermining the attention available for the others. Although he tried diligently in his public remarks to stress the interconnectedness of these proposals, each required a separate vote and, therefore, a separate coalition and, consequently, a separate blend of needs and reasons.

In short, none of the four major strategies of presidential leadership was appropriate for Bill Clinton's presidency. The Nixon analog is instructive. Nixon won election, in part, with creative ambiguity. His "secret plan to end the Vietnam War" invited hawks to expect escalation and doves to anticipate immediate withdrawal, and his theme of "law and order" was widely regarded as a veiled appeal to racist sentiments. As a consequence of his ambiguities Nixon was hamstrung as president, and his first six months were quiet indeed. Clinton, on the other hand, had enunciated a variety of specific policies and objectives and he had committed his administration to a productive hundred days. Hence an unproductive first six months would have been disastrous for President Clinton (Cohen, 1994). In this unusual historic predicament the Clinton White House developed a fifth approach to presidential leadership.

Strategy #5: The Centrist Presidency

Clinton's approach to presidential leadership borrowed selectively from each of the four available strategies. Each of the four major variables—bargaining, public approval, going public, and ideology—has been transformed by Clinton's

White House, and the four have been blended to produce his approach. This centrist approach is based on four strategic assumptions.

Assumption #1: Bargaining Is Crucial Even in the Absence of Discipline and Loyalty. President Clinton surely recognized that legislative action would depend on his ability to muster House and Senate majorities on a variety of bills and that he could not expect the same people to support every bill. From institutional pluralism he drew the objective of persuading individual legislators rather than aggregate public opinion. The appropriate audience for his persuasive efforts would consist not of citizens who *might* pressure their representatives to support his bills; the appropriate audience would be the legislators themselves. This meant that his own skillfulness at facilitating bargains would become an important resource.

But the strategy of institutional pluralism had faded because of the declining ability of party leaders to deliver rank and file votes. To deal with this complication, President Clinton resisted the obvious temptation to bludgeon his opponents and instead allowed them to come and go from his coalitions. Some observers construed this as weakness, and they criticized him for not being tough enough. But the strategy enabled Clinton to have the support of House leaders Richard Gephardt and David Bonior on most issues despite their staunch opposition to his North American Free Trade Agreement, which he saw ratified despite their opposition. Even more dramatically, Senator Sam Nunn, who had spearheaded opposition to Clinton's plan to allow gay military personnel to identify themselves as such, was named to the Carter-Powell-Nunn delegation that persuaded Haitian dictator Raoul Cedras to agree to abdication without an American invasion. Clinton's coalitions resembled the shopping mall food courts where shoppers pause, enjoy a snack, and then go about their business. By respecting the crosspressures impinging on each legislator and by not asking more of them than they could safely deliver, Clinton allowed them to save face and facilitated cooperation.

Assumption #2: Presidential Popularity Is a Lagging Indicator. The conventional wisdom in politics and journalism echoes Neustadt's observation that popular presidents are likely to get what they want and that unpopular presidents invite challenges on all fronts. This perspective values public approval as an indirect route to, and hence a leading indicator of, legislative success. But there is another perspective on approval that is worth considering.

The second view regards presidential approval scores as a lagging indicator of presidential success. From this perspective the president is best advised to line up votes in the legislature to accomplish things that will nurture his public approval. Of course, this renders ongoing public approval tracking polls considerably less important. To oversimplify for the sake of clarity, an inaugurated president need be concerned about his public approval on only one day in his eight years: reelection day. And even then, he needs only to be preferred by a plurality of voters in a combination of states able to produce 271 electoral votes. President Bush's 89 percent approval in April 1991 did not prevent twenty-five of the states he had won in 1988 from throwing their electoral votes to Clinton. Clinton, on the other hand, coasted to electoral victory in 1992 as the first choice of only 43 percent of the people who voted.

The Gallup organization's data on President Clinton's job performance through April 1994 suggest that, as a source of legislative leverage, his ratings have been modest (Moore, 1994a). But only three of their thirty-six surveys found job approval ratings as low as the percentage of voters who had elected him, and two of those three polls were within the margin for statistical error. In short, Clinton's job approval ratings have been unimpressive, but they do not yet portend defeat in 1996 for two reasons: They are aggregate national surveys rather than state-by-state polls that predict electoral votes, and Clinton has yet to begin campaigning on the record of accomplishment that he has been working so hard to build.

On the other hand, President Clinton's disapproval ratings have been above 35 percent since March 14, 1993. This statistic has whetted the interest of journalists and those who might wish to challenge Clinton in 1996. But around whom will Clinton's opponents rally? Moore (1994b, 25) found seven persons to have higher approval ratings than Clinton in April 1994: Colin Powell (66%), Bob Dole (63%), James Baker (54%), Dick Cheney (49%), Dan Quayle (49%), Jack Kemp (44%), and Ross Perot (41%). But when asked whom they preferred as the 1996 Republican candidate, only Dole was preferred for the nomination by as much as 20 percent of the respondents. In fact, the preferences were so varied that Dole was among the top three candidates for only 27 percent of the respondents, followed by Powell (13%), Perot (12%), Quayle (12%), Kemp (11%), Cheney (11%), and Baker (5%) (Moore, 1994b, 25). Although it might be interesting to get them all together to see if they could create an electoral coalition, the point is that disapproval scores fail to illuminate either the reasons for that disapproval or the homogeneity of those reasons. Thus, some people who currently disapprove of Clinton are likely to find that they prefer him to the 1996 alternative, unless so many of them run in the general election that they fragment the vote to the extent that electoral votes can be won with very small pluralities indeed, pluralities that currently appear to be more within the reach of Clinton than any of his challengers. In short, as unimpressive as Clinton's approval/disapproval ratings continue to be, two of three scenarios favor his reelection.

Clinton's 1992 primary campaign provides an interesting template for viewing his presidential popularity. During the multicandidate primaries Clinton focused on winning a majority of the convention delegates by campaigning state by state. As his delegate total grew his national popularity languished, such that he clinched the nomination with less than 25 percent national approval. Once guaranteed the nomination, he went on the Arsenio Hall television show to chat and play the saxophone, and his national popularity began to increase. The Clinton strategy seems to entail the mobilization of the people needed to accomplish specific tasks at specific times. After persuading contributors and organizers, he tried to persuade those voters about to select convention delegates, then the campaign staff worked to persuade a plurality of the voters in closely contested states sufficient to push his safe electoral votes past the 271 total needed for election; as president he persuaded people to serve in his administration and then persuaded a majority of legislators to support the measures before them. The pattern suggests that the Clinton people will not worry too much about his aggregate public approval ratings until 1996, concentrating more on the task of fulfilling his agenda.

Assumption #3: Go Public Only to Win Opinion Leaders and to Undercut Opposition. Clinton used the strategy of "going public," but he used it more strategically than had some of his predecessors. For example, one pitfall of going public is that the president can win public support while alienating legislators. Clinton dealt with this danger by discussing divisive domestic issues from the Oval Office only once, and that was basically an advertisement for the major economic address he would soon deliver to a joint session of Congress. Otherwise, Clinton talked to the nation about domestic issues from the well of the House of Representatives. He expanded upon his predecessors' use of the State of the Union address to speak directly to the legislators whose votes he needed, and he invited the public to witness and to learn.

President Clinton did use Oval Office addresses on matters of foreign policy—Somalia, Iraq, and Haiti. Interestingly, only his second Haiti address was the kind of crisis address that could be expected to boost his public approval. Indeed, Clinton seems to have reserved his Oval Office addresses for the delivery of unwelcome news: There would be no middle-class tax cut and there could well be a tax increase, troops would not be withdrawn from Somalia for several more months, two American helicopters had been shot down by our own plane, and the United States would invade Haiti against the wishes of Congress and some 70 percent of the American people unless General Cedras immediately abdicated. It is difficult to reconcile this approach with Clinton's "Slick Willie" image—one need not be terribly shrewd to figure out the benefits of personally delivering the good news while delegating the delivery of bad news (the Reagan-Stockman model). Why, then, would Clinton evidence such a drastically different pattern?

Clinton was following not the Reagan-Stockman model but the Gerald Ford model. Ford decided that the 1974 convention of the Veterans of Foreign Wars was the ideal audience before which to announce his intent to institute a program of earned pardons for Vietnam-era draft evaders and deserters. Although Ford's choice was rhetorically courageous it was, arguably, politically naive. But Ford demonstrated his good will toward the most hostile public, and he helped them to understand the arguments that had persuaded him toward the policy. The controversial pardon program caused Ford far less political trouble than did the Nixon pardon (Smith and Smith, 1994). In his four Oval Office addresses President Clinton's consistent message amounted to, "You're not going to like this development and neither do I, so let me explain to you why it constitutes the best available alternative at this point.'' These addresses did less to mobilize support than to minimize opposition and to induce quiescence, but quiescent opponents do not pressure legislators to filibuster or to delay.

A second problem endemic in the strategy of going public is that presidents such as Wilson relied too heavily on passionate populist arguments in the hope of creating a public furor, a reliance that complicated the processes of persuading the policy elites to acquiesce or to fine-tune the language of the legislation. President Clinton has instead gone public by addressing audiences functionally related to the legislative proposal rather than addressing the undifferentiated public. This seems an appropriate strategy when the country is increasingly pluralistic and fragmented and when party coalitions are decreasingly able to deliver the support of policy elites.

The complete SUNSITE Internet archive of White House papers (from January 20, 1973, through August 31, 1994) was searched for President Clinton's messages about six controversial issues of the period: taxes, NAFTA, general economics, crime, National Service, and gay issues. Press briefings by Clinton's aides were deleted, as were instances of corrected or duplicate transcripts. The resulting lists provide an empirical profile of President Clinton's speech acts related to these public issues. As Rod Hart observed about the process of analyzing presidential speech acts, ''By choosing to utter words to another, a speaker makes at least these decisions—to speak to A and not to B; to speak now and not then or never; to speak here and not there; to speak about this matter and not about all other matters; to speak for this period of time, not longer or shorter. These rhetorical decisions by a speaker contain 'information' for us as observers if we are wise enough and patient enough to track these decisions'' (1987, xxi; Smith, 1983).

These data tell us several things about President Clinton's speech acts. He spoke about these six issues fifty-three times on his own initiative and twenty-six times in response to reporters' questions. His eighteen discussions of crime accounted for roughly a third of his speeches on these six issues, and he spoke about it with four sets of mayors and three audiences of law enforcement personnel. His discussions of the economy included a nationally televised address to a joint session of Congress, remarks to six business-related audiences, three education-oriented audiences, a NAFTA rally in Kentucky, and a speech in Boston. His ten discussions of NAFTA included four NAFTA rallies, four national press availabilities, and speeches to the United Nations and the Hispanic Caucus.

President Clinton chose to talk with reporters about these six issues a total of twenty-six times, accounting for about one-third of his discussions of them. Roughly 40 percent of those discussions were with regional or local reporters, and they asked him about gays in the military and taxes, rather than the economy, crime, NAFTA, or National Service. The White House press corps, on the other hand, was the audience for four times as many discussions of crime, gays in the military, and NAFTA as for discussions of the economy, taxes, and National Service. The subject of gays arose in about two-thirds of the press encounters and all eleven of the regional press availabilities, although topics and occasions associated with gay people accounted for only about 3 percent of his addresses and remarks—the speech acts initiated and defined by the president himself.

The foregoing observations suggest that Bill Clinton has been going public even though he has rarely addressed us from the Oval Office. Second, he used Oval Office addresses primarily to deliver personally news that would be unpopular, thus taking responsibility for the unpopular and explaining the reasons that had persuaded him. Third, his national addresses about controversial domestic issues were delivered in the Congress, to the Congress, and for the Congress, with the television audience available for enlightenment, for identification with him, and for a solemn witnessing of his congressional leadership. Fourth, nearly 90 percent of his addresses and remarks were to subnational audiences, most of them publics directly and functionally related to the policy in question: mayors and law enforcement personnel on crime, business leaders and educators on the economy, and rallies in support of NAFTA. This set of choices is consistent both with President Truman's successful mobilization of existing organizations to fight famine and with the bargainers need to win the cooperation and acquiescence of policy elites no longer loyal to a political party.

Assumption #4: Help Others to Learn to Think as the President Thinks. Should a president retain or abandon the ideological framework that explained his candidacy to the nation? Although the quick answer would be to retain it, we must recognize that the incongruent electoral and governing coalitions may invite some degree of modification. For example, many presidents have run populist anti-Congress campaigns only to find that those themes do not play well in Congress. Then there are the harsh realities of governance: After campaigning for a middle-class tax cut Clinton found (1) that Perot had established the importance of trimming the deficit and (2) that the deficit would be considerably larger than had been previously projected such that responsible leadership required him to reestablish his priorities.

President Clinton's first rhetorical extravaganza would be his inaugural address. The inaugural genre presents presidential speechwriters with five tasks: reconstituting "the people," rehearsing traditional values, enunciating political principles, enacting the presidency, and fulfilling the expectations of epideictic discourse (Campbell and Jamieson, 1990). Much like Franklin Roosevelt, Lyndon Johnson, and Ronald Reagan before him, Clinton used jeremiadic logic to accomplish those inaugural tasks (Ritter, 1993; Smith and Smith, 1994).

Clinton's campaign jeremiad had warned his congregation about the dangers of following leaders who had drifted rather than led. It had encouraged Americans to find their future in their past by accepting personal responsibility, by working together for their common good, and by embracing change to "make tomorrow better than today." These themes dominated his inaugural address. "We know we have to face hard truths and take strong steps, but we have not done so; instead we have drifted," he said. "And that drifting has eroded our resources, fractured our economy, and shaken our confidence." Jeremiads find the path to the future in the past, and Clinton reminded his audience of the Revolution, the Civil War, the Great Depression, and the civil rights movement. As in each of those eras, "the urgent question of our time is whether we can make change our friend and not our enemy." Because jeremiads find coherence in apparent contradiction, this one turned to the Founders to warrant change: "Thomas Jefferson believed that to preserve the very foundations of our Nation, we would need dramatic change from time to time. Well, my fellow Americans, this is our time. Let us embrace it" (Clinton, 1993a, 75). The jeremiadic logic enabled the president to rehearse traditional values and to enunciate the principles that would guide his administration: change, sacrifice for the common good, and a skeptical view of power and privilege.

As he had during the campaign, the president emphasized on several occasions the importance of understanding and supporting his policies as a holistic package. He told Congress, for example, "The economic plan can't please everybody. If the package is picked apart, there will be something that will anger each of us, won't please anybody. But if it is taken as a whole, it will help all of us" (1993b, 223). He told the middle class that he would be able neither to cut nor to retain their income tax rates, but assured them that by raising modestly their taxes, "Our comprehensive plan for economic growth will create millions of long-term, good-paying jobs. . . . Our national service plan will throw open the doors of college opportunity to the daughters and sons of the middle class" (1993b, 208). And he explained to Atlanta business people, "There are millions and millions of Americans who, in the first 6 months of this year, will save more money in interest payments than they'll pay in the energy tax I propose for the full 4 years of this administration. That is what happens if you gain control of your economic destiny" (1993c, 461).

But as Clinton pressed each proposal in its time his adversaries sought, predictably, to defeat it by breaking the package into parts and then mobilizing potential opponents against each part. They were aided by the legislative realities that have frustrated all rhetorical presidents, as well as by the bitter nature of many of Clinton's prescriptions and by the growing perception that Clinton himself was an old-style tax and spend liberal marketing snake oil cures. How did this happen?

The speech texts from Clinton's first hundred days were not the problem. Many of them, such as his February 26 American University address on the "Global Economy" and his March 1 Rutgers University "Remarks on National Service" were well conceived and argued, expressing many of the themes that had framed the campaign and his inaugural address. Nor can we fault his efforts to communicate directly with voters in his town meetings, a format that enabled Clinton to hear from "real people" and to dramatize his interest in them (Cohen, 1994).

But President Clinton addressed the nation so rarely that his jeremiadic ideology faded from public memory. Word of his subnational addresses reached the public only through the news media and talk shows. And because the news media and talk shows thrive on controversy Clinton and his policies quickly became the subjects of other people's conversations. The more Clinton made his persuasive case to functionally important audiences the more he was pummeled by Rush Limbaugh, "Crossfire," and "The Capitol Gang." Whereas President Reagan had narrated political life for Americans, President Clinton, like President Bush, had become a character in other people's narratives. This was especially unfortunate for Clinton because he is sufficiently charismatic to handle the role of narrator.

Being a character in other people's stories was especially problematic for Clinton because he had dedicated his presidency to reorienting the American people—a task that no president can perform when his adversaries tell his story. As the drama built toward the May 27, 1993, House vote on Clinton's budget that would "make or break" his presidency it was his adversaries who made the news. When it passed by a scant margin of 219–213, CNN's reporters told the story over Clinton's mute gestures. Clinton therefore inherited Bush's problem: How can the president lead when his adversaries dominate the national dialogue?

The key to support for Clinton's policy agenda is an understanding of its dynamic interconnections. For example, a healthy economy was to be achieved by increasing exports, getting people off of welfare and training them for life as productive taxpayers, and by providing consumers with more disposable income. Cutting spending alone, he argued, would not produce a healthy economy because the deficit would continue to grow and push interest rates higher, which would cut still further into consumers' disposable income and increase the cost of the goods to be exported. Instead, he advocated a shift from "spending" to "investing"—in education, training, and improved public health—to create a better work force that would be a good return on the outgoing federal dollars. Thus, deficit reduction would require an increase in some taxes, but the net effect would be to reduce interest rates, thereby leaving consumers with more disposable income with which to buy goods and services from the newly educated and trained workers. Health care was intended not only as a public benefit but as a way to bring the deficit under control and as a crucial step toward welfare reform (since many recipients are reportedly reluctant to take jobs that provide less health care coverage than does welfare). But how many people outside of the Clinton brain trust naturally think along these lines?

It is at precisely this juncture that President Clinton's innovative approach to presidential leadership has run aground. He can facilitate the formation of variegated legislative coalitions by talking to functionally important subnational audiences and by risking soft public approval ratings for a time, *but he cannot do so and win widespread acceptance of his ideology.* This is especially problematic for him because it has kept him from changing the way Americans think about the problems and solutions we face.

The immediate rhetorical problem facing President Clinton was the need to pass specific bills. But for those changes to be perceived as good changes, for his innovations not to be reversed, for sustaining or strengthening the Democratic majorities in Congress, and for facilitating the emergence of a presidential reelection coalition in 1996, Bill Clinton needed to teach Americans how to think as he thinks, much as Ronald Reagan taught Americans to think in the logics of supply-side economics and demonic foreign adversaries. This requires him to explain to the public the arguments that have convinced him, and to do so in forums that permit the president himself, not reporters or critics, to occupy center stage. It is precisely this that candidate Clinton did so well, and it is precisely this that President Clinton has failed to do. Moreover, he is unlikely to teach the nation to think as he thinks if he continues to address universities, chambers of commerce, regional and national press conferences, law enforcement officers, and national radio audiences. On the other hand, a dramatic increase in his frequency of Oval Office addresses might well jeopardize his delicate legislative apparatus.

CONCLUSIONS

This chapter began by posing three questions about the emerging Clinton presidency to which we can now return. The first question asked why this relatively unpopular president has been so much more effective than his recent predecessors in securing the legislative enactment of his agenda. The answer is to be found in the combination of three practices: (1) addressing audiences directly relevant to the legislation at hand (especially to assuage their opposition), (2) allowing legislators to join him or oppose him on specific bills as their crosspressures dictate, and (3) treating public approval ratings as a lagging indicator of his success rather than as a leading indicator.

The second question asked why this legislatively successful president— elected to end gridlock and bring about change—has languished in the public approval polls. The answer lies in the combination of three tendencies: (1) addressing the nation only when he has bad news to deliver, (2) generating too much discourse that invites critical responses, journalistic narration, and national disinterest, and (3) using complicated but potent jeremiadic policy logic without teaching it to his followers.

The jeremiadic logic of Clinton's campaign was an important factor in his victory, but he toned it down in favor of focus by the end of his first hundred days, and he has yet to return enthusiastically to his own ''New Covenant'' rhetoric. By avoiding opportunities to articulate the overarching logic of the Clinton presidency, the White House underestimated the process of presidential leadership in favor of policy results, which have been greeted with relatively little fanfare.

Because Clinton never abandoned his jeremiadic themes they are still available to him, but with each passing day their use becomes more problematic. If the crux of the nation's problem was false leadership, who has been the leader since 1993? If the chosen people return to their first principles and the tribulations disappear, what does the leader do for an encore? And if jeremiadic logic finds hope in recession, what does it find in prosperity? What then can President Clinton do?

It seems advisable for the president to continue to address the issues that are functionally related to the items on his legislative agenda while cutting back severely on the amount of verbiage expended on undefined audiences. The president's practice of delivering weekly radio addresses, in particular, should be discontinued. These addresses sap the president's rhetorical resources to persuade no apparent functional audience, even as they invite responses from his adversaries and invite reporters to repackage his message. This does not seem to be a productive package. By discontinuing these routine addresses the president, his speechwriters, journalists, and citizens alike could focus their discursive energies and trim the fat from the corpus of presidential discourse.

Second, President Clinton should consider more *televised* "fireside chats" with the nation. These should be neither the cardigan-and-crackling-fire speeches President Carter tried nor crisis speeches that increase ego-involvement and undermine compromise. Instead, they should be speeches in the spirit of Franklin Roosevelt's explanation of the banking system that used the Reagan style of "telling America's story" (Lewis, 1987) to foster identification with Clinton's leadership, to establish his narrative authority, and to teach Americans his way of thinking. The objective should not be to advocate specific policies but to frame the issues.

President Clinton used this strategy to advantage in his September 22, 1993, health care address to the joint session of Congress. The address emphasized not his plan but the criteria that a good health care bill should meet: security, simplicity, savings, choice, quality, and responsibility. He operationalized his goal of security as a system in which "those who do not have health coverage will have it and, for those who have coverage, it will never be taken away." By "simplicity" he meant that "our health care system must be simpler for the patients and simpler for those who actually deliver health care: our physicians, our nurses, and our other medical professionals." The goal of savings meant that "reform must produce savings in our health care system." The goal of providing "choice" was twofold, as patients "should be able to choose their own health care plans and their own doctor" and "doctors should have a choice as to what plans they practice in." The quality of health care was to be improved by reform, because, "If we reformed everything else in health care but failed to preserve and enhance the high quality of our medical care, we would have taken a step backward, not forward." And finally, the goal of responsibility meant that any health care reform would "need to restore a sense that we are all in this together, and we all have a responsibility to be a part of the solution" (Clinton, 1993d).

The address was successful in framing the parameters of the health care debate, and there has been little public debate of Clinton's objectives in the year since his speech. Instead, discussion has focused, as the president said he hoped it would, on the ability of the various plans to fulfill all six of these objectives. Does "universal coverage" mean every man, woman, and child, or can there be a margin for error comparable to the operationalization of "full employment" as 3 percent unemployment? Do the plans simplify the health care system adequately for patients, physicians, professionals, and insurers? Do the reform plans save money in absolute or relative terms, and whose figures should be used? Can patients and doctors avail themselves of all possible choices, including abortion, and if not, why not? How is quality to be measured, and who will measure it? How does everyone pay a fair share of health care, and who shall determine that fairness?

At this writing the president's health care bill is, by most accounts, comatose. But it is comatose because he and his allies have been unable to persuade the appropriate audiences that it satisfies the standards he established for it. On the other hand, the standards that he articulated in September 1993 continue to shape the health care debate. Indeed, it may be that Clinton articulated his objectives so well that his opponents have been able to prolong debate by using them long enough to allow two of the president's principal reasons for health care reform— deficit reduction and welfare reform—to be largely forgotten. Nevertheless, Clinton's health care speech illustrates the potential for a president to use televised addresses to frame contentious issues in ways capable of facilitating the formation of legislative coalitions.

The larger theoretical question posed at the outset asked what is happening in the early 1990s and what are the implications for our theories of presidential persuasion. The answer seems to be that Bill Clinton is charting a new course by developing a new approach to presidential leadership that combines old techniques in new ways. It is a rhetorical approach epitomized by a phrase in his health care address: "rough stretches and honest disagreements." If he can make the approach work, Bill Clinton will have dealt a historic blow to legislative gridlock, to the dangers of the plebiscitary presidency, and to the temptation toward presidential demagoguery. But if his approach fails, his successor will have an even more problematic puzzle to solve. The most plausible scenario at this writing is that President Clinton will continue to piece together centrist legislative coalitions in support of policies and objectives that are not well understood by the public. This will continue to leave Clinton at the mercy of those who can characterize his motives and accomplishments to their own advantage as they work toward the day when they can reverse his accomplishments, a reversal made easier by his inability to teach Americans his logic for reasoning about problems and their solutions.

REFERENCES

Arterton, F. Christopher. 1993. "Campaign '92: Strategies and Tactics of the Candidates." In *The Election of 1992,* ed. Gerald M. Pomper (pp. 74–109). Chatham, N.J.: Chatham House.

Bercovitch, S. 1978. *The American Jeremiad.* Madison: University of Wisconsin Press.

Billig, Michael. 1991. *Ideology and Opinions: Studies in Rhetorical Psychology.* Newbury Park, Calif.: Sage.

Campbell, Karlyn K. and Kathleen H. Jamieson. 1990. *Deeds Done in Words: Presidential Rhetoric and the Genres of Governance.* Chicago: University of Chicago Press.

Clinton, William J. 1991. "Announcement of Candidacy for President." October 3. Internet: SUNSITE.

————. 1992. "Campaign Appearance at the University of Notre Dame." September 11. Internet: SUNSITE.

————. 1993a. "Inaugural Address." *Weekly Compilation of Presidential Documents* 29, January 20, 75–77.

————. 1993b. "Address before a Joint Session of Congress on Administration Goals." *Weekly Compilation of Presidential Documents* 29, February 17, 215–24.

————. 1993c. "Remarks to the Business Community in Atlanta." *Weekly Compilation of Presidential Documents* 29, March 19, 458–63.

————. 1993d. "Health Security for All Americans." September 22. Internet: SUNSITE.

Cohen, Richard E. 1994. *Changing Course in Washington: Clinton and the New Congress.* New York: Macmillan.

Dahl, Robert A. and C. E. Lindblom. 1953. *Politics, Economics and Welfare.* New York: Harper & Row.

Edwards, George C., III. 1983. *The Public Presidency: The Pursuit of Popular Support.* New York: St. Martin's.

Florig, Dennis. 1992. *The Power of Presidential Ideologies.* Westport, Conn.: Praeger.

Greer, F. 1993. "Communication in the 1992 Presidential Campaign." International Communication Association, Washington, D.C.

Harre, Rom and Grant Gillett. 1994. *The Discursive Mind.* Thousand Oaks, Calif.: Sage.

Hart, Roderick P. 1984. *Verbal Style and the Presidency: A Computer-Based Analysis.* New York: Academic Press.

————. 1987. *The Sound of Leadership: Presidential Communication in the Modern Age.* Chicago: University of Chicago Press.

Holloway, Rachel L. 1994. "A Time for Change in American Politics: The Issue of the 1992 Presidential Election." In *The 1992 Presidential Campaign: A Communication Perspective,* ed. Robert E. Denton, Jr. (pp. 129–68). Westport, Conn.: Praeger.

Kernell, Samuel. 1993. *Going Public: New Strategies of Presidential Leadership,* 2d ed. Washington, D.C.: Congressional Quarterly Press.

Lewis, William F. 1987. "Telling American's Story: Narrative Form and the Reagan Presidency." *Quarterly Journal of Speech* 73, 280–302.

Lowi, Theodore J. 1985. *The Personal President: Power Invested, Promise Unfulfilled.* Ithaca, N.Y.: Cornell University Press.

Moore, D. W. 1994a. "Clinton's Ratings Hold Steady." *The Gallup Poll Monthly* 343 (April), 12–13, 22.

————. 1994b. "Dole Leads, GOP Hopefuls." *The Gallup Poll Monthly* 343 (April), 24–25.

Neustadt, Richard E. 1960. *Presidential Power: The Politics of Leadership.* New York: Mentor.

Page, C. 1994. "Clinton Can Still Recover." *Greensboro News & Record.* September 4, F4.

Popkin, Samuel L. 1991. *The Reasoning Voter: Communication and Persuasion in Presidential Campaigns.* Chicago: University of Chicago Press.

Ritter, Kurt. 1993. "President Lyndon B. Johnson's Inaugural Address, 1965." In *The Inaugural Addresses of Twentieth-Century American Presidents,* ed. Halford Ryan (pp. 195–208). Westport, Conn.: Praeger.

Seligman, Lester G. and Cary R. Covington. 1989. *The Coalitional Presidency.* Chicago: Dorsey Press.

Smith, Craig A. 1983. "The Audience of the Rhetorical Presidency: An Analysis of President-Constituent Interactions, 1963–81." *Presidential Studies Quarterly* (Fall): 613–22.

———. 1994. "The Jeremiadic Logic of Clinton's Policy Speeches." In *Clinton on Stump, State, and Stage: The Rhetorical Road to the White House,* ed. Stephen A. Smith. Fayetteville: University of Arkansas Press.

——— and Kathy B. Smith. 1994. *The White House Speaks: Presidential Leadership as Persuasion.* Westport, Conn.: Praeger.

Tulis, Jeffrey K. 1987. *The Rhetorical Presidency.* Princeton: Princeton University Press.

Wildavsky, Aaron. 1966. "The Two Presidencies." *Trans-Action* 4 (December).

Selected Bibliography

Abramson, Jeffrey B., F. Christopher Arterton, and Gary G. Orren. 1988. *The Electronic Commonwealth: The Impact of New Media Technologies on Democratic Politics.* New York: Basic Books.

Altheide, David. 1985. *Media Power.* Beverly Hills: Sage.

——— and Robert P. Snow. 1979. *Media Logic.* Beverly Hills: Sage.

Ansolabehere, Stephen, Roy Behr, and Shanto Iyengar. 1993. *The Media Game: American Politics in the Television Age.* New York: Macmillan.

Anthony, Carl S. 1991. *First Ladies: The Saga of the Presidents' Wives and Their Power, 1961–1990,* Vol. 2. New York: William Morrow.

Barkin, Steve M. 1984. "The Journalist as Storyteller: An Interdisciplinary Perspective." *American Journalism* 1: 27–33.

Bedient, David O. and David M. Moore. 1985. "Student Interpretations of Political Cartoons." *Journal of Visual/Verbal Learning* 5: 29–35.

Bellah, Robert N. 1985. *Habits of the Heart: Individualism and Commitment in American Life.* Berkeley: University of California Press.

Bennett, W. Lance. 1975. *The Political Mind and the Political Environment.* Lexington, Mass.: Heath Publishing.

———. 1985. "Communication and Social Responsibility." *Quarterly Journal of Speech* 71: 259–88.

———, Patricia Dempsey Harris, Janet K. Laskey, Alan H. Levitch, and Sarah E. Monrad. 1976. "Deep and Surface Images in the Construction of Political Issues: The Case of Amnesty." *Quarterly Journal of Speech* 62: 109–26.

Berkovitch, Sacvan. 1978. *The American Jeremiad.* Madison: University of Wisconsin Press.

Berry, Joseph P., Jr. 1987. *John F. Kennedy and the Media: The First Television President.* Lanham, Md.: University Press of America Inc.

Bertelsen, Daniel A. 1992. "Media Forms and Government: Democracy as an Archetypal Image in the Electronic Age." *Communication Quarterly* 40: 325–37.

Billig, Michael. 1991. *Ideology and Opinions: Studies in Rhetorical Psychology.* Newbury Park, Calif.: Sage.

Bormann, Ernest G. 1982. "A Fantasy Theme Analysis of the Television Coverage of the Hostage Release and the Reagan Inaugural." *Quarterly Journal of Speech* 68: 133–45.

———. 1985. *The Force of Fantasy: Restoring the American Dream.* Carbondale: Southern Illinois University Press.

Bostdorff, Denise M. 1992. "Idealism Held Hostage: Jimmy Carter's Rhetoric on the Crisis in Iran." *Communication Studies* 43: 14–28.

———. 1994. *The Presidency and the Rhetoric of Foreign Crisis.* Columbia: University of South Carolina Press.

Brooks, Charles, ed. 1994. *Best Editorial Cartoons of the Year.* Gretna, La.: Pelican Publishing Company.

Brummett, Barry. 1979. "A Pentadic Analysis of Ideologies in Two Gay Rights Controversies." *Central States Speech Journal* 30: 250–61.

Burke, Kenneth. 1969. *A Rhetoric of Motives.* Berkeley: University of California Press.

———. 1989. *On Symbols and Society,* ed. Joseph R. Gusfield. Chicago: University of Chicago Press.

———. *The Philosophy of Literary Form: Studies in Symbolic Action,* 3d ed. Berkeley: University of California Press.

Burleson, Brant R. 1987. "Cognitive Complexity and Person-Centered Communication: A Review of Methods, Findings, and Explanations." In *Personality and Interpersonal Communication,* ed. James C. McCroskey and John A. Daly. Newbury Park, Calif.: Sage.

Campbell, Karlyn K. and Kathleen H. Jamieson. 1990. *Deeds Done in Words: Presidential Rhetoric and the Genres of Governance.* Chicago: University of Chicago Press.

Cappella, Joseph N. 1985. "Controlling the Floor in Conversation." In *Multichannel Integrations of Nonverbal Behavior,* ed. Aron W. Siegman and Stanley Felstein. Hillsdale, N.J.: Lawrence Erlbaum.

Carl, Leroy M. 1968. "Editorial Cartoons Fail to Reach Many Readers." *Journalism Quarterly* 45: 533–35.

Caroli, Betty B. 1987. *First Ladies.* Oxford: Oxford University Press.

Cathcart, Robert and Gary Gumpert. 1983. "Mediated Interpersonal Communication: Toward a New Typology." *Quarterly Journal of Speech* 69: 267–77.

Chilton, Paul and Mikhail Ilyin. 1993. "Metaphor in Political Discourse: The Case of the 'Common European House.' " *Discourse and Society* 4: 7–31.

Cohen, Richard E. 1994. *Changing Course in Washington: Clinton and the New Congress.* New York: Macmillan.

Conn, Earl. 1993. "The Press and the Omnipresent President." *Editor & Publisher,* August 14, 18 and 33.

Crable, Richard E. and Steven L. Vibbert. 1983. "Argumentative Stance and Political Faith Healing: 'The Dream Will Come True.' " *Quarterly Journal of Speech* 69: 290–301.

———. "Mobil's Epideictic Advocacy: 'Observations' of Prometheus-Bound." *Communication Monographs* 50: 380–94.

Daly, John A., Anita Vangelisti, and Suzanne M. Daughton. 1987. "The Nature and

Correlates of Conversational Sensitivity.'' *Human Communication Research* 14: 167–202.

Denton, Robert E., Jr. 1988. *The Primetime Presidency of Ronald Reagan.* New York: Praeger.

———, ed. 1994. *The 1992 Presidential Campaign: A Communication Perspective.* Westport, Conn.: Praeger.

——— and Dan F. Hahn. 1986. *Presidential Communication: Description and Analysis.* New York: Praeger.

——— and Gary C. Woodward. 1990. *Political Communication in America,* 2d ed. New York: Praeger.

DeSousa, Michael A. and Martin J. Medhurst. 1982. ''The Editorial Cartoon as Visual Rhetoric: Rethinking Boss Tweed.'' *Journal of Visual Verbal Languaging* 2: 2.

DeVito, Joseph. 1988. *Human Communication: The Basic Course.* 4th ed. New York: Harper and Row.

Dionisopoulos, George. 1986. ''Corporate Advocacy Advertising as Poltical Communication.'' In *New Perspectives on Political Advertising,* ed. Lynda L. Kaid, Dan Nimmo, and K. R. Sanders. Carbondale: Southern Illinois University Press.

Dovidio, John R. Steven L. Ellyson, Caroline F. Keting, Karen Heltman, and Clifford E. Brown. 1988. ''The Relationship of Social Power to Visual Displays of Dominance between Men and Women.'' *Journal of Personality and Social Psychology* 54: 232–42.

Drew, Elizabeth. 1994. *On the Edge: The Clinton Presidency.* New York: Simon & Schuster.

Duck, Steve. 1991. *Friends, for Life: The Psychology of Personal Relationships,* 2d ed. London: Harvester Wheatsheaf.

Eagly, Alice H., Wendy Wood, and Shelly Chaiken. 1978. ''Causal Inferences about Communications and Their Effect on Opinion Change.'' *Journal of Personality and Social Psychology* 36: 424–35.

Edelman, Murray. 1977. *Political Language: Words that Succeed and Policies that Fail.* New York: Academic Press.

Edwards, George C. III. 1983. *The Public Presidency: The Pursuit of Popular Support.* New York: St. Martin's.

Entman, Robert M. 1989. *Democracy Without Citizens.* New York: Oxford University Press.

Ferrarotti, Frank. 1988. *The End of Conversation.* Westport, Conn.: Greenwood Press.

Flanigan, William H. and Nancy H. Zingale. 1991. *Political Behavior of the American Electorate.* Washington D.C.: Congressional Quarterly Press.

Florig, Dennis. 1992. *The Power of Presidential Ideologies.* Westport, Conn.: Praeger.

Frederick, Howard H. 1993. *Global Communication and International Relations.* Belmont, Calif.: Wadsworth.

Frentz, Thomas and Thomas Farrell. 1976. ''Language-Action: A Paradigm for Communication.'' *Quarterly Journal of Speech* 62: 333–49.

Gamson, William A. and David Stuart. 1992. ''Media Discourse as a Symbolic Contest: The Bomb in Political Cartoons.'' *Sociological Forum* 7: 55–86.

Garland, Nicholas. 1988. ''Political Cartooning.'' In *Laughing Matters: A Serious Look at Humour,* ed. John Durant and Jonathan Miller. New York: John Wiley & Sons, Inc.

Garramone, Gina M. 1985. "Effects of Negative Political Advertising: The Role of Sponsor and Rebuttal." *Journal of Broadcasting and Electronic Media* 29: 147–59.

———, Allen C. Harris, and Gary Pizante. 1986. "Predictors of Motivation to Use Computer-Mediated Political Communication Systems." *Journal of Broadcasting and Electronic Media* 30: 445–57.

Germond, Jack and Jules Witcover. 1993. *Mad as Hell.* New York: Warner Books.

Gitlin, Todd. 1980. *The Whole World Is Watching.* Berkeley, Calif.: University of California Press.

Goffman, Erving. 1973. *The Presentation of Self in Everyday Life.* New York: The Overlook Press.

Gonzales, Hernando. 1989. "Interactivity and Feedback in Third World Development Campaigns." *Critical Studies in Mass Communication* 6: 295–314.

Gorrell, Bob. 1981. "A Responsibility to Fairness." *Target: The Political Cartoon Quarterly* 1: 12–13.

Graber, Doris. 1988. *Processing the News: How People Tame the Information Tide.* New York: Longman.

———. 1993. "Making Campaign News User Friendly." *American Behavioral Scientist* 37: 328–36.

Grimes, Ann. 1990. *Running Mates: The Making of a First Lady.* New York: William Morrow.

Gurevitch, Michael and Mark R. Levy, eds. 1985. *Mass Communication Review Yearbook 5.* Beverly Hills: Sage Publications.

Gwyn, Robert J. 1970. "Opinion Advertising and the Free Market of Ideas." *Public Opinion Quarterly* 34: 246–55.

Hainsworth, Brad E. 1990. "The Distribution of Advantages and Disadvantages." *Public Relations Review,* 33–39.

Hart, Roderick P. 1984. "The Functions of Human Communication in the Maintenance of Public Values." In *Handbook of Rhetorical and Communication Theory,* ed. Carroll C. Arnold and John Waite Bowers. Boston: Allyn and Bacon.

———. 1984. *Verbal Style and the Presidency: A Computer-Based Analysis.* New York: Academic Press.

———. 1987. *The Sound of Leadership: Presidential Communication in the Modern Age.* Chicago: The University of Chicago Press.

———. 1994. *Seducing America.* New York: Oxford University Press.

Hawkins, Robert P., John M. Wiemann, and Suzanne Pingree. 1988. *Advancing Communication Science: Merging Mass and Interpersonal Processes.* Newbury Park, Calif.: Sage.

Heath, Robert L. 1988. "The Rhetoric of Issue Advertising: A Rationale, a Case Study, a Critical Perspective—and More." *Central States Speech Journal* 39: 99–109.

——— and Richard A. Nelson. 1983. "An Exchange on Corporate Advertising." *Journal of Communication* 30: 114–18.

Heim, Michael. 1993. *The Metaphysics of Virtual Reality.* New York: Oxford University Press.

Hellweg, Susan A., Michael Pfau, and Steven R. Brydon. 1992. *Televised Presidential Debates: Advocacy in Contemporary America.* New York: Praeger.

Henry, William A. III. 1985. *Visions of America: How We Saw the 1984 Election.* Boston: Atlantic Monthly Press.

Hewitt, Glenn A. 1991. *Regeneration and Morality: A Study of Charles Finney, Charles Hodge, John W. Nevin and Horace Bushnell.* Brooklyn, N.Y.: Carlson Publishing.

Holloway, Rachel L. 1994. "A Time for Change: The Issue in the 1992 Presidential Election." In *The 1992 Presidential Election: A Communication Perspective,* ed. Robert E. Denton, Jr. Westport, Conn.: Praeger.

Horton, Donald and Richard R. Wohl. 1956. "Mass Communication and Para-Social Interaction: Observation on Intimacy at a Distance." *Psychiatry* 19: 215–29.

Howard-Pitney, David. 1990. *The Afro-American Jeremiad: Appeals for Justice in America.* Philadelphia: Temple University Press.

Huizinga, John. 1950. *Homo Ludens.* Boston: Beacon Press.

Hunter, John Mark, David M. Moore, and Edward H. Sewell, Jr. 1992. "The Effects of Teaching Strategy and Cognitive Style on Student Interpretations of Editorial Cartoons." *Journal of Visual Literacy* 11(2): 35–55.

Jamieson, Kathleen H. 1988. *Eloquence in an Electronic Age.* New York: Oxford University Press.

Johnson-Cartee, Karen S. Copeland and Gary A. Copeland. 1991. *Negative Political Advertising: Coming of Age.* Hillsdale, N.J.: Lawrence Erlbaum.

Jones, Steven G., ed. 1994. *Cybersociety: Computer-Mediated Communication and Community.* Thousands Oaks, Calif.: Sage.

Kamber, Victor. 1993–94. "How to Win and Really Lose in Washington." *Public Relations Quarterly* 38: 5–7.

Katz, Elihu and Joseph J. Feldman. 1977. "The Debates in Light of Research: A Survey of Surveys." In *The Great Debates: Kennedy Vs. Nixon, 1960,* ed. Sidney Kraus. Bloomington: Indiana University Press.

——— and Paul Lazarsfeld. 1955. *Personal Influence.* Glencoe, Ill.: Free Press.

Kemmis, Daniel. 1990. *Community and Politics of Place.* Norman: University of Oklahoma Press.

Kerbel, Matthew. 1994. *Edited for Television.* Boulder, Colo.: Westview Press, 1994.

Kernell, Samuel. 1985. *Going Public: New Strategies of Presidential Leadership.* Washington, D.C.: Congressional Quarterly Press.

Langer, John. 1981. "Television's 'Personality System.' " *Media, Culture, and Society* 4: 351–65.

Lazarsfeld, Paul. 1948. *The People's Choice.* New York: Columbia University Press.

Lenart, Silvo. 1994. *Shaping Political Attitudes.* Thousand Oaks, Calif.: Sage, 1994.

Lowi, Theodore J. 1985. *The Personal President: Power Invested, Promise Unfulfilled.* Ithaca, N.Y.: Cornell University Press.

Mailer, Norman. 1966. *Cannibals and Christians.* New York: Dial Press.

Martel, Myles. 1983. *Political Campaign Debates: Images, Strategies, and Tactics.* New York: Longman.

McLuhan, Marshall and Quentin Fiore. 1967. *The Medium Is the Message.* New York: Bantam Books.

Meadow, Robert G. 1981. "The Political Dimensions of Nonproduct Advertising." *Journal of Communication* 31: 69–82.

Meyer, John and Diana Carlin. 1994. "The Impact of Formats on Voter Reaction." *The 1992 Presidential Debates in Focus,* ed. Diana Carlin and Mitchell McKinney. Westport, Conn.: Praeger.

Meyrowitz, Joshua. 1985. *No Sense of Place.* New York: Oxford University Press.

Morello, John T. 1988. "Argument and Visual Structuring in the 1984 Mondale-Reagan

Debates: The Medium's Influence on the Perception of Clash." *Western Journal of Speech Communication* 52: 277–90.

———. 1988. "Visual Structuring of the 1976 and 1984 National Televised Presidential Debates: Implication." *Central States Speech Journal* 39: 359–69.

———. 1992. "The 'Look' and Language of Clash: Visual Structuring of Argument in the 1988 Bush-Dukakis Debates." *Southern Communication Journal* 57: 205–18.

Myers, Dee Dee. 1993. "New Technology and the 1992 Clinton Presidential Campaign." *American Behavioral Scientist* 37: 181–84.

Neuman, W. Russell. 1986. *The Paradox of Mass Politics.* Cambridge, Mass.: Harvard University Press.

Neustadt, Richard E. 1960. *Presidential Power: The Politics of Leadership.* New York: Mentor.

Nimmo, Dan. 1994. "The Electronic Town Hall in Campaign '92: Interactive Forum or Carnival of Buncombe?" In *The 1992 Presidential Campaign: A Communication Perspective,* ed. Robert E. Denton, Jr. Westport, Conn.: Praeger.

——— and James E. Combs. 1983. *Mediated Political Realities.* New York: Longman.

Paletz, David L., Roberta E. Pearson, and Donald L. Willis. 1977. *Politics in Public Service Advertising on Television.* New York: Praeger.

Patterson, Miles L., Mary E. Churchill, Gary K. Burger, and Jack L. Powell. 1992. "Verbal and Nonverbal Modality Effects on Impressions of Political Candidates: Analysis from the 1984 Presidential Debates." *Communication Monographs* 59: 231–42.

Patterson, Thomas E. 1994. *Out of Order.* New York: Vintage Books.

Pavlik, John V. and Everette E. Dennis, eds. 1993. *Demystifying Media Technology.* Mountain View, Calif.: Mayfield.

Pearson, Paul. 1983. "Personality Characteristics of Cartoonists." *Personality and Individual Differences* 4: 227–28.

Peters, Mike. 1985. *The World of Cartooning with Mike Peters: How Caricatures Develop.* Dayton, Ohio: Landfall Press.

Pfau, Michael. 1990. "A Channel Approach to Television Influence." *Journal of Broadcasting and Electronic Media* 34: 195–214.

——— and Jong Kang. 1991. "The Impact of Relational Messages on Candidate Influence in Televised Political Debates." *Communication Studies* 42: 114–28.

——— and Henry C. Kenski. 1990. *Attack Politics: Strategy and Defense.* New York: Praeger.

Popkin, Samuel L. 1991. *The Reasoning Voter: Communication and Persuasion in Presidential Campaigns.* Chicago: University of Chicago Press.

Postman, Neil. 1985. *Amusing Ourselves to Death: Public Discourse in the Age of Show Business.* New York: Penguin.

Pratkanis, Anthony and Elliot Aronson. 1992. *Age of Propaganda.* New York: W.H. Freeman.

Procter, David E. 1992. "Bridging Social Change through Mythic Regeneration." *Communication Studies* 43: 171–81.

Reardon, Kathleen K. and Everett M. Rogers. 1988. "Interpersonal versus Mass Media Communication: A False Dichotomy." *Human Communication Research* 15: 284–303.

Rice, Ronald E. and William J. Paisley, eds. 1981. *Public Communication Campaigns.* Beverly Hills: Sage.

Ritter, Kurt. 1980. "American Political Rhetoric and the Jeremiad Tradition: Presidential Nomination Acceptance Speeches, 1960–1976." *Central States Speech Journal* 31, 153–71.

――――― and David Henry. 1992. *Ronald Reagan: The Great Communicator.* Westport, Conn.: Greenwood Press.

Robinson, John P. and Mark R. Levy. 1986. *The Main Source: Learning From Television News.* Beverly Hills: Sage.

Rogers, Everett M. 1986. *Communication Technology.* New York: Free Press.

Rosenberg, Shawn W. and Patrick McCafferty. 1987. "The Image and the Vote: Manipulating Voter's Preferences." *Public Opinion Quarterly* 51: 31–47.

Rosenman, Samuel I. and Dorothy Rosenman. 1976. *Presidential Style: Some Giants and a Pygmy in the White House.* New York: Harper & Row.

Ryan, Halford, ed. 1993. *The Inaugural Addresses of Twentieth-Century American Presidents.* Westport, Conn.: Praeger.

Salmon, Charles T., Leonard N. Reid, James Pokrywczynski, and Robert W. Willett. 1985. "The Effectiveness of Advocacy Advertising Relative to News Coverage." *Communication Research* 12: 546–67.

Schram, Martin. 1987. *The Great American Video Game: Presidential Politics in the Television Age.* New York: William Morrow and Co.

Schram, Sanford. 1991. "The Post-Modern Presidency and the Grammar of Electronic Engineering." *Critical Studies in Mass Communication* 8: 210–16.

Schwartz, Tony. 1973. *The Responsive Chord.* New York: Anchor Books.

Seligman, Lester G. and Cary R. Covington. 1989. *The Coalitional Presidency.* Chicago: Dorsey Press.

Sethi, Suresh P. 1976. *Advocacy Advertising and Large Corporations.* Lexington, Mass.: D.C. Heath.

Sewell, Edward H., Jr. 1986a. "Taking Aim—The Liminality of Political Cartoonists." In *Communication as Performance,* ed. Janet L. Palmer. Tempe: Arizona State University.

―――――. 1986b. "Rhetorical Analysis of Visual Discourse: A Defense of the Study of Cartoons as Speech Communication." In *Miteinander sprechen und handeln: Festschrift für Hellmut Geissner,* ed. Edith Slembek. Frankfurt am Main, Germany: Scriptor Verlag.

―――――. 1987. "Narrative Communication in Editorial Cartoons." In *On Narratives,* ed. Hellmut Geissner. Frankfurt am Main, Germany: Scriptor Verlag.

Shapiro, Ian. 1994. "Three ways to Be a Democrat." *Political Theory* 22: 124–51.

Smith, Craig A. 1983. "The Audience of the Rhetorical Presidency: An Analysis of President-Constituent Interactions, 1963–1981." *Presidential Studies Quarterly,* 613–22.

――――― and Kathy B. Smith. 1994. *The White House Speaks: Presidential Leadership as Persuasion.* Westport, Conn.: Praeger.

Smith, Stephen A., ed. 1994. *Bill Clinton on Stump, State, and Stage: The Rhetorical Road to the White House.* Fayetteville: University of Arkansas Press.

Stephenson, William. 1967. *The Play Theory of Mass Communication.* Chicago: University of Chicago Press.

Traber, Michael. 1986. *The Myth of the Information Revolution: Social and Ethical Implications of Communication Technology.* London: Sage.

Tuchman, Gaye. 1978. *Making News.* New York: Free Press.

Tulis, Jeffrey K. 1987. *The Rhetorical Presidency*. Princeton: Princeton University Press.

Turner, Victor. 1977. "Process, Systems, and Symbols: A New Anthropological Synthesis." *Daedalus* 106: 61–80.

———. 1982. *From Ritual to Theatre*. New York: Performing Arts Journal Publications.

Walster, Elaine H., Elliot Aronson, and Darcy Abrahams. 1966. "On Increasing Persuasiveness of a Low Prestige Communicator." *Journal of Experimental Social Psychology* 2: 325–42.

Wattenberg, Martin. 1991. *The Rise of Candidate-Centered Politics*. Cambridge, Mass.: Harvard University Press.

WAUDAG [University of Washington Discourse Analysis Group]. 1990. "The Rhetorical Construction of a President." *Discourse and Society* 1: 189–200.

Whillock, Rita Kirk. 1994. "Dream Believers: The Unifying Visions and Competing Values of Adherents of American Civil Religion." *Presidential Studies Quarterly* 24: 375–88.

Wober, J. Mallory. 1988. *The Use and Abuse of Television*. Hillsdale, N.J.: Lawrence Erlbaum.

Woodward, Bob. 1994. *The Agenda*. New York: Simon and Schuster.

Zarefsky, David. 1980. "Lyndon Johnson Redefines 'Equal Opportunity': The Beginnings of Affirmative Action." *Central States Speech Journal,* 31: 85–94.

———. 1986. *President Johnson's War on Poverty*. Tuscaloosa: University of Alabama Press.

———. 1992. "Spectator Politics and the Revival of Public Argument." *Communication Monographs* 59: 411–14.

———, Carol Miller-Tutzauer, and Frank E. Tutzauer. 1984. "Reagan's Safety Net for the Truly Needy: The Rhetorical Uses of Definition." *Central States Speech Journal* 35: 113–19.

Index

About the Editors and Contributors

LISA M. BENITEZ is a graduate student teaching assistant at George Mason University, where she is studying for her Master's degree. Her major focus is Organizational Communication with an emphasis on gender relations. Other interests focus on the role of women in politics and their influence on society.

DENISE M. BOSTDORFF is an assistant professor of communication at the College of Wooster. She teaches in the areas of rhetorical theory and criticism and argumentation. She conducts research in rhetorical criticism, political communication, and public affairs/issue management. Her essays have appeared in *Communication Studies Presidential Studies Quarterly, Quarterly Journal of Speech,* and *Western Journal of Speech Communication.* Her book, *The Presidency and the Rhetoric of Foreign Crisis,* appeared in 1994.

ROBERT E. DENTON, JR., is professor and head of the department of communication studies at Virginia Polytechnic Institute and State University. In addition to numerous articles, he is author and editor of several books. Recent works include *The Primetime Presidency of Ronald Reagan* (Praeger, 1988), *Ethical Dimensions of Political Communication, The Media and the Persian Gulf War* (1993), and *The 1992 Presidential Campaign: A Communication Perspective* (Praeger, 1994). Denton serves as associate editor of *Presidential Studies Quarterly* and as editor for the Praeger Series in Political Communication and the Praeger Series in Presidential Studies.

KENNETH L. HACKER is an assistant professor of communication studies at New Mexico State University. He teaches in the areas of political communication and organizational communication technologies. In addition to numerous scholarly articles and presentations, he is editor of *Candidate Images in Presidential Elections* (Praeger, 1995).

RACHEL L. HOLLOWAY is an associate professor of communication studies at Virginia Polytechnic Institute and State University. She teaches courses in public affairs and issue management. Her work has appeared in *Oratorical Encounters* (Greenwood, 1988), *Eisenhower's War of Words, Public Relations as Rhetorical Inquiry* (Praeger, 1995), and *The 1992 Presidential Campaign: A Communication Perspective* (Praeger, 1994). She is author of *In the Matter of J. Robert Oppenheimer: Politics, Rhetoric, and Self-Defense* (Praeger, 1993).

LYNDA LEE KAID is professor of communication at the University of Oklahoma, where she also serves as the Director of the Political Communication Center and supervises the Political Commercial Archive. She is coeditor of the Political Communication Review. She teaches and conducts research in the areas of political advertising and news coverage of political events. She is coauthor of *Political Campaign Communication: A Bibliography and Guide to the Literature* (1985) and coedited *Mediated Politics in Two Cultures* (Praeger, 1991), *New Perspectives on Political Advertising, Massenmedien im Wahlkampf,* and *Political Communication Yearbook, 1984.* Her articles have appeared in numerous books and journals including *Journalism Quarterly, Communication Research, Social Science Quarterly, Journal of Communication,* and *Communication Quarterly,* to name only a few.

JANETTE KENNER MUIR is the basic-course director and assistant professor in the Department of Communication at George Mason University. She has published articles in a variety of communication journals as well as several book chapters and is currently editing a volume on the uses of C-SPAN in the communication classroom.

DAVID E. PROCTER serves as interim department head and associate professor of speech at Kansas State University. He teaches and writes in the areas of political communication, rhetorical criticism, and qualitative methods. Procter has published articles in *Quarterly Journal of Speech, Communication Studies, Western Journal of Speech Communication,* among others. He is also author of *Enacting Political Culture: Rhetorical Transformations of Liberty Weekend 1986* (Praeger, 1990).

KURT RITTER is associate professor in the Department of Speech Communication and Theater Arts at Texas A & M University. He is editor of *The 1980 Presidential Debates* (1981), coauthor of *The American Ideology: Reflections of the Revolution in American Rhetoric* (1978), and *Ronald Reagan: The Great Communicator* (1992). Other recent works appear in *The Modern Presidency and Crisis Rhetoric* (1994), *Rhetorical Studies of National Political Debates,*

1960–1988 (1994), and *The Inaugural Addresses of Twentieth-Century Presidents* (1993).

EDWARD H. SEWELL, JR., is associate professor of communication studies at Virginia Polytechnic Institute and State University. He teaches in the areas of visual media and photojournalism, communication theory, and research methods. He is the author of numerous book chapters, journal articles, and proceedings. He is currently working on a book entitled *Editorial Cartoons as Political Discourse.*

CRAIG ALLEN SMITH is professor of communication at the University of North Carolina-Greensboro, where he teaches courses in political communication, rhetorical criticism, and speechwriting. His previous works include *Political Communication* (1990), *Persuasion and Social Movements* (3rd ed., 1994) with Charles J. Stewart and Robert E. Denton, Jr., *The President and the Public: Rhetorical and National Leadership* (1985), edited with Kathy B. Smith, and *The White House Speaks* (Praeger, 1994), as well as several book chapters and numerous journal articles.

JULIA A. SPIKER is a graduate student at the University of Oklahoma. Her research interests include political communication, media influence, and legal communication.

JOHN C. TEDESCO is a graduate student at the University of Oklahoma. His research interests include political communication and advertising.

RITA K. WHILLOCK is associate professor of communication at Southern Methodist University. She is the author of several articles in journals such as *Presidential Studies Quarterly, Political Communication, Southern Communication Journal,* and *World Communication Journal.* She is the author of *Political Empiricism: Communication Strategies in State and Regional Elections* (Praeger, 1992), which was named Outstanding Book in Applied Communication for 1992 by the Speech Communication Association. She is coediting a forthcoming book entitled *Hate Speech.*

ISBN 0-275-95109-X

HARDCOVER BAR CODE